THE BATTLE FOR THE FALKLANDS

Max Hastings, author of over twenty books, was editor of the *Daily Telegraph* for almost a decade and then for six years edited the *Evening Standard* in London. In his youth he was foreign correspondent for newspapers and BBC television. He has won many awards for his journalism, particularly for his work on the Falklands War. He was knighted in 2002.

Simon Jenkins is an award-winning journalist and author of over fifteen books. He writes for the *Guardian* and the *Sunday Times*, as well as broadcasting for the BBC. He has previously been political editor of the *Economist* and editor of *The Times* and the *Evening Standard*. He was knighted in 2004.

Hastings and Jenkins were awarded the *Yorkshire Post*'s Book of the Year prize for *The Battle for the Falklands* when it was first released in 1983. The book became an instant bestseller.

MAX HASTINGS
AND SIMON JENKINS

THE BATTLE FOR THE FALKLANDS

PAN MILITARY CLASSICS

PAN BOOKS

First published 1983 by Michael Joseph Limited

First published by Pan Books 1997 with a new Introduction

This edition published 2010 by Pan Books
an imprint of Pan Macmillan, a division of Macmillan Publishers Limited
Pan Macmillan, 20 New Wharf Road, London N1 9RR
Basingstoke and Oxford
Associated companies throughout the world
www.panmacmillan.com

ISBN 978-0-330-51363-0

A CIP catalogue record for this book is available from
the British Library.

Typeset by SetSystems Ltd, Saffron Walden, Essex
Printed and bound by CPI Group (UK) Ltd, Croydon, CR0 4YY

Contents

Maps

SOUTH   ATLANTIC

(May 25)
COVENTRY ●

*Pebble
Island*

Saunders Island

Byron Sound

WEST FALKLAND Port
Howar

King George Bay

*Swan
Island*

Falk'

Queen Charlotte Bay

Fox Bay

Weddell Island

WEST
FALKLAND

Falkland   Sound

*Speedwell
Island*

Eagle P

George Island

ARGENTINA

SOUTH ATLANTIC

Falkland Islands

● BELGRANO
(May 2)

OCEAN

(May 25)
● ATLANTIC CONVEYOR

Cow Bay

North Falkland Sound

Douglas Settlement

Teal
Inlet

(May 24)
ANTELOPE
(May 21)
ARDENT ●

San Carlos
Water

Teal Inlet Settlement

Berkeley Sound

● Port San Carlos

Top Malo House

Estancia House

Mt Low

San Carlos

Mt Longdon

Grantham
Sound

Sussex Mts.

EAST FALKLAND

Mt Kent

Moody Brook

STANLEY

Two Sisters

Tumbledown

Sapper Hill

...and Sound

Camilla Creek House

Darwin

Fitzroy Settlement

Bluff Cove Settlement
(June 8) SIR GALAHAD

Goose Green
Settlement

Choiseul Sound

Swan Inlet

LAFONIA

Lively Island

Low Bay

Bay of
Harbours

Sea Lion Islands

...ssage

(May 4) SHEFFIELD
●

Introduction

The 1982 South Atlantic war was one of the strangest in British history. At the time, many Britons saw it as a tragic absurdity. Most accepted that some military response to the Argentine invasion was necessary, but necessary only after a serious breakdown in British policy and diplomacy. Any dispute that required the dispatch of 20,000 men to fight for a tiny relic of empire 8,000 miles from home was bizarre. Even in victory, the government felt obliged to examine its own performance prior to the crisis, with a commission of inquiry under Lord Franks. Its limited remit and careful exoneration of the politicians involved was and remains unconvincing.

The war itself has sunk into history, a glow of military success tinged by only the occasional doubt. The British won, and against the odds. The war confirmed the quality of British arms and the effectiveness of British command and control in the field, a quality reconfirmed in the Gulf and Bosnia. The reckless Goose Green adventure and failures in the handling of 5 Infantry Brigade, as well as the shortcomings of naval tactics and equipment, have not obscured an overall success. Sending troops by sea halfway round the globe to seize a well-defended island was a huge gamble, and its outcome therefore a remarkable triumph. Those who risk their lives at their government's bidding deserve the tribute of history, especially when they win.

The aftermath has been chequered. The Tory government, whose political fortunes were greatly boosted by the success, was obliged by continued Argentine belligerence to spend some £2 billion fortifying the islands, building a vastly expensive air base and deploying there a garrison. These measures conceded a strategic importance to the Falklands which the same British government had emphatically denied in negotiating with the Argentines before the war. The Falklands encounter blighted every subsequent review of defence procurement policy.

For the enemy, the outcome was benign. The Buenos Aires junta under General Galtieri and his colleagues collapsed, ushering in a period of hesitant democracy under President Carlos Menem. As so often in war, the vanquished gained as much from the conflict as the victor. The Falklands defeat was probably the best thing to happen to Argentina in half a century. But it did nothing to diminish the vigour of that nation's claim to the islands, which still sit offshore, an enticing target for dissident adventurers.

The account of the war that we wrote immediately it was over has not been superseded in any important respect since its publication. Few military or political revelations have emerged since 1982 to discredit our conclusions, although many details have been inked in. We now have a clearer idea of Argentine planning and strategy before and during the war. Some new material has come from military and political memoirs (less so from the latter) and from investigative journalism. Military and regimental memoirs do not, in our view, change the basic story as told in 1983 – though some books are enlivened by their authors' personal spleen towards colleagues and rival units.

Some commentators have criticised censorship by the Ministry of Defence during the war. The weight of literature on this issue chiefly reflects the media's inflated view of its own importance in war. We believe that any government has a right, and probably a duty, to conceal information that might be of value to any enemy when the outcome of a war is at stake. Such a right might even embrace deliberate deception. That said, in the Falklands as in much of the Gulf war, the military authorities on the ground enjoyed a virtual monopoly of communication. This is unlikely to be repeated in the age of the portable satellite phone.

Much investigation has been devoted to what supposedly went

wrong in the conduct of the fighting. This has suffered from hindsight – notably the completeness of the eventual British victory – and from an exaggerated lay expectation of how military units perform in combat. Wars rarely go according to plan. If they are lost, every decision was a mistake. If they are won, every excess on the part of the eventual victor was a barbarity. The much-publicised casualties at Goose Green, including the death of 2 Para's CO Lieutenant Colonel Jones, indeed arose from what has been criticised as a reckless 'political battle'. The bombing of *Sir Galahad* and *Sir Tristram* stemmed from sins of commission and omission by middle-ranking officers. Yet battles cannot be scrutinised like peacetime train crashes. War is characterised by uncertainty, surprise and overcaution followed by overreaction. Both sides blunder in ignorance, in circumstances seldom of their own choosing. Few journalists have personal military experience, and thus the temptation to deploy in war the techniques and values of domestic peacetime journalism proves hard to resist.

One instance of foolish hindsight has been the controversy over 'friendly fire' casualties. These are a feature of every battle. British casualties from friendly fire in the Falklands were trivial by comparison with similar losses suffered by bombing and artillery during the Second World War and even the Gulf war. The Ministry of Defence has been criticised for concealing the circumstances of some such deaths from relatives. In previous wars, it has been judged humane to allow next of kin to suppose that their loved ones died by enemy action. This approach has nothing to do with a desire to cover up mistakes, but rather with intended kindness. This may no longer be a sustainable policy, but it is not an immoral one.

The publication in 1993 of a sensational memoir by a former member of 3 Para who saw service on Mount Longdon, alleging that Argentines had been wantonly shot by British troops, provoked a frightened Defence Secretary, Mr Malcolm Rifkind, into ordering a costly inquiry. Its report was passed to the Director of Public Prosecutions. After intense controversy, the DPP accepted

counsel's advice against charges for manslaughter. It was extraordinary that anyone, least of all a Tory cabinet minister, should
ever have thought such charges appropriate. There was no suggestion of the Argentines taking action against any of their own
veterans for alleged misbehaviour on the islands.

Similar argument has surrounded the sinking of the Argentine
cruiser *Belgrano*, by the British submarine, HMS *Conqueror*. This was
pursued by many journalists and MPs, including notably Labour's
Tam Dalyell. The British government lied in its initial explanation
of the *Belgrano*'s course when attacked. The ship was not directly
threatening the British task force at the time. That deceit created
the foundation on which an edifice of hostile comment has been
built. Our view was, and remains, that the attack was justified. The
two navies were at war, with the odds heavily favouring the
Argentines. The sinking went some way to restoring the balance:
crucially it drove the Argentinian carrier, *The 25th of May*, back into
port for the duration of the war. At that point, the carrier's mere
presence at sea constituted a major threat to the entire British
operation.

The government's problem was that it could not admit the full
scale of the danger facing the task force. It had both to sustain a
belief in British invincibility, and yet to take every possible step to
improve the odds. The enemy's navy and air force were deployed
close to their home bases. As we report, many American analysts
at the time predicted that Britain could not possibly win and were
arguing fiercely over whether a rescue of their British ally was
politically feasible.

Two final questions remain to be considered, material for
which was not available at the time of writing this book. The first
concerns the Argentine side. In 1983, we examined why the
Argentines initiated this venture, but not how. Books by Jimmy
Burns and Lawrence Freedman have gone some way to answering
the first question. We now know for sure that the Argentines
brought forward their planned July invasion to April because the
preliminary testing occupation of South Georgia had gone badly

wrong. Yet by July, winter weather would have made a British response near inconceivable. 'General winter' would have triumphed. Thus does the accident of war determine its outcome.

The Franks inquiry was set up to answer the second question, but failed so to do: why was Britain taken so completely by surprise? As Simon Jenkins argued in a series of articles for the *Sunday Times* in May 1987, the intelligence failure was not so much one of raw material as of its assessment within the government machine. As we show in our book, copious warning messages were flowing from Buenos Aires through the Foreign Office and Ministry of Defence in February and March 1982. In London these messages were distorted and suppressed to suit diverse interests within the Whitehall system. Government failed to distinguish correctly between 'signals' and 'noise', as intelligence jargon has it, chiefly because the political will to do so was lacking. Neither the Ministry of Defence nor the Treasury nor the Cabinet collectively wanted to accept the need for costly precautionary measures in the South Atlantic, a distant place for which it cared little and of which it knew less. The culture of the Thatcher government at the time was hostile to defence and overseas affairs, and even more so to spending money on them (apart from nuclear weapons). Such attitudes, above all else, gave comfort to a prospective enemy and supplied the essential precondition for the war.

Of this Franks made no mention. The wounding of the reputation of the Foreign Secretary, Lord Carrington, was most unfair. But he recovered, and is today revered as almost the sole honourable resigner from the Tory government between 1979 and 1997. Success healed all the wounds and Britain's introverted political culture closed over them. If the cabinet system was at fault, so much the better. No individual need take the blame. Accountability can be lost in collectivity.

Within a decade, the Falklands war was overshadowed by the much larger deployment of British forces in the Gulf. But the South Atlantic conflict retains its fascination as a freak of imperial history. It was a clean British victory – albeit one that required extensive American help. The war was of no wider significance for British interests and taught no lessons. Other British colonies, such as Diego Garcia, had their inhabitants evacuated without compunction when it suited the British government. Likewise Hong Kong. The Falklands was essentially a political war, a war of pride, a war to save a government's skin. It taught a dictator a lesson, but not dictatorship. Many dictators enjoy aggression unthreatened by task forces. That was not why the task force set sail in April 1982.

But a task force did set sail. It set sail and it won. Here is the tale of that adventure.

Max Hastings
Simon Jenkins
January 1997

Foreword

This is the story of a freak of history, almost certainly the last colonial war that Britain will ever fight. So extraordinary an event was it that, even after men began to die, many of those taking part felt as if they had been swept away into fantasy, that the ships sinking and the guns firing round them had somehow escaped from a television screen in the living room.

As a correspondent with the task force, Max Hastings did not trouble to ask himself whether the war was desirable or necessary. He merely felt privileged to have the opportunity to witness the drama at first hand and see the British services go about their business as they always have done: amidst muddle and controversy, showing the capacity for laughter, professionalism, courage and determination that has been their inheritance from Blenheim to Belfast. While the war was in progress, the prime concern of almost everyone in Britain was that it should be won. Once it had ended, the long and complex process of investigation began. Why was it fought? Should it have been fought? What really took place? Might it have been done differently?

The day before the task force sailed, we agreed that, if a war indeed broke out in the South Atlantic, we would write a book about it together. Simon Jenkins possesses an extensive knowledge of Westminster and Whitehall, and closely watched the politicians, officials and diplomats as they steered Britain through one of her most acute postwar traumas. Hastings could draw on the experience of accompanying the task force from Southampton to Port Stanley.

Our book is primarily an account of British political decision-

making and of naval and military operations. It is not a study of
the problem of the Falkland Islands and their inhabitants, nor,
though it draws on a number of first-hand Buenos Aires sources,
does it purport to show the war from Argentina's point of view. In
writing the book we have divided our responsibility very simply:
Jenkins describes events in London, Washington and Argentina.
Hastings has written the narrative of the conflict in the South
Atlantic. We have united to reach our conclusions.

In the months since the war ended, each of us has interviewed
scores of those who participated. We can claim to have seen almost
every central figure of the war, often for many hours. Most have
been remarkably frank, recognising that the struggle was a unique
event and that few of its secrets needed to be shielded from
posterity. Most wanted to talk off the record and, though it is an
irritating convention to quote simply 'an officer', 'a civil servant'
or 'a minister', it has sometimes proved necessary, to convey the
flavour of what men say in time of war. Their words could not
have been used had they been attributed. Occasionally the resulting views, particularly of key meetings, conflicted. We can only say
we did our best to resolve these conflicts and await the 'truth',
which under Britain's ridiculous secrecy rules will not emerge until
2012, if at all.

Hastings would like to pay special tribute to the officers and
men of the task force who endured his company at close quarters
not only in the Falklands but in the months that followed. He
hopes that, given time, Chris Keeble of 2 Para will stop dining out
on the story of how his attached correspondent fell asleep beside
him during the battle for Wireless Ridge. Through the generosity
of scores of officers and men, Hastings has had access to reports,
diaries and letters written both in the South Atlantic and during
the post-mortems on the war. He would also like to recognise the
immense assistance and patience of the Commander in Chief,
Fleet's staff at Northwood in arranging for him to meet so many
officers and men of the naval staff and battle group home from
the South Atlantic. Having preserved their reputation as 'the silent

service' while the war was being fought, the Royal Navy could not have been more forthcoming and helpful when it had ended. They will find much to disagree with in what we have written, but we hope they will accept that we have attempted honestly to reach for the reality of what took place. The manuscript was read before publication by a number of senior officers of the task force, whose comments and corrections have been invaluable. They do not, of course, bear any responsibility for the authors' errors or judgements.

Jenkins must thank the many anonymous ministers, civil servants, diplomats and officers who helped him in London, New York and Washington, generously sparing their time and often laying bare their reputations with no more than an 'off the record' to protect them. Librarians at Chatham House, Canning House and the *Economist* were indispensable. Of the many sources on Argentina, Andrew Graham-Yooll, Malcolm Deas and Guillermo Makin were invaluable, as was Jimmy Burns in Buenos Aires. Richard Natkiel prepared the maps with great speed and efficiency.

We both owe a great debt of thanks to our wives, who had to live with the Falklands for an obsessive eight months. Louis Kirby, editor of the London *Standard*, not only sent Hastings to the Falklands but offered him immense kindness and support after his return and put up with his absence while this book was being written. Andrew Knight, editor of the *Economist*, showed the same understanding towards his Political Editor, Simon Jenkins. Jennie Davies and Henrietta Heald made possible a remarkable effort of book production at great speed, and helped with the collation of photos and the correction of the manuscript.

The Franks Report on the preliminaries to the Falklands war appeared in January 1983, after the first impression had been printed. It has since been read alongside our text, which, except in a few chronological details, has not required material adjustment. Only our conclusions differ, as can be seen in our concluding chapter. For convenience and for the record, Franks's conclusions are reproduced as Appendix D.

We would like to think that this book is more than instant journalism, if necessarily less than instant history. Let us call it an interim report on Britain's war in the South Atlantic, based overwhelmingly on the testimony of the participants, at home and abroad, at sea and ashore.

Max Hastings
Simon Jenkins
February 1983

1 » FORGOTTEN ISLANDS

All this country is bare with not a bit of wood, very windy
and very cold, because eight months in the year it snows
and the prevailing winds are south-west.

Log of unknown ship out of Seville, 1540

The 14th wee were driven in among certain Isles never
before discovered . . . lying fiftie leagues or better from the
shoare, in which place unlesse it had pleased God of his
wonderfull mercie to have ceased the wind, wee must of
necessitie have perished.

Passenger with Captain John Davis, 1592

On the 24th day about dawn, three little islands were
sighted, hitherto neither noted nor drawn on any map.
These were given the new name Sebaldes . . . in the same
place they found an extraordinary number of penguins.

Ship's surgeon under Sebald de Weert, 1600

The Falkland Islands' misfortune has always been to be wanted
more than they are loved. They loomed up out of mountainous
seas and freezing fog, disorienting and terrifying early sailors
blown east from Cape Horn. Navigators unsure if they were still
off the South American mainland would merely record in their
logs a barren but lethal coastline of rocks and inlets, and pray they
lived to tell the tale. No one knows who saw the islands first.
Vespucci, Magellan, Davis, Hawkins, Sebald de Weert may all make
their claims. As a result, the islands acquired a bewildering variety

of names: the Sansons, the Sebaldes, Hawkins Land, the Malouines, the Malvinas. For those concerned with theories of discovery, Spaniards, Britons and Dutchmen are almost equally entitled to credit.

We do at least know who first set foot on the Falklands. In 1690, Captain John Strong was voyaging to Chile when he was driven east from the Cape in a violent storm. He found himself off the northern tip of the islands, which he identified from a previous sighting by Captain Richard Hawkins. 'Here are many good harbours,' Strong wrote. 'We found fresh water in plenty and killed an abundance of geese and ducks. As for wood, there is none.' Strong did no more than chart the sound between the two main islands and name it after the First Lord of the Admiralty, Lord Falkland. He then sailed on.

Strong was soon followed by others in the period of intense trade rivalry between eighteenth-century Spain, Britain and France. Under the Treaty of Utrecht of 1713, Spain's control of its traditional territories in the Americas – which embraced the Falklands – was formally confirmed, but this appears to have done little to restrain English and French ambitions. Covetous eyes were cast at islands which, in Lord Anson's hyperbolic words, 'even in time of peace might be of great consequence to this nation and in time of war would make us master of the seas'. The basis of Anson's enthusiasm was that the islands would be a refuge and refreshment base for British ships rounding Cape Horn. Whether he envisaged a fully fledged naval base is not clear. Little immediate action was taken on Anson's advice. But the concept of the Falklands as a maritime key to various El Dorados was already planted in the political consciousness.

The first man to carry through a plan to take and settle the Falklands was a French nobleman, Antoine de Bougainville, eager for revenge against Britain after the loss of Quebec. Sailing from St Malo on 5 April 1764, he formally claimed the islands in the name of Louis XV. Along with rights derived from the general Spanish dominion in those parts, this occupation lies at the root of all subsequent Argentine claims to the Falklands. The French landed north of the site of the present Port Stanley on East Falkland. It was, de Bougainville wrote, 'a countryside lifeless for want of inhabitants . . . everywhere a weird and melancholy uniformity'. Nonetheless he and his band of colonists built a small fort and settlement, which they called Port Louis. This was replenished with supplies the following year. Despite its bleak location, the colony put down firm roots. However distant and trivial an event this may seem to British eyes, the strength of present-day Argentine feeling cannot be understood without an awareness of it.

At almost exactly the same time, the British, perhaps warned of de Bougainville's expedition, conceived of a similar venture. Commodore John Byron, who rejoiced in the nickname 'Foulweather Jack', was sent out by the Admiralty to survey the islands and lay claim to them. He arrived on West Falkland a year after the French in 1765 and, unaware of the presence of the French on the other island, hoisted the Union Jack. He named the spot Port Egmont, planted a small vegetable patch and immediately sailed away.

Yet another year passed and Captain John McBride was sent out to consolidate Byron's landing, with orders to build a fort and eject any other settlers who might be on the islands or question Britain's right to the territory. For the first time, the British now encountered the French at Port Louis, numbering some 250. The French pointed out that theirs was a properly constituted colony and it was McBride who should leave.

The Falklands thus stumbled onto the stage of world politics. The Spanish were furious at what they regarded as a blatant breach of the terms of the Treaty of Utrecht by both British and French expeditions. France was at this time considered an ally of Spain and an agreement was reached by which the Port Louis colony was ceded to the Spanish in return for substantial compensation to de Bougainville. The transfer was accomplished at a ceremony on East Falkland in 1767 and a new Spanish governor, Don Felipe Ruiz Puente, appointed under the captain general of Buenos Aires. The colony was renamed Puerto Soledad. The French cannot have been sorry to vacate so desolate a spot. Certainly the Spanish were none too happy on arrival. 'I tarry in this miserable desert, suffering everything for the love of God,' wrote Father Sebastian Villanueva, the community's first priest. A British lieutenant stationed at the time at Port Egmont added his amen: 'The most detestable place I was ever at in all my life.'

It took Spain two years to act against the British on West Falklands. In 1769, the Buenos Aires captain general, a spirited character named Francisco Bucarelli, was instructed by Madrid to drive any British from the islands, by force if necessary. He set about his task with evident relish. Five ships and 1,400 men were sent from the mainland. The British commander in charge at Port Egmont, Captain George Farmer, duly quit the settlement 'under protest' with his small band of marines. He arrived home in England in September 1770. The Falklands historian Julius Goebel, writing in 1927 of Farmer's reception by Lord North's hard-pressed government,* provides us with a premonition of the events which were to occur two centuries later: 'The ministry, which had clearly been disposed to an accommodation at the outset of the trouble and might even have gone so far as to acquiesce in an arrangement suggested by Spain . . . now found itself in the situation where only extreme measures would silence popular clamour.'

The result was Britain's first Falklands crisis. The enemy this time was Spain and the dispute was dominated by the domestic insecurities of the respective governments. A year of frenetic diplomacy ensued, with threats of war from both sides. Finally an agreement was reached under which Britain would be allowed to return to Port Egmont 'to restore the King's honour', Spain nonetheless reserving her claim to sovereignty. The Spanish maintained, however, that the British return was only permitted as a result of a promise by Lord North that the British would subsequently leave again. This promise had had to be kept secret

---

* Julius Goebel, *The Struggle for the Falkland Islands*, Yale, 1927.

because of the outcry it might have produced from Lord Chatham's opposition.

At the same time the government commissioned a pamphlet from Dr Samuel Johnson in an effort to lower the temperature and diminish the importance of West Falkland in British eyes. Johnson wrote that it was a place 'thrown aside from human use, stormy in winter, barren in summer, an island which not even the southern savages have dignified with habitation, where a garrison must be kept in a state that contemplates with envy the exiles of Siberia, of which the expense will be perpetual.'

A British expedition indeed returned to Port Egmont, but evacuated it three years later. A plaque was left, which stated: 'Be it known to all nations that Falkland's Ysland, with this fort, the storehouses, wharfs . . . are the sole right and property of His Most Sacred Majesty George III, King of Great Britain.' (Most British sources have made the 'Ysland' plural, thus extending the claim beyond West Falkland.) There was no British suggestion that the Spanish should leave Puerto Soledad. Indeed, on a number of later occasions, the British effectively acknowledged Spanish jurisdiction on the islands. In 1790, the two nations signed the Nootka Sound Convention, by which Britain formally renounced any colonial ambitions in South America 'and the islands adjacent'. The Falklands were now occupied as a Spanish colony for forty years, until the collapse of Spain's New World empire in the early nineteenth century.

The first stirrings of a move towards independence from Spain occurred in Buenos Aires in 1810 and, as a result, the colonial authorities decided the following year to remove Spanish settlers from Puerto Soledad and from neighbouring Patagonia on the mainland. The Falkland Islands were now left to their fate as a refuge for sealing and whaling vessels from a number of nations, under no other justice than that administered by passing ships' captains. In 1820, however, the new state of the United Provinces of Rio de la Plata, forerunner of the present Argentina, sent a frigate to claim them as part of its post-colonial legacy from Spain.

The commander told the fifty or so vessels at the Puerto Soledad settlement that all fishing and hunting on the islands lay within the jurisdiction of his government. Successive attempts during the 1820s to assert this authority appear to have fallen on deaf ears in the anarchic, largely maritime community. Nonetheless, Buenos Aires appointed its first governor in 1823, and by 1829 matters had improved sufficiently for another, Louis Vernet, to ally governor-ship with substantial farming and trading interests on the islands. He also imposed restrictions on the indiscriminate slaughter of the seal population, then in danger of extinction. The British consul in Buenos Aires, Woodbine Parish, felt obliged to sustain Britain's old claim to the islands (despite Nootka Sound), protesting at Vernet's appointment though taking no further action.

Vernet proceeded to execute his commission by arresting an American ship, *Harriet*, for engaging in what he regarded as illegal sealing and confiscating some of her property. He sailed with her to Buenos Aires to put her captain on trial. With some encourage-ment from Parish, the American consul in the city took umbrage at this action, claiming that American vessels could do what they liked on the Falklands, as America had never recognised Vernet's jurisdiction there. Finding himself fortuitously with an American warship in port, USS *Lexington*, the consul dispatched it to Puerto Soledad to secure the restitution of the property, mostly sealskins, that Vernet had confiscated from the American ship.

If any action in history can be said to have been the cause of the 1982 Falklands war, it was that taken by the reckless captain of *Lexington*, Captain Silas Duncan, on arrival at Puerto Soledad. He not only recovered the confiscated sealskins, but also spiked the Argentine guns, blew up their powder, sacked the settlement buildings and arrested most of the inhabitants. He then declared the islands 'free of all government' and sailed away. His action was pure piracy. The result was recrimination between Washington and Buenos Aires over reparations – for Vernet's and Duncan's actions respectively – which continued into the present century. Meanwhile the Argentinians sent another governor to the islands,

Juan Mestivier, who unfortunately was murdered on arrival by the few Argentinians left by Duncan, most of them convicts.

Alerted by Parish, the Admiralty now took its chance. On 2 January 1833, the British returned to the Falklands with two warships, *Tyne* and *Clio*, under the command of Captain James Onslow. He had been instructed by the Palmerston government to take and hold the islands for Britain. Onslow found the commander of an Argentine frigate, Don Jose Maria Pinedo, in the midst of suppressing the rebels who had murdered Mestivier. Onslow ordered him to lower the Argentine flag and depart. Outgunned, Pinedo was forced to leave: yet another officer departing the Falklands under a 'protest' which cannot have been too heartfelt. It took the British another six months to hunt down a group of vagrant gauchos who refused to accept British rule. One of them, a bandit named Antonio Rivero, was finally arrested and returned to Montevideo and has since been cast as a heroic Argentine 'guerrilla'. With the exception of two months in 1982, the British have remained in possession of the Falklands ever since – though for eight years after 1833 they did little to restore the rule of law which the Argentinians had been struggling to maintain before their ejection.

*

The Falklands were never of any great strategic importance – certainly not before the advent of coal-powered vessels. Yet from the moment of their discovery they seem to have embodied the national pride of whoever held them. All Argentinians are convinced the 'Malvinas' belong to them, outrageously seized by a colonial power in 1833. Likewise, as the British Foreign Secretary, Francis Pym, asserted in 1982, 'Her Majesty's government is not in any doubt about our title to the islands and we never have been.' In an era of at least rudimentary international justice, the claims of each cannot simply be subordinated to the principle of 'might is right' and 'possession is nine tenths of the law'. Some adjudication of the issue is appropriate.

The Argentine case rests on the argument that discovery alone has never been accepted by international lawyers as the foundation of sovereignty. Discovery is only a valid basis if allied to occupation and settled administration. The first colony on the islands was French, but this was ceded by de Bougainville to Spain – virtually the only straightforward deal in the whole history of the Falklands. The British claim to first occupation must be confined to West Falkland, and did not involve any settled community. After a major dispute with Spain, this occupation was terminated: the famous plaque is legally immaterial. Spain then operated a peaceful colony on the islands for forty years. When Spain left, in 1811, the British did not claim the Falklands back and the government of what became Argentina declared sovereignty by inheritance from Spain in 1820. It appointed governors, installed them and at least attempted to enforce administration and justice. It was only a fortuitous act of American piracy which permitted the British seizure.

The British case is three-fold. First, Britain asserted a claim in 1765 and never renounced it. In 1833 this was merely being reasserted to fill a political vacuum on the islands. This argument is not strong, and is known to have caused the Foreign Office some hesitancy when Argentina again revived her claim late last century. American 'neutrality' on the issue of sovereignty is based on similar doubts, expressed in a secret State Department memorandum of 1947.

Since before the Second World War, the British have moved to a second area of argument, the doctrine of prescription. This broadly states that continuous possession over a period of time constitutes a right to ownership. The right is clearly reinforced if that possession is not contested by the world at large. Nor is it annulled by another claimant persisting in a competing demand. In international law, this is little more than an affirmation that might, sustained for long enough, is right.* The best that can be said in its defence is that, if all nations reopened 150-year-old

---

* For an elegant dispatch of this argument, see Malcolm Deas, *London Review of Books*, August 1982.

claims whenever they felt strong enough, the world would be a bloodier place than it is.

The strongest British argument rests on a third principle, that of self-determination. The islands have a two-thirds indigenous population, who passionately want to stay British. Respect for the wishes of inhabitants on matters of sovereignty is enshrined in the United Nations charter and has underlain decades of decolonisation. The Argentinians protest that any nation can thus take another's land, implant settlers and claim it. Yet, undoubtedly, the fact of the islanders' presence and their freely expressed desire to remain British has dominated the last seventeen years of negotiation over their future.

*

Argentina can at least argue that she has never allowed her claim to lapse altogether. Buenos Aires objected when Britain formally declared a colonial administration in the Falklands in 1842. In the 1880s, when Argentina was being 'rounded off' to the south with Chile, she again asked for the islands back. In 1908, Britain unilaterally declared sovereignty over uninhabited territory south of the Falklands. South Georgia, the South Sandwich, Orkney and Shetland Islands and Graham Land were all grouped under the Falkland Islands Dependencies. Argentina declared they were firmly hers, and thereby began half a century of genteel squabbling between British, Argentine and Chilean warships and scientists. They would sail south and put down plaques and build sheds to test each other's resolve before retreating from the hostile weather.

By the end of the Second World War, the Argentine government, the British Foreign Office, the Falklands people and the British navy were all setting out on a collision course. Most had started as the best of friends. In the 1930s, Argentina was still part of Britain's commercial, if not political, empire. Under the 1933 Roca-Runciman pact she was even granted the same import preferences for her foodstuffs as those given to the new Commonwealth dominions. Massive European immigration from Italy and Germany as well as Spain began to weaken Argentina's links with Britain. Argentina was proud that its population was almost exclusively European with little negro or Amerindian stock. She chose to distance herself from her Latin American neighbours to the north, and in 1930 a military coup instilled a new nationalism into her politics. A booming economy established an industrial base and the interest groups to match. Argentina was a nation of rising expectations, active trade unions and diversifying political power.

In Germany, Italy and Spain – 'home' to tens of thousands of Argentinians – such a society had produced the phenomenon of national socialism. The phenomenon took another decade to flower in Argentina but, from 1945 onwards, Colonel Juan Peron and his followers were able to build on this base some three decades of charismatic nationalism. Since his death in 1974, Peron's memory has sustained one of South America's most destructive political vendettas, that between Argentina's 'Peronistas' and her military class. No one in the dramatis personae of the Falklands war cast a darker shadow across the counsels of the Argentine junta than Juan Peron. He was commendatore to Galtieri's Don Giovanni.

Peron's army background, his visits to prewar Spain and Italy and his overt admiration for Mussolini led him towards what he termed 'integral nationalism'. After the Second World War, in which Argentina had sided until the last minute with the axis powers, she found herself a nation apart from the new US-sponsored pan-Americanism. This independence determined a fierce restatement of her right to various disputed borders, chiefly in Tierra del Fuego, the South Atlantic and the Antarctic. Maps, commissions, expeditions, 'scientific' bases, all flowed south from Buenos Aires, challenging Britain's traditional supremacy in this area of the world. In 1959, Antarctica was regularised and in theory demilitarised by one of the few successes of international law, the Antarctic Treaty. Britain now narrowed the ambit of the Falkland islands Dependencies to the three groups of islands north of the

60th parallel laid down in the treaty; the South Sandwich Islands, South Georgia and the Falklands themselves. In doing so, she once again intensified Argentine feeling that these islands were not and never should be British.

Peron appears to have been content to leave all this to his diplomats. The islands were of no economic and only limited strategic significance. There was no zest for colonising them and the presence of a settled British community was at least a complicating factor. The British navy also still had a base at Simonstown in South Africa. Nevertheless, all Argentine schools were instructed to teach 'The Malvinas are Argentine', a cry which was even set to music. A generation of Argentinians thus grew up regarding the British occupation as an affront to their nationhood. Repossession was not a matter of legal or diplomatic nicety. It was a challenge to national honour. British ministers visiting Buenos Aires in the 1960s and 1970s were constantly baffled by the emotion the subject aroused. Such relics of empire were fast fading from the minds of the European 'regionalists' at Westminster. It was a mystery why they should arouse such feeling among emergent regionalists elsewhere in the world.

Most British politicians were perhaps dimly aware that the Falklands were a welcome respite from the anguish of imperial retreat. As one nation after another threw off the British connection, the Falklanders desperately wanted the connection to stay. Here was imperialism and self-determination marching for once side by side. Yet both required defence against a hostile neighbour. The Falklands had long sheltered under the umbrella of imperial defence. As that umbrella was removed they became increasingly exposed, dependent not on real military power but on the memory of it. They were protected by a form of historical bluff.

The political party on which had fallen the burden of much of Britain's decolonisation was ironically the party which had traditionally grasped the empire to its bosom. By the end of the thirteen years of Conservative rule in 1964, the major British possessions in Africa and Asia were either independent or becoming so. Yet the military bases designed to defend them were still in place. From Hong Kong and Singapore, through Aden and Simonstown to Cyprus and Gibraltar, the Union Jack still flew. Tories who had resented the pace of imperial retreat now fought, from the opposition benches, to maintain this military umbrella.

Such MPs argued that a reduced empire did not entail a reduced world role as long as British forces were deployed. Like the nuclear bomb, British bases were a 'ticket to the top table' of nations. The new Labour Prime Minister, Harold Wilson, was not averse to this argument. Yet, just as the Tories had had to guard their backs against their right wing in matters of foreign and defence policy, so Wilson had to guard against his left. Withdrawal from east of Suez became a rallying cry to Wilson's party opponents, and one which he ultimately conceded. A crucial consequence of this front-bench insecurity over post-imperial policy was to remove foreign and defence affairs out of the limelight of parliamentary and public debate into the more secret world of Foreign Office working parties, Ministry of Defence committees and backbench study groups. Within these nether regions of the British constitution, policy could be formulated and implemented (or obstructed) with a minimum of public scrutiny or controversy.

The major responsibility for sustaining the defence of the Falklands lay with the Royal Navy. More than any other service, it had found little consolation in the retreat from empire. As each patch of red faded from the globe, so too did the need for aircraft carriers, amphibious landing ships and overseas bases. The advent of seaborne nuclear weapons and the lengthening time-span required for ship design called for frequent and usually pessimistic reviews of naval strategy. A service grown doubtful of its role began to turn in on itself and defend its institutional territories – which mostly meant ships. Navy ministers, sea lords, admirals of the fleet now earned their battle honours in the linoleum corridors of the great white Ministry of Defence building in Whitehall. Their defeats were recorded in the leaden prose of successive defence white papers. Their victories lay gleaming on the slipways of the

Tyne and the Clyde. Their arguments were not without force: Britain's foreign-policy makers could not sustain a wide range of alliance commitments on the hot air of diplomacy alone. But what ships the navy really needed was a matter of bitter debate.

In the 1960s and early 1970s the navy was led by such strong personalities as Sir Michael le Fanu and Sir Peter Hill-Norton. Their periods of office seemed dominated by a single obsession: the fate of Britain's carrier force. The aircraft carrier symbolised not merely the majesty of naval power but the navy's ability to perform a full range of operational tasks worldwide. The carriers' existence demonstrated Britain's continuing role as world policeman. Admirals and their parliamentary supporters fought for their carriers with a determination – and, through the letters column of *The Times*, an insubordination – unheard of in other public services. It was the Labour Defence Secretary, Denis Healey, who first set out to sink the carriers in 1966, in what was intended as the most radical defence white paper since the war. He stated categorically that the only sort of operation for which aircraft carriers would ever again be required would be a 'landing or withdrawal of troops against sophisticated opposition outside the range of land-based air cover'. (The Falklands war in a nutshell.) Yet he could envisage no such operation in which Britain might be engaged 'unaided by our allies'. Britain, in other words, would be a policeman only in concert with the Americans.

The navy maintained its campaign throughout the 1970s. Plans for 'Harrier carriers' and 'through-deck cruisers' came thick and fast across defence secretaries' desks. This campaign was sufficiently successful for one 'mini-carrier', *Invincible*, to be available for the South Atlantic while a second, *Illustrious*, was under construction on the Tyne. Britain also still possessed the old carrier *Hermes*, now officially designated as a 'Landing Platform Helicopter'. The strategic justification for these ships, which could take only Harriers and helicopters, was that they provided anti-submarine defence for Nato. By the time of John Nott's 1981 white paper, this function was considered better (and certainly more cheaply) performed by destroyers and frigates. *Hermes* was scheduled for the scrapyard and *Invincible* had been sold to the Australians. In the late 1970s, financial restrictions on the Royal Navy were also so severe that warships were crippled by lack of spare parts. Some Leander-class frigates were unable to operate their primary sonars. Naval pay had fallen so low that many sailors based ashore were 'moonlighting', taking second jobs to increase their incomes. 1980 was the blackest year of all, with a total moratorium on defence contracts, and fuel allocations so severely cut that many ships could not put to sea for months.

Carriers were not the only victims of naval retrenchment. Just as Healey had tried to predict the strategic requirements which Nato would make of the navy ten years from 1966, so John Nott had to make the same prediction in 1981. He came to a remarkably similar conclusion. To Nott, the navy should concentrate on anti-Soviet and anti-submarine defence. Not only were carriers no longer a requirement, but 'needs do not warrant the replacement of specialist amphibious ships' intended for out-of-area landings. The assault ships *Fearless* and *Intrepid* found their days were numbered.

The whole tenor of Nott's 1981 review – inspired by the most sustained attack ever mounted by the Treasury on defence spending – was to curtail the surface role of the navy and reduce its need for costly surface warships. It was this cut in the navy's conventional capability which secured Nott the resignation of the Navy Minister, Keith Speed (a carbon copy of that of Healey's minister, Christopher Mayhew, also over carriers), and the enmity of the First Sea Lord, Admiral Sir Henry Leach. Blessed with a pleasant manner but a devastating directness of approach, Leach had run up his battle colours over his corner of the Ministry of Defence and laid down a withering fire in Nott's direction. His defeat only made him the more outspoken. It seemed that not since de Ruyter sailed up the Medway in 1667 had such havoc been wrought on the British navy. Nott showed considerable political courage in resisting this bombardment to the end.

To most defence strategists, Nott had finally called the Royal Navy's bluff. Set-piece sea battles, mass convoys, amphibious landings and land-support gunnery – the textbook manoeuvres of the first half of the twentieth century – had finally been sent to the museum. To the Prime Minister, Margaret Thatcher, Nott's review was the cause of much political anguish and her support for it was conditioned largely by her desire to cut spending. It alienated those among her backbench MPs such as Julian Amery, Winston Churchill and Alan Clark, whose enthusiasm for her leadership had been built on her declared intention to expand Britain's defences. These tended to be the same MPs as were deeply offended by her 'sellout' to the black majority in Rhodesia and by any concessions made to the Common Market. Ironically, the Ministry of Defence came to join the Foreign Office – two ostensibly 'conservative' departments – as the Whitehall institutions which the Tory right disliked most intensely.

Despite being cast by most critics as the villain of the Falklands piece, the Foreign Office had been more adaptable than most arms of government to Britain's changed postwar role. It had been forced to build new alliances with many nations who were either careless of Britain or actively hostile to her. For diplomats working in such a climate, the lingering relics of empire were a patent embarrassment. Far from being paternalist havens of order in a troubled world, the surviving colonies tended to be sources of revolution, terrorism and instability. By the early 1970s, admittedly, there were not many of them left. With the exceptions of Rhodesia and Hong Kong, they were scattered islands and enclaves still 'clinging close to nurse for fear of something worse'. Most were in the Caribbean and Polynesia, but there was also a disparate group including Mauritius, St Helena, Diego Garcia and the Falklands. These were the true orphans of post-imperialism. History had left them on Britain's doorstep and few had any desire to go back on the street.

Two of these possessions, Gibraltar and the Falklands, fell into a special category. They were occupied by people of British background and citizenship but were also claimed by their adjacent foreign states. Unlike, for instance, the Solomons or Bermuda, they could not be included in some regional defence arrangement. They were British colonies and proud of it. The task of running these territories had originally lain with the Colonial Office. As its responsibilities diminished, this office was in 1966 merged with the Commonwealth Office and two years later with the Foreign Office. Veterans of colonial government, many of them former soldiers, found themselves junior partners in a department dominated by the ethos of diplomacy rather than administration.

Here, old colonial functions lived on in divisions with titles such as 'Gibraltar and General' and 'Oceanic Territories'. Governorships were seldom prized, indeed they often signified the end of a career. Money for colonial development had to be prised from the new Overseas Development Ministry (later Agency), where it competed with more needy and politically significant clients for generosity. Indeed, the Falklands were notorious in Whitehall for being per capita the wealthiest recipients of ODM funds. The Falklands' population comprised only 1,800 people living in utterly self-contained circumstances. In the eyes of the new Foreign and Commonwealth Office, they could not possibly weigh heavily against British policy towards South America, a continent of 240 millions.

Last in the Falklands cast list – but by no means least – comes the British Parliament. Successive governments have, as we have seen, had devious reasons for steering foreign policy away from the House of Commons. This desire for secrecy has been equalled only by Parliament's apparent lack of interest in overcoming it. William Wallace, in his study of the Commons' supervision of foreign affairs,* has argued that such supervision is now virtually non-existent. Neither full-dress debates nor Foreign Office question times exercise any proper scrutiny of policy. Even ministers seem to act as little more than mouthpieces for decisions taken behind

---

* *The Foreign Policy Process in Britain*, Royal Institute of International Affairs, 1976.

their backs, and usually before their time. As these decisions rarely involve resources, they are deprived of the red meat of public controversy, a row with Treasury. Foreign affairs barely registers on any poll of issues taxing the mind of the electorate. Why should MPs bother?

Just occasionally, this complacency can backfire. Events can enforce a policy change. The government must adapt accordingly. A small handful of MPs may not understand this change or may represent an interest to which it is a threat. Shut out from the process of decision, they can resort only to suspicion and antagonism. The issue may be unimportant. The cabinet of the day may feel the change demanded of it not worth the political aggravation. At this point, the process of foreign-policy formation becomes tense and embattled. Having neglected for so long to make friends in the wider political community, the Foreign Office finds itself hamstrung, with no allies, no constituency and no supportive lobby. Diplomats have to prevaricate and stall. Ministers have to dissemble. For over seventeen years this is what happened to the FO's Falklands policy. This policy ended in failure and the nation went to war.

2 » THE SEVENTEEN YEARS' WAR

> If the problem of the Falkland–Malvinas Islands leads to
> tragedy, the disaster will be a prime instance of the effects
> of non-communication all round, a national dilemma ren-
> dered lethal by separate and total ignorance.
>
> H. S. Ferns, *Argentina*, 1968

'The interests of the inhabitants of these territories are para-
mount.' In August 1964, with these ringing words, the British
representative at the United Nations, Lord Caradon, declared his
nation's future motto for a long-drawn-out diplomatic battle and a
three-month war with Argentina. Caradon was responding to a
declaration on the part of the Falklanders, conveyed to the UN
General Assembly, that under all circumstances they wished to
remain a British dependency. The rights of the islanders to self-
determination, he said, lay squarely within the terms of Article 73
of the UN Charter.

The cause of this sudden interest in the Falkland Islands by the
highest forum of world affairs was a decision by Argentina to use
the UN 'committee of 24' on decolonisation to demand the 'return'
of the Falklands to Argentine sovereignty. The committee was
turning its attention to Britain as a result of the independence
crisis in Rhodesia. Argentina, in collaboration with Spain over
Gibraltar, felt the time was ripe to play the anti-imperialist card.
Nothing happened for a year. Then Ian Smith declared unilateral
independence for his white regime in Salisbury and Britain found
herself suddenly vulnerable. In December 1965, a resolution was

rushed through the General Assembly calling on Britain and Argentina to 'proceed without delay with negotiations . . . with a view to finding a peaceful solution to the problem'. From this simple resolution (No. 2065), so easy to pass in the panglossian atmosphere of the UN in New York, all else in this book follows.

The Falkland Islands had been the most somnolent of sleeping dogs. The UN resolution meant this could no longer be. The Wilson government had enough problems with the UN over Rhodesia not to go flouting a General Assembly resolution on so vague and trivial a matter as the Falklands. Negotiations commenced. These negotiations and the international auspices under which they were conducted gradually lent legitimacy to the Argentine claim. They implied that there was indeed an issue about which to negotiate and when they ran into any obstacle, notably islander resistance, Buenos Aires was enabled to feel a grievance, a sense of injustice.

The Foreign Office minister charged with the first talks was a former soldier and defence journalist, Lord Chalfont. Appointed by Harold Wilson in 1964 to the novel post of Minister for Disarmament, Chalfont had expected to spend his time commuting between London and Geneva. But the Foreign Office is no respecter of fancy titles. Chalfont found himself expected to accept his share of ministerial responsibilities, and these included relations with Latin America, which in turn embraced the Falklands negotiations. As Chalfont approached the task, his staff, departmental interest and personal reputation as a skilled negotiator were thus all directed towards honouring the negotiating remit and seeking a compromise, rather than allowing the islanders the final say and resting the case on that. In other words, the British 'national interest' overrode that of the islanders. The basis of the Foreign Office view on the Falklands was laid.

The view received reaffirmation with the first-ever tour of Latin America by a serving British Foreign Secretary, Michael Stewart, in 1966. The tour was a gesture towards what had always been regarded as a 'Cinderella' continent, and Stewart used it to prepare a critique of British diplomatic practice since the war. He said that the diplomats had been over-preoccupied with political work and neglectful of commercial.* In Latin America British investment and management had enjoyed a high reputation. Yet sheer inertia was permitting Germans, French and Americans to steal markets which should be British. The foreign service had to realise that modern diplomacy was the handmaid of economics as well as that of politics. The commercial attaché was king. To such a philosophy, a footling dispute with Argentina over the Falklands was a nuisance, a cloud over the Latin American landscape where the sun of British salesmanship ought now to shine. 'Reaching some agreement with Buenos Aires' became a prerequisite for improved trade.

The Argentine foreign ministry at the time was in the hands of a lawyer and former ambassador to Chile named Nicanor Costa Mendes. A short perky man, cosmopolitan, fond of English clothes and pretty women, Costa Mendes loved to flaunt his expertise in international relations. (He has even been a visiting lecturer at St Anthony's College, Oxford.) Yet his politics were firmly conservative and nationalist. He saw in the pursuit of Argentina's territorial claims against both Chile and Britain a means of strengthening the nation's identity and resisting the countervailing social appeal of Peronism. Under Costa Mendes, Argentina's claim to the Falklands entered the country's political arena to become more than just a slogan. It was also a valuable diversion from domestic ills. His attempt to put this concept into practice straddled the history of the Falklands dispute. Early in 1966, Costa Mendes established the Instituto y Museo Nacional de las Islas Malvinas y Adjacencias, an offshoot of the old Antarctic Institute in Buenos Aires. A Peronist committee for the recovery of the Malvinas was revived. Even the backing of the Anglo-Argentine community was obtained: its senior figure, Sir George Bolton of the Bank of London and South America, told Michael Stewart during his visit that the issue was a 'running sore' in relations between the two countries.

There now followed a series of meetings in London in July 1966

---

* An opinion elaborated in the Duncan Report, Cmnd 4107, 1969.

between a senior Foreign Office diplomat, Henry Hohler, and an official from the Argentine embassy, Juan Carlos Beltramino. Like all Argentine diplomats in London, Beltramino was (and has remained) a Falklands expert. Hohler had just arrived by way of postings in Europe and an ambassadorship in Saigon. Throughout the years of talks with Britain, Argentina's official negotiators were a relatively constant and experienced team. Few British representatives lasted more than two years. 'Which regime is supposed to be the stable one?' an Argentinian once murmured as he saw yet another strange face across the table.

The Hohler–Beltramino talks were conducted in secret and were clearly predicated on an eventual transfer of sovereignty. The chief concern was to find a means of protecting the rights and way of life of the islanders and to secure the continued development of the islands' economy. Both sides were abruptly reminded of the sensitivity of the issue when, in September 1966, a group of armed Peronist youths attempted to take the matter into their own hands. They hijacked a Dakota over Patagonia, flew to Port Stanley, landed on the racecourse (there then being no airstrip) and 'arrested' two British officials who approached them.

The group was called the New Argentina Movement and the exploit, codenamed Operation Condor, turned to farce as the plane sank into the soft ground. The group were rounded up by the marines and later returned to Argentina. (Their leader was eventually murdered as a *Montonero*.) Significantly, the Peronist trade union confederation referred to them as national heroes and threatened a twenty-four-hour strike if they were punished. Costa Mendes was appalled at this display of Argentine crudity in the midst of what were intended as peaceful negotiations.

The incident demonstrated the islands' vulnerability to surprise attack from the mainland. The previous April, Denis Healey had stated that 'protection for island territories in the Atlantic, Indian and Pacific Oceans can readily be provided from our major areas of deployment'. In the case of the Falklands, the relevant area was Simonstown in South Africa. But the continued withdrawal from east of Suez was casting doubt on the future of this base, and even Simonstown was a week's sailing from Port Stanley. What if the Argentinians failed to give a week's notice? The only answer was to increase the islands' small 'tripwire' force of marines to forty, allocate them a hovercraft (which later broke down) and divert warships as and when required. While this would not stop a full-scale assault, it would at least necessitate the shedding of blood in any invasion attempt. It was assumed, especially in the course of UN negotiations, that the Argentinians would not risk such action.

*

By September 1967, the negotiations had reached foreign-minister stage and a meeting took place in New York between Costa Mendes and the new British Foreign Secretary, George Brown. Observers felt that Brown's grasp of the subject was uncertain, though his instinctive ebullience found a response in Costa Mendes's more calculating diplomacy. The issue of islands opinion, previously emphasised by Lord Caradon at the UN, was acknowledged. The British intended to win the islanders round by demonstrating the benefits which a link with the mainland would bring. The Argentinians were happy to provide guarantees of continuity of customs and lifestyle. It was sovereignty, not a colony, which they craved. Meetings would continue to produce various heads of agreement.

It was now two years into the negotiations and not a word had been said about them either to Parliament (apart from a brief 'written answer') or in Port Stanley. The Foreign Office policy had been to prepare a satisfactory package of safeguards as well as economic benefits, to be presented to the islanders in such a way that the good news outweighed the bad. Aware of the sensitivity involved on both sides, officials wanted to avoid publicity 'until ministers were ready'. This could not last. The islands' governor at the time was Sir Cosmo Haskard, the last to be appointed before the Colonial Office merged with the FO. He travelled to London, was told of the Costa Mendes–Brown talks and permitted to inform his executive council of them but only under oath of secrecy. His

taciturnity on returning to Port Stanley in February 1968 predict-
ably aroused widespread alarm.

A letter was immediately sent from a number of islanders to
MPs in London, and to *The Times*, warning of their fears over the
course of possible negotiations. They complained bitterly of lack of
consultation and emphasised that, whatever was going on, they
'did not want to become Argentinians'. Among those who received
letters was a somewhat eccentric barrister and former diplomat in
the British embassy in Buenos Aires, William Hunter Christie. He
was a well-known Falklands enthusiast and author of the standard
work on the politics of Antarctica.*

Christie duly approached Patrick Ainslie, chairman of the
116-year-old Falkland Islands Company (FIC), owner of two-thirds
of the farms on the islands and virtual controller of its modest
economy. Christie suggested to Ainslie the formation of a Falkland
Islands Emergency Committee which, if the company would fund
it, he would run from his office in Lincoln's Inn. This room, a
Dickensian stage-set of yellowing papers and dusty tomes, became
the centre of activity. Support was assured from a number of MPs,
largely on the right of the Conservative Party, including Michael
Clark Hutchison and Bernard Braine. Ainslie agreed, and with
commendable tact Christie managed to get a Labour MP, a farmer
named Clifford Kenyon, to act as the committee's first secretary.

The committee's aim was simple: to represent in London the
views of the islanders independent of the channels provided by
the governor and his executive council. The intention, in other
words, was ostensibly democratic. The Foreign Office took the view
that the committee was little more than a front for the FIC. Even
its representative on the islands, Arthur Barton, was the company's
retired local manager. No one has ever maintained, however, that
the committee was at variance with islands opinion. Barton himself was a popular local figure and was an elected member of the
Falkland Islands' eight-man legislative council. (The governor's

---

* *The Antarctic Problem*, Allen and Unwin, 1951.

separate executive council included two members of this body, plus ex-officio members.) The FIC's stance throughout the dispute with Argentina was to be paternalist and strongly pro-British, even when this might have conflicted with its shareholders' interests.

British pressure groups are never so effective as when they are convinced that ministers and civil servants are hatching plots behind their backs. The rights and wrongs of a policy matter less than the secrecy with which it is being formulated. The implementation of the UN resolution was not discussed by Parliament until March 1968, when Lord Chalfont was asked in the House of Lords whether it was true that negotiations were under way with Argentina. He admitted that they were, but said they were 'confidential between governments'. He refused an invitation to deny that they were about sovereignty.

Lord Chalfont is the first of many ministers who recall the Falklands as causing them their worst moments in Parliament. Time and again such ministers were hoist on the petard of their own words – or words prepared for them by their civil servants. Were they or were they not prepared to transfer sovereignty to the Argentinians even if the islanders objected? What did the perennial phrase 'guided by the islanders' interests' really mean? Why were the islanders not present at any talks? What did the Foreign Office understand by self-determination: was it determination by the islanders or by the British people as a whole? These questions, put to Chalfont with searing directness, were never truly answered throughout all the years of negotiations. Officials felt they were political and for ministers to resolve. Ministers mouthed one evasion after another and hoped someone else would take on their job before the talks became critical.

Hardly had the new Falklands policy been formulated than the Foreign Office found it crumbling before its eyes. Tory backbenchers were enraged at what John Biggs-Davison MP called a 'solution of shame and infamy'. Argentine expectations were running high. Any change would require consent in both Port Stanley and the House of Commons. Both had now been encouraged to fear the worst. Officials had therefore to find a form of words to pour oil on troubled waters without actually denying the UN resolution. On 26 March, Michael Stewart (back at the Foreign Office after George Brown's resignation) told the House that any concession on sovereignty would occur 'only if it were clear to us . . . that the islanders themselves regarded such an agreement as satisfactory to their interests'. Stewart could hardly have put it more categorically, but whenever he and his colleagues were asked if this meant the islanders had a veto over any deal, they were reluctant to give a definitive yes. Such a veto would effectively render the negotiations meaningless.

Talks with Buenos Aires continued throughout the summer of 1968 but with a new hesitancy on the British side. In meetings with the Argentine ambassador, Eduardo McLoughlin, and with Beltramino, Chalfont began to refer to the need to 'create a climate in which one day sovereignty can be discussed'. The climate he referred to was not in London but in Port Stanley. The thrust of the talks was towards what came to be known as the 'hearts and minds' approach: encouraging the islanders themselves to want the benefits of closer links with the mainland. At the end of the year, Chalfont detached himself from a royal visit to Chile to preach this new gospel personally in Port Stanley.

Chalfont spent three days traversing the islands, extolling the virtues of a new deal with Argentina: an air service to the mainland (the Falklands were then only accessible by sea), better schools and hospitals and a more immediate market for local produce. He was greeted with hecklers, banners and placards: 'No Sellout' and 'The Falklands are British'. Local opinion seemed totally deaf to Chalfont's warning that Britain could not sustain the islands indefinitely from 8,000 miles away. Chalfont formed a personal aversion to this combination of isolationism and dependency, an aversion shared with many other visitors before and since.

The report Chalfont prepared for Stewart on his return was brisk. The Argentinians' strong feeling should not be underestimated. They had shown some willingness to compromise on their claim for outright possession. The islanders had shown none. If Britain simply broke off talks, relations with Argentina and with the UN would deteriorate. In a prophetic phrase, Chalfont said it might become a 'casus belli'. The Falklands was discussed in cabinet, and – not for the last time in this matter – the outcome did not find favour at the Foreign Office. The Wilson government decided that, as long as the islanders did not want any transfer of sovereignty, it was not worth the political price to force it onto them. On 11 December 1968, Stewart announced categorically that 'no transfer could be made against the wishes of the islanders'. The issue remained on the table in the light of the UN resolution, but that was all. For good measure, the Tory opposition spokesman, Sir Alec Douglas-Home, pledged that the Tories would 'strike sovereignty from the agenda' when they returned to office.

Just as Costa Mendes had succeeded in putting political bite into the Falklands issue in Buenos Aires, so the Falklands lobby and its parliamentary friends had done the same in London. Papers such as the *Daily Express* and *Daily Telegraph* could be relied upon to leap to the attack at the slightest mention of dealings with Argentina. It was established in the minds of both front benches that any Falklands settlement had a 'political price' attached to it. The size of the price was unknown. Yet, on so minor an issue, why bother to pay it? Not just successive Parliaments but successive cabinets became instinctively hostile to Whitehall's determination to pursue negotiations, whenever they appeared on any agenda.

Why did the Foreign Office not now simply give up? The Argentinians could have been told there was nothing doing. The UN could have been told that talks had foundered on its own oft-stated principle of self-determination. Instead, the Foreign Office ploughed on. In November 1969, letters were sent to U Thant, the UN Secretary General, promising to continue talks on communications and economic cooperation. These talks survived the fall of the Wilson administration and the advent of Sir Alec Douglas-Home to the Foreign Office in 1970. Douglas-Home's only provisos were that sovereignty should not be on the agenda and that the islanders should be involved throughout. To reinforce this down-grading, talks were to be conducted not by the junior minister responsible for Latin America, Joseph Godber, nor even by an official from the Latin America department. The chosen envoy was the under-secretary in charge of 'dependent territories', David Scott.

Scott's appointment was a rare stroke of Whitehall tact. A former Commonwealth Office civil servant, Scott had been more concerned with the problems of colonial status than with the demands of Britain's trading relations with South America. His avuncular manner betrayed none of the smooth aloofness which had so often grated on the Falklanders. He also displayed the flair possessed by many with experience of colonial administration for projecting a sympathetic personality in public. He was a civil servant playing a quasi-political role. He had not only to negotiate a deal with Buenos Aires but also to obtain political consent for it in Port Stanley.

Some new arrangement for links with the islands was now urgent. The Falkland Islands Company's vessel, *Darwin*, which ran monthly to Montevideo, was losing money heavily and was to be withdrawn at the end of 1971. The only other regular communication was a charter cargo ship, *AES*, commuting four times a year to Tilbury with the wool crop and general supplies. A study by the accountants Peat Marwick had looked into both sea and air connections and reached the conclusion that an air link was the most economic. The question was who should provide it.

The 1971 Communications Agreement with Buenos Aires was the highpoint of British Falklands diplomacy. The basis of the deal reached between Scott, McLoughlin and Beltramino was that the British would build an airstrip and provide a new shipping link to the Argentine mainland, if the Argentinians would run the air service. Considerable haggling surrounded the status of documentation for islanders landing at Comodoro Rivadavia: to the Argentinians it was an 'internal' flight, to the British an international one. It was agreed that there should be a 'white card' of nondescript markings. The Argentinians had to promise not to hold the Falklanders liable for taxation or military service – a long-standing Buenos Aires threat.

The essence of the agreement was simply contact. Scott's often proclaimed principle was 'rape of the Falklands, no; seduction, by all means'. The air service would take islanders to mainland schools, hospitals and entertainments. Tourism would develop. Supplies of fresh produce, especially fruit, would arrive. The Falklanders could begin to feel a new regional identity more in keeping with their location. In June 1971, Scott crossed to Port Stanley to sell his package to the islanders. His reception contrasted with that given to Chalfont three years earlier. On radio and at meetings, he repeated time and again that he was 'not here to sell you up the River Plate'. He wanted to talk not about sovereignty but about a better standard of living. He proved a master communicator and the very fact of his non-ministerial status seems to have calmed nerves.

Scott returned immediately to Buenos Aires with the consent in his pocket, accompanied by a posse of islanders. Ten days of intense talks followed, and the agreement was signed on 1 July. Scott's main constraint was Joseph Godber in London, insistent that no inch be conceded on sovereignty. Afterwards, Beltramino told Scott in confidence that he regarded sovereignty as having been shelved for the time being. Scott added his personal view that the islanders would be under an Argentine flag within twenty-five years. Such was the confidence of the officials on both sides in the efficacy of the 'hearts and minds' policy.

Scott's deal obeyed the first law of complex negotiations. It avoided the crucial issue in dispute and concentrated on establishing confidence in areas where minor accord seemed feasible. Both sides knew that islander opinion was a stumbling block which could not be disregarded. Confidence in the agreement now had to be built up in Port Stanley, requiring time and tact and money. They were to prove scarce commodities.

The policy adopted by the Foreign Office, both before and since the agreement, was founded on a belief that the Falklanders could eventually be assimilated into the essentially European mainland community. No attempt was made, for instance, to buy them out and resettle them elsewhere in Britain or the commonwealth. Yet the mainland community could hardly have less in common with the 'kelpers'. The Anglo-Argentinians of Buenos Aires have their roots in the middle-class commercial life of the capital. The descendants of Scots and Welsh settlers in adjacent Patagonia might superficially seem to possess similar characteristics to the Falklanders. Yet even the Welsh of Puerto Madryn are fully fledged Argentinians and proud of it. Their lingua franca is Spanish (or Welsh), not English. The Falklanders, as one of them proudly said, have 'not an ounce of Latin America' in them.

The Falklands people have lived for over a century as tenants to the Falkland Islands Company, plus nine other absentee land-lords based in Britain. The Shackleton Report of 1976 (see pages 42 to 45), a document determinedly optimistic about the islands' potential, nonetheless referred constantly to the sense of depend-ency this had created in the workforce. There was virtually no local private sector. Almost everyone was employed either by the FIC or by the government. This had bred, in Shackleton's words, 'a lack of confidence and enterprise at the individual and community level, and a degree of acceptance of their situation which verges on apathy'. A report subsequently written by a marine major, Ewen Southby-Tailyour (who served in the Falklands war), was less complimentary. He explained the problems of island development firmly in terms of the poor quality of the workforce. They were, for the most part, 'a drunken, decadent, immoral and indolent collection of drop-outs'. These characteristics, he said, 'are evident at all levels of society with only a frighteningly few exceptions'. It should be added that, despite these strong words, Southby-Tailyour had an affection for these people which is evident throughout his report.

The Falklands have long suffered from emigration and from a surplus of men to women. On West Falkland this ratio is more than two to one. The presence of a marine garrison, even just forty strong, marrying one or two girls a year and taking them back to England, has been a constant source of complaint. Girls of child-bearing age in a community of just 1,800 people are a crucial local resource. One consequence has been a divorce rate estimated at three times that of a roughly equivalent Scots island community.

In addition, the nature of the islands' one export, wool, encourages the settlers of the Camp – the territory outside Port Stanley (from Spanish *campo*) – to a solitary existence. They demonstrate little of the intense interdependence of communities which live off the sea. There is no island fishery – despite no apparent shortage of fish. Cohesion lies in human intercourse between families and neighbours rather than in strong local institutions and cultural traditions. The Falklands are a fragile society, threatened by any intrusion or change, including that represented by the younger generation. Visiting teachers, soldiers, scientists, government officials – their presence hinting at a better life elsewhere – have all been seen as part of that threat.

The Falklanders share a collective fragility with small isolated communities the world over. Sociologists have detected it even in the urban villages of major city centres. Yet, in the 1970s, the Falkland islanders' predicament seemed stark: they felt they were being handed over to an enemy. The islands' population may have been almost comically small, but in the context of post-imperial self-determination it had an emotional weapon to arm itself against change more effectively than any other community under the rule of the British Parliament.

*

The Communications Agreement began fruitfully enough. Local enthusiasm was considerable, especially among the younger islanders. Scholarships were offered and taken up at mainland schools. There were jokes about oranges, gauchos and a possible replenishment in the supply of women. In January 1972 an Albatross flying-boat landed off Port Stanley to commence temporary twice-monthly flights to Comodoro Rivadavia, prior to an airstrip being built. The cruise liner *Libertad* arrived with 350 Argentine tourists, who cleaned Port Stanley out of its limited stock of souvenirs. Arthur Barton was sufficiently encouraged to tell the Falkland Islands Committee in London that they could wind up their operations.

The first back-sliding was a British one. Whatever agreement Scott might have signed in Buenos Aires, he was not plenipotentiary over the Treasury. There was no sign of the promised maritime link to an Argentine port to replace *Darwin*. This placed correspondingly greater emphasis on the importance of the Argentine air link and on Argentine ships to supply it with aviation fuel. British engineers made a survey of Cape Pembroke outside Port Stanley as site for the promised airport, but this indicated a need for costly foundation work well beyond the resources of the Falkland Islands' budget. The Foreign Office had not secured the necessary finance from the Overseas Development Agency, and were thus unable to honour the British side of the agreement.

The Argentinians offered to lay a temporary runway themselves if the British would obtain from the Americans the necessary steel-mesh strip. This was done at an estimated cost of $1 million, reportedly as part of a defence package which included an exchange of information with the Americans on jump-jet technology. In the second week of May 1972, the Argentine naval transport *Cabo San Gonzalo* sailed from Buenos Aires carrying forty workmen and technicians and loaded with 900 tons of construction and air-control equipment. They were waved off at the quay-side by the British ambassador, Sir Michael Hadow, himself. The local correspondent of the *Financial Times* opened his report with the words: 'The Argentines have finally established a beach-head on the Falklands.' He laconically listed the items aboard the ship and reported the comment of a local magazine: 'Each item in a certain way implies the ratification of Argentina's sovereignty.'

Whitehall now experienced a severe bout of interdepartmental warfare. As the temporary airstrip was down, the Overseas

Development Agency, with far more pressing claims on its tight budget, began to wonder what possible reason there was for any permanent airport. Why not wait and see what market there might be for the new Argentine Fokker Friendship service? Might a longer runway not make an Argentine invasion easier? If one were built, should it be of domestic length or suitable for international jets – perhaps a South Pole route to New Zealand? Approval was finally given for the project to go out to tender, but only for a short runway. The promise of a new sea link to the mainland vanished without trace. Every nuance of this argument was read, and mis-read, in Buenos Aires. Britain's commitment to the Communications Agreement, and thus to the future of the Falklands, was apparently less than wholehearted.

Argentine politics, after a period of comparative stability under the military regime of General Ogania, was deteriorating into chaos. Haunted by the still-powerful presence of Peron in his Madrid exile, the military authorities finally allowed him home on a visit in November 1972. They hoped the sight of the ageing dictator in the flesh would demythologise his name and divide his supporters. They were wrong. Within a year, Peron was back in the presidential palace. Though he was now a dying man his return was an extraordinary comeback for an essentially prewar fascist leader. Once again the crudest sort of nationalism was on the Argentine political agenda.

If the British had dishonoured the letter of the Communications Agreement, the Argentinians had been less than careful to preserve its spirit. Beltramino and Scott had meticulously negotiated that the opening of the air link would be a civilian affair, even though it would be run by the military air service, LADE. When Scott arrived at Buenos Aires for the ceremony to celebrate the launch of the service – his last function before becoming High Commissioner to New Zealand – he was horrified to see the inaugural flight filled with senior officers in full uniform. Events worthy of an Ealing comedy ensued. The Falkland Islands' governor, Toby Lewis, was ordered to run up the British flag at the airstrip and appear in full-dress regalia, his plumes blowing proudly in the strong wind. The islanders took fright and feared a covert invasion, engineered as much by the British Foreign Office as by the Argentinians. There was even rumour of a demonstration. The islands' secretary, John Laing, overreacted and called out the marine detachment on patrol. A supposedly joyful event was overshadowed by high tension.

Buenos Aires, now overtaken completely by a Peronist revival, effectively abandoned the Scott–Beltramino 'hearts and minds' policy. The Argentine ambassador to the UN reopened the sovereignty question, warning that his government might be forced to 'seek the eradication of this anachronistic colonial situation'. Peronist journals such as *Cronica* and *Mayoria* took up the cue. The ambassador was praised for his new departure from the 'history of our pusillanimous and colourless diplomacy'. In Port Stanley, the LADE staff, blatantly military and resentful at being posted to such a spot, provoked the growing hostility of the islanders. In London the Falkland Islands Committee was reformed, again on Hunter Christie's initiative. Joseph Godber left the Foreign Office, to be replaced by the hardest of hard-liners, Julian Amery.

Implementation of the Communications Agreement passed in 1973 to the new head of the Latin America department, Hugh Carless, and his superintending under-secretary, Robin Edmonds. Carless had already served in Brazil and achieved a certain unwonted fame as a butt of Eric Newby's satire in *A Short Walk in the Hindu Kush*. He was also one of the few outstanding Latin American experts produced by the Foreign Office since the war. To the Falklands Islands Committee, Carless, Edmonds and his successor as under-secretary, George Hall, became the embodiment of the Whitehall Falklands policy.

Two supplementary Communications Agreements were reached by the Foreign Office aimed at encouraging economic links with the mainland and permitting the Argentinians to build and supply fuel tanks at the airfield. Fuel oil, including that for the islands' modest internal air service, would be provided exclusively by the Argentine state oil concern, YFP, and the base would be staffed by Argentine military personnel. At the same time, the British belatedly announced the commencement of work on a concrete runway at Cape Pembroke. These agreements, signed in June 1974, did more than anything to increase the islanders' suspicions of the Foreign Office. They had lost their monthly British supply ship, and received instead a less than reliable Argentine air service. They had seen an influx of Argentine supplies and officials, and Argentina had now gained control of their fuel oil. To cap it all, in December 1974, the Argentine ambassador to London, Manuel Anchorena, was summoned back to Buenos Aires after negotiating the new agreements and insulted publicly as a 'lawyer for the British'.

A month later, Buenos Aires imposed immigration controls on all air travel to the Falklands. The 'white card' was now replaced by one declaring the holder to be an Argentine citizen of the Malvinas. Without submitting to this unilateral breach of the 1971 agreement, no Falklander could get to or from the rest of the world (except on an occasional British ship). By conceding this measure – and with no new British sea link in sight there was no option – Britain granted Buenos Aires effective passport control over the islanders. It was a major advance in Argentina's fight for sovereignty.

*

Whatever might have been the rhythm implied by the Scott–Beltramino accords, it was now replaced by an ad hoc combination of sticks and carrots, largely directed at breaking down Falklander intransigence. The return of a Labour government in 1974 brought to the issue yet another minister, David Ennals, and yet another feeling, instilled by officials, that some new initiative was needed to outflank the sovereignty barrier and maintain the commitment to the UN talks. Seminars were held, the Falklands Committee carefully consulted, options tabled and, last resort of Whitehall despair, a major study commissioned. The Foreign Office intention was that the study, ordered from the ebullient Labour peer Lord Shackleton (son of the explorer), should paint a rosy future for the islands, but only on the condition that the islanders settled their differences with Buenos Aires.

This proved a miscalculation. In the first place, the Argentinians worked themselves into a synthetic fury at what they saw as a direct challenge from London. The failing Peronist regime – ruled uncertainly by Peron's widow, Isabella, and wracked by *Montonero* terrorism – was already sensing the 1976 coup which brought the military junta to power. In January 1976 Lord Shackleton's team were denied permits to fly through Argentina. He was portrayed as a 'pirate and buccaneer', to his evident delight. As a result, the naval Antarctic survey vessel *Endurance* had to be sent to convey him from Montevideo to Port Stanley, and this in turn led to Buenos Aires severing ambassadorial relations between Britain and Argentina. Five years of patient diplomacy lay close to ruins.

The Shackleton mission boosted morale on the islands – if only by the hysteria it evoked in Buenos Aires. For once here was someone sent by the Foreign Office who did not want to discuss sovereignty or links with the mainland, but merely mutton, alginates, fishery and oil. In February 1976, Shackleton sailed on to South Georgia to visit for the first time the grave of his father. By way of response, an Argentine naval vessel, *Admiral Storni*, was ordered to fire across the bows of a British scientific research ship, *Shackleton*, in the belief that the peer himself was aboard. A flurry of naval activity followed, including the diversion of the British frigate *Chichester* to Port Stanley on its way home from Hong Kong. Relations with Argentina had never been at such a low ebb.

Shackleton's report was delivered to the government in June 1976, shortly after Harold Wilson had given way to James Callaghan as Prime Minister. Anthony Crosland was now Foreign Secretary, with Ted Rowlands as his junior minister – yet another new face on the Falklands desk. The 400-page document immediately became, and remains, the point of departure for all discussion of the Falklands economy and society (supplemented by another from the same team in July 1982). It admirably illustrates its author's maxim that an island is an area of land entirely surrounded by advice.

Shackleton laid great stress on the fact that the islands were in no sense a drain on the British taxpayer, who on balance made a profit from them. (By the early 1980s, this was no longer the case.) He was most critical of the past exploitation of the local economy. The policy of the Falkland Islands Company and the nine absentee farming companies was, he wrote, 'to keep investment in the Falklands as low as possible without putting the farming operations in jeopardy and to channel any undistributed profits into UK investment'. He estimated that between 1951 and 1974 the absentee companies took £11½ million more in profit than they invested back in the Falklands.

These findings instilled in the islanders a sense of grievance which further increased their suspicion of the British government. Yet their economy was as well protected as in theory was their territory. The Aliens Ordinance, under which colonial land can be protected from foreign purchase on the decision of the local governor, prevented Argentine economic encroachment and effectively forestalled any Argentine immigration. For the owners, this kept the price of land low and its yield relatively high. For the islanders, there seemed little to threaten their apparently contented dependence on the company and the government beyond the one menace of emigration.

Shackleton's ninety proposals presented the islands as a potential paradise of economic progress: trawler fishing, land improvement, alginates from seaweed, salmon farming, road construction, tourism and oil exploration. The key to most of this was that 'the permanent airfield should be strengthened and extended to a length necessary to receive short-/medium-haul jets and part-loaded long-haul jets'. Although the team were excluded from considering political or defence matters, Shackleton pointed out privately that a longer runway would make rapid troop deployment possible in the event of a threatened invasion from the mainland.

In only two areas did Shackleton show any sympathy to White-hall's ambitions for his report. In the case of the harvesting of deep-water krill (a small crustacean) and oil exploration, both involving operations well outside Falklands waters, he said that 'major policy formulation must be seen as taking place within a highly political arena'. Nonetheless, he poured cold water on the more extravagant predictions made for hydrocarbon exploration in the Malvinas Basin. Extraction would be difficult and costly in so hostile a climate and 'not only because of the political risks involved'. The theory, widely held in Latin America and the USA, that Britain's attachment to the Falklands is based on the prospect of glowing oil riches has never been given credence by the UK.

Shackleton now reads as a monument of British paternalism. The islanders were to be elevated from their cultural immaturity and economic dependence, primarily through large injections of British money. The most constructive suggestion was that land hold-ings be diversified out of the hands of the FIC, but the report fought shy of suggesting outright nationalisation of the FIC and enforced disposal. In addition public-investment projects totalling some £13 million were recommended. It was hard to envisage where within Whitehall Shackleton expected to find support for these proposals. The ODA was already resenting the £1 million a year spent on the islands' administration; the runway extension alone would require £4 million. The Foreign Office Latin America depart-ment had hoped for a sledge-hammer to bludgeon the islanders into concessions. It was hardly likely to champion the provision of cash from the Treasury to promote their greater independence.

What Shackleton did provide was fuel for the Falklands lobby. Parliamentary support for the re-established Falklands Islands Com-mittee was swelling, with airborne visits by MPs under the aegis of the Commonwealth Parliamentary Association. Argentina's repu-tation for political extremism was also widening the committee's

ideological appeal to embrace Liberal and Labour MPs. Already the
Falkland Islands Company had found itself taken over by Slater
Walker and passed to the coal firm of Charringtons (later to Coalite).
To Labour MPs as much as to Tories, the idea of sacrificing the
victims of capitalism to the torturers of Buenos Aires was
unthinkable.

*

There was worse news yet for the Foreign Office. There is no
evidence that, before the 1970s, Argentine threats to invade British
territory in the South Atlantic were more than political or journal-
istic rhetoric. However, it is known that a draft plan for the
'recovery' of Argentine territory in the South Atlantic had existed
in the Argentine navy headquarters since the late 1960s, prepared
or at least revised by none other than Captain Jorge Anaya (head
of the navy in 1982). With the return of Peron in 1973, a 'retirement' of senior officers took place and the navy was put in charge
of the comparatively junior Admiral Emilio Massera.

Not content with the subordinate role his chosen service had
traditionally played to the army in Argentine politics, Massera
initiated a period of intensive naval aggrandisement. The navy
became virtually an independent military command. It developed
its own air force, equipped with modern American and French jets,
purchased on the admiral's freewheeling trips abroad. It strengthened its marine commando force and established land and air
bases at strategic points along the coast. It was active to a fault in
the 'dirty war' against opponents of the government: the Naval
Mechanical School became the most notorious of Argentina's torture centres. All young officers were expected to play their full
part in this work. No service or section of a service should be able
to claim afterwards that its hands were clean of involvement. Many
naval officers were so traumatised by the experience that they
ended up in psychiatric clinics.

Massera and his colleagues had long been impressed by the ease
with which the Indian government had taken military possession

of the Portuguese colony of Goa in 1961. An almost total lack of international condemnation greeted this action. To Massera, the fastidious diplomacy of Costa Mendes and his foreign ministry successors was based on a false premise: that world opinion was intrinsically averse to force. A swift and preferably bloodless operation in the cause of anti-colonialism would soon be accepted as a fait accompli. So why not an operation to recover the Falklands?

The Massera–Anaya plan, 'Plan Goa', involved a surprise landing on the islands and is believed to have included the total removal of the existing population to Montevideo and its replacement by Argentine settlers. This would neatly reverse the 1833 action and forestall any wrangling about the status of the islanders under Argentine rule. Nonetheless, the Argentine navy had a healthy respect for the British submarine fleet, and the plan accepted that sustaining a garrison by sea would not be easy. It would be better to put just a hundred or so marines ashore alongside the civilian settlers to complicate any British military response, should there be one. It is believed that Plan Goa was put to the new Videla junta after the 1976 coup and again at the height of Videla's prestige after the World Cup triumph in 1978. On both occasions, sceptics managed to quash it. (The British lawyer Hunter Christie was told by a naval commander in 1975 that British submarine strength was the crucial factor.)

The navy did, however, win for the regime one patch of British territory. Late in 1976 some fifty 'technicians' were put ashore on Southern Thule in the South Sandwich group. This was done with no publicity and initially with a flat denial that any such landing had occurred. The first indications came from radio ham operators on the Falklands. At least one catalyst to the occupation of Southern Thule was the British decision, taken the year before, to withdraw the ice-patrol ship *Endurance* from the South Atlantic. This ship was the last British naval presence in the Antarctic and her impending removal was taken as a clear sign of reduced British commitment to her possessions in the area. (*Endurance* was subsequently saved by the Foreign Office, only to find herself again threatened in 1981.) When the occupation of Southern Thule was finally revealed to the Commons in May 1978 (over a year later), the Callaghan government said it had rejected a suggestion that a force of marines be sent to repossess the island.

For the second time since the passage of the UN resolution, the British government would now have been justified in ceasing negotiations on the Falklands. In the past two years, the Argentinians had broken the Communications Agreements, fired on a British ship, unilaterally severed ambassadorial relations and invaded British territory. James Callaghan would have been supported both in Parliament and at the UN in any stand he took against the junta. For good measure, he could have seen the Argentinians off Southern Thule with a couple of frigates.

Instead, in February 1977, the Foreign Secretary, Anthony Crosland, stood up in the Commons to give his official response to the Shackleton Report. It was a highly distorted gloss. He drew attention to the 'enormous potential waiting there to be exploited', especially of fish and oil. However, Shackleton was made to imply this wealth was dependent on Britain being 'willing to have economic cooperation with Argentina'. Crosland added, in a remarkable leap of judgement, that 'we cannot have that unless certain political issues are raised'. More talks would therefore commence between his junior minister, Ted Rowlands, Buenos Aires and Port Stanley. Sovereignty would be 'in no way prejudiced' by the talks and nothing would be settled without the islanders' acceptance, though he confirmed that they would 'raise fundamental questions in the relationship between the islands, Britain and Argentina'. A report carefully (indeed optimistically) written in support of establishing the Falklands' economic independence was thus stood on its head to serve the Foreign Office view. Dismissing the more costly investment proposals, Crosland even turned the knife further: 'There are more urgent claims from much poorer communities. The right political circumstances do not exist.'

*

The Foreign Office now simply gritted its collective teeth. Shackleton – whatever he had really said – was to be used as the bait in bringing both sides to realise their mutual self-interest. Diplomacy is nothing if not the art of persistence. If the islanders would not receive the Argentinians into their hearts, perhaps they might into their bank balances.

Rowlands arrived in Port Stanley in February 1977 to be greeted by the usual demonstration of affection for Britain and aversion to Foreign Office policy. The visit was considered a success. A wiry extrovert from the Welsh valleys who likes to be liked, Rowlands proved adept at the public-bar conviviality which consumes much of the Falklanders' leisure time. More important, he brought from London a message which appeared definitive. The dispute with Argentina had gone on long enough. It had to be settled. Nothing would or could be done against the islanders' wishes, but he wanted their agreement to enter full negotiations. They simply had to trust him. The island leaders who met Rowlands appear to have been impressed that continued intransigence would be futile. They were being offered a share in the process of deciding their future. They should now take it for fear of worse. For the first time, the distant crack of a Westminster three-line whip could be heard in Port Stanley.

Hugh Carless, who was in Argentina and was shortly to become chargé d'affaires in Buenos Aires, and Robin Edmonds in London now seized the moment. The Foreign Office immediately put out a statement on the strength of the Port Stanley meetings to the effect that negotiations would take place between Britain and Argentina on both economic and political ties with the Falklands. In a subtle extension of Crosland's position, the statement added, 'In such negotiations the basic issues affecting the future of the islands, including sovereignty, would have to be discussed.'

The Foreign Office was now on the brink of a political coup. It had restored sovereignty to the Falklands agenda nine years after a Labour government had removed it and seven years after a Tory government had done so. Its aim had been wholly laudable: to heal a running sore in Britain's relations with Latin America. This sore would only fester as time passed and could not be cured merely with a series of uncompromising statements. Transient politicians might not like it, but constructive negotiations and settlement were clearly in the interests of the islanders and of Britain's relations with Argentina. Yet a Whitehall policy is only effective if its creators can convince a government of the need to implement it. Successive Foreign Office ministers were convinced: Chalfont, Godber, Ennals, Rowlands, and later Ridley and Luce. But successive cabinets could never see why they should pay the price of enforcing such a compromise on their followers in Parliament. The Foreign Office was thus a Sisyphus, pushing the ministerial stone uphill every two years or so, only to see it crash down again.

Rowlands was now almost at the top of the hill. The Falklands negotiations became peripatetic for the remaining two years of the Labour government, visiting successive neutral locations, Rio de Janeiro, Rome, Lima and New York. The basis of the talks was an economic package which could be sold to the islanders in return for some understanding on sovereignty and administration. The British toyed with a variety of constitutional concepts: treating the land as separate from its inhabitants; 'transfer and leaseback' on the Hong Kong model; and joint Anglo-Argentine sovereignty and administration, known as condominium.

Rowlands's efforts had stimulated the Falklands lobby to new heights of activity. Hunter Christie had established his committee in what must have been London's smallest office, a cubby-hole off Victoria Street. It now had a full-time director, Air Commodore Brian Frow, and a £15,000 budget. It worked marvels of pressure-group activity. Parliamentary interventions requiring a ministerial response increased from an average of one a year since 1971 to five in 1977 alone, two of them full-dress debates. Yet somehow the political drive did not match the official enthusiasm. As in 1968–9 and 1973–4, a government struggling with economic tribulation and electoral unpopularity found it hard to commit itself to difficult change, however minor.

The Argentine negotiators appeared troubled by equally conflicting pressures. Rowlands's opposite number, Captain Gualter
Allara, found in mid-1977 that a freebooting Buenos Aires business-
man, Cao Saravia, had calmly offered '$1 million more than any
current asking price' for the FIC from its current owners, Charringtons. The bid was stopped under threat of invoking the Aliens
Ordinance. Then in November, shortly before another round of
talks in New York, the Argentine navy abruptly (albeit temporarily)
cut the fuel supply to Port Stanley and said their ships would no
longer fly the British flag in Falklands waters.

*

There now occurred one of the most curious incidents of the
Falklands saga, its origins deep in Britain's most obscure freema-
sonry, the intelligence services. These services comprise the domestic MI5, the overseas MI6 and the Government Communications
Headquarters (GCHQ) at Cheltenham, monitoring overseas signals
intelligence. Through their various hands passes material from
spies, government missions abroad and friendly agencies such as
the CIA and the National Security Agency in Washington. This
material is processed with the Downing Street Cabinet Office by a
secretariat comprising two current intelligence groups, one for the
eastern hemisphere and one for the western. Here it is sifted and
given an 'assessment' or political/ strategic overlay.

These groups, known as 'Cigs', report to a weekly meeting of
the Joint Intelligence Committee (JIC), held each Wednesday (or
more often in a crisis). This body is the fulcrum of British intelligence activity. Its chairman is customarily the deputy head of the
Foreign Office and its membership includes the government's
security coordinator, the head of the intelligence secretariat and
the chiefs of MI5, MI6 and GCHQ. This committee pulls together
the various assessments into a ten-to-twelve-page booklet under
red covers which normally goes to members of the cabinet's
overseas and defence committee with their weekend boxes. A
highly confidential annex, placed as if to indicate its sensitivity in

a black box, contains selected 'raw material' of a topical nature and is sent only to those who 'need to know', invariably the Prime Minister, and the Defence and Foreign Secretaries.

Ministers, and particularly Prime Ministers, vary in their addiction to these boxes. Some, such as Harold Wilson, find them a compelling real-life spy story to round off a weekend's reading. Those with little experience of foreign, or defence affairs can, on the other hand, regard them as yet more barely relevant paper amid the welter already claiming their attention. James Callaghan, Prime Minister in 1977, was a fanatic. He had a map inserted into his box each week indicating the location of every ship in the fleet so he could counter Ministry of Defence protests of non-availability. He devoured the red book and loved to jump items from it on his colleagues. At this time, such items included two 'American' trouble spots, Belize and the Falklands.

In November 1977 the JIC had taken the view that another exploit similar to the Southern Thule expedition might be in hand in Buenos Aires. The unprovoked cutting of fuel supplies was a possible prelude. Naval exercises were due. Imminent New York talks could provide an incentive, were they to turn sour. Callaghan saw this assessment, raised it with Rowlands and the new Foreign Secretary, David Owen, and put it to the cabinet's defence and overseas policy committee. The Prime Minister and Foreign Secretary wanted a submarine sent immediately to be on station should any trouble occur. The Defence Secretary, Fred Mulley, was reluctant to send more than two frigates. Callaghan overruled him and demanded both frigates and a submarine. These were duly diverted from the Caribbean. Ironically, the commander in chief of this task force was Admiral Henry Leach, later to be First Sea Lord and prime mover of its 1982 successor. Another meeting of Callaghan's committee drew up rules of engagement for Leach's captains, based on a 25-mile exclusion zone round the Falklands.

Callaghan disclosed the fact of this operation to the Commons in March 1982 at the height of the South Georgia crisis. The result was an intense argument about its true significance. It had been kept secret both during and after the event, the intention being to declare its presence only if an invasion seemed imminent. Otherwise it would seem a flagrant provocation. Yet, if the Argentinians never knew of the submarine's presence, how could it be said to have deterred them, as Callaghan has claimed? Callaghan said that he had told the head of MI6, Sir Maurice Oldfield, of the committee's action but did not know whether this information was passed on. (Oldfield is now dead.) Both the Foreign Office and the Ministry of Defence vigorously maintain that the Argentinians knew nothing about it. As the Franks Report has since shown, however, the crucial point was that the deterrent force was activated and put on station. Deterrence was potential, even if not actual. Clearly in 1977 the cabinet and intelligence machine worked smoothly in response to a perceived threat.

What is more questionable about the 1977 incident is the impact it had on future intelligence assessment of Falklands threats. The movement of modern warships is a costly business. It disrupts Nato and sorely inconveniences the navy. There is little doubt that, to some in the British intelligence community, the 1977 submarine operation came to seem an excessive response to what was a low level of threat. This might not matter after the event. But how might the JIC assess future alarmist material from Buenos Aires, and how might the diplomatic and defence establishments react? Might they not be tempted to treat 1977 as a case of someone crying wolf and avoid making the same mistake again?

*

In selecting her ministers on assuming office in May 1979, Margaret Thatcher consciously sought a balance between the different wings of her party. She was well aware that many of her cabinet colleagues had not supported her bid for the leadership in 1975. Yet expediency and party unity required that certain of these dissenters be offered senior posts. For the Foreign Office, only one individual seemed remotely qualified by seniority and experience, and that was Lord Carrington. Mrs Thatcher and Carrington were not bosom friends. As a hereditary peer he had never been elected to Parliament, and he embodied an aristocratic and wealthy self-assurance, characteristic of a certain breed of Tories, which Mrs Thatcher always found difficult to stomach. Nor did she possess any great respect for the department of which he was to be head. Its international view of Britain's interests, its obsession with the Third World and its rampant Europeanism, all made it an object of suspicion. To have it in the charge of a supporter of the moderate Toryism of her predecessor, Edward Heath, would surely test her blandly right-wing approach to foreign policy. This was exacerbated when Carrington chose Sir Ian Gilmour, an outspoken critic of Mrs Thatcher's economic policies, as his deputy and spokesman in the Commons.

The Prime Minister therefore made no mistake in her third Foreign Office appointment. Nicholas Ridley may have been no more her class of Tory than Carrington and Gilmour (all were old Etonians). Yet he was clever, an ardent supporter of her leadership and had the signal distinction of having fallen out with Edward Heath as a junior industry minister in the 1970 government. Were British politics ever so crude, Ridley would have been termed a Thatcherite fifth column in the Foreign Office.

Ridley was well aware that few ministers ever shine in junior office. He also knew that the spotlight of Carrington's foreign policy would be on Rhodesia, Europe and the Middle East, none of which proved to be within his area of responsibility. This area included the Americas, and with it the poisoned chalice of the Falklands issue. Was there anything here, he wondered, to which he could modestly put his name before fortune and Mrs Thatcher moved him on?

Both Robin Edmonds and Hugh Carless had departed from the Latin America department in 1977, though Carless remained as chargé d'affaires in Buenos Aires until 1980, later to be ambassador in Caracas. The newly named South America department was headed from 1979 by Robin Fearn. Above him as under-secretary for the Americas was John Ure. Like Carless, Ure was an enthusiast for Latin American history and culture. He had seen service in Chile, Portugal and Havana. His travelogue, *Cucumber Sandwiches in the Andes*, is a delightful work of diplomatic erudition. Civil servants like to get their ministers on the road as soon as possible and Ridley had not been in office for a month before Ure and Fearn had him across the Atlantic and touring his bailiwick. His itinerary naturally included his two 'trouble spots', Belize and the Falklands. Belize, where a black population of 150,000 was threatened by Guatemala, was already on the way to independence. The only outstanding negotiation concerned a continuing defence agreement. The Falklands were a different matter. Winter in Port Stanley is not the best of times and the islanders did not warm to Ridley's message, which was yet again to advocate a change in their relationship with Argentina. They had heard this from Rowlands just eighteen months before. Why did London not get on and do something about it? They were like patients constantly promised a ghastly operation, yet never actually having it performed.

Ridley returned to London determined to 'sort this one out once and for all'. He briskly set about cohering the options so far tabled under three headings: a freeze on sovereignty but not on economic talks; joint Anglo-Argentine sovereignty and administration (condominium); and a transfer of sovereignty to Argentina with a long-term leaseback to Britain. He was aware that a freeze would be unacceptable to Buenos Aires and condominium equally so in Port Stanley. His hopes were pinned on leaseback. It honoured the Edmonds–Rowlands concept of different types of sovereignty. Provided the lease was long enough – 99 years, even 999 years were mooted – it ensured security for existing islanders and their children. It was surely the ideal solution to this vexed problem. The only alternatives were 'Fortress Falklands' or a serious risk of Argentine impatience leading to military action. Britain had at least to show a sense of momentum towards settlement.

Ridley now had some formidable obstacles to surmount. He

had to convince Carrington, the Prime Minister, the cabinet's overseas and defence (OD) committee and the parliamentary Conservative Party, in roughly that order. Carrington thought that Ridley's initiative was probably 'right but rash' – so rash, indeed, that Carrington felt he should broach the subject himself with the Prime Minister. On this as on all matters of foreign affairs, she responded with an instant dogmatism – indeed her reply to Carrington was described by Whitehall sources as 'thermonuclear'. As so often, she implicitly challenged her Foreign Secretary to argue her round. Why, she asked, go bruising the feelings of her backbenchers, already rubbed so sore by the Foreign Office over Rhodesia?

In September 1979, having failed to deter Carrington, Mrs Thatcher decided to try Ridley direct. She clearly suspected that a Foreign Office scheme was afoot and she wanted it nipped in the bud. She knew that Carrington and Ridley could obtain substantial support in OD committee and is thought to have asked Ridley to withdraw his proposal lock, stock and barrel, repeating the argument she used to Carrington, that there was no need to stir the issue at such a delicate moment with the backbenchers. The Foreign Office believes that Ridley argued strongly that some movement had to be made; if negotiations were not seen to be proceeding, there was a serious risk of invasion. Ridley held his ground and eventually won access to OD. At a meeting of this committee on 29 January 1980, argument was intense, again centring on the likely reaction of Tory backbenchers to any sign of weakening on British sovereignty over the islands. Ridley found himself in the unusual position for a Thatcher supporter of relying on 'wets' such as William Whitelaw and Francis Pym for support. He won approval to prepare a plan to be put to the islanders on a consultative basis. This plan, basically for 'leaseback', was drawn up over the summer and approved at an OD committee in July. Again there was a marked lack of enthusiasm for its possible parliamentary reception.

Ridley arrived back in Port Stanley in November 1980, pursued by a horde of Argentine journalists, to commence what proved to be the last effort to settle the Falklands dispute by peaceful means. It was not a relaxed visit. The new governor, Rex Hunt, was amiable enough but not a subtle diplomat. The islanders were punch-drunk with Foreign Office pressure. Ridley claimed to be offering them three options. One of them, a freeze on the status quo, was what they had always wanted. Why did he keep trying to sell them leaseback? Under the circumstances, it is to Ridley's credit that he left with a clear impression that at least half of those to whom he spoke accepted the virtues of leaseback. To many, he had seemed aloof and intolerant of what he regarded as the short-sightedness of many Falklanders. Yet the younger people, and most of those living in Stanley itself, seemed to acknowledge the need for some long-term stability in their relations with Argentina. The editor of the local *Penguin News*, Graham Bound, confirmed this assessment. A future member of the islands council, John Cheek, was harsher: 'If anyone other than Ridley had tried to sell us leaseback, then it would have had a chance.' Despite such hostile comments, the Foreign Office policy seemed on course.

House of Commons question time rarely presents British politics in the best light. Ministerial answers are skilfully drafted to give as few openings for embarrassing supplementary questions as possible. As a result, most MPs attend question time to witness a performance, not scrutinise the work of government. Yet the Commons has a nose for a plot. When it feels it is being taken for a ride it can deliver a minister a verbal punishment more savage than any Old Bailey cross-examination. The attack is seldom coherent but it can demoralise a minister, his department and even a government. As such, it constitutes a rudimentary democratic deterrent.

Ridley's report back to the Commons on his return from Port Stanley on 2 December produced just such a savaging. He explained quietly the difficulties caused to the islanders by the continuance of the dispute. He set out his three options and emphasised that 'any eventual settlement would have to be endorsed by the islanders and by this House'. It was precisely the position adopted by ministers for a decade and a half. It was no plot. No one listened. Alerted by the Falkland Islands Committee to the minister's leaseback enthusiasm, MPs gave Ridley a battering worse than anything MPs could recall in the course of the Parliament. The opposition spokesman, Peter Shore, who had sat in the cabinet which approved the Rowlands mission, loudly demanded 'paramountcy' for the islanders' wishes. One after another, the Falklands lobby then piled in. Sir Bernard Braine spoke of 'fresh anxieties' created by Ridley's visit. The Liberal Russell Johnston attacked the Foreign Office's 'shameful schemes . . . festering for years'. Julian Amery asked curtly if Ridley was aware that 'for years, and here I speak with some experience, his department has wanted to get rid of this commitment'.

Nothing Ridley said in his defence could be heard. Eventually Hansard recorded the grim stage direction: 'Several Hon. Members *rose*. Mr Deputy Speaker: *Order.*' Ridley left the chamber pale and trembling. One MP said he had just watched a man wreck his career on a pile of rock. At a meeting of OD committee held shortly afterwards, the mood was 'We told you so.' Ridley acknowledged that the parliamentary reaction was a setback. It was also clear that the islanders were not totally enthusiastic. The meeting agreed to wait and see what the islanders felt formally on the subject. Once again, a cabinet drew back from supplying leadership on the issue at the moment when leadership was most needed. Ironically, when the Falkland Islands Committee met later to discuss leaseback, they were evenly divided on the question, and conveyed this fact to their Falklands representatives. Yet, just as political opinion might have begun to accept the need for compromise with Argentina, the opposition generated at Westminster by past suspicion gained the upper hand.

Might Nicholas Ridley's leaseback have worked? When he met his opposite number, Carlos Cavandoli, in Buenos Aires, the latter had impressed on him the need for 'something, anything' to give the junta. Throughout Ridley's visit to Port Stanley, the Argentine press had heaped odium on the options of condominium and freeze, but had scrupulously avoided the subject of leaseback. Privately, Cavandoli had said he would find ninety-nine years hard to accept, but this looked like a negotiating position. John Ure, on a visit in June 1981, found Buenos Aires 'well disposed towards leaseback'. It is hard to avoid the conclusion that, had the British cabinet had the courage of its own minister's convictions at this time, leaseback could have been negotiated between Port Stanley and Buenos Aires. The result would almost certainly have been no war and little disruption to the islanders' lifestyle.

*

Falkland Islands politics now followed the Commons in a Dutch auction of intransigence. The legislative council formally voted for a freeze on all negotiations other than purely economic ones. After further OD discussion, Ridley, in February 1981, travelled to New York accompanied by two Falklands Council members, Adrian Monk and Stuart Wallace, to tell Cavandoli that any political solution was off the agenda. He forlornly suggested that the Argentinians might talk to the islanders direct; their wishes were now the sole key to any future settlement. Cavandoli's conversation with the council members was later regarded in Port Stanley as akin to Satan's temptation of Christ. He offered them 'most pampered region status' within Argentina; they could keep their laws, local government, language and customs, yet receive roads, schools, television. Just let him have the one word: sovereignty. It was by all accounts a most persuasive performance. Monk replied that he would have to report back to his council, but he doubted any response until the new elections the following October.

For all the politicians in New York, this was their last throw. Within a year, both Cavandoli and Ridley had been relieved of the task of representing their governments on the Falklands issue. Monk and Stuart likewise departed at elections unusual on the Falklands for their political intensity. Despite earlier ambivalence, island opinion rapidly hardened behind outright opposition to any deal with Argentina. Local leadership went to an outspoken police-man, Terry Peck, and an engineer named John Cheek. In September Ridley secured promotion, to the job of Financial Secretary to the Treasury. Mrs Thatcher showed that even a Commons debacle was not enough to finish a man when the issue was as trivial as the Falklands.

The Foreign Office now drifted into the critical phase of the Falklands saga with its policy in shreds. As Nicholas Ridley had frankly said when departing for the New York talks, he could only 'stall for time'. A bid by Shell to explore the Magallanes Est sector of the Malvinas Basin (straddling Falklands waters) under an Argentine licence was resisted. A formal protest from Argentina at the lack of progress with the talks was received and noted in July 1981. A government firmly tied to the apron strings of the islands' council had no room whatsoever for negotiating manoeuvre.

On 30 June, shortly before he was moved to the Treasury, Ridley had called back the Falklands governor, Rex Hunt, and the ambassador in Buenos Aires, Anthony Williams, for a meeting in London. He was bravely determined that, despite the reverses in the Commons and in New York, the momentum towards a settlement should not be lost. The meeting, attended also by Fearn and Ure, reviewed various contingencies against a possible stepping-up of Argentine pressure. This pressure was expected to take three stages: first, renewed protests at the UN; second, an economic squeeze on the islands by withdrawing the air service and denying them fuel; the third stage would be military. The old Falklands defence file was taken down and given its first formal review since the 1977 crisis. Drawn up in the late 1960s, it covered procedures for reinforcing the marine garrison and for the dispatch of surface and submarine units as a deterrent to Argentine attack. In the latter case, it was accepted that only a 'large task force' capable of engaging the Argentine navy would be suitable, including at least one carrier and assault ship. It was based on the belief that Britain would have a measure of advance warning.

The expectation of graduated pressure from Buenos Aires prior to any military action now underlay all Foreign Office and intelligence assessments of the Falklands crisis up to the moment of invasion.

*

The Foreign Office was now hit by two decisions taken by other government departments which immeasurably weakened any bargaining position it might have had with Buenos Aires. Despite the protests of Carrington and Ridley in the spring of 1981, the Ministry of Defence again pushed through a plan to withdraw *Endurance* from the South Atlantic at the end of the 1981–82 tour. Carrington warned the Defence Secretary, John Nott, in a succession of notes that this would be taken as a clear sign of Britain's reduced commitment to the Falklands.

The MoD was adamant. *Endurance* had for some time featured on the ministry's 'List A' of items which, when under acute Treasury pressure, could be cut 'without seriously damaging our defence capability'. (Lists B and C involved cuts with more savage implications.) In the public-spending climate of mid-1981, virtually every item on List A was by definition vulnerable. *Endurance* might cost no more than £2 million a year, but there it was. When the decision was surreptitiously announced by Lord Trefgarne in the House of Lords on 30 June, an Argentine official rang Lord Shackleton to ask whether this indeed meant that the British were climbing down over the South Atlantic. Shackleton despairingly assured him not. Yet the Foreign Office now found itself accused of the one gesture of disengagement it had bitterly opposed. Lord Carrington continued to protest the decision up to the moment of his resignation.

At the same time, the new British Nationality Bill came before Parliament sponsored by the Home Office. It had been intended to clarify the status of British colonial citizens whom for reasons of race relations the government did not wish to see migrating to Britain. It was aimed primarily at the Hong Kong Chinese. The rules had to be drawn up with care (and not a little cynicism), so as not to deny right of entry to white colonials of British descent. The method, as with Commonwealth citizens, was to admit to full citizenship those with 'patrial' status, conferred where at least one grandparent had been born in Britain.

This did not cover third- or fourth-generation settlers in colonies such as Gibraltar and the Falklands. The bill would now deprive them of their most valued security: full British citizenship with right of abode in the UK. Right-wing Conservatives promptly allied themselves with Labour and Liberal members already opposed to the bill and, on 2 June, the government narrowly survived defeat on an amendment to exclude Gibraltar from the bill. When the bill reached the Lords, the Gibraltar amendment had mustered enough support to be pushed through against the government by 150 votes to 112, despite a plea by Lord Soames that 'if there are to be special cases then every dependent territory will make its special case', mentioning in particular the Falklands. The Gibraltarians were saved from the ignominy. On a similar amendment to exclude the Falklands, Soames's argument prevailed and the amendment was defeated by one vote.

Consistency now demanded that the cabinet either reinstate Gibraltar's inclusion in the bill when it returned to the Commons or else similarly exclude the Falklands (which would leave Hong Kong almost alone). In the event, Whitelaw decided to capitulate on Gibraltar but still deny full citizenship to the Falklanders, on the argument that half a loaf was better than none. The Gibraltarians were ecstatic. The 800-odd Falklanders who did not qualify as patrials were dumbstruck. They were to be treated as no different from the Hong Kong refugees from mainland China. They had been deserted by precisely the MPs who had declared, 'Britain would always stand by the Falklanders.'

These apparently random occurrences in the course of 1981 did not seem random to the Argentinians. Ambassadorial relations had been resumed in 1980 and the old game of Falklands-watching from Belgrave Square was taken up with renewed fervour. Every subtle variation in British policy, however disparate, was plotted on the same graph. Its vertical axis was British commitment to the South Atlantic, its horizontal axis was time. As 1981 progressed, that graph appeared to be moving steadily down.

3 » GALTIERI'S GAMBLE

... the simple plan:
That they should take who have the power
And they should keep who can.

R. B. Armstrong, *History of Liddesdale*

Argentina in 1981 was enjoying a novel and exhilarating experience. She was being courted openly by the most powerful nation on earth. The previous year had seen American visitors whose concern, for once, was not prisons and torture chambers, and who asked no questions on human rights. Roger Fontaine and General Daniel Graham, advisers to the new presidential candidate, Ronald Reagan, averted their attention from such obsessions of previous American envoys. They discussed ending the Carter arms embargo and greeted the Argentinians as fellow fighters against marxism in Latin America. They held out the vision of a new anti-communist alliance in the South Atlantic. Following in their footsteps came General Vernon Walters, former deputy head of the CIA and a roving freelance for the State Department. Other military officials of the new Reagan administration arrived. The new army chief of staff, General Leopoldo Galtieri, received them all, and in August he was invited back as guest of his US opposite number, General Edward Meyer. A handsome, hard-drinking cavalry officer who wasted little time on the subtle nuances of international politics, Galtieri was a great success with his hosts.

At the same time, the Videla regime which had held power

since 1976, backed by a junta of the leaders of the three armed forces, began to crumble. The conservative economic policies of Dr Martinez de Hoz had failed (or been insufficiently ruthless) to stem rising inflation and falling growth, and had brought about a collapse in middle-class real incomes. Videla resigned the presidency in March 1981, thrusting the former army commander Roberto Viola forward as his replacement. Power clearly lay with the three-man military junta, of which Galtieri was already a member. Viola's assumption of power was accompanied by the usual prelude to political unrest in Argentina: much talk of an early return to democracy, a marginal freeing of political activity and a consequent conspiracy among the military to stop it.

By October it was clear that Viola's days as President were numbered. A reshuffle of junta members (normally taking place every two years) led to new air force and navy representatives, Brigadier Basilio Lami Dozo and Admiral Jorge Anaya respectively. The latter, known to be a hard-line opponent of any return to civilian rule, pushed aside a number of more senior officers for the post. He also possessed one characteristic rare in recent Argentine history: as a naval officer, he was nonetheless a personal friend of the army commander, Galtieri.

In November, Galtieri paid another lightning visit to Washington, where his appointments included dinner with Caspar Weinberger and a meeting with Reagan's national security adviser, Richard Allen. Already regarded as the next ruler of his country, Galtieri was described in public by Allen as 'possessed of a majestic personality'. Such talk would have turned the head even of a humbler man than Leopoldo Galtieri. The prospect of a new strong man in Buenos Aires was understandably appealing to the Reagan team. A conspicuous if messy victory had now been won against left-wing guerrillas, and the human-rights implications of that victory were receding into the past. Galtieri seemed ambitious and aware of Argentina's yearning for charismatic leadership in the style of Peron. Equally, he was politically unsophisticated and biddable. He was the perfect client-state leader. To America's renascent anti-communism, he would make an ideal southern bulwark against Latin American revolution.

Walters believed that Galtieri was strongly advised in Washington not to surrender the army command if he took power. To keep the command, he would need the agreement at least of one other junta member, presumably his friend Anaya. It is said by associates of both men that this agreement, forged in December 1981, shortly before Galtieri ousted Viola as President, involved assurances on a range of policy issues. One of these was an understanding that the recovery of the Falklands should be achieved within the two years of Galtieri's presidency term, preferably before January 1983, the 150th anniversary of the British seizure. The lion's share of glory would go to the navy, in whose sphere of operational responsibility the Malvinas lay.

Viola retired from the presidency on grounds of ill-health in December and Galtieri took office with a clean sweep of cabinet portfolios. The civilian component increased and included two names likely to find favour in Washington. One was the economy minister, Dr Roberto Alemann, a keen follower of Professor Milton Friedman. He differed from his predecessor, de Hoz, largely in his determination to impose the same deflationary medicine even more ruthlessly. The other was Dr Nicanor Costa Mendes, returning to the foreign ministry after an absence of more than a decade. Alemann's first package of measures, introduced in January 1982, was of devastating severity. Under the slogan 'deflate, deregulate, denationalise', he floated the exchange rate, froze public-sector wages (no mean step with a 150 per cent inflation rate), increased indirect taxes, and even reduced defence spending. The last item did not include Anaya's German frigates or Super Etendard jets. At a time when the political process was just emerging from five years of total repression, the package was bold to the point of recklessness.

Costa Mendes offered a strategy no less tough, though ostensibly far less painful. Alongside the rapprochement with the USA there was to be a reassertion of Argentina's regional supremacy. This included active participation in the anti-communist struggle in Central America, especially Nicaragua and El Salvador, and a forceful prosecution of territorial disputes with Britain and Chile. The dispute with Chile over a group of islands in the Beagle Channel had supposedly been resolved first by the British crown (as arbiter under a 1902 treaty) and then by the Vatican. Both decisions were in Chile's favour. Galtieri, as army commander, had already put his weight behind rejecting the Vatican arbitration and, in January 1982, Costa Mendes formally repudiated Argentina's 1972 treaty with Chile. Troop detachments were moved to the southern border area and relations between the two nations reached an unprecedented low. Throughout the Falklands war, Argentina was afraid of a Chilean opportunist attack on her rear and kept some of her best winter-trained commando troops away from the Falklands near the Chilean frontier as a precaution.

Both Costa Mendes and his deputy, Enrique Ros, were veterans of the Falklands dispute. To Costa Mendes it was quite absurd that negotiations should have dragged on for more than a decade since he had apparently resolved them with George Brown in 1967. He knew the British Foreign Office were keen for a settlement. The Treasury had shown not the slightest interest in the development of the islands. The ten-year-old Communications Agreement remained unhonoured by the British side. The Shackleton Report lay gathering dust. In addition, and within the past year, HMS *Endurance* was to be withdrawn; the islanders had been denied full British nationality; even the British Antarctic Survey was about to close its South Georgia station for lack of funds. If ever a nation was tired of colonial responsibility, this was it.

Within Argentina, recovery of the 'Malvinas' would not stifle internal dissent, but at least it would unite the nation for a time. It would serve as a vindication of military rule and cleanse the reputation of the armed forces after the horrors of the dirty war (the desire to do this was one reason why the notorious Captain

Alfredo Astiz was later chosen to recapture South Georgia). It would also elevate the junta to an authority which was certainly required to enforce Alemann's economic package.

Within weeks of Galtieri's assumption of power, the navy's old invasion plan was revised. The proposed date for an invasion was believed to be between July and October 1982, by when *Endurance* would have been withdrawn and any British naval response made near-impossible by the winter weather. The joke was that, to reach the Falklands, British troops would be 'pasteurised' by having to sail through the tropics to the freezing South Atlantic. Equally important, by July, the navy would have taken delivery of its new French planes and Exocet anti-ship missiles, and any conscript troops required would have been fully trained.

The essence of the military operation would lie in surprise. There would be none of Massera's population transfusion. Minimum force would be used and there should be no islander casualties whatsoever. The world would be presented with a fait accompli and Britain given no emotional stick to wave at the United Nations. There should be no advance warning, since this might lead to reinforcements being sent to the islands. It is believed that at the start of 1982, no more than nine individuals knew of any firm intention by the junta to invade.

The diplomatic arguments pointed in a slightly different direction. The Argentine foreign ministry is not a cohesive institution. Its senior ministers and officials move in and out regularly and many are serving military officers. Abroad, Argentine diplomats must work alongside a parallel network of service attachés with independent lines to their commanders in chief. The naval mission to London, for instance, has (or had) its own building in Vauxhall Bridge Road. The senior military attaché in Washington, General Mallea Gil, was considered far more influential with Galtieri than the ambassador, Esteban Takacs, and was treated as such by the administration.

Costa Mendes was aware that, for a Falklands invasion to be accepted as a fait accompli in the style of Goa, the diplomatic ground required preparation. A sense of legitimate grievance had to be created. Latin American support would be important, as would American neutrality and possibly a Russian veto in the UN Security Council. At no point do Costa Mendes or any of his advisers appear to have believed a British military response was likely. Nevertheless, financial and economic sanctions in themselves could do Argentina immense harm. Costa Mendes needed to know what would happen in the event of invasion.

The result was a conflict between the need for secrecy and a desire for information. Agents were told to ask 'hypothetical' questions of their contacts. Indications of Argentina's intentions appeared in the Buenos Aires press, most publicly in columns by the well-informed Jesus Iglesias Rouco in *La Prensa*. Writing in January, he said, 'the Argentine government is about to submit a number of conditions to the British before proceeding any further with negotiations ... It is believed that, if the next Argentine attempt to resolve the negotiations with London fails, Buenos Aires will take over the islands by force this year.'

In Washington, General Mallea Gil was in regular contact with the assistant secretary for Inter-American affairs at the State Department, Tom Enders, as well as with the US ambassador to the UN, Mrs Jeane Kirkpatrick, a long-standing Latin American expert. Both have denied steering the junta towards invasion in anything they said at this time. Yet their overt friendliness clearly said all the junta wanted to hear. Newspaper editors were clumsily asked to get hypothetical 'reaction' stories from their foreign correspondents. Raul Fain Binda, London correspondent for *Siete Dias*, ingeniously came up with an idea for a front page of *The Times* with the headline 'Mrs Thatcher sends the fleet'. He even suggested Admiral Woodward as commander. It appeared the actual week of the invasion and seems to have been the only accurate prediction in the junta's entire intelligence operation.

Reports from foreign agents and correspondents generally enabled Buenos Aires to build up a relatively glowing picture of how the world saw the new Argentina. Because it had had to be allusive in its nature, none of the intelligence gathering could be certain. Much of it came through military channels and was liable to the distortion inherent in military lines of command. Officers were conscious that evidence of minimal response was what their superiors wanted to hear. Yet everything pointed to the same conclusion: the British would not respond militarily; the Third World countries at the UN would side with Argentina; there would be insufficient support for a vote favourable to Britain in the Security Council; even if there were sufficient support, Russia would honour the anti-colonialist ticket and veto it; and sanctions imposed by Britain would be ineffective and short-lived.

*

Like a relentless grandfather clock, the old Falklands negotiations were due to chime at the UN in New York in February 1982, having been postponed from the previous December by the Galtieri upheaval. The British delegation was led by yet another newcomer to the subject, Richard Luce. A junior Foreign Office minister who had previously specialised in Africa, Luce added the Americas to his portfolio following Ridley's departure. He was a quiet-spoken Tory of liberal views. Rare among Falklands negotiators, he had actually visited the islands himself as a Commonwealth Parliamentary Association delegate. Of the pile of papers given him by his under-secretary, John Ure, on his arrival, the Falklands file was by far the thickest.

Luce was by nature a cautious man and he had not the slightest intention of seeing himself strung up on the same gallows as the backbenchers had erected for Nicholas Ridley. He therefore pressed the South America desk's Robin Fearn to reassure him that the various belligerent noises coming out of Buenos Aires contained no new ingredient. Costa Mendes's latest messages had indicated a particular impatience. Ros had even been mobbed by journalists at the airport before his departure for New York. What did it mean?

Fearn was able to reply with the full support of his department in London and of Anthony Williams, the ambassador in Buenos

Aires, that such hysteria was normal before each round of negotiations and Luce should not allow himself to be over-anxious
about it. Williams had prepared a full brief on the Galtieri government the previous December. His view was that the new regime
would be harsh internally and would increase the pressure on
Britain over the Falklands, but the junta would have too much on
its plate for any dramatic initiative for the time being. Williams
repeated this view to Luce personally while in New York.

Ros began the talks clearly under intense pressure from home.
A sophisticated international lawyer, he could sometimes ill conceal his distaste for his military masters. As a result, the British
were treated to a performance of stagy intolerance. Ros elaborated
on demands for a standing permanent commission on the Falklands issue, under alternating British and Argentine chairmanship.
He wanted monthly meetings and, most significant, a deadline on
the talks set for the end of the year. Nothing did more to confuse
subsequent British intelligence than this mention of a year-end
deadline.

After much haggling, Luce eventually agreed to the commission, adding that two island councillors should be present all the
time. He would also accept the proposals for 'regular' meetings, an
'open' agenda and a 'review' after a year. Ros consulted continually
with Buenos Aires. Finally, a deal was struck subject to ratification
by both sides. Luce had agreed to nothing but to keep talking,
albeit at an increased tempo. A joint statement was prepared for
release in each capital. It referred to the 'cordial and positive spirit'
of the talks but made no mention of details.

Ros then visited the UN Secretary-General, Javier Perez de
Cuellar, and privately told him he was delighted at the outcome.
He had achieved more than any of his predecessors and there now
seemed a real urgency in the negotiations. Luce, Williams and the
two islanders present at the talks all felt at least reassured. Their
collective view was that they had 'bought three to six months'.
Luce now embarked on the other half of his mission: a visit to
Washington to discuss El Salvador at the State Department. Here

he met Tom Enders, then about to leave on a trip to Buenos Aires, and took the opportunity to ask him to impress on Costa Mendes Britain's good faith in the new round of talks. Enders's mind was filled with El Salvador and Nicaragua and he clearly found it hard to believe that the matter of the Falklands was worth the bother. America had also maintained a traditional neutrality on the sovereignty issue. He agreed, however, to act as a conduit.

Now, at the start of March 1982, miscalculation crowded on miscalculation. Costa Mendes appears to have blown his top on reading Ros's 'cordial and positive' communiqué from New York. Cordiality with Britain and a deadline a full year away was the last thing he wanted in the run-up to an invasion. He bluntly refused to issue the communiqué. Instead, a wholly different statement was put out by his First Secretary, Gustavo Figueroa, saying that Argentina had been negotiating in good faith for long enough. Unless Britain would cede sovereignty in the near future, Argentina reserved the right to 'employ other means' to regain the islands. It was, in retrospect, the first stage in the Foreign Office prediction of 'graduated pressure'. It was not read as such in London.

A week later, Enders passed Luce's message on to Costa Mendes and, he maintains, to Galtieri. Both listened to him but did not react, confirming Enders's view that Luce had been over-concerned. He did not offer, nor was he asked, any opinion on what America's attitude might be to invasion. Only in discussion with Ros was any great play made of the year-end deadline, but then Ros is believed to have been unaware of the invasion plan. Enders's talks ranged over central America, security cooperation, European agriculture, the Organization of American States. At no point did the Falklands arise. 'It was after all a private UK affair,' said Enders later. Only in retrospect did he realise how significant was this omission. Relations between Washington and Buenos Aires remained close.

If Ros returned home to be all but disowned by a hawkish boss, Luce returned to a department of doves. He was genuinely shocked by Buenos Aires's volte-face on the New York communiqué. He and Carrington now discussed what it might mean. The advice of officials was clear, as was that of the ambassador on the spot. The tension was not yet ominous and was not unprecedented. They should beware of provocation which might give Buenos Aires excuse for escalation. Luce remained anxious. What did Carrington advise?

High on the walls of the Foreign Office building in Whitehall are the portraits of men who would not have given the question a moment's thought. If in doubt, they would have sent a gunboat. To many of his admirers, Lord Carrington was the last of such Palmerstonian Foreign Secretaries. Yet he did not react with any such belligerence. The reasons were partly internal, rooted in the procedures of the Foreign Office and perhaps in Carrington's own imperturbable cast of mind. But they were also external, the result of relations established between departments and individual ministers throughout Mrs Thatcher's administration.

Even for a Foreign Secretary, to summon up the British navy is no easy matter. He must approach the cabinet's OD committee with a case. He will find the Ministry of Defence averse to the cost and dislocation of ships. The Treasury will likewise be unsympathetic. He will therefore need substantial evidence of a threat to national interests, presumably in the form of a JIC assessment from Cabinet Office. He will need to square the Prime Minister in advance. Everyone will want to know what collateral action from allies and at the United Nations is proposed, how long the defence requirement may last and what will happen if open hostilities break out.

Carrington and Luce felt they had insufficient evidence of increasing tension to justify such a concerted appeal to their ministerial colleagues. There was circumstantial evidence. But this they chiefly derived from the Argentine press, and the Foreign Office, guided by Williams, was playing it down. JIC assessments, informed in large part by Foreign Office diplomats, were adding a similar gloss. Galtieri, they pointed out, had shown no belligerence on the issue. Relations between Argentina, Britain and the USA were good. The New York talks had ended constructively with the prospect of a full year of negotiations before any deadline was reached. (These talks were still being cited as evidence of Argentine moderation by the JIC even after they had been disowned by Buenos Aires.) Messages warning of increased Argentine pugnacity sent to the defence ministry by Captain Barker of *Endurance* were being discounted as part of his campaign to save his ship from withdrawal.

A yet greater obstacle lay across Carrington's path – one mentioned time and again by participants in this stage of the Falklands crisis. Relations between departments in Mrs Thatcher's government had, by spring of 1982, become utterly dominated by budgetary considerations. The cash-limit system introduced under the Callaghan administration had been elevated by Sir Geoffrey Howe into what seemed the be-all and end-all of policy. This may not have done much to restrain public expenditure, but it did make anathema any policy change involving additional spending. In particular, departments resisted strongly any claims for spending imposed on them by other departments which might worsen their relations with the Treasury. In spring 1982, no department was having a worse time with the Treasury than the Ministry of Defence. Severe fuelling restrictions had had to be imposed on the navy to save money. It was something of a comfort for Nott that, in resisting Carrington's demands for the retention of *Endurance*, he had secured the public support of the Prime Minister in the Commons in February 1982.

Luce gave his first statement to the Commons on the New York talks on 3 March. It was immaculately rehearsed and gave his listeners no cause for their traditional alarm on the topic. Yet he had to meet a direct question from Julian Amery: 'Will [the minister] assure us that all necessary steps are in hand to ensure the protection of the islands against unexpected attack?' Luce gave an evasive answer, knowing at this stage that the cabinet would not even let him keep *Endurance* on station. Amery did not forget his question, and every nuance of Luce's answer was transmitted back to Buenos Aires by the Argentine embassy.

Two days later, on 5 March, Luce and Carrington gathered together their officials, including Fearn and Ure, at the Foreign Office to review the Falklands position in the light of Costa Mendes's belligerent response. This meeting was crucial to government actions in March. The view of Fearn and Ure, supported by Williams in Buenos Aires, is believed to have been that it was by no means clear whether the junta was stimulating the new tension or seeking to play it down as promised. Officials advised that Williams see Costa Mendes to clarify this point, and that a strong letter be drafted for sending to Buenos Aires if required. The meeting ran through once again the three predicted phases of increased pressure and began to plan possible responses. Despite the renewed tension, the Argentinians had yet to return to the UN. After that, a blockade of the Falklands might be expected, cutting air and fuel links. A precautionary paper was proposed for sending to the OD committee outlining the financial implications of any additional measures to meet this threat. Third and last, there was the question of military pressure, probably taking the form of a covert landing on an outer island.

To cover this last contingency, the military file for the Falklands was again reviewed. This coincided with a request for contingency plans from the Prime Minister (stimulated by intelligence reports) to the Foreign Office and the Ministry of Defence on 8 March. In addition, a formal request went in once more to the OD committee for a cancellation of the withdrawal of *Endurance*. It appears to have been at this point that officials first told ministers of the affair of 1977. A convention of British government dictates that advice given by officials to one administration is not revealed to another. The 1977 operation had been kept secret and it was felt that it should remain so, but those present thought it important at least to mention the previous task force. They emphasised that the circumstances which had caused it to be sent had been far graver than they looked now – for instance, ambassadors had been withdrawn. Carrington asked whether the Argentinians had been told of it. The answer was no, which further weakened its significance. The question of sending submarines was never raised. The evidence and the advice before the meeting did not seem remotely to justify such a response. Had such a request gone forward to the OD committee at this stage, the same evidence and the same advice would have been proffered in the briefing material prepared for ministers. None of those interviewed for this book is in any doubt about what would have been the outcome: 'The request would have been laughed out of court.'

*

Two weeks later, with still no meeting of OD and no answer from the Ministry of Defence on *Endurance*, an incident occurred which appears to have taken both Buenos Aires and London by surprise. Early in March, an Argentine scrap-metal merchant named Constantino Davidoff applied to the British embassy for permission to implement a contract negotiated with a Scottish-based shipping firm, Christian Salvesen. The contract was to clear the whaling station at Leith in South Georgia, which Davidoff had personally surveyed the previous December. The station, abandoned in 1965, was an eyesore of sheds, old barges and scrap iron, nestling amid the glaciers and alpine scenery of an island more akin to the Antarctic than to the Falklands.

Davidoff has since vigorously maintained that his decision to go to South Georgia at this point was his alone and was prompted solely by commercial motives. He denies that the Argentine navy had anything to do with it. However, it is believed that he had had a meeting at navy headquarters in January, when he was given assurances of navy 'support' should he ever wish to take up his contract and return to South Georgia. His charter vessel was the Argentine navy transport *Bahia Buen Suceso* and, from the moment it sailed, the navy were clearly in a position to command events. The British embassy agreed to the expedition and merely told Davidoff that his men would need formal authorisation on arrival from the British Antarctic Survey base 20 miles down the coast at Grytviken. Whether through lethargy, bravado or instructions from a naval officer, the party of some forty workmen failed to comply with this request. Landing at Leith on 19 March, they hoisted the Argentine flag and set about their work.

The presumption is that at this stage Anaya's navy, whose exclusive military preserve the South Atlantic had always been, decided to use Davidoff s incursion to mount a similar exercise to that of 1976 on Southern Thule. It would register Argentina's claim as obliquely as possible in order to confuse and ultimately minimise British responses. These would be unlikely to be military. Another toe-hold would thus have been secured on a British possession and Britain would find it the harder to complain about a Falklands expedition later in the year. To this extent, James Callaghan's failure to react militarily in 1976 was a far more significant 'signal' than his covert reaction in 1977.

The Argentine navy's initial assumption about the British response was at least partially wrong. The flag-waving incident was observed by scientists on patrol from Grytviken and reported back to Rex Hunt in Port Stanley. The scientists were told to order the Argentine captain by radio to lower the flag and seek proper authorisation. The Argentinians agreed to do the former but not the latter. The British embassy in Buenos Aires thereupon commenced two weeks of constant pressure on the foreign ministry, now plainly in the picture, to get Davidoff's workmen removed or at least properly accredited.

Had this been all that happened, the Anaya strategy would have been on target and there is no reason to believe an imminent invasion of the Falklands would have been launched. As it was, Davidoff s exploit suddenly gave the Foreign Office the weapon it needed against Downing Street. On Saturday, 20 March, Mrs Thatcher with remarkable promptness agreed with Lord Carrington to send *Endurance* from Port Stanley, taking with her two dozen marines from the Port Stanley garrison under the command of a twenty-two-year-old lieutenant named Keith Mills. They arrived off the BAS station at Grytviken four days later and were told to await orders.

At the same time, Mrs Thatcher requested from the Foreign Office a memorandum for the cabinet's OD committee on options in the South Atlantic. To this, John Nott was asked to submit a defence minute. This drew on the existing Falklands contingency file and listed the defence implications of the various diplomatic options. These ranged from shipping in a commando group to sending a submarine or even a full task force to take on the Argentine navy. It was not a particularly encouraging document. It stressed the logistical problems of operating at this distance. There might also be substantial difficulties in meeting Nato commitments at the same time. As for retaking the islands *after* an Argentine invasion, there was 'no certainty' that even the largest available task force could do the job. Nott thought no more of the matter and departed for a Nato meeting in Colorado.

The prompt dispatch of *Endurance* did not accord with the Argentine strategy. Buenos Aires was at this stage unprepared both militarily and diplomatically for a sudden escalation in the Falklands dispute. Yet Argentine citizens were ashore on territory which Argentina claimed as her own. The British were demanding the formal acknowledgement of sovereignty through the obtaining of permits, on pain of removal by force. This would constitute a conspicious loss of face for Buenos Aires, the last thing the junta could afford just then. Yet any dramatic increase in tension might attract British ships to the Falklands and sabotage plans for an invasion later in the year. The South Georgia incident had come at least six months too soon. *Endurance*, which should have been safely back in Britain before any invasion, was a crucial complicating factor.

Costa Mendes now played for time. On 23 March, *Bahia Buen Suceso* sailed from Leith with all but a dozen of the workmen aboard. However, the following day the armed Argentine naval survey ship *Bahia Paraiso* took her place, entering Leith harbour unmolested by *Endurance* offshore. With orders to 'protect' the Leith workmen, a full marine detachment was put ashore under Captain Alfredo Astiz. In Buenos Aires, Costa Mendes was replying to each British protest by repeating that the men would be removed in due course and that London would only aggravate matters by doing anything rash with *Endurance*. However, this was something of a gamble. The mere presence of British marines meant that sooner or later some sort of confrontation was probable on South Georgia. Meanwhile the likelihood of British reinforcements to the Falklands was overwhelming. Suddenly everything was pointing towards an abrupt bringing forward of the July/October invasion plan.

If the junta thought the South Georgia affair must be leading London to drastic responses, it was wrong. Indeed, it appears to have had a mesmerising effect. The idea of a gang of scrap-metal merchants causing an international crisis had a humorous ring to it: it was repeatedly described in the press as a 'comic opera'. Although he was kept constantly in touch, Lord Carrington at this time was diverted by yet another Common Market budget dispute and by the predictions of an Israeli invasion of the Lebanon. An overt threat to the Falklands might have sounded warning signals in Whitehall, but the scrap men of Leith surely merited no more than a rap over the knuckles: 'a problem best solved by diplomatic means,' said the Foreign Office. Spokesmen pleaded with commentators not to 'blow the matter up out of all proportion'.

Pre-crisis political and military intelligence must have two components to be of use. First, it must quantify the degree of instability in a given situation and chart its likely development. Second, and far more difficult, it must indicate as precisely as possible when that development will precipitate a trauma – and do so in time for the information to be of use to policy-makers. The fall of the Shah of Iran and the Yom Kippur invasion of Sinai were both 'predicted' by western intelligence reports, but neither was predicted with dates attached. By contrast, in the mid-sixties, the CIA told the State Department that Venezuela was going to occupy disputed areas of Guyana, probably within a week. US officials approached the Caracas government and told them in no uncertain terms that America would not tolerate such action. It did not take place. The CIA maintains that it also predicted the Argentine invasion of the Falklands, even circulating Rouco's *La Prensa* column in its Latin American bulletin. Yet no intelligence material in Washington or London (or, for that matter, in Chile or Brazil) was able to give any indication of when this invasion might occur nor at what point Argentina's familiar belligerence might turn critical. Worse, British intelligence was clearly indicating a breathing space of months, if not a year, preceded by a measured increase in pressure.

The British Cabinet Office current intelligence group covering Latin America was headed at this time by Brigadier Adam Gurdon, reporting to the JIC through the head of the assessment staff, a diplomat named Robin O'Neill. His inputs were political reports from the Buenos Aires embassy, including material from the first secretary charged with 'Falklands-watching', Mark Heathcote, and from the defence and naval attachés, intelligence from 'friends' (spies) in Argentina and US material passed from the CIA and the National Security Agency (NSA). This last included satellite and signal intercepts, known colloquially as sigint, to be collated with intercepts from GCHQ at Cheltenham.

The British maintain that CIA material of any value before the invasion was 'sparse to non-existent'. In fact, the CIA had tended to leave Argentina to Britain to watch, given her long-standing Falklands interest. Britain on the other hand had been progressively reducing covert activities in South America to cut costs – British intelligence officials tend to sound like civil service shop stewards on the subject. As a result the balance of 'human intelligence', known as humint, to sigint shifted drastically in favour of the latter. (Satellite photo-reconnaissance played virtually no part in the Falklands crisis: American Landsat pictures were of such poor quality that Washington actually showed them to the Argentinians to prove they were not helping the British.)

Sigint was copious, pouring out of the NSA in Washington and from GCHQ at Cheltenham down a teleprinter line to the Cabinet

Office. America intercepts came primarily from tracking stations in the south of Chile. Later, *Endurance* also supplied invaluable material as she cruised off South Georgia. The problem with such material, vexing intelligence services round the world, is that it is very 'raw': hundreds of intercepts, demanding ever more costly and sophisticated interpretation. Thus Gurdon's group did not need telling in the fourteen days which separated the South Georgia landing from the Falklands invasion that a large number of Argentine ships were at sea. There was an immense amount of radio traffic, though this could equally well be caused by the annual naval exercises with Uruguay, already publicly announced in Buenos Aires and Montevideo. What did it all mean? Here the JIC had ultimately to rely on human judgement and this judgement was based on three principles which dominated JIC assessments right up to the hours immediately prior to the final invasion.

The first was that, as we have seen, any military pressure on the Falklands would not come until the end of the year. When it came it would be preceded by a clear sequence of signals commencing with pressure at the UN and public sabre-rattling to emphasise Britain's unreasonableness. The second was a conviction that, whatever the tension, it was nothing like as bad as it had been in 1977 when the JIC had cried wolf, and there had been no planned invasion by Argentina. Assessments, in other words, were based on a crucial input: the intelligence community's fear of crying wolf a second time. It is believed this input did not appear in the assessments. Remarkably, it appears to have been ignored (except, with hindsight, by the Franks Committee).

The third principle, which increasingly became dominant, was that no response should provoke Argentina into a pre-emptive strike which Britain could not forestall militarily. Britain was, and always had been, wholly vulnerable to a surprise Argentine attack. Only 'Fortress Falklands' could have removed that vulnerability. A de-escalation and diplomatic settlement of the South Georgia incident was therefore the prime end of policy. It was understated response carried to an extraordinary extreme. This tactic was strongly advocated by Ambassador Williams and by Foreign Office ministers right up to the breaking of the crisis.

The understated response went sadly awry. In theory, it is meant to provide a cover of de-escalation in order to put a deterrent defensive force in place without provoking any preemption by the enemy. This obviously requires diplomatic and military liaison of the most meticulous kind, with clear signals going to the enemy and absolute secrecy maintained at home. As it was, the key decisions over South Georgia were taken by Mrs Thatcher in bilateral meetings with individual ministers rather than in the more deliberative forum of OD committee. They were also subject to near barrack-room reception on the floor of the House of Commons.

There is now considerable evidence – both published and from sources close to the junta – that the sending of *Endurance* from Port Stanley by Mrs Thatcher and Lord Carrington on 20 March was the first of the two triggers which caused the junta to bring forward their original invasion plan. Far from removing provocation, *Endurance* intensified the pressure on the junta to commit themselves immediately or face a humiliating climbdown. Yet, at the same time, the other limb of the strategy of understated response – the covert sending of deterrent forces – was delayed a whole week. Downing Street asked the Foreign Office and Ministry of Defence for no more than a position paper for a future meeting of OD committee. This lack of urgency in view of the general climate in Buenos Aires must be considered a serious error. It contrasts with the procedure followed in 1977 (see page 44).

The Argentine junta is believed to have brought forward its invasion at a meeting held to review the South Georgia crisis on Friday, 26 March. The factors involved can only be surmised, but they would have included the realisation that a confrontation at Leith could hardly be avoided by the mere exercise of diplomacy. Strengthening of the Port Stanley garrison by Britain in some form was a certainty. In addition, domestic tension was increasing as Alemann's measures began to bite, and demonstrations were threatened on the streets of the capital the following week. A military diversion was fast becoming imperative. Costa Mendes also continued in his firm view that the diplomatic consequences could be contained and no military reoccupation by Britain would be attempted. In his defence, it should be said there were sound empirical grounds for his view (including Mr Nott's contingencies paper).

Intelligence reports on the Saturday indicated that two Argentine missile corvettes, with the robustly English names of *Drummond* and *Granville*, had broken away from the Uruguayan manoeuvres and sailed south to reinforce *Bahia Paraiso*. This was clearly a direct challenge to London. Whether it was a decision of the full junta or just of the navy – and opinion differs on this – whoever took it cast the die. That weekend, naval leave was cancelled, stores and equipment were rushed to the major naval base of Puerto Belgrano and to Comodoro Rivadavia, the nearest air base to the Falklands. Overflights of Port Stanley by Hercules transports, not a wholly unusual occurrence, became frequent. A meeting of high-level career diplomats at the foreign ministry was told by Costa Mendes that the invasion decision had been taken. On Sunday night, the ministry formally told Ambassador Williams that 'the door is now closed on all further negotiations on South Georgia'. At the same time, Argentine embassies abroad were ordered to cancel Easter leave and await developments.

These moves were duly registered by British intelligence. They appeared in the assessments prepared for ministers on Sunday, 28 March. Mrs Thatcher and Lord Carrington discussed them over the phone that evening and again at length on the Monday morning as they flew together to Brussels for a Common Market meeting that day. The JIC gloss was still that no invasion was imminent. But both Prime Minister and Foreign Secretary were now aware that the threat in the South Atlantic had extended beyond South Georgia to the Falklands themselves. By the time their plane landed at Brussels, they had agreed that three nuclear submarines should be sent south immediately. John Nott at the MoD was telephoned from the airport and instructed accordingly. Considering the abuse heaped on British ministers and their cabinet staffs in the prelude to the Falklands invasion, it is worth pointing out that a submarine force was ordered to sea within two and a half days of the junta's probable decision to proceed with an early invasion. Yet as the contingency planners had always predicted, this was bound to be too late.

4 » THE ADMIRAL'S HOUR

The Falklands, even in time of peace, might be of great consequence to this nation, and in time of war would make us master of the seas.

Lord Anson, 1740

The events of the final week before the Argentine invasion of the Falklands seem with hindsight to have possessed an awful inevitability. In Argentina the invasion machine was now in forward gear, though it is still maintained in some quarters (including American intelligence) that the final decision to go on 2 April was not made until 31 March (the Wednesday). In London, politicians and officials appear to have been bemused and hesitant as crisis swirled towards them. Only one institution seems to have responded to the assessments of 28 March with total single-mindedness: the Royal Navy. In its case there were ulterior motives.

At the time the order to dispatch three nuclear submarines reached the Ministry of Defence on Monday, the 29th, the navy had only one which could be sent immediately. She was HMS *Spartan*, then taking part in Exercise Spring Train with the First Flotilla off Gibraltar. Submarines, in the words of one official, 'do not appear out of thin air', and the first reaction of the submarine staff at Fleet Headquarters at Northwood was one of surprise: 'We've got better things to do with our submarines than mess about in the South Atlantic.' Nonetheless, *Spartan* was recalled immediately to Gibraltar dockyard, where her practice torpedoes were exchanged for live ones from the submarine *Oracle*. She sailed within forty-eight hours. *Splendid* followed on 1 April, the day before the Argentine invasion, and *Conqueror* three days later, both from Faslane in Scotland. All maintained a remarkable average speed of 23 knots on the passage south. But even so, *Spartan* did not take up station off Port Stanley until 12 April. The Royal Fleet Auxiliary *Fort Austin* sailed from Gibraltar on the 29th to provide support for them and for *Endurance*.

Whatever the initial surprise of some junior officers, others in the Royal Navy were blessed with wider vision. A meeting of the First Sea Lord, Sir Henry Leach, and his senior operations staff took place on the Monday afternoon at the Ministry of Defence in Whitehall. They reviewed the options presented in Nott's paper of the previous week in the light of the new intelligence and the decision to send submarines. What if a 'larger task force' should be required, one 'capable of taking effective action against the Argentine navy'? Argentina possessed a substantial navy, with surface, underwater and air capability. She had at least six ships fitted with Exocet sea-skimming missiles, also the principal surface weapon of the Royal Navy. She had four submarines, two of them formidably difficult to detect with sonar, and an air force with more than two hundred planes capable of striking at a British sea or land force. The logistic and strategic difficulties of conducting operations against such a force 8,000 miles distant would be immense. Conventional wisdom decreed that, with the ships available to the Royal Navy in 1982, it would be most dangerous to take to sea against a force of this strength. The meeting therefore decided immediately to reject any task-force contingency which did not embrace all the resources available, including carriers, submarines and an amphibious assault element.

There now grew in the minds of Leach and his staff a most remarkable prospect, that of a full British battle fleet putting to sea in earnest against a not inconsiderable foe. To most senior officers, such a concept was not merely fantastic in the context of the 1980s. It would also become entirely impossible within a few years when the carrier and amphibious assault groups had been

phased out. This was precisely the unforeseen contingency Leach
had always argued that the navy had to be equipped to meet, and
the one which the policies of successive defence secretaries had so
nearly rendered impracticable. There were certainly overwhelming
strategic arguments for sending a large task force, which Leach
began to assemble that very day. He would be the first to admit
that there were overwhelming political ones as well.

The core of such a force would have to be made up from the
First Flotilla, some twenty ships then conveniently placed in
the mid-Atlantic on Exercise Spring Train under their flag officer,
Rear Admiral John 'Sandy' Woodward. His superior (and Leach's
immediate subordinate), the Commander in Chief Fleet, Sir John
Fieldhouse, was observing the exercise aboard the County class
destroyer *Glamorgan*. Late on that same Monday night, Fieldhouse
received a message from Fleet Headquarters in the north-west
London suburb of Northwood that the situation in the South
Atlantic was worsening and the MoD were considering a larger
'balanced' task force than the submarines already ordered. At fifty-
three, Fieldhouse had already achieved the pinnacle of naval command and was clearly destined, like Leach before him, for
promotion from Fleet Headquarters to Whitehall. A man who
radiated imperturbable urbanity, in voice, manner, even appearance, he had something about him of the actor Charles Laughton.
Shrewd and able, he was greatly respected both by the Americans
and by his Nato counterparts. Like many naval officers that week,
he must have sensed that a crucial moment in naval history could
be at hand. On receipt of the signal from London, he promptly
summoned Admiral Woodward to join him 'with all dispatch' from
his flagship, *Antrim*, then some 250 miles away. The two men met
for an hour at 4.30 a.m. on the Tuesday morning in the admiral's
big day cabin on *Glamorgan*. They discussed the role of First Flotilla
in any larger task force and the wider implications of naval
operations in the South Atlantic. Before dawn Fieldhouse was
helicoptered to Gibraltar and flown direct to London. From then
on, contingency planning was in progress for the sending of the

largest naval fleet Britain had seen since the war. Leach's opposite
number, Admiral Jorge Anaya, had yet to take the action which
would precipitate its sailing. Were he to decide on an invasion, he
knew and London knew that all the British ships in the world
could not stop him.

*

Richard Luce appeared at a Foreign Office reception on the Monday
night leaning exaggeratedly on a walking stick and declaring, 'This
week I am going to need it.' The next morning he had to wrestle
with the swift evolution of the policy of understated response. He
had been told that *Spartan*'s sailing time to the Falklands was ten
days. All endeavours now had to be directed towards lowering the
temperature with Buenos Aires in the meantime. That Tuesday
morning, Carrington decided to break into his planned trip from
Brussels on to Israel to make a joint statement with Luce to
Parliament. They had been authorised by the Ministry of Defence
on 24 March to announce that *Endurance* would remain 'on station
for as long as is necessary'. Luce added in the Commons that
'further escalation of the dispute is in no one's interest . . . It is
clearly right to pursue a diplomatic solution.' He then produced a
crucial sentence intended to satisfy MPs without alerting the
Argentinians to the sending of submarines: 'The question of security in the Falklands area is being reviewed, although the House
will understand that I prefer to say nothing in public about our
precautionary measures.' It was a pious hope.

The Commons once again demonstrated its unsuitability as a
forum for discussing the conduct of a crisis. Few appeared aware
of Luce's dilemma, except insofar as they could make party capital
out of it. The opposition foreign affairs spokesman, Denis Healey,
remarked that ministers had shown a 'grave dereliction of duty in
putting themselves in a position where they are totally incapable
of making any response to a threat which has been mounted for
the past three weeks'. This was true, but the time was long past
for pointing it out. Next, James Callaghan rose to reveal to the

House the details of his 1977 task force, supposedly a state secret. 'While I do not press the minister on what is happening today,' he said, 'I trust that it is the same sort of action.' Luce was now in a hopeless predicament. It was becoming politically impossible to deny the submarine force, yet it was military lunacy to confirm it. MPs might as well have publicly challenged the junta to get to Port Stanley first. Ministers have since argued that, from the time of South Georgia, the climate in the Commons ruled out strict 'non-provocation' such as not moving *Endurance* from Port Stanley. In which case, Parliament bears partial responsibility for precipitating the early Argentine invasion.

The game of cat and mouse with Luce continued upstairs, at a meeting of the Conservative backbench committee. Luce emphasised that he could add nothing to his Commons statement. This proved no deterrent to right-wing MPs yearning for news of the British navy gloriously at sea. After the meeting, some of those present felt sufficiently reassured to nod the wink to certain lobby correspondents that indeed submarines appeared to have been sent. The fatal word appeared on the television news that night. It was reported as fact in the early editions of the morning newspapers. The information was flashed to Buenos Aires where it confirmed rumours already current in top military circles. When a junior defence minister, Peter Blaker, called Luce's office to tell him of the leak, a member of Luce's staff felt physically sick at the news. Britain's Parliament, a citadel of secrecy when openness is required and of partisan garrulity when discretion should be all, had turned a covert deterrent to invasion into a public invitation to one.

Before Carrington departed for Israel, he had one matter to resolve with the Americans. On 28 March he had sent a formal message to the Secretary of State, Alexander Haig, informing him of the danger of warships becoming involved in the South Georgia area and requesting his intercession with the junta. To his astonishment, he received a message from Haig's deputy, Walter Stoessel, pointing out that both Britain and Argentina were 'good friends' of the USA and counselling caution. America's ambassador in Buenos Aires, Harry Schlaudemann, would nevertheless see what he could do. (Indeed, Schlaudemann approached Costa Mendes that same Tuesday and was rebuffed.) By all accounts Carrington hit the roof. He summoned the US ambassador, John Louis, and finding him away delivered the rough edge of his tongue to his long-suffering number two, Ed Streator. Carrington told Streator to inform Haig that aggression had been perpetrated in the South Atlantic and the United States had better decide fast which side she was on. The skeleton of US perfidy over Suez was already rattling in the Foreign Office cupboard.

The tempo of the crisis now quickened. The news of the dispatch of submarines finally tightened the junta's finger on the invasion trigger. Anaya's pride and joy, the carrier *Veinticinco de Mayo*, had already put to sea from Puerto Belgrano. On Tuesday a statement from naval high command said the service was 'in a high state of readiness', though for what was not mentioned. That night, the streets of Buenos Aires erupted not to the exultant cries of war fever but to anti-government demonstrations and mob violence of a ferocity not seen in Argentina since before the military coup of 1976. It made the junta's decision final. As *La Prensa* had prophetically remarked a month earlier, 'The only thing which can save this government is a war.'

*

Wednesday dawned with British intelligence poring over sigint from the South Atlantic. It clearly indicated that the Argentine fleet was now at sea and moving into a position from which an assault on the Falklands was possible inside forty-eight hours. A full assessment landed on John Nott's desk that afternoon. Lord Carrington's went at once to Richard Luce at the Foreign Office. Neither needed any prompting to scrutinise it. Nott, who was at the House of Commons, hurried along with the briefing papers to see the Prime Minister, who was also in her Commons room. It was already early evening. Luce took identical action. He sum-

moned Fearn and Ure for their advice, then told Humphrey Atkins
– acting Foreign Secretary in Carrington's absence in Israel – that
he was going to see the Prime Minister immediately. Accompanied
by Ure, he walked over to No. 10 Downing Street, only to find that
Mrs Thatcher was at the Commons, already closeted with Nott.
They pursued her there.

From all over Whitehall that evening, the bees began to buzz
round the hive of impending disaster. By seven o'clock, Mrs
Thatcher's Commons office contained John Nott and Richard Luce
as well as Humphrey Atkins. The prospective Foreign Office permanent secretary, Sir Antony Acland, attended as head of the JIC
(in the process of handing over to Patrick Wright). Mrs Thatcher's
private secretary, Clive Whitmore, was there and later her parliamentary private secretary, Ian Gow. Nott's permanent secretary,
Sir Frank Cooper, was summoned from a dinner party. The First
Sea Lord, Sir Henry Leach, was a later, arrival. Significant absentees
were both Lord Carrington, in Tel Aviv, and the Chief of the
Defence Staff, Sir Terence Lewin, away on a visit to New Zealand.
Lewin telephoned London each day during this crisis week to ask
if he should return. Each time he was told it would only cause
alarm for the Chief of the Defence Staff publicly to cut short an
official visit.

The Wednesday meeting lasted four hours. It reviewed the
intelligence reports and debated at length the continued Foreign
Office and JIC conviction that invasion was by no means a certainty. At most, a submarine landing might be planned as a means
of increasing the pressure on Britain in South Georgia – a view
communicated to Rex Hunt in Port Stanley. At any rate, if a full
invasion was imminent, there was no possible British military
action which could stop it. Britain's best hope at this stage was
diplomacy. The first decision was therefore to galvanise the Americans into putting pressure on Galtieri immediately and urgently.

That evening, the British ambassador in Washington, Sir Nicholas Henderson, duly called on Haig and Enders and sought to
convince them of the seriousness of the position. He went armed

with the Wednesday intelligence reports. The Americans were unaware of them (much to the subsequent satisfaction of British intelligence) and Haig asked his staff, 'Why have I not been told of this?' He immediately set up a working group under Enders and alerted the White House that the British Prime Minister might be trying to reach the President. Mrs Thatcher's message was transmitted at 9 p.m. London time in the form of a telegraph requesting Reagan to get in touch with the Argentine President and warn him off British territory.

What if this approach should fail? Most of those gathered in Mrs Thatcher's room were men whose instincts were to counsel caution. Humphrey Atkins and the Foreign Office officials were strongly of the view that, since there was nothing Britain could do to avert an imminent invasion, she should at least avoid giving Buenos Aires any excuse for one by provocative action. John Nott's position was more complex. An emotional man in a spare frame, he had never found it easy clearly to state his view in cabinet when there were powerful arguments on all sides. He gave his colleagues the impression of bottling his worries inside himself and then suddenly letting them burst out, often at unpredictable moments. On this particular evening he had before him a minute from the previous day's Defence Operations Executive (no relation of the service-oriented navy staff) highly sceptical of a Falklands expedition. He argued the logistical difficulties of the sort of operation necessary to retake the islands in the event of an Argentine occupation. More germane, he pointed out that, if the task force were sent, it would develop a momentum of its own which would be politically very difficult to halt. It was a major undertaking on which the chiefs of staff should take a view. Nott did not add that it was precisely the sort of 'out-of-the-area' operation which his naval review philosophy had sought to render impossible. Of those present at the start of the meeting, only Mrs Thatcher could be regarded as temperamentally averse to caution. But what could she alone do?

There now appeared a deus ex machina – and dressed for the

part. The First Sea Lord and Chief of the Navy Staff, Admiral Sir Henry Leach, was announced by Ian Gow as being outside the door. Should he come in? Leach was very much an admiral's admiral. Sharp, erect and precise, he appeared in full naval uniform after a day spent fulfilling an official engagement in Portsmouth (though with his helicopter in constant communication with London). He had arrived back in Whitehall shortly after 6 p.m. to find Nott's Falklands briefing material on his desk together with the new intelligence reports. Fearful once again that his Secretary of State was going to sell the navy short, Leach phoned Fieldhouse to ascertain the state of contingency planning, picked up the suspect briefing papers and strode along the corridor to Nott's office. Finding him already at the Commons, he set off in pursuit, baulked only by the policeman in the central lobby who proved to be no respecter of First Sea Lords even in full regalia. Leach ended up waiting a full quarter of an hour in a junior whip's office while Nott was found. Only when the news of his presence in the building was brought to Mrs Thatcher's notice was he asked to join the critical discussion. He was, after all, not the government's senior service adviser (who is the Chief of the Defence Staff) nor even the acting CDS, Sir Michael Beetham, Chief of the Air Staff.

Most participants at the meeting agree that Leach's arrival made a marked difference to its tenor. Asked by the Prime Minister if he could mobilise a full task force and how soon, he replied that he could and by the weekend. He added that it had to be a balanced fleet, not just a small squadron, and it would require full logistical support. He also hazarded the wholly political view that, if an Argentine invasion did occur, the navy not only could but should respond. When the Prime Minister asked him, in terms redolent of Good Queen Bess, what his reaction would be to such a force were he the Argentine admiral, he replied, 'I would return to harbour immediately.'

To his colleagues, John Nott seemed embarrassed to have this old man of the sea overriding his own hesitancy so confidently – and with the Prime Minister hanging on every word. For his part,

Leach would have been less than human if he did not revel in the irony of his position and the moral victory it represented over his adversary. It was a modern sea lord's prayer come true. The defence staff was now instructed to see if they could reinforce the Stanley garrison urgently. The fleet was put on initial alert. No one yet dreamed that a task force would sail, let alone be used in anger. Nott's view at this stage – that a task-force operation would be unwise – appears to have prevailed, though he did not oppose the alert. Leach, however, had injected into the discussion two crucial elements: first, an insistence that any task force would have to be a large one; and second, that it could and should be mobilised by the weekend.

Opinion differs as to how that Wednesday meeting might have gone had the Chief of the Defence Staff, Sir Terence Lewin, been there in place of Leach. Though himself a sailor, Lewin was less consumed by naval politics than Leach and might have been more in tune with the strategic considerations taxing the minds of Nott and the defence staff. This would certainly have been the case with a non-naval Chief of the Defence Staff such as Lord Carver. As it was, Lewin was never consulted on the advisability of sending the task force, merely informed in New Zealand that it was being sent. Leach has argued that, throughout the preparatory phase of the task force, it was 'exclusively a navy matter'. Certainly without his personal dynamism it is unlikely that the fleet would have sailed so soon, and as a result more cautious counsels might have gained wider currency.

Late that night, the senior fighting commander of the Royal Marines, Brigadier Julian Thompson, was telephoned at his home on Dartmoor near the marines' headquarters at Plymouth. He was told simply, 'I think you should know there is a problem on the Falklands.' In the light of the South Georgia incident, this did not come as a total surprise to Thompson; indeed, he had discussed the matter with his brigade major the previous Sunday. Yet of his three operational infantry units, 45 Commando was at its base in Scotland, 42 Commando had just dispersed on leave after exercises in Norway, and 40 Commando was training in north-west England. Since the last was the most accessible, its 600 men were ordered to return to Plymouth immediately.

*

The following morning saw a flurry of Whitehall meetings. The cabinet's OD committee gathered to review both the intelligence and the military position. Luce attended in place of Carrington. His anxious state was enough to produce a comment among the Cabinet Office staff – still infused with JIC sang-froid – that he was grossly overreacting. At the Ministry of Defence, the chiefs of staff met to review Leach's proposals for the dispatch of the fleet. It is believed that, at this meeting, Sir Edwin Bramall of the army expressed some reservations, as did Sir Michael Beetham of the air force. But the issue remained one of feasibility and that was a navy matter. Leach's contingency planning since Monday now stood him in good stead. As a senior ministry official remarked later, 'Every one of Leach's commanders would have been shot if those ships had not been ready to sail by the weekend. Leach knew that not just the Falklands were at stake.' Although both Bramall and Beetham have since been scrupulously discreet, it is known that at this time they were communicating considerable disquiet about Leach's operation to their staffs. This, however, in no way diminished their subsequent commitment to providing the task force with maximum logistical support.

At the same time and elsewhere in the ministry building, a Royal Marine generals' meeting was taking place, the first to be chaired by the corps' senior officer, Sir Steuart Pringle, since his return to duty after being seriously injured by an IRA bomb. The Falklands were mentioned, though the subject was by no means top of the agenda. The issue of reinforcing the island garrison was extremely complicated. There was no means of flying direct. The RAF's C-130 Hercules could not be refuelled in the air, and the only hope was perhaps to route them via a friendly Latin American country, such as Chile.

At various stages in the course of the day, Brigadier Thompson in Plymouth was ordered to alert and then stand down first the whole of 40 Commando, then one company, then one and finally two air defence troops. However, by the day's end, the Ministry had abandoned the almost absurd attempt to convey men to the South Atlantic in a matter of hours. In service parlance everyone was back 'as you were'. Thompson's immediate superior, Major General Jeremy Moore, travelled home from the ministry meeting to Plymouth thinking chiefly about his impending retirement and his search for a new job.

That evening, the group of ministers and officials who were later to form the core of the war cabinet gathered again in Mrs Thatcher's upstairs study at No. 10. In addition to most of those present the night before, the Deputy Prime Minister, William Whitelaw, was called in. Lord Carrington arrived back from Tel Aviv in the course of the evening. Mrs Thatcher herself hurried back from a planned stay with the Queen at Windsor. Intelligence reports indicated clearly that a large Argentine fleet was approaching Port Stanley.

Phone calls were now made to and from Haig as Reagan's aides frantically tried to brief the President on his impending conversation with Galtieri – a conversation which had yet to be fixed. Ambassador Schlaudemann in Buenos Aires tried to prepare the ground for it with approaches to both Costa Mendes and Galtieri but received no response. Each Argentinian was convinced that, whatever Reagan might say for the record, the Americans would ultimately remain neutral in the dispute. Galtieri therefore had no desire for a discussion with Reagan which could be merely embarrassing.

The general evaded Reagan for four hours but eventually agreed to speak with him. The conversation lasted, with translation, for an hour. Reagan was at least effective in impressing on Galtieri Britain's resolve to resist any invasion. He also told him that the USA could not have a conflict between two allies in the South Atlantic. He said Argentina would be the aggressor and any invasion would end the USA's good relations with Buenos Aires. He added an offer of his Vice President, George Bush, as mediator. This was refused. Reagan's call must have given Galtieri a bad attack of cold feet. The Argentine President told Anaya of the American message and the admiral is said to have replied, with the air of a practised conspirator, that it was too late for second thoughts. His ships were already in formation off the Falklands. He might have added, with Lady Macbeth, 'Was the hope drunk wherein you dress'd yourself!'

All attention in the Prime Minister's study now concentrated on deciding Britain's response. As one participant put it, 'We sensed a missile had already been launched; we could only wait to see where it might land.' This time John Nott, following the meeting of his chiefs of staff that morning, presented a less hesitant message. He told the Prime Minister that since the previous evening he had come to the view that a task force should be Britain's response to any invasion. Leach, summoned from the ministry, was more than ready to confirm that view. Indeed, to many present, a task force already seemed the only garment with which they could cover their political nakedness should the worst occur. The fleet was accordingly to be put on the fullest state of alert. Still no one seems to have believed that it would come to blows. Indeed, ministers' readiness to accede to the alert was partly conditioned by its unreality. There was no discussion of rules of engagement, strategy or the likely balance of advantage against the Argentine fleet. As Sir Terence Lewin was later to declare, although the creation of a task force was the product of a contingency plan, its deployment was not. 'We had no plan for a campaign of this sort in the South Atlantic, nor for the reoccupation of the Falkland Islands,' he told a Commons select committee. At this stage, the task force was seen essentially as a show of strength. This perhaps goes some way to explain one of the mysteries of the Wednesday and Thursday night meetings: why was there no consideration of a direct ultimatum to Buenos Aires? A number of anti-invasion Argentinians were later to complain bitterly that Britain had given the junta nothing but 'come-on' signs for three months. Mrs Thatcher had even left Argentine troops unmolested on South Georgia. Now, as invasion approached, no indication whatsoever was signalled to Buenos Aires that it would be met with massive retaliation. This curious omission is discussed below (pp. 423–4).

*

In the early hours of Friday morning, as the Argentine fleet was moving into position off East Falkland, the meeting at Downing Street broke up, grim and deeply worried. Only one participant seems to have drawn any satisfaction from it. Sir Henry Leach returned directly to the naval operations room at the Ministry of Defence, where his staff were assembled and waiting for him. He issued a terse and confident directive: 'The task force is to be made ready and sailed.' A signal was sent immediately to Woodward in mid-Atlantic: he was ordered to 'consolidate his task group' and 'prepare covertly to go south'. It is perhaps no more than a constitutional curiosity that at this stage such an expedition had been approved by neither the British cabinet nor the British Parliament. Nor indeed had the Argentinians yet invaded the Falklands. We are tempted again to quote Leach himself: 'it was exclusively a navy matter'.

5 » TASK FORCE

Rightly to be great
Is not to stir without great argument,
But greatly to find quarrel in a straw
When honour's at the stake.

Hamlet, Act IV, Scene IV

Argentina's long-running battle for the Falklands ended quickly at dawn on Friday, 2 April. As if in acknowledgement of their help-lessness, the members of the British cabinet were sound asleep at the time. The climax was pathetically easy.

Rex Hunt in Port Stanley had been informed the previous day that he was now threatened with far heavier metal than the solitary submarine of which he had earlier been warned. A full invasion fleet was on its way. Hunt had at his disposal not one marine detachment but two: Major Mike Norman's forty-strong incoming relief group and Major Gary Noott's outgoing group, twelve of whom had left on *Endurance* for South Georgia. The governor summoned the two officers to Government House and told them, in a phrase that has passed into Falklands history, 'It looks as if the buggers mean it.'

Possible landing beaches near the airport were earmarked for the laying of barbed wire. A two-man watch was posted on the headland overlooking the harbour entrance. Marines were sent to guard the airfield, the road into town and Government House itself. The islands' territorial defence force, supposedly some 120 strong, was summoned to muster. Only twenty-three turned out, to be given rudimentary tactical instruction. There was later some caustic comment that the islanders were more eager for others to fight for their territory than to fight for it themselves – though this seems ungenerous given the level of their training and the shock of the moment.

At 8.15 that evening, the governor made a radio broadcast. He announced to his shocked listeners that 'there is mounting evidence that the Argentine armed forces are preparing to invade the Falklands'. This was the first most islanders had heard beyond rumour. It left them little time to organise civil defence or leave the capital for the safety of the Camp. In retrospect, no aspect of British unpreparedness was more serious. Had the Argentine fleet been less restrained in its approach – had it begun its assault with a bombardment – there could have been considerable loss of life which elementary civil defence could have prevented.

Hunt ordered the radio station to remain on the air and told the inhabitants of Port Stanley to keep off the street. He made further broadcasts through the night, culminating in the declaration of a State of Emergency at 4.25 a.m. The small marine force was now deployed round the outskirts of Port Stanley, with orders to resist attack and retreat if necessary for a final stand at Government House. Hunt and Norman were aware that this could be only a gesture against the force now reported to be approaching.

The Argentinians are believed to have planned originally to land a small force of 150 'Buzo Tactico' marine commandos under cover of darkness at Mullett Creek, some three miles south of Port Stanley. These men would then trek overland and capture the garrison barracks at Moody Brook outside the town. With the British forces thus neutralised, the governor would be arrested and the way cleared for the full invasion fleet to enter Port Stanley Harbour. Minimum force was to be used. It is even said that a court martial was threatened to any soldier injuring a Falklands civilian.

Whatever the intended strategy, the course of the fleet through the South Atlantic on Thursday, ship-to-ship radio at full blast, deprived it of any element of surprise. Nor was Buenos Aires any more cautious. Faced with the collapse of domestic order, the junta had let it be known that 'by tomorrow the Malvinas will be ours'. Broadcasting stations relayed the news. Newspapers were told to prepare special editions.

The commandos indeed landed at Mullett Creek, about 4.30 a.m., and reached Moody Brook ninety minutes later. But their subsequent tactics suggested no misgivings about causing casualties. In a noisy full-scale attack, they hurled phosphorus grenades into the barracks and raked the rooms with automatic fire. Only the fact that the British marines had already been deployed prevented heavy loss of life.

The commandos, dressed in black, now joined the force which had marched direct to Government House, apparently with the intention of seizing Rex Hunt. A fierce exchange of fire ensued with Major Norman's group dug in round the house. This lasted some two hours and left at least two Argentinians dead. The commandos could now do little more than pin down the British until the arrival of heavy support with the main landing force. This entered Port Stanley harbour and began disembarking at 8 a.m. A group of British marines overlooking the harbour, commanded by Norman's deputy, Lieutenant Bill Trollope, managed to hit one of the landing craft with an anti-tank weapon before deciding to fall back on Government House.

By 8.30, with armoured troop carriers and guns coming ashore, Hunt realised that further resistance was useless. He ordered a surrender. The British had suffered no casualties. The Argentinians swiftly seized both the radio station and the Cable and Wireless office. Cut off from any communication with London, Hunt was unable to tell the Foreign Office what had happened. He refused to shake the hand of the invading commander, General Oswaldo Garcia, much to the latter's dismay. He then changed into full gubernatorial regalia and made his way in his official taxi to the airport to be flown by Argentine Hercules to Montevideo. The marines were photographed face-down on the ground to emphasise their humiliation, and flown out shortly afterwards. Any islander who wished was allowed to go with them.

For the British, the only redeeming aspect of the nation's humiliation was the vigorous resistance put up by Lieutenant Keith Mills and his twenty-three-man marine detachment previously landed from *Endurance* on South Georgia. The young officer had received orders reflecting the confusion and contradictions in London. He was to shoot only in self-defence; not endanger life; yet not surrender. At 10.30 a.m. on 3 April, Captain Astiz, aboard the Argentine vessel *Bahia Paraiso* at Leith, radioed news of Rex Hunt's surrender to the British detachment around Grytviken, urging that Mills and his men should follow suit. Two hours later, the corvette *Guerico* and two Alouette helicopters approached the harbour, followed by a big Puma troop-carrying helicopter. The Royal Marines opened fire with every weapon they possessed, damaging the helicopter and forcing it to beat a hasty retreat. They hit the corvette with three 84 mm Carl Gustav anti-tank rockets and more than 1200 rounds of small-arms fire. After two hours, with a much superior Argentine force established ashore, four Argentinians dead and one British NCO badly wounded in the arm, Mills concluded that he had done as much as any man could expect to force the Argentinians to pay a price for South Georgia. His country agreed with him. He returned to Britain after his surrender to receive a hero's welcome and the Distinguished Service Cross.

*

Unable to contain its delight, Buenos Aires was proclaiming the recovery of the Falkland Islands to the world at least two hours before the formal surrender. The news reached London in time for the Friday morning newscasts. With the lines to Port Stanley dead, the British government now had no means of checking these claims. The Foreign Office frantically called the office of the Falkland Islands Committee to ask for a list of radio hams on the islands, but it was not until 4 p.m. London time that an operator in Wales picked up an on-the-spot confirmation of the invasion.

Buenos Aires now erupted in a day of ecstasy. In a morning broadcast, Galtieri announced that his government 'had no alternative other than to do what has been done'. He promised no disruption to the lives of the islanders and hoped there would be no breach in good relations with Britain. A communiqué announced that the fifty-two-year-old commander of the Buenos Aires first army corps, General Mario Benjamin Menendez, had been appointed governor of the 'Islas Malvinas'. At a rally later outside the Casa Rosada presidential palace, Galtieri told a jubilant crowd that 'the three commanders in chief have only interpreted the sentiment of the Argentine people'. For once, an Argentine leader was telling his people the unvarnished truth. Military adventurism was working its time-honoured magic and Galtieri's voice constantly broke with emotion at the spectacle before him. Not since the days of Peron had a soldier so conspicuously implemented the popular will. Three days earlier, his police had been shooting at civilians in this same Plaza de Mayo. Now the square was filled with men and women weeping tears of joy.

Meanwhile in London, a brilliant spring day could do nothing to rouse Westminster and Whitehall from its sense of paralysing shock. Civil servants and politicians seemed to talk only in hushed tones as if contemplating a momentous bereavement. Suddenly the future seemed utterly uncertain. For no group was this more true than those who had met the previous night in Mrs Thatcher's study. Then, they had been engaged in what seemed a paper exercise in diplomatic brinkmanship. They had been discussing deterrence. Now the event they had been seeking to deter was an accomplished fact. They were staring at catastrophe. Worse, they had no evidence on which to base a response. Throughout Friday morning, they remained incredulous that a full invasion had occurred. With no link of any sort established with Port Stanley, they prayed that the reports from Buenos Aires were bravado. As a result, for a crucial eight hours, they could offer the nation neither comfort nor leadership. For nuclear strategists, it was a classic demonstration of the hiatus in authority which can follow a failure in communications at the outbreak of war (see page 416).

The first emergency cabinet after the Argentine invasion met on the morning of Friday, 2 April, with both Leach and the acting CDS, Sir Michael Beetham, in attendance. It was a miserable and inconclusive gathering. Leach reported on the fleet's preparedness and the movements of his Royal Marines. He said that *Invincible* would be ready to sail by Monday. *Hermes* was being rushed out of maintenance. But no firm decisions could be taken because the cabinet had no information beyond that issuing from Buenos Aires. It could only stand by and await news.

Humphrey Atkins, as senior Foreign Office minister in the Commons, then made a disastrously misleading statement from the dispatch box. He said that his department had been in communication with Hunt two hours earlier and no invasion had been reported. In fact, the contact with Hunt had been four hours earlier, shortly before the invasion. Although the announcements from Buenos Aires were undoubtedly premature, no one believed what Atkins was saying. Matters were made worse at 2.30 p.m. With British radio reporting dancing in the streets of Buenos Aires and the Commons crowded with worried MPs, the Leader of the House, Francis Pym, rose to give yet another 'holding statement'. He could offer only the promise of an emergency session of Parliament the following day, Saturday, 'if the situation in the Falklands deteriorated'. The cabinet had wholly lost touch with events.

At 6 p.m., Lord Carrington and John Nott at last held a press conference to confirm the invasion. Both looked shocked and bemused. They announced that diplomatic relations with Argentina were being broken off and that a large task force was ready to sail. (As we have seen, the First Flotilla had already been dispatched.) The Commons would meet the following day for statements and debate. It was the first such meeting since Suez, and to MPs it seemed an ominous precedent. The cabinet then immediately began its second emergency session of the day.

The full British cabinet played a minor role in the Falklands war. Mrs Thatcher, its chairman, had never found it an easy body to handle. Still dominated by men of the liberal Tory tradition – Carrington, Whitelaw, Francis Pym and James Prior – it had never offered her the cohesion and collective loyalty to which she felt entitled. As a result, she had come increasingly to take key decisions in sub-committees and at bilateral meetings from which her opponents could be excluded. It was a tactic she might have borrowed from one of her predecessors, Sir Harold Wilson. At Friday's second meeting, however, Mrs Thatcher knew she had to gain total cabinet support in what was clearly the greatest crisis yet to confront her three-year-old government.

There was no attempt by the service chiefs to conceal the huge logistic problems posed by the dispatch of a South Atlantic task force. In the first place it required a full complement of warships equipped with air-defence systems, Sea Harriers and their support vessels. There would be tankers, supply ships and hospital ships. An amphibious assault group would be required. This would demand the urgent requisitioning of civilian ships (ships taken up from trade, or STUFT for short). Leach himself was absolutely determined to sail the first group by Monday, fearful that there might be political pressure for a delay pending diplomacy. But an early departure would in turn require a major airlift to Ascension, which posed enormous problems for the Royal Air Force.

In addition to Leach's own clear enthusiasm, three factors made the cabinet's decision that evening a foregone conclusion. The first was the sheer momentum of actions already in hand. Monday's dispatch of submarines, Wednesday's fleet alert, Thursday's go-ahead, had all seemed prudent responses to Argentine threats. Now, the British bluff had been called. The South Atlantic seemed a different, far more hostile, place. Yet Mrs Thatcher and her colleagues could scarcely order the services to stand down merely because the invasion they were intended to confront had occurred.

The second factor was that, even with the invasion confirmed, the sending of the ships seemed light years removed from all-out hostilities. Mrs Thatcher went round the cabinet table meticulously ticking off each member in turn. One after another reiterated what had been and still was John Nott's primary concern: that the navy should not be sent if Britain was only going to turn it round in mid-operation. Yet just as the Foreign Office had never entirely believed the Argentinians to be so dedicated to the possession of the Falklands as to invade them, so the cabinet could not believe they would remain unmoved by the threat of violent retribution. It was agreed that Argentine assets in Britain would be frozen, export credit suspended, imports banned. The US and the EEC would be asked to join in these measures. The UN would be mobilised. To all this, the task force was simply a supportive gesture of resolve. All those interviewed for this book agree that on 2 April no cabinet minister believed for a minute that the outcome of their decision would be open war.

It was the third factor, however, that was decisive. Bluntly, the government could not face Parliament the following day without a task force. In the emphatic words of William Whitelaw, 'the government would have to resign'. Whitelaw had long been regarded as the Trollopian embodiment of party consensus, even when – as on law and order – he seemed personally most at odds with it. In Friday's highly charged atmosphere, his view seemed incontrovertible. In clubs and drawing rooms all over London, Tory MPs were awaiting Saturday's debate like time bombs on short fuse. The fleet was known to be on alert. To stand it down would be more than political flesh and blood could bear. A strategic gamble the task force might be, but a political imperative it unquestionably was. Only one minister, the Trade Secretary, John Biffen, is understood to have dissented from the collective decision, a dissent his colleagues put down to his slightly lugubrious eccentricity. We return to these issues in our conclusion.

*

To some, the debate in the Commons on Saturday, 3 April, represented British democracy at its best. The House rose almost as one voice to speak the collective shame of the nation and did so in terms that no government could ignore. Yet to others, the debate was a depressing re-run of the negative qualities which for years had prevented any sensible resolution of the Falklands dispute.

Mrs Thatcher made the best of an impossible task in her opening remarks. Clearly tired and in a speech which bore the traces of many hands – most of them in the Foreign Office – she pointed out that, 'it would have been absurd to dispatch the fleet every time there was bellicose talk in Buenos Aires.' As for keeping a permanent deterrent force on station, 'the cost would be enormous . . . no government could have done that.' Stepping painfully across the no-man's-land between past failure and future restitution, she announced only that, 'A large task force will sail as soon as preparations are complete.'

As she sat down, contempt rolled like thunder from the benches round her. It was the culmination of a dozen Falklands question times over the past decade, a demonstration of distrust not just of the Foreign Office but of executive government in general. Those excluded from the joys of office could at last take their revenge on the placemen of power. MPs seemed to revel in the self-righteousness of their rhetoric.

Given the cabinet's decision to send the task force, there was little of substance MPs could add. The opposition leader, Michael Foot, who had once proudly proclaimed himself a 'peacemonger', found himself bellowing for 'action not words' alongside the most rabid rightwingers. Few were bold enough to question the military implications of sending the task force. Apart from an intervention by a Conservative ex-diplomat, Ray Whitney, for which he was accused of defeatism, no one had the courage to examine the long-term consequences of a military response. As in Buenos Aires so in London, the hour seemed to call for emotion rather than a clear head.

Never was the absence of the Foreign Secretary from the Commons more painful. While Carrington was presenting a careful apologia to a respectful audience in the Lords, John Nott had to face the final firestorm in the lower house. His speech, which he later admitted could 'only have been a disaster', received scant attention for its content. No amount of government bellicosity would appease his audience. His plea for support for the armed forces as they set sail was brushed aside amid uproar and cries of 'Resign!' MPs left the Commons blinking into the sunlight of Parliament Square, to find it packed with tourists eager to witness the bizarre spectacle of the wounded British lion sending its fleet to war.

Still the Commons had not exacted its full toll. The previous day, Richard Luce had suggested to Lord Carrington that as junior minister responsible he should resign. Carrington had strongly resisted the implication that he as Foreign Secretary might be any less responsible. He said they had both better see the crisis through, and put Luce in charge of coordinating the diplomatic offensive then under way. The events of Saturday caused Carrington to change his mind. The Commons debate, attacks on his department at a subsequent backbench meeting upstairs, and his own inability as a peer to answer back at the Commons dispatch box, all filled him with gloom. He told Mrs Thatcher that he felt after all he should step down.

Mrs Thatcher had publicly resisted Nott's proffered resignation on the grounds that his department had in no sense been responsible – an argument which did nothing for Foreign Office morale. He was also badly needed where he was. Carrington might have borne more responsibility, but he was even more badly needed. However uncomfortably, Mrs Thatcher leaned on him for advice and support. She also knew that, when it came to responsibility for a number of Falklands decisions, she might prove no less vulnerable than he. She pleaded with him to remain at his post. He agreed to sleep on it. On Saturday the 4th, in the midst of her other travails, the Prime Minister had to mount a major operation to save her Foreign Secretary. The Chief Whip, Michael Jopling, was summoned to soothe Carrington's sensitivity to backbench criticism. Whitelaw spent hours in gentle persuasion. Even two ex-Prime Ministers, Lord Home and Harold Macmillan, were wheeled into the line.

It was all to no avail. As a peer, Carrington undoubtedly had a thinner political skin than those who have sought office through the rough and tumble of election. He was crushed by further attacks on himself and his department in the Sunday and Monday press. An editorial in Monday's *Times* telling him to 'do his duty' was particularly depressing. Other factors also came into play. Carrington's resentment of the anti-Foreign Office Conservative backbenchers was deep and long-standing. He objected to Mrs Thatcher's continual appeasement of them, her pitting of their opinions against his department's considered view. In a nutshell, he was fed up. The Falklands was the last straw. On Monday he told Mrs Thatcher he would go.

Humphrey Atkins resigned as well, despite having had no connection with Falklands policy. Luce also departed, in a gesture that was a parody of the principle of ministerial responsibility. Throughout the succeeding three months, not one of these ministers was asked for advice by the war cabinet, although in Luce's case he could clearly call upon considerable experience of Argentine negotiators.

The job of Foreign Secretary went to the only plausible candidate who could be moved without a major reshuffle: the Leader of the House of Commons, Francis Pym. The appointment was not an easy one for Mrs Thatcher to swallow. Pym had already been moved from the Ministry of Defence in 1981 for what she regarded as excessive spinelessness in his control of defence spending as well as a general lack of thrust in confronting his civil servants. He was a well-known 'wet', though of an always indefinite point of view, and his intuitive political mind had made him a focus for Mrs Thatcher's opponents in the party at Westminster. Despite his appearance, not unlike that of an old-fashioned family solicitor, he was her most widely tipped successor and thus the inevitable challenger to her leadership should the Falklands operation turn sour. Pym's promotion was the true price Mrs Thatcher had to pay for the Falklands fiasco. She felt she paid for it dearly over the coming weeks.

The Prime Minister spent at least part of the weekend making her governmental dispositions. If the genesis of the Falklands dispute had shown up the weaknesses in the British machinery of government, the response to the task force showed up some of its strengths. The decision sent an electric shock through Whitehall, aided by the brutal clarity of Mrs Thatcher's stated objective of 3 April: 'to see the islands returned to British administration'. For the Cabinet Office machine, business as usual was clearly out of the question. This in itself traumatised Whitehall's normal lines of communication.

Prompted by Harold Macmillan and guided by the Cabinet Secretary, Sir Robert Armstrong, Mrs Thatcher decided that the conflict did not merit the implementation of the full wartime contingency machinery, but it did require a small steering group of ministers. Sir Robert's quaint solution was a sub-committee of the OD committee, dubbed ODSA (for South Atlantic). It swiftly became known as the war cabinet, but the initials ODSA appeared on its papers throughout and officials referred to it as 'Odza'.

The committee's initial membership selected itself. It included the Prime Minister; her deputy, the Home Secretary, William Whitelaw; the Foreign Secretary, Francis Pym; and the Defence Secretary, John Nott. The official team comprised the Chief of the Defence Staff, Sir Terence Lewin, who was finally collected from New Zealand by an RAF VC10 and delivered to London on Monday morning; the new permanent secretary to the Foreign Office, Sir Antony Acland; Sir Robert Armstrong; and the Cabinet Office head of foreign and defence liaison, Robert Wade-Grey. The outgoing head of the Foreign Office, Sir Michael Palliser, was also invited by Mrs Thatcher to head a 'communications group' within the Cabinet Office. Its task was to keep other ministers and other departments fully briefed whenever they 'needed to know'. Palliser was also to prepare papers for the war cabinet on non-immediate issues, such as constitutional options for the Falklands.

A more controversial addition to the war cabinet, in its first week of operation, was the chairman of the Conservative Party, Cecil Parkinson. He had been plucked by Mrs Thatcher from junior ministerial office the year before to take over from the increasingly dissident Lord Thorneycroft. For an as yet little-known MP of fifty, this was considered by many of his colleagues to be promotion enough. The declared purpose of his further elevation was to maintain links with other members of the government and party – a function some thought William Whitelaw could perform equally well. The true reason for Parkinson's presence was more Machiavellian. John Nott, who had worked with Parkinson in the Trade Department, sensed at an early stage that he would be needing support against the Foreign Office team, where he assumed Pym would form an early alliance with Whitelaw. In addition, Nott's relations with Mrs Thatcher had recently been under some strain. Nott felt that the support of someone who knew his complex thought processes and was at the same time trusted by Mrs Thatcher could prove invaluable. His request for Parkinson was duly granted by the Prime Minister on the straightforward argument that 'Francis has Willie'.

In addition to these fixed members, other ministers and officials would be called in as and when required. Thus John Biffen, when still Trade Secretary, was involved in decisions over sanctions and ship requisition – which involved a swift dash to Windsor on the first Sunday to get the Queen to sign the necessary orders. (Biffen replaced Pym as Leader of the House.) The Attorney General, Sir Michael Havers, was frequently consulted over rules of engagement and over the legal terms of the various settlement proposals. The chiefs of staff would attend when required, and were regularly invited to weekend sessions at Chequers, where they would mingle less formally with the politicians. The Foreign Office legal adviser, Sir Ian Sinclair, was also much in evidence.

Thus disposed, Whitehall went to war. Most of its senior personalities were quite new to such a crisis. They knew only that the last time Britain had been involved in hostilities on this scale, at Suez, total disaster had followed. The cloud of Suez hovered over all their deliberations. Whitelaw admits that he shuddered each time he thought of Eden.

*

If politicians approached the month of April with trepidation, the same could not be said for the sailors and soldiers who were to form the naval task force. From the start of invasion week, when Sandy Woodward was instructed to prepare his task group, the mood was of guarded anticipation. With the news of the Argentine invasion, this changed to open excitement extending from the men of the First Flotilla in mid-Atlantic, to fleet command at Northwood, to the marines, the SAS and SBS, who would form the assault group, and on through the carriers, escorts and dock-yard personnel. Years of routine suddenly achieved meaning and purpose.

First there was the issue of command. The First Flotilla, of destroyers and frigates, was clearly to be the spearhead of the task force. It was already at sea, under the fifty-year-old Woodward. In the course of his conversation with Woodward on the Monday night, Fieldhouse had asked him what his reaction would be if a more senior, three-ring admiral were sent down to take overall command. Woodward naturally answered that he would defer to Fieldhouse's decision.

The Royal Navy is traditionally believed to be run by a changing sequence of fraternal societies: first, destroyer captains; then Fleet Air Arm officers; in 1982, it was thought, submariners dominated the fleet command. Both Fieldhouse and Woodward were sub-mariners. Some officers expected that another admiral with more experience of surface and amphibious operations would take com-mand of the task force. Derek Reffell, of the Third Flotilla, and

Sir John Cox, an expert on carrier operations, were mentioned.
Fieldhouse wanted Woodward; neither Leach nor Lewin dissented.

The politicians initially expressed concern at the choice. The
war cabinet had never met Woodward. Nott asked anxiously, 'Who
is he? Was he in the war?' and seemed to favour dispatching a
more experienced admiral. But Woodward was in command of the
units already at sea and the leaders of the navy expressed their full
confidence in him. Besides, although to the British public Sandy
Woodward was the sole custodian of the fate of the task force, in
reality final decision-making lay firmly with Fieldhouse at Northwood.

Fieldhouse's task was now immense. Even if the Royal Navy
was merely to conduct a major demonstration in the South Atlantic, the difficulties of deploying and supporting a force at the end
of an 8,000-mile line of communication would be enormous. Above
all, any task force would need air cover. The only aircraft carriers
Britain possessed were *Invincible* and *Hermes*. The first was very
small, the second seemed very old, and each could carry only a
fraction of the aircraft of a full-size fleet carrier. If both were
loaded to capacity with the Fleet Air Arm's only relevant aircraft,
the Sea Harrier, Woodward's ships should possess the barest minimum of credible air support to operate in the South Atlantic. The
force would also need defence against air attack. Taking part in
Exercise Spring Train were three highly modern air defence ships,
the Type 42 destroyers *Coventry*, *Glasgow* and *Sheffield*, armed with
Sea Dart. For close air defence, the only ships armed with modern
missiles were three Type 22 frigates equipped with Sea Wolf,
although these had been designed principally as anti-submarine
ships. One of the Type 22s, *Battleaxe*, was suffering shaft trouble
and was unfit to steam south. But the other two, *Broadsword* and
Brilliant, it was immediately evident, would be critical to the
defence of a task force. Beyond these ships, the officer commanding would simply be given all the frigates and destroyers that could
be made available. In the South Atlantic winter, wear and tear on

the ships would be formidable, even before possible battle damage was considered.

Even when a substantial number of ships had been mustered, doubt remained about their suitability for conventional war against the sort of opponent they now faced. Over the past three decades, as both Britain's world responsibilities and the navy's budgets had contracted, so also had the versatility of the fleet diminished. The Royal Navy in 1982 was overwhelmingly an anti-submarine force designed for war in the Atlantic against the Soviet Union. Yet the fleet was now being presented with its first, its greatest, challenge for a generation, a unique opportunity to prove what it could do. If its senior officers had any secret reservations about the dispatch of a task force, they kept them to themselves.

In the early hours of 2 April, before the Argentinians had completed their conquest of the Falklands, Woodward was instructed by Northwood to 'consolidate' his task group and begin to move towards Ascension Island. The ships which had taken part in Exercise Spring Train split into two groups: those which would sail with Woodward, and those which, because of their mechanical state of unsuitability for the South Atlantic, would return to Britain. As the force divided, one ship from the northbound and one ship from the southbound group came alongside each other and began a complex and exhausting 'crossdecking' operation that continued for some twelve hours. The northbound ships handed over every pound of surplus food, ammunition and spare parts they could provide. The southbound units offloaded drill ammunition and compassionate cases who wished to return home for weddings or funerals. *Coventry*, for instance, lost five men. The homebound *Aurora* sent across five volunteers from her own ship's company to replace them. Many of the fighting group asked homeward-bound ships to telephone wives and families on their return. Some sent over consignments of telegrams to be dispatched.

Among the men, there was much less of the exuberant eagerness for action that had infected the marines and paras. Many had already been at sea for weeks – in some cases, such as the crew of *Sheffield*, for months. They had been looking forward to returning home for Easter. The entire history of British foreign policy since Suez suggested that, after a period of prolonged dithering, a diplomatic settlement on the Falklands would be reached. Even the enthusiasts remained flippant. 'Today we have heard the news that we are off to the Falklands Islands to bash the Argentines,' Lieutenant David Tinker, secretary to the captain of *Glamorgan*, wrote home to his parents. '. . . very much a 1914 affair, with the Royal Navy going off to defend her colonies (or should I be thinking of Suez?). Of course the whole thing may blow over in a week, but the thrill of some real confrontation, away from the nuclear bombs of the northern world, in a "colonial war" is quite exciting compared to the routine of exercises and paperwork. The captain is of course delighted; he may be able to finish his career in a blaze of glory.'* His commanding officer, Mike Barrow, had joined the navy on the same day as Admiral Woodward and was now within a few months of retirement.

*

Major General Jeremy Moore of the Royal Marines had been asleep just two hours when the telephone rang at 3 a.m. on 2 April. One of his staff reported that the Argentinians were in the midst of an armed invasion of the Falklands. Like scores of other men who were called from their beds that morning, Moore suffered a moment of total disbelief. He demanded to be assured that this was not a belated April Fool's joke. Then, like Brigadier Julian Thompson, he dressed and drove to his headquarters at Hamoaze House, high on a hill above Plymouth overlooking the river estuary. Already it had been determined that a British land force was to be sent to the South Atlantic. Since the disbandment of

---

* This and other letters from Lieutenant Tinker quoted in the text are taken from *A Message from the Falklands: The Collected Letters and Poems of Lieutenant David Tinker*, published by Junction Books, 1982.

16 Parachute Brigade in 1974, 3 Commando Brigade was Britain's only thoroughly trained and prepared all-arms force capable of carrying out immediate amphibious operations. In any event, it was evident that this would be overwhelmingly a Royal Naval expedition. The navy would want their marines to form the spearhead of any landing force. In a hotel room in Denmark, Thompson's brigade major, John Chester, was called to the telephone and ordered to gather together the entire staff, who had been reconnoitring for a Nato exercise, and bring them home forthwith. All that day they trickled in to Heathrow, having struggled with British Airways for whatever seats could be found on a succession of civilian flights from Copenhagen.

Other servicemen had similar experiences. At his home in Hampshire, Captain Jeremy Larken of the assault ship *Fearless* was awakened to be informed enigmatically that his ship and certain others 'had been placed in a high category for the acquisition of stores'.

Lieutenant Colonel Nick Vaux, CO of 42 Commando, walked out on that Friday morning to the staff car which he believed was taking him to the airport to fly to America, only to discover that he was being driven immediately to his own headquarters to begin recalling his unit from leave by every means available. Vaux had been through this before. As a young subaltern, he landed with the Royal Marines at Suez.

At the Hereford base of the 22nd Special Air Service Regiment, the principal special forces unit of the British army, the commanding officer, Lieutenant Colonel Michael Rose, placed one squadron on standby as soon as he heard on BBC News of the invasion and of the alert of the Royal Marines. Then he telephoned Julian Thompson to suggest that, if there was to be an operation in the South Atlantic, presumably some SAS would be wanted.

One of the most remarkable figures immediately summoned to duty was winkled out of a London flat where he was staying after a Cruising Club dinner. Major Ewen Southby-Tailyour was an exuberant romantic who had always placed professional ambition well behind personal fulfilment. With his white hair resembling a slight swell in mid-Atlantic, his infectious charm and enthusiasm, he was a familiar celebrity among Royal Marines. The son of a colonel commandant of the corps, he was commissioned in 1960 after Pangbourne Nautical College and Grenoble University. He boasted proudly that, in the ensuing twenty-two years, he had spent only two in an office; this had done little for his chances of promotion, but had enabled him to sail halfway round the world – he was a superb helmsman and ocean racer – speak and write Arabic, paint watercolours of seabirds, explore the wildest corners of Arabia, and, above all, to know the Falklands.

In 1978, Southby-Tailyour commanded the marine detachment in the islands. He fell in love with the place and, even more improbably, with its people. He spent much of his tour at sea, exploring every creek and settlement along the coastline. He could claim to know the Falklands as well as any man alive, and wrote a navigational guide to the islands for private circulation. He cherished a passionate ambition to return. On 2 April, he was taking time off from his job as officer commanding the marines' landing-craft unit to attend a course on the Middle East at London University. On Brigade's urgent orders, he was rushed by staff car to Hamoaze House to meet Julian Thompson. The brigadier demanded to hear all that Southby-Tailyour could tell him about the Falklands. 'Hang on,' said the major firmly – he and Thompson were old friends – 'I'm not going to tell you a thing until you've promised to take me with you.' 'Don't worry, Ewen,' grinned Thompson. 'You'll be coming.' Southby-Tailyour was one of those remarkable, freakishly English enthusiasts who had suddenly caught his moment in military history.

The Royal Marines are a small, tightly knit family of some six thousand officers and men. Serving together for a lifetime, they declare proudly that almost everybody in their ranks knows each other. They cherish their independence, their own rank structure and pay system under naval jurisdiction, and their specialised fighting skills. The commando artillery regiment, for instance, which is made up of volunteers from the Royal Artillery who are seconded to the unit after passing the commando course, accepts only one in four of the men who apply to join. In recent years, 3 Commando Brigade's Nato role – defending the northern flank in Norway – had provided them with unique training, experience and equipment for arctic warfare.

Yet, in the previous decade, the very existence of the marines had come into question. As Britain's armed forces contracted, the corps' relations with its naval parent had become strained. Many marines were increasingly convinced that the Admiralty would be happy to be rid of them. The commando-brigade budget could then be spent on ships and weapons systems. As the navy's amphibious capability shrank – both the assault ships *Fearless* and *Intrepid* were at that time threatened with sale to foreign powers – the marines believed that the admirals' interest in their survival had waned. Some senior army officers argued that their marine counterparts moved in too narrow and private an orbit and lacked the breadth of experience for commanding modern forces in a Nato context. Less than a year earlier, at the height of the bitter debate about John Nott's proposed navy cuts, the Secretary of State dismayed the corps by publicly saying that, if the marines were disbanded, the blame would lie with the Admiralty Board for failing to make out a comprehensive case for their retention.

Now, on this spring morning of 1982, Mr Nott had his answer, and the Royal Marines an extraordinary opportunity. If a landing in the Falklands became necessary, 3 Commando Brigade would have to carry it out. The staffs at Hamoaze House began the huge planning operation necessary to take their force to sea, undaunted as yet by any great fears about what they might be called upon to do. This period, Jeremy Moore said later, 'was one of the best I have ever spent. Everybody was so elated, everybody was working so hard for a common end, overcoming difficulties. We had nothing but help from the army, the navy, the dockyard. I found people crossing the road to salute. Even the children seemed to catch the mood.'

The broad concept for the deployment of the amphibious task force was established early that weekend. Thompson's brigade would be strengthened by the addition of the 3rd Battalion the Parachute Regiment and all the supporting elements necessary to create a balanced landing force – above all, defence against air attack. The greatest initial problem was to gather the shipping to carry them. As Thompson's officers worked on the staff tables which decreed the loading scales necessary for units embarking for war, they discussed which ships might be available. They could count upon *Fearless* as their command platform. But her sister ship *Intrepid* was laid up, out of commission. Presumably they would have the use of *Hermes*, officially designated as a helicopter platform and commando carrier. They began to study the red book listing ships of the Merchant Navy available for charter or requisition in the event of war. They were mindful of Suez, when political fiasco was compounded by such appalling confusion in the loading of shipping that the British could have been in grave difficulty if they had met a resolute enemy. Many of the ships now earmarked for use by the army in the event of war were only suitable for a Channel or North Sea passage, and were quite unfitted for the South Atlantic.

Then, to their acute dismay, Thompson's officers learned that they could not have the use of *Hermes*, because she was required for the Sea Harriers. Even if they used both *Hermes* and *Invincible* and every available aircraft, the task force would sail with only twenty Harriers to provide air cover, a pitifully small force when battle casualties and inevitable flying accidents began to take their toll. *Hermes* would carry one company of 40 Commando as a contingency force, in case action ashore became necessary before the main amphibious group arrived. For the bulk of the brigade, however, there appeared to be only the navy's six elderly logistics landing ships, and the supply ship *Stromness*. Thompson's staff were in momentary despair about the shipping problem.

Then, at a stroke, most of their difficulties evaporated. They were told that the 45,000-ton cruise liner *Canberra* was to be requisitioned. She alone would be able to transport some two thousand men in much greater comfort than any ordinary troop-ship. The requisition of *Canberra* was an imaginative decision by Northwood and the Ministry of Defence, for it ensured that the brigade could remain at sea – and, above all, continue training – for far longer than would normally be possible. The flexibility of the whole task force increased dramatically. In secret, a small team was dispatched in civilian clothes to Gibraltar, to board the liner on her passage home from the Mediterranean, still laden with paying passengers. These officers would use the two remaining days at sea to select sites for helicopter pads, hospital facilities, unit accommodation.

Meanwhile, Northwood had set in motion the greatest oper-ation for the mobilisation of civilian shipping in support of the Royal Navy undertaken since the Second World War. The Admir-alty's STUFT cell was expanded. Commander Brian Goodson had held his posting as fleet logistics coordinator at Northwood for just a fortnight, yet it was now his responsibility to determine what ships the constantly expanding task force would need to maintain itself at sea. The list was awesome: storeships, tankers, dispatch vessels, hospital ships, repair ships, container ships – some fifty-four from civilian sources alone before the operation was com-plete, 500,000 tons in all. The Directorate of Naval Operations and Trade was expanded from one commander to four, and began the huge task of deciding which British ships were suitable to operate with the task force, then feeding these requirements to the govern-ment broker to supply through the charter market, or if necessary by requisition. About half of the ships for the South Atlantic were finally obtained by each method. While some vessels were in commercially depressed categories, readily available, others, such as passenger liners, were in profitable service, and much more difficult to secure.

Then the routine began of appointing senior naval officers to each ship to work alongside the civilian captains, providing naval parties to carry out specialist duties such as ciphering and refuelling at sea – and even a hundred-strong technical team for the repair ship *Stena Seaspread*. There were helicopter pads to be fitted on many ships; three-hour briefings for their captains on naval procedures and evolutions; naval survival suits to be found for the crews, rates of pay to be fixed with the National Union of Seamen. It was one of the great achievements of the Falklands war that this remarkable transition was carried out in a matter of weeks. Within six days of the Argentine invasion, *Canberra* had been fitted with two helicopter pads, replenishment-at-sea facilities and naval communications equipment. She was ready to carry a large part of 3 Commando Brigade to war.

*

On Sunday, 4 April, while the Prime Minister was seeking to dissuade her Foreign Secretary from resignation, Julian Thompson presided over a major meeting at Hamoaze House to brief his commanding officers for their departure. Some forty men filed into the old ballroom on the ground floor: General Moore and Sir Steuart Pringle, the brigade staff, the COs of the major units, Major Jonathan Thomson of the Special Boat Squadron. Julian Thompson himself – a slightly built, black-haired man of forty-six, wearing spectacles and smoking his customary pipe – might have been mistaken for a thoughtful university don. He possessed a reputation for quick intelligence, and an explosive, highly strung temper when roused. He had immensely enjoyed commanding 40 Commando as a lieutenant colonel, and had feared that, after that experience, the remainder of his career might seem 'a trifle flat'. The Royal Marines are sometimes derided by the other services for offering brawn rather than brains on the battlefield. They are nicknamed the bootnecks – 'the booties'. Some of their senior officers in the past have indeed been more muscular than thoughtful. Almost every man at Hamoaze House on 4 April was grateful that the chance of fortune had fallen upon Thompson to take 3 Commando Brigade to sea. He was one of his corps' rare intellectual soldiers, a man who had studied military history deeply, and understood his own business very thoroughly indeed.

Ewen Southby-Tailyour began the meeting by giving a presentation on the Falklands Islands. He described the sodden peat and tussock grass, sheep and snipe, persistent winds and a chill factor that bitterly intensified the winter cold. He emphasised that there would be no local food or pure water – every ounce of both would have to be provided for the landing force. British planning for war in Europe had taught a generation of soldiers to assume that troops crossing the sea would be received by a friendly government and population, able to offer vital support facilities. Yet there would be no local resources to call upon in the Falklands. Southby-Tailyour was dismayed by the number of officers who talked as if they would be able to use the familiar woods and hedgerows of Europe to screen reconnaissance and tactical movement. There would be no cover whatever in the Falklands, he warned, except that of darkness. By land as by sea, the South Atlantic presented an entirely hostile environment for men to live or fight in. Southby-Tailyour was followed by Lieutenant Bob Veal, a young naval officer who had recently commanded a joint services expedition to South Georgia. His vivid description of that lonely, ice-clad pinnacle sounded even more sobering than the image of the Falklands.

Then came Captain Vivian Rowe, Thompson's brigade intelligence officer. Rowe, a tall, quiet-spoken Welshman of thirty-two, had been working since Friday amidst almost absurd difficulties to evaluate the strength of the enemy. His principal source of information had been Plymouth City Library, which yielded standard reference works such as the Institute of Strategic Studies' annual *Military Balance*. For more than a generation, in the matter of intelligence, as in every other area of budget-conscious defence, attention had been focused decisively upon eastern Europe. Even the defence attachés in most British embassies had concentrated more on selling arms to their host countries than upon intelligence gathering. Argentina had always enjoyed close defence links with Britain, sending officers to British training establishments, buying substantial quantities of British weapons, most recently Blowpipe and Tigercat ground-to-air-missiles, and two Type 42 destroyers. But although British intelligence improved markedly as the Falklands conflict escalated – with critical assistance from American sigint – on the battlefield information about enemy formations, their condition and tactics remained sketchy in the extreme. Contrary to public belief at home, the British commanders in the South Atlantic never received a single satellite photograph of the battlefield, from American or any other sources. As far as it is possible to discover, Britain was able to mount no useful Secret Intelligence Service effort within Argentina and only limited SAS surveillance of her airfields. It is not surprising that Rowe's briefing on 4 April was very thin on hard information. As far as anybody could judge, there were now about 3,000 Argentinians on the Falklands. Thompson's force of some 3,500 men would outnumber them, but the British would have nowhere near the 3 to 1 superiority which the rule book considered essential for offensive operations. Thompson himself took the floor to begin a cool, precise exposition which almost exactly foretold the pattern of the war. The amphibious force would do nothing until the naval battle had been won, he said. The brigade could expect to spend a long time at sea. A direct assault on Port Stanley was out, because the British possessed such a limited assault capability, and such scanty helicopter assets. Thompson envisaged securing a beach-head into which reinforcements could be fed. The British would be foolish to underestimate the Argentinians, who had carried out their invasion of the Falklands exceptionally efficiently. 'Advanced phase operations' – the landing of SAS and SBS teams for reconnaissance – were being planned. Many of those present, like many of the British public, were privately sceptical that the vast juggernaut now being set in motion would ever reach a battlefield. But from the outset Thompson had little doubt: 'I was quite sure that with our Prime Minister, if the

Argentinians didn't fold, we would fight them.' Officers who had never before worked with marines left Hamoaze House that morning much impressed by an experienced brigade staff thoroughly on top of its job.

*

In the days that followed, service officers, conditioned by years of petty economy, niggling bureaucracy and chronic supply problems, were astounded by the efficiency of the machine that now moved them towards war. Whatever Sir Edwin Bramall's initial reservations about the role of the task force, that week he and the British army committed themselves wholeheartedly to a huge effort to equip the men who were to sail. The whole of southern command was ransacked, an immense transport plan put into effect to move the stores to the docks. The war maintenance reserves of equipment and ammunition were broken open and moved to the ships exactly as planned. Supplies of arctic clothing, new radios, handheld laser rangefinders and spare parts flowed into units as fast as the indents were signed. 'It was like Christmas, that Monday,' said Lieutenant Colonel Hew Pike of 3 Para. Men poured back from leave, alerted by signs at railway stations, telegrams, phone calls. Scores of officers, soldiers, sailors besieged their units to be allowed to join the embarking force. Some were accepted. A few, inevitably, took as much trouble to be left behind. The parents of a seventeen-year-old junior rating on one of the warships agitated successfully for their son to be posted ashore, although Northwood had decided as a matter of policy to allow seventeen-year-olds to sail. A few long-serving ratings whose time was almost up chose to escape the risk of months trapped at sea. Most of the pressure was the other way. The Fleet Air Arm base at Yeovilton in Somerset was ruthlessly stripped of every serviceable helicopter. Thompson emphasised from the outset that his force would need the strongest possible airlift.

At this stage, there were critical space constraints upon the quantities of men and equipment that could be embarked on the ships. Southby-Tailyour had told Thompson that wheeled vehicles were useless in the Falklands. The marines possessed some Volvo tracked vehicles which they normally employed on the Norwegian snow, but which it seemed reasonable to hope might operate on peat. As it was impossible to load all the equipment required, they worked on the principle of taking something of everything. Seven or eight Volvos per unit – perhaps a quarter of the total stocks – were moved to the ships. As Thompson pondered the Argentine order of battle he became more and more concerned about the air threat. After an initial request for just one troop of Rapier anti-aircraft missiles, he increased this to an entire Rapier battery – twelve launchers. He also wanted Scorpion and Scimitar armoured reconnaissance vehicles, whose cross-country capability was said to be remarkable. He was told that there was space for only two troops – eight vehicles. When the Blues and Royals' squadron commander wished to sail in command of them, he was told there was no room for him on the ships. This little armoured force accordingly put to sea in the hands of a twenty-four-year-old lieutenant. Still uncertain about conditions in the Falklands winter, the marines debated whether to take full ski equipment. They compromised by providing it for thirty men per commando.

Throughout those days, the logistics officers were conscious of the imperfections of their ship loading. Columns of trucks were streaming into Portsmouth and Plymouth, driven by exhausted young men from all over England often ignorant of the nature of their cargoes. Crates were stowed unmanifested aboard the ships. It was obvious that the naval force under Admiral Woodward would require weeks in which to do its business before the commando brigade could land. Would it not be more sensible, the staff asked, for the landing force to use this period of grace for intensive training and proper ship loading in Britain, rather than put to sea in a state of confusion? They received a clear, unequivocal answer. The government was determined to send the task force to sea while the public and political will existed to launch it. If

3 Commando lingered in England, the vital impetus, the sense of national purpose, could slip away. They would sail the moment that the ships were loaded, and reorganise and restow at Ascension Island, which had been appointed as their rendezvous.

Hew Pike of 3 Para was one of the few unit commanding officers convinced from the outset that they were going to war. He said as much when he addressed his battalion for the first time at their base at Tidworth in Hampshire on the day following the invasion: 'It seemed very clear that we were likely to fight. I felt that we were very fortunate, and said so.' A crisp, sharp, clever Wykehamist of thirty-nine, Pike was the son of a general, and widely regarded as a future general himself. Like most British officers of his generation, he had served in Aden, Oman and Northern Ireland, but had never been shot at by anything heavier than small arms. As his battalion prepared to leave for South-ampton, he felt no great fears about what lay ahead: 'I was confident that we were reasonably well prepared. There is enor-mous residual self-confidence in a parachute battalion. People don't wonder whether they can do things.'

Nick Vaux, the slightly built former amateur steeplechase rider commanding 42 Commando, privately believed that 'Ascension was as far as we were likely to get' before some sort of settlement was reached. But he let none of his reservations get through to his men, who were irrepressibly exhilarated by the whole experience. At forty-six, Vaux was older than most of his fellow colonels, but much respected for his quiet, penetrating judgement. In his younger days, Vaux had rivalled Ewen Southby-Tailyour's enthusi-asm for high living and female company. Now, as a CO, he radiated a relaxed calm and common sense which inspired enormous confidence among his men on the battlefield. But when his com-mando mustered on their parade ground before embarking on *Canberra*, he allowed himself a moment of pure theatre. Major General Moore delivered a moving and effective speech about the feelings of young men on the edge of possible action. Then Vaux called the parade to attention. 'For the South Atlantic . . .' he shouted. '. . . Quick . . . March!' The marines loved it.

＊

On the afternoon of 4 April, Brigadier Thompson flew from Plymouth to Northwood with Southby-Tailyour and Michael Clapp, the commodore amphibious warfare. Clapp, an almost boyish-looking fifty-year-old whom Noël Coward would not have been surprised to find beside him on the bridge in *In Which We Serve*, would be commanding the landing force – as distinct from Wood-ward's battle group – until the brigade had been put ashore. Fleet headquarters at Northwood, a large office complex set in an obscure corner of suburban Metroland and incongruously given the name HMS *Warrior* (complete with 'decks'), was now hum-ming with activity. Major General Moore was to become Sir John Fieldhouse's military deputy, and his staff were already estab-lishing themselves in the unused Nato operations room deep in the underground command bunker – 'the hole'. All manner of additional army and naval personnel were moving in: intelligence cells, RAF officers controlling the airlift of stores and men already under way to Ascension Island, communications specialists, liaison officers.

Southby-Tailyour promptly repeated his morning briefing on the Falklands for the benefit of Fieldhouse and his chief of staff, Vice Admiral Hallifax. Clapp favoured taking his own ships down in consort with the main battle group. But Fieldhouse emphasised that they would sail separately, then pause at Ascension until Woodward's naval battle had been fought. He also eased one of Thompson's major preoccupations by declaring firmly that a Falklands landing would not take place under air threat. They were all impressed by the commander in chief's directness and his unshakeable urbanity. In the corridor after the meeting, Field-house turned to the party and said, 'This is going to be a sad and bloody business. I only wish that I could give you more ships.' To

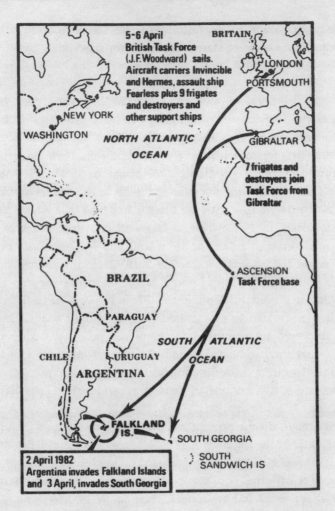

5-6 April
British Task Force (J.F. Woodward) sails. Aircraft carriers Invincible and Hermes, assault ship Fearless plus 9 frigates and destroyers and other support ships

BRITAIN

LONDON
PORTSMOUTH

NEW YORK

WASHINGTON

NORTH ATLANTIC OCEAN

GIBRALTAR

7 frigates and destroyers join Task Force from Gibraltar

ASCENSION
Task Force base

BRAZIL

PARAGUAY

CHILE   URUGUAY
ARGENTINA

SOUTH ATLANTIC OCEAN

FALKLAND IS.

SOUTH GEORGIA

SOUTH SANDWICH IS

2 April 1982
Argentina invades Falkland Islands and 3 April, invades South Georgia

Thompson he said, 'This thing must be approached soberly and coldly.' When they arrived back at Hamoaze House that evening, Thompson said, 'Well, thank goodness there's somebody with some sense in charge up there.'

Monday was a day of movements. Ewen Southby-Tailyour flew with Clapp and Thompson to Brize Norton airfield to debrief Mike

Norman and his Royal Marines, repatriated after their capture in Port Stanley. Sitting in the VIP lounge, they ran urgently over the details: Where did the enemy come ashore? With what equipment? How good did their morale appear? What defences were they building? Little of value for the future emerged, except a general impression that the first Argentinians to land had been impressive, while those who followed were much less so. As they were talking, elsewhere on the airfield Michael Rose was seeing off his D Squadron for Ascension Island – sixty-six 'badged' SAS, plus fourteen signallers and support personnel with 50,000 pounds of equipment, which the regiment maintains at constant readiness for emergency deployments.

At Portsmouth, amid the tower blocks and masts and cranes that dominate the flat horizon of one of the great naval towns of Britain, the crowds had been watching quietly all weekend as the convoys of trucks rolled through the dockyard gates. Red flags fluttered above ships in process of ammunitioning. The flight-deck crews of Britain's only two operational aircraft carriers received the Fleet Air Arm squadrons of Harriers and Sea King helicopters. Now, as the ships cast off their lines and began to move out of the harbour, vast throngs of flag-waving, cheering people gathered to bid them goodbye and good luck. The crews lined the ships' sides. A Harrier crowned the flight deck of *Invincible*, moored precariously at the very tip of her 'ski ramp'. Bands played, women wept. It was the beginning of a unique episode in modern British history, a throwback Edwardian or even Victorian in character. Many civilians and not a few servicemen were privately dismayed that so vast an operation, straining the dwindling resources of the nation to the limits, should be launched in such a cause. Yet most still believed that once Galtieri's invasion had taken place, Britain possessed no choice but to react to it. Tragic or grotesque this expedition might seem, yet it was also deeply emotional. Britain remained one of only three, or at most four, nations in the world which could mount such an operation. The British were going to war as they had always gone, in haste and some confusion but with confidence and great pride. The launching of the task force was of itself a marvellous feat of speed and efficiency. Even the most ardent cynic must have been moved by the spectacle of the Royal Navy's surface fleet, which so many had come to regard as an anachronism in the age of the nuclear submarine, sailing forth out of the ports from which Nelson and St Vincent, Rodney and Collingwood had gone.

Most of Julian Thompson's staff spent that Monday quietly in their homes, packing and enjoying a few final hours with their families. The following afternoon, 6 April, they were summoned to muster on the football field beside Stonehouse Barracks, the huge, square, stone base built in the Napoleonic era that now housed 3 Commando Brigade headquarters. Julian Thompson had to deal with one last-minute change of plan. Northwood was considering the use of a small independent assault force to retake South Georgia. M Company of 42 Commando, highly trained for mountain and arctic warfare, were to fly to Ascension Island led by the unit's second in command, the mountaineer and explorer Major Guy Sheridan. Thompson sorted out the arrangements, then made his way to the landing zone. It was a windy, overcast day, with a soft Devon rain falling steadily. On the edge of the field, a cluster of wives watched.

At last, in from the sea clattered the three big naval Sea Kings. Clapp, Thompson, and their staffs, accompanied by Michael Rose and a handful of key support personnel, pushed their kit up in front of them, and clambered into the noisy holds. They lifted away over the sea towards their mid-Channel rendezvous with *Fearless*, which had sailed from Portsmouth a few hours earlier. They set down aft, on her big flight deck. As the helicopters were moored and the rotors lashed, they made their way along the ship's companionways, over layers of packing cases and stores, to the overcrowded cabins that would be their homes for the next three months. Southby-Tailyour made up his bed in a spare bath. Thompson went forward to meet Jeremy Larken, the captain. Sailors and marines alike were exhausted after the frenzied days of preparation. The crew had also been unsettled by watching close-up television pictures of naval families in tears on the quayside as they sailed.

The brigade staff possessed no directive except to put to sea and begin considering how they might make a landing in the Falklands. Thompson was conscious that, if there was to be war, the navy could lose it. And naval support was essential to make victory possible. But only his landing force could ultimately regain the Falklands for Britain. That night, his staff – less those suffering from seasickness – settled down in the brigadier's day cabin for the first of many sober discussions about the options that now lay before them.

*

Three days later, on Good Friday, amid scenes of emotion as great as for the departure of the carriers, 3 Commando Brigade sailed from Southampton aboard the liner *Canberra*. Max Hastings, standing by the rail listening to the strains of 'Rule Britannia' drift up from the quayside as the lines were cast off, caught a marine officer's remark: 'Now I know this is serious. You can't let the nation see us go off to war with bands playing and then bring us back without doing anything.' There were still many men, including some in high command, who believed that Britain was mounting a mere military demonstration. But it is now possible to see what one commander calls 'the ghastly political inevitability' of all that followed the sailing of the task force. Once the great machine had been set in motion, only the most astonishing change of heart in Buenos Aires could have halted it.

6 » HAIG'S DOVES

Peace hath her victories
No less renowned than war.

Milton, *Sonnets*

Military historians have long said that war is no more than an extension of diplomacy. Falklands diplomacy reached that crisis after the diplomats had been at work for nearly two decades. The sending of the task force by Mrs Thatcher gave them a respite of just fifty days. As a result, those involved were not so much diplomats as medieval envoys. They hastened back and forth between London, Buenos Aires, Washington and New York with bargain after bargain, eventually seeking to forestall battle by no other argument than that one or other side was bound to get beaten.

The British Foreign Office at the start of April was a shattered institution. It was like an army recoiling from a disastrous engagement in which it had lost its beloved commander in chief – murdered, many believed, by traitors on his own side. Yet like an army it had now to regroup, repair its defences and counterattack. Just as the Royal Navy discovered a new challenge in proving itself to its critics through the mobilisation of the task force, so the Foreign Office turned disaster to at least temporary triumph with two remarkable diplomatic coups, first in New York and then in Brussels.

Britain's ambassador to the United Nations, Sir Anthony Parsons, had been posted to New York after leaving Teheran with the fall of the Shah. It was not an easy assignment, even for this gregarious diplomat of liberal inclinations. The UN under both Waldheim and his current successor, Javier Perez de Cuellar, appeared bogged down in a morass of Third World politics, its pronouncements ignored and its peace-keeping operations, notably in Cyprus and the Lebanon, ossifying rather than resolving divisions. The principle of self-determination which underlay its foundation was mocked as one dictatorship after another took the rostrum to rant against the world's surviving democracies, while the leaders of two of its most important members, Britain and the USA, treated its proceedings with either neglect or open contempt.

A sympathetic UN response to Argentina's invasion was central to Costa Mendes's diplomatic offensive. Yet another indication of the junta's unpreparedness was that the distinguished lawyer, Eduardo Roca, had only just arrived to head the Argentine delegation in New York when the crisis broke. He had no time even to learn UN procedure, let alone build up a constituency of support for his government. Costa Mendes had always been convinced that Britain would not be able to summon the Security Council, and even if she did and gained enough votes for a condemnatory resolution, he was sure the Russians could be persuaded to veto it. The US ambassador, Mrs Kirkpatrick, is known even to have hazarded the view that no western power would dare use the Security Council procedure to sustain a colonial possession in a Third World continent.

As it was, Parsons displayed what a UN admirer called 'good old-fashioned diplomatic legwork' to obtain the nine votes he required to have the Security Council summoned on Thursday, 1 April, even before the invasion had occurred. He announced that an Argentine assault on the islands was imminent and secured an immediate call from the council's Zairean President, Kamanda wa Kamanda, for both sides to show restraint. The hapless Roca was clearly not sure what had hit him, and remained silent. So much for Costa Mendes's fait accompli. Invasion would now be in flagrant defiance of a Security Council presidential call.

With the Argentine occupation of the Falklands a fact on the Friday, Parsons again moved with speed. Thatcher might share with President Reagan the view that the less heard from the UN the better. But no nation likes to go to war without right on its side, and even Thatcher was not averse to the banner of a Security Council's resolution fluttering over her task force. Throughout the war, Parsons's strategy was dominated by two considerations. The first was to secure a UN demand for Argentine withdrawal, to 'legitimise' Britain's military response; the second was to avert any subsequent demand that Britain stall or recall the task force.

As soon as invasion was confirmed, the Security Council was again summoned to confront a straightforward British request that it pass a binding resolution ordering the Argentinians to leave the islands. Rather than follow the normal procedure of circulating an advance draft to sound out opinion, Parsons presented a 'take-it-or-leave-it' final resolution. Such 'black drafts' as they are known entitle the presenter to a vote within twenty-four hours. The vote would be held on the Saturday evening. Costa Mendes raced to New York to support Roca, still confident he could avert a diplomatic disaster. The Security Council has fifteen members, of whom five are permanent and ten are chosen on rotation every two years. Two-thirds support is needed for a binding resolution, which means a proposer must secure the votes of at least some of the 'non-aligned' members. This seemed a near-impossible task for Britain and Costa Mendes's confidence was understandable.

Parsons now set about the challenge. Of the western bloc, he could assume he had the UK, the US, France and Ireland in the bag, as well as Japan. The communist states, China, Russia and Poland, had to be ruled out, as did Latin Spain. Panama had already agreed to sponsor Argentina's case. That meant Britain needed all the remaining five for her two-thirds majority, a mixed bag of Third World nations comprising Jordan, Togo, Zaire, Uganda and Guyana. At times like this a diplomat must draw on every resource at his disposal – an old favour done, a personal contact kept in good repair, a trade deal or cultural exchange in the offing, perhaps simple friendship. Parsons had less than two days for his manoeuvring.

Guyana gave her vote to Britain, agreeing to any resolution which might deter Venezuela from pursuing a border dispute with her. Zaire did the same, as the nation of the affronted UN President, Kamanda. France was asked to square the Togo vote, which she did. Uganda remained doubtful until the last minute, but eventually sided with Britain on the grounds of Argentina's 'aggression'. But it was Jordan who found herself in the sort of confusion normally reserved for the US delegation. The Jordanian delegate declared in favour of Britain, but was then instructed from Amman not to vote with any colonialist cause. Parsons tried every pressure, but the Jordanians' hands were tied. Finally he wheeled out his biggest gun. His office telephoned London, tried to reach Carrington, failed and went for the Prime Minister herself. Mrs Thatcher, who had other things on her mind that Saturday, responded to this buccaneering spirit. Parsons had gained her respect (rare in the Foreign Office) when she had previously visited his embassy in Teheran. While Parsons ingeniously stalled for time (even suggesting a retyping of the resolution to include the word 'Malvinas'), Mrs Thatcher telephoned King Hussein and personally pleaded with him to support Britain. Parsons got his ten votes.

Costa Mendes now went into conclave with the Russian delegate to induce him to use his veto. He cited non-alignment, anti-imperialism, Argentine grain sales to Moscow, anything. It was Russian policy not to use the veto except on resolutions directed specifically at their interests, but in an atmosphere of tension rare for the UN, Costa Mendes kept up the pressure to the end. Parsons's staff still felt the chances of a Russian veto were evens: Parsons's personal betting was 6–4 against. In the event, the Russians abstained. What became the Security Council's Resolution 502 went through as drafted by Britain.

Argentina was now faced with a demand for the 'immediate withdrawal' of her forces, followed by one instructing both governments to seek 'a diplomatic solution to their differences and to respect fully the purposes and principles of the charter of the United Nations'. The charter reference was crucial, enabling Britain to cite the principle of self-determination for the Falklanders in any subsequent negotiation over their future. It also gave her, under Article 51, 'the inherent right of individual and collective self-defence if armed attack occurs . . . until the Security Council has taken measures necessary to maintain peace and security'. The article, often considered a belligerent's charter, was a particular favourite of Mrs Thatcher in the weeks to come.

Resolution 502 turned out to be a minor classic of British postwar diplomacy. To many at the UN, Britain's dispatch of a task force was a gross overreaction to what was seen as an anti-colonialist peccadillo by Argentina. To call the Security Council in aid, to win a two-thirds vote there, and to avoid the veto, all in forty-eight hours, was remarkable. A senior US delegate described it as 'a stunning example of sheer diplomatic professionalism'. Even Mrs Kirkpatrick, who could ill conceal her pro-Argentine sympathies, later used the incident to compare British diplomacy with American 'amateurism'. Parsons had handed his Prime Minister a precious victory even before the task force set sail. 'All the Argentines have to do,' she would intone to all who cared to listen, 'is honour UN Security Council Resolution 502.' It was an improbable handrail for someone of her views to grasp, but all the more effective for that.

*

The Foreign Office's Falklands Emergency Unit, set up under the indestructible head of the South American desk, Robin Fearn, was now pouring out justificatory paper through its embassies abroad. Within a week, Australia, Canada and New Zealand had promised full support. The new socialist government of France particularly gladdened Thatcher's heart by the promptness of its backing. Germany's Helmut Schmidt, strong in his distaste for Thatcher, was only slightly more dilatory. Japan came down on Britain's side. Even the communist states seemed little attracted to Argentina's brand of anti-colonialism. China counselled caution. Russia initially maintained a guarded neutrality.

Britain's most urgent need was cooperation over sanctions, especially from the US and the Common Market. First and foremost, these had to embrace arms sales, with Germany due to build Argentina two frigates, and France to supply her with Super Etendard jets and Exocet missiles. Both orders were immediately frozen, confirming the fears of the more cautious Argentine planners who had wanted the invasion to await their delivery. Over the weekend, Britain banned virtually all trade with Argentina and blocked Argentina's financial assets in London. However this would be largely symbolic without foreign support. Britain imported some £160 million worth of goods from Argentina in 1980 against £1 billion imported by the rest of the EEC.

The Common Market is normally the most lethargic of diplomatic animals. With the Easter break beckoning at the end of the first week of the sailing of the task force a concerted initiative which would actually hurt member states' pockets was almost inconceivable. It was the more so at the request of Britain, whose relations with the EEC at this time were anything but good. On Tuesday, 6 April, a senior Foreign Office diplomat, Sir Julian Bullard, arrived in Brussels to support the number two there, Bill Nicholl – the ambassador being away on holiday. There followed a sustained lobby of the members of the European Commission and of national representatives, not unlike that mounted the previous week by Parsons in New York. By Good Friday, with everyone yearning for his limousine, the British made their bid: first a statement of political support and then, most remarkably, a package of economic sanctions including a six-week import ban and a suspension of trade preferences. As in New York so in Brussels, there is little doubt that the task force was the major factor in bringing the issue to a head.

Economic sanctions are rarely effective in their aim of forcing a government to alter a course of policy on which it has embarked. Their chief value is not financial but political: an emphatic act of

world ostracism. Argentina was unlikely to withdraw from the
Falklands because Italy would not import her leather. But, as with
the UN vote, Buenos Aires was shaken by the solidarity of the
European response. It also meant that other Latin nations thought
twice before being sucked into the conflict.

Argentina's economy in fact suffered far more from an almost
automatic consequence of the invasion. In April 1982, she was
one of the world's most severely overdrawn nations, with international debts totalling $32 billion. Loans from individual banks,
including Lloyds and National Westminster in London, and Morgan
Guaranty and Citibank in New York, were believed to total hundreds of millions of dollars each. These borrowings were commercial. Throughout the war, and despite the freezing of $1 billion of
Argentine assets in London, Argentina was careful never to default
on her interest payments. But from the moment of invasion, no
banker would lend Buenos Aires more. This was a devastating blow
to Galtieri's hopes of a Malvinas-backed economic revival. His new
economics minister, Roberto Alemann, reportedly offered his resignation in despair, only to be told that he would be drafted to the
job if he did.

*

There remained one large blot on Britain's diplomatic escutcheon
as the task force set sail: the United States. Nuclear strategists have
a dread of incidents such as the Falklands invasion. One of their
scenarios for a third world war was of a Russian-stimulated diversion in an obscure corner of the globe, taking political attention
and military resources away from Europe, and thus offering the
Russians the opportunity for a pre-emptive strike. (Worries about
such a diversion were voiced by British intelligence before the
invasion.) Washington's initial response suggested that the Falklands did not even rate the status of a diversion. On the evening of
invasion day, Jeane Kirkpatrick, accompanied by Haig's deputy,
Walter Stoessel, and Tom Enders, went to a dinner in her honour
given by the Argentine ambassador to the US, Esteban Takacs. The

British ambassador, Sir Nicholas Henderson, remarked that it was as if he had dined with the Iranians the night of the Teheran hostage seizure. Kirkpatrick, never one to waste good oil on troubled waters, responded that America had always been neutral on the issue of Falklands sovereignty and 'if the Argentines own the islands then moving troops into them is not armed aggression'. Kirkpatrick, an American spokesman patiently explained, was an academic, not a professional diplomat.

London's suspicion of American attitudes and actions in the early days of the crisis was understandable. The casual response to Carrington's early warnings, the delayed call to Galtieri, the emphasis on 'even-handedness' and on US friendship towards Argentina, the vacuous pleas from Reagan for restraint, all suggested that America would prove as unreliable an ally as she had over Suez. In addition, the public rifts between Haig and Reagan, and within the State Department between Haig and Kirkpatrick, were grimly reminiscent of the Dulles–Eisenhower disagreements in 1956. Over that first weekend Haig's 'Falklands unit' was embroiled in discussion over what America's role should be. The administration sailed a sea of conflicting views and indecisions. There were those who advocated leaving the crisis to the Organization of American States or at least to individual Latin American nations. Some saw the UN as the proper forum for mediation. Others regarded it as a US function to bring two supposed allies of America together in negotiations. Vice President George Bush, officially appointed trouble-shooter by Reagan for just such a crisis, was standing by.

Washington is not the most discreet of cities. By Tuesday the argument had crystallised into a row in Haig's office between Enders and the more extrovert assistant secretary for European affairs, Lawrence Eagleburger. Enders argued that for America to sacrifice its new and hard-won position in South America, where a number of nations teetered on the brink of marxism, all for the sake of the Falklands, was lunacy. Eagleburger, like Haig, was an Atlanticist. He felt strongly that the certainty of support for a Nato ally was crucial to European security. It was the classic dilemma of modern American foreign policy.

Eventually mediation won the day. Its advocates could at least argue that it would postpone the moment when the administration might have to 'tilt', as it was termed, to either side. Much against the better judgement of many of his aides, Haig himself decided to act as mediator and informed the White House accordingly. The following day, Reagan held what was dismissively billed as a 'mini-National Security Council'. Sensing the strong part ambition was playing in Haig's decision, he simply told the Secretary of State to do his best and left on a visit to Miss Claudette Colbert in the Caribbean with an air of unconcern.

Alexander Haig certainly saw the Falklands as the perfect stage on which to put in some safe and, he fondly hoped, relatively easy practice for his vocation as a world statesman. His use of shuttle diplomacy for the Falklands mission was in patent emulation of his predecessor, Henry Kissinger, though the venue was hardly as glamorous as the Middle East. Initially, at least, the auguries did not look too bad. Neither Britain nor Argentina could conceivably want war, let alone a costly sea and air war. The issue was itself ludicrous: sovereignty over an almost valueless group of desolate islands. Although America accepted that the wrong lay with Argentina, few in Washington could believe the British would not compromise to a sufficient extent to avert hostilities. They had after all been negotiating some sort of transfer of the islands to Argentina for years.

Haig's Boeing 707, equipped with bunks, writing desks, radio telephones, photocopying machines and high hopes, duly lumbered into the air on the night of Wednesday, 7 April, and headed for London. It contained a relatively small team, headed by Enders and with David Gompert, Eagleburger's deputy, as 'European' representative. Vernon Walters joined the party later. Haig had insisted that no press were to accompany him. He was still an apprentice and had yet to acquire Kissinger's effortless manipulation of the media.

The British were by no means pleased to see him. 'American treachery' was already being whispered in Whitehall, and 'even-handed' negotiators on a matter of clear principle were viewed with suspicion. Haig's mission had received the prompt support of Costa Mendes, but Thatcher would only agree to it on the understanding that Resolution 502 would be honoured before any negotiations and that Haig would be 'supporting efforts to this end'. To ram home this point, the cabinet announced a 200-mile maritime exclusion zone round the Falklands from the following Monday, the estimated date of arrival of *Spartan* in the area. The zone was declared while Haig's plane was airborne.

*

The British war cabinet had by now found its stride. Meetings at Downing Street commenced each morning at 9.30 (or at Chequers most weekends). By that time the Ministry of Defence had sorted out its overnight reports from the task force and the Foreign Office had digested its telegrams, including the end-of-day messages from the US. Proceedings began with Lewin's own report, followed by Nott's comments, Pym's presentation of the negotiating position, and then general discussion. Decisions were disseminated round Whitehall well before lunch and the senior civil servants involved reassembled after lunch to review their implementation and prepare material for the following day. The essence of this machinery was that it was so close-meshed. There was a minimum of participation by departments or agencies other than those directly involved: hence the importance of Palliser's communications operation. Towards the end of the war, some members felt this system's arteries had begun to harden – which usually means too much power is going to Cabinet Office. But it gave the war cabinet both flexibility and total power. As Churchill found, government by a small, all-powerful cabinet is a state of grace for a Prime Minister which Westminster and Whitehall will tolerate in war but which cannot be recreated in peace.

The other key to the war cabinet's success as an instrument of government was its military command structure. The central institution of British armed services command is the chiefs-of-staff committee, chaired by the Chief of the Defence Staff at the Ministry of Defence. In war, this body is normally closely integrated with the war cabinet, acting in effect as its military executive. Leach presented the dispatch of the task force as a strictly senior service affair: it was a conventional naval deterrent in support of diplomacy. Mobilisation of warships, merchant ships and marines was his business. 2 and 3 Para, the Blues and Royals contingent and the RAF Harriers were assigned to the task force. Its commander in chief was the C-in-C Fleet at Northwood, Sir John Fieldhouse. The other services, notably the Royal Air Force, were simply to lend logistical support as required.

As the fleet moved south and the prospect of Britain waging a land war increased, it might have been expected that the command structure would broaden. If anything, it narrowed. The chiefs of staff met after Lewin returned from war cabinet each morning, ran over its decisions and reviewed any strategic options outstanding. By then Lewin had already been in telephone communication with Fieldhouse. There was little concealing the fact that the chiefs of staff, including even Leach himself, were being sidetracked by the exigencies of the operation. Not until late April, for instance, did the army get a senior man, General Richard Trant, into Northwood. It was to Nott's credit that, despite pressure from within his department, he maintained the simplicity of the cabinet–Lewin–Fieldhouse command structure throughout the conflict.

The structure was subject to one limitation: it tended to conceal from the war cabinet the nature of military doubts about the efficacy of the operation. Assessing operational risks is a complicated business. Conveying those assessments to ministers who have other interests at stake is even more so. The Prime Minister, abetted by Leach, had effectively ordered the chiefs of staff to war without even meeting them. Any reservations which might have been felt by Sir Michael Beetham of the air force and Sir Edwin Bramall of the army – and they were known to have at least some

– were never on the cabinet agenda. Their job was to carry out the order to put the task force to sea. Only later, when it had established a continuous momentum, did any reservations gain a hearing.

Many of these conflicting pressures came to rest on John Nott's shoulders. Lewin's reports were regarded as model documents of politico-military relations. They were intended to convey information and certainly risk, but they also had to convey reassurance. Whenever the going looked rough, the Prime Minister would ask him again and again, 'Are you sure you can do this?' Lewin would reply, with a winning combination of authority and charm, 'Yes, Prime Minister.' In the early days of the task force, members of both the war and full cabinets believed that, if the navy had to fight, they would achieve a walkover. As a result, when the chiefs of staff made their first formal presentation to the war cabinet at the Ministry of Defence a week after the task force sailed, ministers were decidely shaken by the warnings of possible losses and casualties, by the news of Argentine naval strength and particularly by a predicted 50 per cent Harrier attrition rate. It seemed a sobering, even depressing, meeting. Ironically, it was the supposed 'doves', Whitelaw and Pym, who drew on their past military experience to assure their colleagues that chiefs of staff are always gloomy about risk before battles.

*

The war cabinet's initial and sheltered self-confidence undoubtedly played a part in Britain's first response to the Haig mission. Haig brought with him on 8 April only the three themes which were to dominate the whole negotiating phase: military withdrawal by both sides, an interim administration and a long-term settlement. The last included a job lot of solutions borrowed from successive Falklands negotiations in the past. The Americans also brought an apparent lack of understanding of the essence of the British position, which worried those who met them.

Haig's team was first briefed by Pym at the Foreign Office.

Then, at 6 p.m. they walked across Downing Street to see Mrs Thatcher. This was followed by a working dinner, with Nott, Lewin and Acland also present. If Mrs Thatcher appeared to the Americans theatrically intransigent – certainly more so than the Foreign Office – the American approach seemed uncoordinated to the British. In the wider exchanges, one of them after dinner, Haig seemed heavy-handed in his insistence that America could not have two allies at war, and that Britain had to give him room for manoeuvre. More privately – especially in talks with Mrs Thatcher herself – he hinted that he had to talk tough to impress the Argentinians and, it seemed, his own team as well.

The war cabinet's response left no room for doubt. The nation would return to the negotiating table as and when Argentina honoured Resolution 502. Meanwhile, Britain was sustaining her rights under Article 51 of the UN charter. For good measure, Haig was deluged with details of the horrors of winter in the South Atlantic and of the need for speed. He left that night overwhelmed by the strength of the British stance – as he admitted to his ambassador during a stopover in Brazil.

Not until Haig's team arrived in Buenos Aires did they realise the full scale of the task ahead of them. Vast demonstrations packed the Plaza de Mayo, summoned with tactical aplomb by opposition newspapers. Headlines, placards and graffiti cried: 'Death to Margaret's Swine' and 'Goodbye Queen, Long Live Argentina'. Posters showed Mrs Thatcher with a piratical black patch over one eye. Street gossips vied with each other in the crudity of their jokes at the expense of her sex. Radio and television poured out a stream of propaganda, interrupting regular programmes with subliminal messages: 'The Malvinas are Ours'. At one point, Haig had to be helicoptered out of the presidential Casa Rosada to avoid the crowds massed outside.

Haig found Galtieri only marginally more rational than the mob. The junta had clearly been utterly taken aback by the speed and strength of the British military response. They could not believe that it was anything but bluff. The past inaccuracy of their diplomatic intelligence seemed to have no effect on the credibility of their military predictions. No amount of persuasion by the Secretary of State that he knew the British to be in deadly earnest could sway them.

Haig spent four hours with Costa Mendes and held two meetings with Galtieri, at which the President's whisky consumption awed and then alarmed the Americans. Haig left with little more than an impression, gained from Costa Mendes, that the Argentinians might withdraw their troops alongside a British withdrawal, provided some symbol of the islands' altered status was left in place. They accepted that the British could hardly concede sovereignty in advance of negotiations. But the Argentinians insisted that their flag should stay on the Falklands.

This apparent flexibility gave Haig his first building block. If he could postpone the sovereignty issue for the time being, his only task was to find a formula for an Argentine withdrawal which did not look like a climb-down, and for a British return which did not look as if Buenos Aires had profited by aggression. In other words, he had to create an interim administration for the Falklands, prior to restarting long-term talks, on a basis acceptable to both sides. This task, apparently so straightforward, remained beyond the grasp of all the Falklands intermediaries. Time and again the issue of long-term sovereignty raised its head. Nor did the Americans at any time discern a real yearning on either side to avert the impending hostilities. 'Like two schoolboys itching for a fight,' said one of Haig's aides, 'they'll not be satisfied until there's some blood on the floor.'

Haig's plane headed back to London on Sunday night, 11 April, with his staff complaining bitterly of the 'machismo' which appeared to dominate the dispute. The Secretary of State was cast in gloom. In a radio telephone conversation with Reagan – later embarrassingly leaked – they discussed whether, if Mrs Thatcher was able to sink one Argentine vessel, it might vindicate her desire for 'retribution'. The White House was now openly questioning the wisdom of committing any further American prestige to an apparently hopeless mission. Yet Haig pressed doggedly on. He landed at Heathrow at 5.40 a.m. on Monday, 12 April, his body clock in ruins and no one at the airport to meet him. A hastily arranged fleet of cars took his team to the Churchill Hotel to recuperate before meeting the war cabinet.

An entire day of talks in London added little to Haig's understanding of the British position. From Pym, he gleaned a slight hope that Britain might agree to some sort of joint administration on the islands and would accept sovereignty on an agenda for later talks. Resolution 502 had to come first. There would be no tight deadline on a long-term solution; no Argentine access to the islands in the interim; affirmation of the principle of self-determination. The best Pym could offer was that the 'trauma of invasion' might have induced the islanders to soften their previous intransigence. Mrs Thatcher unhelpfully added that they would hardly be softening in a pro-Argentina direction.

Haig's team was now in regular communication with Buenos Aires, where the Argentine cabinet met that Monday evening. Haig assumed that it was discussing its final terms for the interim administration. To his dismay, Costa Mendes reported that his government was now demanding a fixed timetable for a transfer of sovereignty: a direct betrayal of the understanding with which Haig had left Buenos Aires. To Haig's team this was not shuttle diplomacy, it was a madhouse.

Not for the first time, the Americans sensed Costa Mendes's inability to deliver his government. Haig postponed his departure from London and saw Mrs Thatcher again on the Tuesday morning. Was there no flexibility she could offer him? Her sole concessions were a shift from a demand for the status quo ante to just a 'recognisably British administration', and at least a downplaying of the British demand for paramountcy for the islanders' own wishes. At the same time, the war cabinet was becoming impatient of Haig's lumbering progress. Britain was looking for America's support. Pym pointedly told a press conference he was sure 'the US wouldn't be neutral between a democracy and a dictatorship'. It was even quietly put about that the Queen was less than enthusiastic about welcoming an 'even-handed' President Reagan on his proposed June state visit.

Haig now returned again to Buenos Aires by way of Washington, professing to find the situation 'exceptionally difficult and dangerous'. He saw Reagan, and told him that he could see no give on either side. Despite the continued strong reservations of Enders and Kirkpatrick, he felt that the time had come to threaten Buenos Aires with the full weight of American support for Britain if they did not honour Resolution 502. Reagan agreed. The second week of the shuttle thus found Haig back in Argentina and ready to wave the big stick. Galtieri by now had few doubts that the Americans meant business. He even called Reagan before Haig's return to assure him of his 'desire for a peaceful solution' and to express the hope that Washington would not desert its new ally. Yet Galtieri was already a prisoner, trapped on one side by a navy colleague convinced that his service was on the brink of a major triumph and on the other by a foreign minister who seemed to be losing one poker hand after another. From now on he cut an increasingly pathetic figure.

Costa Mendes infuriated the Americans. Like the lawyer he was, he would leap from wild affirmations of principle – apparently to ingratiate himself with the military – to an obsession with trivial detail: How high should a flagpole be? What should the observers be called? What should be the shape of a withdrawal zone? Intermediaries began to realise that hours spent with him were probably wasted. Even the 'three stooges' from each of the armed forces, Admiral Benito Moya, Brigadier Jose Miret and General Iglesias, who sat in on the Costa Mendes talks, brought no greater authority to the proceedings. Indeed, by requiring interpreters they slowed them to a snail's pace (Costa Mendes negotiated in English). The power of decision clearly lay with Admiral Anaya. Without him, a Costa Mendes concession was no concession at all.

Haig's ideas had by now begun to cohere into what was grandly called a five-point plan. This involved withdrawal by both sides; a three-flag administration to last until December; restored communication with the mainland; talks in the new year on a long-term settlement; and consultation to ascertain the islanders' views. This was plainly a reasonable splitting of the difference between the two sides, but it was a little more than that. There was no certainty that Haig could get London to accept a year-end deadline on the interim administration (after which, what?); nor could he offer Buenos Aires any assurance that at the end of the year Argentina would be any nearer sovereignty. Military working groups discussed the Haig plan far into the night of 17 April. Only the air force seemed at all willing to compromise.

On Sunday, 18 April, Haig played his final trump card in person before the full junta. He told them bluntly, with particular emphasis towards Anaya, that Britain was not bluffing in her determination and that America could not see two friends at war. He said that Washington would not tolerate the fall of Thatcher's government. Argentina had to enter realistic negotiations on the basis of Resolution 502 or America would side with Britain. Anaya remained spectacularly unmoved. He stated his view that the British had no stomach for a fight; that democracies could not sustain casualties; and that the task force ships would simply break down in the South Atlantic winter. Anaya was also aware, through his own independent intelligence network, of the divisions within the American administration: he did not believe Haig could deliver a Washington 'tilt' towards Britain. In a dramatic rejoinder, he leaned across the table and told Haig to his face he was lying. Haig was flabbergasted.

The junta did not reject the Haig plan outright. As one of the Americans sarcastically observed, that would have required of them a decision. Instead, they continued the laborious processes of military consultation. British ministers described Argentina as a dictatorship, in coy recollection of the struggle against Hitler and Mussolini. It was no such thing. It was an oligarchy: weak, unstable and extraordinarily brutal. The regime's methods of suppressing opposition, by 'disappearance' and non-juridical execution, were

callous, wasteful and ineffective – even by the standards of neighbouring Chile and Uruguay. The nation's constitution, such as it
was, has been classified by Professor Finer* as 'direct military rule
arising out of a coup d'état'. Legitimacy derived from the junta's
pretensions to protect the state from internal disorder. The institutions of that legitimacy were the service councils, direct parallels
of the 'committees of public safety' of revolutionary societies.
These councils were Argentina's parliaments, her ruling elite in
conclave.

It was before such bodies that the junta members had to defend
any compromises they might offer Haig. The fifty-four-man army
council met at least twice over the weekend under General Jose
Antonio Vaquero, head of its general staff. Galtieri declared that
his troops would 'stay on the Malvinas dead or alive'. For the navy,
Anaya had withdrawn his precious carrier to Puerto Belgrano,
apparently following a serious mechanical failure. But the rest of
his fleet was at sea, determined to uphold the navy's glory as the
redeemers of the Malvinas. No senior commander seems to have
doubted their ability to inflict unacceptable losses on the British
task force. Any hierarchical responsibility now collapsed as each
junta member guarded his rear. At consultative meetings, hands
would shoot up, hard-liners would form factions, moderates would
be heckled into silence. Surely the junta were not going to turn
back now? Had they not said the Malvinas were theirs? Did they
not possess air superiority, submarines, Exocet, 8,000 men dug in
round Port Stanley? Why on earth negotiate on sovereignty?

Such proceedings signalled death to diplomacy. By Monday the
19th, Haig had realised that he was dealing with a regime quite
unable to take coherent decisions, let alone stick to them. Galtieri
would agree some detail, go out onto the Casa Rosada balcony,
breathe in the plaudits of the crowd and find himself promptly
repudiating it. Buenos Aires was now rife with rumour: the
invasion had been Anaya's alone; Lami Dozo was in revolt; Galtieri

---

* Professor S. E. Finer, *Man on Horseback*, Pall Mall, 1962.

was insensible with drink. Incredibly, Haig battled on. He set out with Costa Mendes what he understood to be Argentina's 'bottom line': a shared Anglo-Argentine administration under US supervision; a shared islands council; sovereignty to be resolved at the UN by the end of the year. This was formulated into a Costa Mendes 'plan'. But everything remained in doubt. How far should the task force withdraw? Would there be free access for Argentine nationals, clearly unacceptable to Britain? What did 'joint sovereignty' really mean? As Haig's plane was about to leave, a flurry of messages reached his team from Costa Mendes. There might be more concessions. No, there might not. Costa Mendes might offer concessions. The junta might yet draw back.

The new Costa Mendes proposals had been telegraphed to London at 9 p.m. on the Monday evening. It was more than two weeks since the task force had sailed, and they were received with outright hostility by the war cabinet. None of the new ingredients was acceptable. The only factor which saved Haig from receiving a raspberry was the war cabinet's desire not to be seen as the prime cause of breakdown. Haig was called during a refuelling stop in Caracas – where he had staggered from his bunk to 'brief' the Venezuelan foreign minister – and informed that there was no point in his heading for London. He would hear nothing new.

Haig's shuttle now ground to a halt in Washington. He had been absorbed exclusively in the Falklands for twelve days and had covered 32,965 miles – a record of sorts. At home, opposition to his mission was growing. The New York Times headlined an editorial 'Stay at Home Al Haig', arguing that there were bigger crises to occupy his energies. In addition, America, and particularly its east coast, was experiencing an extraordinary upsurge of pro-British sentiment. The British ambassador in Washington, Sir Nicholas Henderson, had mounted a political public relations campaign on the Falklands quite as sophisticated as that conducted at the UN by Sir Anthony Parsons. He was indefatigable. Each morning his crumpled suit and wayward hair appeared on one television network after another, seemingly the embodiment of European rectitude and reliability. In a city of images, he managed to convey one of a Britain engagingly down-at-heel and yet resolute in the cause of justice. The very eccentricity of the task force seemed to tell in its favour.

Henderson succeeded in unlocking ancient, almost atavistic, emotions tying Britain to America. These had nothing to do with Nato or Europe or the fate of Reagan's Latin America policy. As one senator emphatically told him, he was not interested in the rights or wrongs of the Falklands: 'Why am I with you?' he asked rhetorically. 'It's because you're British.' As Henderson daily padded the corridors of Capitol Hill, lobbying senators and congressmen or anyone who cared to listen, he was also calling forth a similar enthusiasm to that seen in Britain, from people yearning to witness a government, any government, responding uncompromisingly and with main force to an adverse turn in world affairs. A Lou Harris poll on 29 April showed the American people 60 per cent for Britain and only 19 per cent for Argentina. Haig's staff now settled down in Washington to review progress and prepare their final bid to save their Secretary of State from humiliation and the Falklands from war.

7 » ASCENSION TO SOUTH GEORGIA

The elements of the British task force converging upon Ascension Island at the end of the second week of April were under orders to prepare a range of options for the war cabinet. Commodore Clapp and Brigadier Thompson, aboard *Fearless*, were wrestling with the implications of 'repossessing the Falkland Islands'. Thompson and his planning cell – the 'R' Group – had been specifically instructed that they need only concern themselves with land operations, since the air and sea battle would be fought and won before their arrival.

To achieve these conditions, Sir John Fieldhouse and Admiral Woodward could call upon the three nuclear-attack submarines already on their way to the South Atlantic; the most powerful force of destroyers and frigates that Britain could put to sea, headed by the three Type 42s – *Glasgow*, *Sheffield* and *Coventry* – and two Type 22s – *Brilliant* and *Broadsword* – which had left Gibraltar with the Spring Train force for Ascension; and the carrier group, *Invincible* and *Hermes*. Woodward's ships began to sail south at a cracking 25 knots, but quickly reduced speed when it became apparent that they could do little until the carrier group caught up. Even then, for all the speculation in the British press about a possible two-week passage to the Falklands, there was never the remotest chance that the ships could steam south without their accompanying tankers, which cruised at 15 knots.

Flag Officer First Flotilla, or FOFI as Admiral Woodward was customarily referred to, sailed for the South Atlantic with a reputation as an exceptionally dynamic and brilliant officer. He radiated energy and aggression, threw out ideas in a manner that those who knew him well had come to admire deeply over the years: 'an absolutely super chap,' said one of his frigate captains decisively. In command of a submarine and later of a Type 42 destroyer, he worked very hard for the interests of his men, but he was too abrasive to win affection easily, and seemed to have few close friends. One of his captains, who admired him, said that Woodward suffered from a deep-seated shyness, which he masked in tough talking and sharp signalling. 'Sandy has an undisciplined intellect' he added. The son of a Cornish bank clerk, unlike most of his officers Woodward came from a family with no naval tradition. A mathematician and chess player, he had risen through the ranks by sheer brains, speed of intellect, force of personality. If indeed he suffered from self-doubt, no outsider was likely to sense it. The task force was under the control of an uncommonly clever naval officer full of confidence about what he and his ships were about to do. Most of the criticism of the admiral and his actions in the weeks that followed came from those who considered that this confidence was overdone.

On Sunday, 11 April, Woodward entertained his captains aboard *Glamorgan*. At a meeting before lunch, he invited the officers to put forward their own ideas about what was likely to happen, and how they would confront the Argentine threat if they were obliged to fight. Many men shared the view of the captain of *Glasgow*, Paul Hoddinott: eager to show what their ships could do, but believing that, after some sort of armed demonstration, perhaps a skirmish with the Argentine navy, the enemy would make terms. David Hart-Dyke of *Coventry* argued that the air threat was extremely serious, but he did not think the enemy fleet would dare to come out of port. Other officers could not see how the Argentine navy could politically afford to refuse battle, having stimulated their own people to a frenzy of excitement about the seizure of the Falklands. The admiral himself seemed to regard surface action against elements of the Argentine navy as most likely, with a serious threat from the enemy's two modern German 209 submarines, and the possible further risk of attack from the air. Most officers of all ranks admitted later that, at this stage, they gravely underrated the power of the Argentine air force. 'We were not as worried as we should have been,' said a captain whose ship was severely damaged by bombing. 'We underestimated their will to press home their attacks.' While Woodward was very conscious of the sheer weight and size of the enemy air force, his assessment in April was not assisted by intelligence reports from London that the enemy possessed only one Super Etendard aircraft capable of launching AM39 Exocet missiles, and only five of the weapons themselves.

The surface threat seemed very real indeed. 'When you are fighting your own weapons system, it is difficult to feel superior,' as one officer put it. The Argentinians possessed at least six destroyers and frigates fitted with Exocet ship-to-ship missiles. Before the carrier group sailed from Portsmouth, its captains had met on board *Invincible* for a conference with the director of the Naval Tactical School at Fort Southwick. They discussed the Argentine capabilities in some detail. 'Exocet v. Exocet,' said Jeremy Black of *Invincible* thoughtfully. 'Hmm. That's not nice.' The British submarines would be doing everything in their power to mark the key units of the enemy's fleet, but the British believed that a determined Argentine attempt to break out could succeed. Woodward was not happy about the shape of the 200-mile maritime exclusion zone around the Falklands Islands, already announced in London, and due to come into effect on the following day, 12 April. The politicians and chiefs of staff had drawn a simple circle. Woodward would have preferred a much wider zone east of the islands, to give himself plenty of searoom and to preclude one British nightmare – that of the enemy carrier lying in safety on the 200-mile limit, whence it could launch air attacks against the fleet within comfortable range.

No ship in the British task force – with the exception of the two Type 22 frigates, equipped with close-range Sea Wolf missiles – possessed an active counter to Exocet. Most ships depended solely upon firing 'chaff', which laid a curtain of radar-decoying tinsel across the sky, and flying helicopters trailing radar decoys whenever there was sufficient threat warning to do so. From the outset, Woodward's hopes of avoiding missiles were based on destroying their launching ships or aircraft before they fired, or keeping his carriers out of range. If the Argentine navy broke out, Woodward proposed to withdraw his carriers eastward at high speed, confident that the enemy must outrun their tanker support if they were compelled to steam far. Meanwhile, two British 'attack groups' would seek to engage and destroy the Argentine ships. One would be composed of the three Type 42 destroyers, and the second of *Glamorgan* with two Type 21 frigates.

The principal burden of air defence would fall upon the Sea Harriers. At this stage, the aircraft was still entirely untested. To many naval officers, it seemed little better than a toy by comparison with the Phantom and the Mirage, just as *Invincible* seemed a shadow of the lost glory of *Ark Royal* and the big fleet carriers. Above all, there were pitifully few Harriers. Only thirty-two Sea Harrier airframes existed in the world. When they were gone, there would be no replacements. Beyond the air group, the next layer of fleet air defence – the 'inner skin of the onion' as the navy puts it – would be formed by the Type 42 destroyers, with their much-vaunted Sea Dart missiles. During Exercise Spring Train, *Sheffield*'s Sea Dart had destroyed a target moving at 1,500 m.p.h. at 51,000 feet. The system was a source of great pride to the navy, though it was well known to be less than totally reliable. And, since the Argentine navy also possessed Sea Dart, it seemed likely that their pilots would be aware of its one, overwhelming weakness: designed to meet high-flying Russian aircraft and missiles, it could not engage targets at low level. If Argentine aircraft came in low, the ships' defence would rest solely upon the Sea Wolf missiles fitted to only two vessels and, after that, guns. Woodward's ships were equipped with only a handful of 40-mm Bofors and 20-mm Oerlikon anti-aircraft guns, regarded by ship designers as mere historical leftovers, hand-pumps on the village green.

Above all, Woodward's fleet possessed no airborne early-warning system. In this respect, his ships would go into action less effectively protected than any squadron of the Royal Navy since 1954, when AEW was first introduced. The 965 surveillance radar fitted to most ships in the task force was a generation out of date and notorious for its declining effectiveness in a heavy sea state. There were likely to be many heavy sea states in the South Atlantic in May. One captain said that, until long after the fleet passed Ascension Island, he continued to believe that the British government must have arranged some highly secret access to AEW, either by using aircraft with Chilean markings or with the assistance of the Americans. He was simply unable to accept that the task force was sailing to war against a substantial air threat with no AEW capability whatever.

The deployment and capabilities of the naval battle group were riddled with paradoxes which neither Northwood nor Whitehall had attempted to resolve. The most senior officers of the British army and RAF were at pains to emphasise after the war had ended that they had supported the sailing of the task force initially as a deterrent, demonstrative move. They had been satisfied by the Royal Navy's assurance that its ships could 'look after themselves' in the South Atlantic. But in the critical first days of April, there had been no hardheaded calculations about the difficulties of fighting a major war in the South Atlantic, far less of conducting an amphibious landing. It was only now, day by day, while the fleet sailed south, that hard thinking began in London about the strategic options ahead. Many politicians still trusted that a mere demonstration in the South Atlantic, or at worst the enforcement of a blockade, would bring the Argentinians to reason. Although some senior naval officers still believed that the confrontation would never come to war, they were also privately convinced that a blockade alone would never force the Argentinians to withdraw if negotiations had not done so. Admiral Woodward and most of his captains saw an obvious escalation of options at the disposal of the British government: first, the mere advance into the South Atlantic; then the establishment of a blockade; the recapture of

South Georgia; and thereafter an increasingly delicate stepladder of attacks on Argentine ships and aircraft until total war broke out. If it became necessary to go all the way, to mount a British amphibious landing, senior naval officers in London privately envisaged Woodward's battle group destroying 30 per cent of the enemy's air capability before 3 Commando Brigade was sent in.

Yet to do this, to fight a war in the South Atlantic against an enemy with the known capabilities of the Argentinians, Woodward's force was extraordinarily underarmed. The lack of weapons and especially guns on modern British ships had been a matter of controversy for years. Some experts believed that the hull designs created by the navy's ship department at Bath emphasised speed at the expense of ability to carry armament. In an age when the importance of man management loomed large in British society, British warships were built to very high standards of comfort. It was because of this that a force such as the South Atlantic battle group could put to sea and stay there for months. But the cost of increased comfort was reduced armament. The huge radar arrays fitted to the masts of modern ships created a chronic problem of excessive topweight, which had never been satisfactorily resolved.

To send Admiral Woodward into the South Atlantic, with the specific task of challenging the enemy's air and surface forces, was a vastly risky enterprise, much more so than most British politicians or the British public began to understand. Some naval officers and many defence specialists and planners were deeply alarmed. Throughout its history, the Royal Navy's record of seamanship was unequalled. Yet again and again its uncertain mastery of technology had exposed it to disaster. Admiral Beatty at Jutland, Admiral Holland with *Hood* and *Prince of Wales*, Admiral Phillips with Force Z, had all put to sea radiating the confidence and courage inherited in full measure by Admiral Woodward and his generation, only to suffer appallingly for the shortcomings of their technology against that of the enemy.

Nor were these fears restricted to soldiers and civilians ashore. Before Woodward's fleet sailed south of Ascension, one

experienced captain felt moved to write to a friend in England
with access to the Prime Minister and urge that he should convey
to her the reality of the risks the fleet faced: 'I was really quite
concerned that her decision to send us was the wrong one. I
reckoned that this was a highly risky war. I thought it was essential
to be sure that the politicians understood what they were getting
themselves into. Watching the signal traffic from UK during those
weeks, it seemed to some of us that the politicians' belligerence
was persistently outpacing naval and military thinking about what
we could do.'

*

On 12 April, the submarine *Spartan* arrived off the Falklands to
enforce the British maritime exclusion zone. At Ascension Island,
Woodward's ships were loading spares and equipment from the
vast stocks being flown to the airfield by the Royal Air Force. For
the next three months, Ascension's lonely pinnacle of lava, inhabited by a few hundred mostly American communications specialists, was to be the hub of the greatest British logistics operation
since 1945. Of all the factors disturbing British commanders
throughout the war, it was the awesome distance between the
theatre of operations and the home base that remained the most
potent. Any form of disaster – damaged ships, stranded men, lost
aircraft – would take place more than 3,000 miles from any secure
source of support.

The first group of ships to move into the South Atlantic was
quickly on its way. As early as 6 April, planning had begun for the
retaking of South Georgia. At Ascension, *Plymouth*, *Antrim* and the
tanker *Tidespring* embarked Major Guy Sheridan and M Company
of 42 Commando, Major Cedric Delves and D Squadron of the SAS,
together with a party from the Special Boat Squadron. They sailed
immediately southwards, to rendezvous with *Endurance*.

Woodward's other ships embarked upon brief but intensive
exercises, above all in launching the 'attack groups' against
approaching surface threats. Without the carriers, they had no

means of practising air defence. There would now be no time for most ships to do so, for in London the war cabinet had become anxious urgently to establish a British force as deep as possible in the South Atlantic pending the progress of diplomacy. Woodward was ordered to send the bulk of his force – the three Type 42 destroyers and the frigates *Brilliant* and *Arrow* – to a holding position equidistant some 1,000 miles from Buenos Aires, South Georgia and Port Stanley. Under the command of the doughty Captain John Coward in *Brilliant*, they were to sail immediately in radar and radio silence.

Before they did so, Woodward personally visited each ship by helicopter. He addressed the officers and senior ratings in each wardroom, the junior ratings in the messhalls. He spoke frankly about the prospect of war. But, in his anxiety to instil confidence in the men, he appears to have underplayed his assessment of the enemy's capabilities in a manner that closely mirrored his controversial newspaper interview on *Hermes* almost two weeks later: 'Our chaps could read their *Jane's Fighting Ships* as well as he could,' an officer said later, 'and they didn't like being treated as idiots.' Another said, 'He was trying to be human, and not succeeding.' Lieutenant Tinker wrote bitterly to his brother some weeks later, after the first air attacks had exposed the critical deficiences of the task force: '. . . The Navy felt that we were British and they were wogs, and that would make all the difference. The Admiral said as much to us on the task force TV . . .' Few men in the task force would have put the issue so bluntly, but many harboured their private misgivings.

The *Brilliant* group went on its way, to reach its holding position on 15 April. *Glamorgan*, meanwhile, turned north, to rendezvous with the approaching carriers on 14 April. There was then a pause at the Ascension Island anchorage, during which large quantities of stores and G Squadron of the SAS were embarked. A series of important meetings also took place. On 16 April, Woodward landed on *Fearless* as it approached the island, to meet Clapp, Thompson and the staff of 3 Commando Brigade.

The marines' passage south had not been happy. For more than a week, they had worked day and night assessing the options for an amphibious landing. They received little information of value from Northwood or the Ministry of Defence about Argentine deployments on the islands, but a great deal of disconcerting news about the size of the enemy garrison. This was now believed to number at least 8,000 men. For 3 Commando Brigade, even reinforced by 2nd Battalion the Parachute Regiment, now earmarked to join them, the notion of attempting to retake the Falklands when outnumbered by more than two to one seemed increasingly hazardous, even foolhardy. Nor had they been finding it easy to conduct joint planning with the Royal Navy. Thoughtful naval officers concede that staffwork has never been one of their service's greatest strengths. The autocratic command structure that is necessary in a warship at sea militates against the military approach, which is for a commander to offer his staff great flexibility in presenting a range of alternatives for achieving an objective. A naval staff is more accustomed to being arbitrarily informed by its commander, 'This is what I want to do. Arrange to do it.'

Commodore Clapp, in charge of the landing-force ships, had a peacetime staff only four strong. This had been hastily increased before *Fearless* sailed, but inevitably the officers appointed were those who happened to be available at short notice. They had never had the chance to work as a team. The marine staff set about preparing their landing plans almost completely independent of Clapp's staff. When they finally produced their assessment, Clapp and Captain Larken of *Fearless* were obliged to recast the plan drastically, to give some impression that the naval problems had also been considered. Larken, a tall, bony submariner of exceptionally catholic tastes and artistic interests, was to play an important role in keeping 'combined operations' combined. His personal charm and great skill in sympathising with other men's points of view contributed enormously to the eventual success of the amphibious operation.

The fruit of their joint labours on the passage to Ascension was a forty-six-page appreciation with eleven annexes, outlining the amphibious options for a landing in the South Atlantic. Thompson's strongly preferred course was to take his entire brigade to South Georgia, partly to guarantee the seizure of the task force's first objective, but, more importantly, because the island could provide a rehearsal for his brigade and a base from which to conduct further operations against East or West Falkland. Thompson did not conceal his reluctance to risk his force in an immediate assault on the Falklands: 'We were a one-shot operation, you see. It couldn't be like Dieppe, where if we tried and it didn't work, we could make sure we did better next time. We had to get it right in one go.'

At the meeting on the 16th, Woodward heard out the amphibious planners' exposition without obvious enthusiasm. Then he suggested that the staff consider, first, establishing a bridgehead on West Falkland which they could defend while an airstrip was built to receive Hercules transports and Phantom fighters; or second, a landing on the flat plain of Lafonia in the south of East Falkland. He flew back from *Fearless* believing that it had been a good meeting, at which some useful ideas had been exchanged. On the command ship, however, he left behind an enraged commando brigade staff. 'He made us feel like a bunch of small boys under the scrutiny of the headmaster,' one of them said. He introduced himself to Ewen Southby-Tailyour with the words, 'And what do you know about the Falklands, boy?' He brushed aside Viv Rowe, the intelligence officer, when he began a briefing on the air threat with a dismissive, 'I don't think we need bother about all that.' In justice to the admiral, he had been receiving the same information as 3 Commando Brigade about the enemy's air force. His proposal for the creation of an airstrip reflected his urgent anxiety to remove the dependence of the task force on his carriers. It was Woodward's style to throw out ideas in order to stimulate debate. This is what he believed he had done on this occasion. But, while his manner might not trouble close colleagues and friends, it exasperated a group of Royal Marines already much concerned about what they might be called upon to do.

Brigadier Thompson's 'R' Group worked all night to prepare new appreciations in accordance with the admiral's demands. The following morning, 17 April, they flew to *Hermes* to attend a meeting chaired by Sir John Fieldhouse, who had flown out from Northwood with Major General Moore for a final discussion with Woodward and Thompson before they departed southwards. Almost a hundred naval and land-force officers crowded into the briefing room to hear him. Fieldhouse began with an impressive declaration of purpose: the government, he said, was utterly committed to the recapture of the Falklands by whatever means necessary – 'without limitation'. If diplomacy failed, the task force could depend on absolute political support for its operations. He then talked briefly about the next stage. The battle group would proceed south to enforce the blockade; begin the sea and air battle; and launch the reconnaissance operations essential before a landing. Then the meeting broke up into independent naval and military cells, each discussing its specialist problems. There was one disappointment for the marines: it was finally made clear that they would not have use of *Hermes* even as a crossdecking platform before a final landing. But the C-in-C listened sympathetically to Thompson's request for time to train and rehearse for this purpose – giving him the impression that he was willing to consider sending the entire brigade to South Georgia. Fieldhouse departed for the airfield leaving behind a vastly reassured brigade staff. They had begun to grasp that it would be Fieldhouse, at Northwood, who would take the vital strategic decisions about when and where the landing force went ashore, rather than Woodward on *Hermes*. Woodward would be responsible for the conduct of naval operations. He would not have the authority to compel 3 Commando Brigade to go to Lafonia, where they feared that a landing would be devastated by air attack. But the C-in-C had not entirely opened his mind to the task force officers. From beginning to end of the conflict Fieldhouse was convinced that it was essential to move with all possible speed upon the vital objectives, above all Port Stanley. South Georgia was politically significant, but strategically irrelevant. It was essential to ensure its removal as a threat before the main landing on the Falklands, but – unless the Argentinians had dramatically reinforced their garrison on the island – the marine and SAS detachment already earmarked should be capable of doing the job. After the war, Thompson agreed that Fieldhouse's view had been entirely vindicated. Yet it was rapidly becoming apparent that more troops would be needed for a battle on East Falkland. Thompson's force should be able to make a landing and secure an initial beach-head. But thereafter they would have to be reinforced. The dispatch of 5 Brigade was already being considered. And, if the operation were to expand to divisional strength, Major General Jeremy Moore would become its commander.

The amphibious staffs now settled down in the Ascension anchorage for a long period of debate and preparation, awaiting the arrival of *Canberra* and all their men and equipment. For logistical reasons alone, it was agreed that the earliest possible date for a British landing was 14/15 May. To their great relief, as a consequence of the 17 April meeting at Ascension, Clapp and Thompson's remit was modified from taking responsibility 'for the repossession of the Falklands' to planning 'for a landing with a view to repossessing the Falklands', an incomparably more manageable concept. Rather than burden themselves with the enormous problems of considering how the overall campaign against the Argentinians could be won, the British could now concentrate on their initial, strictly limited, objective: to land and secure a beach-head on the islands. They would worry about what then followed when the time came, although the issue of responsibility for planning further offensive operations would later become one of the most vexed of the campaign.

On 18 April Woodward and his battle group left the marines at Ascension and sailed to confront the Argentine navy. If diplomacy failed in the weeks to come, the entire weight of British hopes rested upon a graduated escalation of the campaign at sea by the

Royal Navy. The admiral's staff at this stage appeared to be addressing themselves overwhelmingly to this process, rather than to the
possible future landing. Much of the friction between officers of
the battle group and those of the amphibious force stemmed from
the ill-concealed conviction of the former that, once the landing
force was put ashore, the chief problems of the campaign would
be over. For those soldiers responsible for planning a campaign in
the appalling climate and terrain ashore in the Falklands, this was
an exasperating attitude. Yet, in an important sense, the navy was
right. The hazards that the landing force would face were possible
to anticipate and measure. Whatever the virtues of the Argentine
army, it was reasonable to assume that, on the battlefield, the
exceptional quality and training of the British army, whose finest
units were on their way to the South Atlantic, would sooner or
later prove decisive. There was a great deal more room for doubt
about the outcome of the war at sea. 'I hope that people realise,'
said Fieldhouse at Ascension, 'that this is the most difficult thing
we have attempted since the Second World War.' At this stage,
however, even the Royal Navy was far more optimistic about
achieving its objectives than its officers would become a month
later – and few of their private fears and reservations about the
difficulties they would face in the South Atlantic reached the eyes
and ears of politicians or civil servants.

*

In the first fortnight following the dispatch of the task force, when
the service chiefs' overwhelming preoccupation was logistics, the
war cabinet could safely be left to address itself to diplomacy. But,
by late April, the time had come to present the politicians with
some of the more complex implications of the course upon which
they had embarked. Sir Terence Lewin had immense admiration
for the Prime Minister, but was conscious that some of her colleagues were totally unfamiliar with naval and military affairs, and
would need to have decisions presented to them in the simplest
possible terms.

The first politico-military dilemma concerned rules of engagement. The Royal Navy has always issued sets of instructions to its captains about the circumstances in which they may fire on an enemy. In peacetime these are naturally based upon the principle of self-defence. But as the task force sailed south, half at peace yet half at war, what rules were to govern its behaviour towards Argentine ships and aircraft? When enemy Boeing 707s began to shadow the task force, Admiral Woodward requested that his ships be permitted to shoot them down. Lewin approached the war cabinet. The politicians, prompted by the Foreign Office, were at first appalled. Great efforts were still being made to achieve a diplomatic settlement. Apart from the risk of misidentification, so blatantly warlike an act would severely damage Britain's cause; the Boeing represented no direct threat to the fleet. Lewin patiently explained to the cabinet that the aircraft could vector Argentine submarines, of which the navy were extremely wary, onto the track of the task force. Permission was only granted to shoot at them shortly before the ships entered the maritime exclusion zone; one unsuccessful attempt was made to hit a Boeing with Sea Dart.

A more complex problem concerned the movements of submarines. The 200-mile maritime exclusion zone had been drawn up to provide the British SSNs with an area small enough to be patrolled effectively, while large enough to provide plenty of searoom. On the day that *Spartan* arrived off Port Stanley, she sighted the Argentine landing ship *Carlo San Antonio* laying mines off the harbour. The news was immediately relayed to Northwood. Was she to be attacked? The war cabinet decided that the enemy was not a warship, and was already inside the MEZ rather than attempting to breach it. In addition, there was a reluctance at this early stage to reveal the submarine's presence. Bigger fish were being anticipated. In reality, these technicalities merely masked the government's deep unwillingness to sink an Argentine ship so early in the war. It was only under pressure that the government agreed ten days later to allow submarines to patrol outside the

MEZ, towards the Argentine coast. Once the initial hesitations of
the politicians had been overcome, however, it was remarkable
what freedom they granted to the task force in opening fire. Sir
Terence Lewin's drafting of rules of engagement, aided by a semi-
permanent committee of officials in Cabinet Office, eventually
gave his captains the widest possible latitude; this, combined with
his skill at getting these agreed by the war cabinet, won him the
greatest admiration at Northwood and among the task force.

Yet another debate concerned the feasibility of a naval blockade
of the islands as an alternative – or sustained preliminary – to a
landing. Blockade appealed to a number of politicians, including
John Nott, who were deeply concerned by the risks of an opposed
landing followed by a land war in a hostile climate. Blockade
obviated the need, at least for a while, of dispatching the landing
force south from Ascension, with the corresponding political
momentum to war that would entail. And even a land victory
would commit Britain to the huge costs of a garrison when the
fighting was ended. Indeed, the Ministry of Defence was as eager
as the Foreign Office to see a negotiated settlement of the Falklands
issue. But Lewin and his fellow service chiefs were unequivocal.
The danger of attrition by weather and enemy action put a sustained blockade out of the question.

The first great strategic debate to face the war cabinet concerned operations against South Georgia. The island was 800 miles
beyond the primary objective – 800 miles of hostile sea and danger
from submarines. It was largely irrelevant to the recapture of the
Falklands, and would probably be surrendered automatically once
the major Argentine positions had been taken. It seemed a major
diversion of effort to dispatch Thompson's entire brigade to South
Georgia, whatever the attractions for the marines of a rehearsal
for greater things to come. Conversely, the use of only the small
force embarked aboard *Antrim* and *Plymouth* seemed too risky. It
would be a devastating beginning to British operations in the
South Atlantic to suffer any kind of failure against such an object-

ive. Virtually the entire navy staff, including Leach and Fieldhouse, advised against it.

The decision to press ahead against South Georgia, like so many others of the campaign, was primarily political. The British public was becoming restless for action, more than two weeks after the task force had sailed. Buenos Aires remained intransigent. Questions were even being asked in Washington about Britain's real will for a showdown. The former head of the CIA, Admiral Stansfield Turner, suggested on television that Britain could face a defeat. British diplomacy needed the bite of military action to sharpen its credibility. To the politicians in the war cabinet, South Georgia seemed to offer the promise of substantial rewards for modest stakes. The *Antrim* group was ordered to proceed to its recapture.

*

The detached squadron led by Captain Brian Young in *Antrim* rendezvoused with *Endurance* 1,000 miles north of South Georgia on 14 April. The British believed that the Argentinians had placed only a small garrison on the bleak, glacier-encrusted island. The submarine *Conqueror*, which left Faslane on 4 April, had sailed direct to the island to carry out reconnaissance for the *Antrim* group. She slipped cautiously inshore, conscious that an iceberg 35 by 15 miles wide and 500 feet high had been reported in the area. Her captain reported no evidence of an Argentine naval presence. The submarine then moved away north-westwards to patrol in a position from which she could intervene either in the maritime exclusion zone, or in support of the South Georgia operation, or against the Argentine carrier, if she emerged. A fifteen-hour sortie by an RAF Victor aircraft confirmed *Conqueror*'s report that the approach to South Georgia was clear.

On 21 April, Young's ships saw their first icebergs, and reduced speed for their approach to the island, in very bad weather. The captain summoned the marine and SAS officers to his bridge to see for themselves the ghastly sea conditions. The ship's Wessex helicopters nonetheless took off into a snowstorm carrying the Mountain Troop of D Squadron, SAS, under the command of twenty-nine-year-old Captain John Hamilton. *Antrim* had already flown aboard a scientist from the British Antarctic Survey team which successfully remained out of reach of the Argentinians through the three weeks of their occupation of South Georgia. This man strongly urged against the proposed SAS landing site, high on the Fortuna Glacier, where the weather defied human reason. Lieutenant Bob Veal, a naval officer with great experience of the terrain, took the same view. But another expert in England very familiar with South Georgia, Colonel John Peacock, believed that the Fortuna was passable, and his advice was transmitted to *Antrim*. The SAS admits no limits to what determined men can achieve. After one failed attempt in which the snow forced the helicopters back to the ships, Hamilton and his men were set down with their huge loads of equipment to reconnoitre the island for the main assault landing by the Royal Marines. One SAS patrol was to operate around Stromness and Husvik; one was to proceed overland towards Leith; the third was to examine a possible beach-landing site in Fortuna Bay.

From the moment that they descended into the howling gale and snowclad misery of the glacier, the SAS found themselves confounded by the elements. 'Spindrift blocked the feed trays of the machine guns,' wrote an NCO in his report. 'On the first afternoon, three corporals probing crevasses advanced 500 metres in four to five hours . . .' Their efforts to drag their sledges laden with 200 pounds of equipment apiece were frustrated by whiteouts that made all movement impossible. 'Luckily we were now close to an outcrop in the glacier, and were able to get into a crevasse out of the main blast of the wind . . .' They began to erect their tents. One was instantly torn from their hands by the wind, and swept away into the snow. The poles of the others snapped within seconds, but the men struggled beneath the fabric and kept it upright by flattening themselves against the walls. Every forty-five minutes, they took turns to crawl out and dig the snow away from the entrance, to avoid becoming totally buried. They were now facing katabatic winds of more than 100 m.p.h. By 11 a.m. the next morning, the 22nd, their physical condition was deteriorating rapidly. The SAS were obliged to report that their position was untenable, and ask to be withdrawn.

The first Wessex V to make an approach was suddenly hit by a whiteout. Its pilot lost all his horizons, fell out of the sky, attempted to pull up just short of the ground and smashed his tail rotor in the snow. The helicopter rolled over and lay wrecked. A second Wessex V came in. With great difficulty, the crew of the crashed aircraft and all the SAS were embarked, at the cost of abandoning their equipment. Within seconds of takeoff, another whiteout struck the Wessex. This too crashed on to the glacier.

It was now about 3 p.m. in London. Francis Pym was boarding Concorde to fly to Washington with a new British response to Haig's peace proposals. Lewin, anxiously awaiting news of the services' first major operation of the Falklands campaign, received a signal from *Antrim*. The reconnaissance party ashore was in serious difficulty. Two helicopters sent to rescue them had crashed, with unknown casualties. For the Chief of Defence Staff, it was one of the bleakest moments of the war. After all his efforts to imbue the war cabinet with full confidence in the judgement of the service chiefs, he was now compelled to cross Whitehall and report on the situation to the Prime Minister. It was an unhappy afternoon in Downing Street.

But an hour later, Lewin received news of a miracle. In a brilliant feat of flying for which he later received a DSO, Lieutenant Commander Ian Stanley had brought another helicopter, a Wessex III, down on the Fortuna Glacier. He found that every man from the crashed helicopters had survived. Grossly overloaded with seventeen bodies, he piloted the Wessex back to *Antrim* and threw it on to the pitching deck. His exhausted and desperately cold passengers were taken below to the wardroom and the emergency medical room.

A disaster had been averted by the narrowest of margins. Yet the reconnaissance mission was no further forward. Soon after midnight the following night, 23 April, they started again. 2 Section SBS landed successfully by helicopter at the north end of Sorling Valley. Meanwhile, fifteen men of D Squadron's Boat Troop set out in five Gemini inflatable craft for Grass Island, within sight of the Argentine bases. For years, the SAS had been vainly demanding more reliable replacements for the 40 h.p. outboards with which the Geminis were powered. Now, one craft suffered almost immediate engine failure and whirled away with the gale into the night, with three men helpless aboard. A second suffered the same fate. Its crew drifted in the South Atlantic throughout the hours of darkness before its beacon signal was picked up the next morning by a Wessex. The crew was recovered. The remaining three boats, roped together, reached their landfall on Grass Island but, by early afternoon, they were compelled to report that ice splinters dashed into their craft by the tearing gale were puncturing the inflation cells. The SBS party in Sorling Valley was unable to move across the terrain, and had to be recovered by helicopter and reinserted in Moraine Fjord the following day. All these operations provided circumstantial evidence that the Argentine garrison ashore was small. But they were an inauspicious beginning to a war, redeemed only by the incredible good fortune that the British had survived a chapter of accidents with what at this stage seemed the loss of only one Gemini.

On 24 April, the squadron received more bad news: an enemy submarine was believed to be in the area. The British already knew that Argentine C-130 transport aircraft had been overflying the island, and had to assume that the British presence was now revealed. Captain Young dispersed his ships, withdrawing the RFA tanker *Tidespring* carrying M Company of 42 Commando some 200 miles northwards. It seemed likely to be some days before proper reconnaissance could be completed, and any sort of major assault mounted. Above all, nothing significant could be done until more helicopters arrived. That night, the Type 22 frigate *Brilliant* joined

up with *Antrim* after steaming all out through mountainous seas
from her holding position with the Type 42s. She brought with her
two Lynx helicopters. Captain Young and his force once again
moved inshore, to land further SAS and SBS parties. British luck
now took a dramatic turn for the better.

Early on the morning of 25 April, *Antrim*'s Wessex III picked up
an unidentified radar contact close to the main Argentine base at
Grytviken. *Endurance* and *Plymouth* at once launched their Wasps.
The three helicopters sighted the Argentine Guppy class submarine
Santa Fe heading out of Cumberland Bay, and attacked with depth
charges and torpedoes. *Plymouth*'s Wasp fired an AS 12 missile,
which passed through the submarine's conning tower, while *Brilliant*'s Lynx closed in firing GP machine-guns. It may seem astonishing that, after so much expensive British hardware had been
unleashed, the *Santa Fe* remained afloat at all. It was severely
damaged, and turned back at once towards Grytviken, where it
had been landing reinforcements for the garrison, now totalling
140 men. There, the submarine beached herself alongside the
British Antarctic Survey base. Her crew scuttled hastily ashore in
search of safety.

There was now a rapid conference aboard *Antrim*, and urgent
consultation with London. The main body of Royal Marines was
still 200 miles away. But it was obvious that the enemy ashore had
been thrown into disarray. Captain Young, Major Sheridan of the
marines and Major Cedric Delves, commanding D Squadron, determined to press home their advantage. A composite company
was formed from every available man aboard *Antrim* – marines,
SAS, SBS – seventy-five in all. In the cramped mess-decks of the
destroyer, they hastily armed and equipped themselves. Early in
the afternoon, directed by a naval gunfire support officer in a
Wasp, the ships laid down a devastating bombardment around
the reported Argentine positions. At 2.45, under Major Sheridan's
overall command, the first British elements landed by helicopter
and began closing in on Grytviken. There was a moment of farce
when they saw in their path a group of balaclava-clad heads on the

skyline, engaged them with machine-gun fire and Milan missiles, and found themselves overrunning a group of elephant seals. Then they were above the settlement, where white sheets were already fluttering from several windows.

As the SAS led the way towards the buildings, a bewildered Argentine officer complained, 'You have just walked through my minefield!' SAS Sergeant Major Lofty Gallagher ran up the Union Jack that he had brought with him. At 5.15 local time, the Argentine garrison commander, Captain Alfredo Astiz, formally surrendered. He was an embarrassing prisoner of war, as he was wanted for questioning by several nations in connection with the disappearance of their citizens while in government custody on the Argentine mainland some years earlier. Britain was eventually to return him to Buenos Aires, uninterrogated. Somewhat reluctantly, the fastidious Royal Navy began to embark a long column of filthy, malodorous and dejected prisoners aboard the ships. The following morning, after threatening defiance by radio overnight, the small enemy garrison at Leith, along the coast, surrendered without resistance. The scrap merchants whose activities had precipitated the entire drama were also taken into custody, for repatriation to the mainland.

The British triumph became complete when a helicopter picked up a weak emergency-beacon signal from the extremity of Stromness Bay. A helicopter was sent, managed to home on it, and recovered the lost three-man SAS patrol whose Gemini had been swept away in the early hours of 23 April. They had paddled ashore with only a few hundred yards of land left between them and the Atlantic. Thus, with a last small miracle, the British completed the recapture of South Georgia, the first operation of the Falklands campaign, without a single man lost. One Argentine sailor had been badly wounded and one was killed the following day in an accident.

The news of the operation was immediately relayed back to London. A sense of relief turned to euphoria. Two days earlier, Mrs Thatcher had personally visited Northwood to be briefed by Fieldhouse and his staff and to endure with them the agonised suspense of the SAS and SBS debacles. Her constant supportive remarks to the fleet staff made a deep impression. The simplicity of her objectives and her total determination to see them achieved came as a welcome change to men used to regarding politicians as hedgers and doubters.

Sunday's news was greeted by the public as a triumph long expected and not a little overdue. The British people had, after all, been led to believe that the task force was irresistible. As a result, when Mrs Thatcher joined John Nott on the steps of Downing Street and called to waiting pressmen, 'Rejoice, just rejoice!' it seemed a curiously hard and inappropriate heralding of the onset of war. Yet it was the reaction of a woman overwhelmed with relief. The first stage of her gamble had only narrowly been rescued from catastrophe.

The euphoria was not confined to London. On 26 April, aboard his flagship *Hermes*, Admiral Woodward gave a rare interview to a task-force correspondent, in which he declared robustly, 'South Georgia was the appetiser. Now this is the heavy punch coming up behind. My battle group is properly formed and ready to strike. This is the run-up to the big match which, in my view, should be a walkover.' The British were told, he said, that the Argentinians in South Georgia were 'a tough lot. But they were quick to throw in the towel. We will isolate the troops on the Falklands as those on South Georgia were isolated.' Woodward subsequently denied much of the substance of that interview as reported in the British press. But, to many of his officers, it had the authentic flavour of the admiral, anxious to inspire the greatest possible confidence in what his task force could do.

*

Now, at last, the battle group was poised to begin direct operations against the Argentine forces on and in the seas round the Falklands. *Plymouth* and *Brilliant* rejoined Woodward at high speed from South Georgia, bringing with them the SAS and SBS who would be needed for reconnaissance operations on the islands. On 24 April the carriers had made their rendezvous with the Type 42 destroyers. Three days later, the group adopted battle formation. *Broadsword* and *Brilliant*, equipped with Sea Wolf, took up the 'goalkeeping' role of close escorts for *Invincible* and *Hermes* which they would retain for much of the campaign. The Type 42s, the specialist air-defence ships, adopted the advanced radar picket positions, covering the fleet's western flank, closest to the enemy.

Each day, as the fleet steamed south listening intently to the faltering progress of diplomacy on the World Service, crews exercised their drills and equipment to exhaustion, above all damage control. Most of these very young men were sobered by the unsmiling routine of defence stations six hours on and six off, filling in will forms and insurance papers, drawing respirators and identity cards, supporting intensive helicopter flying to screen the task force, preparing missiles, fusing shells. All manner of peacetime restrictions had been swept aside, together with a host of bureaucratic difficulties. Ships could steam at full power. Often in the past their engines had suffered from receiving poor-quality fuel; now, when they rendezvoused every two or three days to RAS – refuel at sea – from their accompanying tankers, they found themselves receiving nothing but the best. Supply ships fell in alongside to transfer Sea Skua missiles that were scarcely out of their test programme to arm the frigates' helicopters. Demands for spares and equipment of all kinds were met with extraordinary speed.

A mass of intelligence and tactical data was passed to the ships by signal and parachute drop. There were appreciations of the enemy's air-force capability: intelligence suggested that they could sustain a strike rate of perhaps four waves of aircraft a day, with six aircraft in each wave. That rate would decline in a predicted graph as maintenance problems escalated over a period of weeks. Woodward, however, had to ponder the likely problems with his own aircraft maintenance. It is customary to plan carrier operations on the basis of five days out of the line for rest and recovery for every five days of intensive flying operations. With only two ships and twenty aircraft, there was no hope of such relief. They would have to continue to operate as hard as they could for as long as they could. But how long would that prove to be? Thirty days seemed the maximum they could reasonably hope for.

Most of the data on Argentine capabilities and likely tactics came from their principal trainers and arms suppliers, the French and Americans. In the first days of the operation, the Chief of Defence Staff submitted personal requests for help and information to his counterparts in both Paris and Washington, and was rewarded with thick books of information from each. Yet, overall, the intelligence picture was still sadly inadequate. There was no substitute for the presence of old-fashioned agents on the ground in Argentina. One of the British directors of the war described the command's yearning 'for some chaps whom one could simply give a bundle of pesos to, and tell them to jump over the wall of the naval dockyard and tell us what was going on behind it'.

Fleet debate came increasingly to be dominated by discussion of the best means of evading an incoming Exocet. The Directorate of Naval Warfare sent the fleet a fat sheaf of material on the subject; there was so much data that some captains found it contradictory. A ship could turn bow or stern on, to present the smallest possible target. But what of the problem of being unable to bring one's own weapons to bear in this position? It was agreed that it was desirable to fire at the missile with all possible armament, in the hope of decoying or destroying it. But when should the chaff be fired, and from which projectors? It was widely accepted that one of the most desirable anti-Exocet measures would have been a fully automatic chaff response system. One senior officer dismissed that notion brusquely with the comment that a computer-activated system would have fired itself at seagulls with great frequency, unaware that each British ship carried only seven complete chaff salvos in its magazine. Identifying a small missile on a radar screen was still an inexact science. There were other breaks with normally prescribed tactics. To meet a Russian

supersonic diving missile, doctrine demanded that a ship should
fire its chaff and then remain within its own decoy pattern. To
meet Exocet, it was thought preferable to leave the decoy pattern
as rapidly as possible.

*

For the navy, the contrast between life at peace and at war was
much less dramatic than for the land force. But the traditional
comforts and courtesies of the ships at sea had vanished. Soft
furnishings, trophies, pictures, mess fittings were stowed or
ditched. The Royal Fleet Auxiliary ships fortified their gun
positions with potato sacks. The battle group began to meet South
Atlantic winter weather. Day after day, ships ploughed and pitched
into the huge seas, water crashing over their fo'c'sles, turrets and
missile launchers; gusts of spray obscuring neighbouring ships in
the tearing winds; rain and mist reducing visibility to a few
hundred yards. Off-duty, men wearied by six hours of bracing
themselves against bulkheads or at control positions to counter
the pitch of the ship sought only to sleep, eat or write letters. On
the 23rd, the first Sea King had been lost in atrocious weather, and
with it the first life. Young commanding officers who had hitherto
known only the exhilaration of running a ship began to feel the
weight of its responsibility: 'One felt the loneliness of command
for the first time,' said one. 'I was desperate for somebody to talk
to, an outsider, another captain from whom one could seek advice
or reassurance. There was no longer time to check up on people to
make sure that things were being done – you had to depend on
each man to do what was expected of him. One quickly lost that
peacetime habit of giving orders by saying to people, "Do you mind
doing so and so?" You just said, "Do it."'

A few men found their entire predicament grotesque. 'At times
the situation seems so absolutely silly,' wrote Lieutenant David
Tinker from *Glamorgan*. 'Here we are in 1982, fighting a colonial
war on the other side of the world; 28,000 men going to fight over
a fairly dreadful piece of land inhabited by 1,800 people . . .' Yet

the overwhelming majority of his comrades were convinced of the justice of their cause. The senior ratings' mess on the frigate *Argonaut* was astonished one night to hear a petty officer chef, not normally an outspoken man, declare solemnly, 'We want to sort this out so that our children can walk about in the world with their heads held high . . .' In the messdecks, teenagers who had been in the navy only a matter of months asked themselves, 'How am I going to take it?' A week or two earlier, most had been scarcely aware of where the Falklands were. There had been no dramatic transition from the prospect of a naval demonstration to the likelihood of war in the South Atlantic, only a hesitant, progressive deterioration of the hopes of diplomatic settlement.

Most ships held services of dedication before they entered the total exclusion zone which came into effect on 1 May. Woodward told his captains that he expected ships to be lost. In London, Sir Terence Lewin, with the experience of a man who had served on Malta convoys on which more than half the ships at sea were lost, warned the government of the prospect of casualties. Yet it was very difficult for most men afloat or ashore, in command or in the messdecks, to reconcile themselves to the real prospect of tragedy. 'I could easily believe that we would see ships damaged,' said a frigate captain. 'But it was very difficult to conjure up the image of them actually being sunk.'

8 » FAILURE OF A MISSION

When you've shouted 'Rule Britannia', when you've sung
   'God Save the Queen',
When you've finished killing Kruger with your mouth . . .

            Kipling, *The Absent-Minded Beggar*

The recapture of South Georgia came as a badly needed shot in the arm to British public opinion. As the crisis had entered its third week, Thatcher had left her nation in no doubt that her policy was emphatic, but growing doubts existed as to what it was emphatic about. The task force was clearly not achieving its initial purpose: to threaten the enemy into withdrawal, or at least into making major concessions at the negotiating table. The premise on which many had supported its dispatch – that it would not be used – was in imminent danger of collapse.

The tabloid press, with the undeniably courageous exception of the *Daily Mirror*, was continuing to run pages of near-hysterical war-mongering. 'Haig Double Faults Again,' the *Daily Mail* cried with evident glee. 'No Surrender' demanded the *Express*. The *Sun* tried the obscenity 'Stick it up Your Junta!' in response to a peace proposal. Fleet Street's yearning for an old-fashioned sea battle was equalled only by its suspicion that the Foreign Office might be conspiring to cheat it of one. 'Let's End the War of Politics,' said the *Daily Star* in frustration. The distance of the impending encounter from Britain and from civilian casualties seemed to induce a reckless aversion to peace. At one point, Downing Street became so alarmed that lobby correspondents were urged to persuade their editors to acknowledge the risks the task force was running.

There is little evidence that this belligerent sentiment truly reflected the public mood. The sending of the task force had certainly been approved by a wide range of public opinion, but at a time when it did not appear to entail a declaration of hostilities against Argentina. While the *Sun* could declare, 'It's War!' the day that the task force sailed, papers such as the *Observer*, the *Financial Times* and the *Sunday Times* appeared to accept its dispatch only insofar as it meant the opposite. According to the *Sunday Times*, a counter-invasion of the islands would be 'a short cut to bloody disaster'. The *Financial Times*, which could not bring itself to back the task force at all, argued for economic pressure only. Of the serious press, only the *Telegraph* and *The Times* were out-and-out enthusiasts for the expedition. The *Guardian* was crisply opposed throughout.

Circumstantial and poll evidence supported this impression of ambivalence. Visitors to service communities, where the true price of war would be paid, found local people unconvinced that the cause was worth the loss of life. 'For the task force, but against a war' summed up the sentiment of canvassers in these areas in the early May local elections. A series of opinion polls by MORI for the *Economist* asked whether regaining the Falklands was worth the loss of British lives. Up to the time when lives were indeed lost and other emotions came into play, a narrow majority replied no. The nation seemed to join with the cabinet in believing Britain was engaged in a great game of bluff. Admiral Anaya could perhaps be excused his illusions.

Pessimism over the fate of the Haig mission made it harder to continue this dodging of the war issue. The first strains were political. Michael Foot's initial goading of the government left him little room for manoeuvre when his belligerence caught up with him. Try as he might to plead for more activity at the UN and more time for negotiation, he remained manacled to the task force throughout the conflict. Foot's shadow cabinet, with Denis Healey and especially Peter Shore arguing for a tough stance, remained more or less united. This was not true of the Labour Party at large: Tarn Dalyell and Andrew Faulds were sacked by Foot from his front-bench team for opposing shadow-cabinet support for the task force. Tony Benn, from the start a cogent opponent of the whole operation, campaigned against Foot's line without reserve, supported by the Labour Party chairman, Dame Judith Hart. The Trades Union Congress also backed off, calling on the government not to engage in military action. The future leader of the new Social Democratic Party, Roy Jenkins, was noticeably silent. Prominent centre-party figures such as Shirley Williams and David Steel were known to be deeply worried at the prospect of war.

Nor were doubts confined to the political left. The thirty-three Labour MPs who voted against their party whip later in May were by no means exclusively on the left of the party. The BBC television programme *Panorama* was able to put together a feature on Tories not in favour of the task force. Their opposition was largely as set out by Lord Wigg in a pithy letter to *The Times*: 'I have no confidence in improvised military adventures in pursuit of undefined objectives.' One straw poll in Whitehall estimated that a majority of top civil servants were opposed to the sending of the task force, including such key departments as the Foreign Office, the Treasury and the Cabinet Office. It was quite wrong for outsiders to deduce from a reading of the tabloid press that Britain was united in a lust for nostalgic naval glory. Nor were the supporters of the task force necessarily advocates of its use to clear the Falkland Islands of Argentinians. Many saw it quite literally as a bluff, a strengthening of the negotiating hand which might ultimately involve substantial concessions to the Argentine side but which would gain more rights for the Falklanders than mere economic sanctions. When the bluff was clearly treated as such by Buenos Aires, such people had to make a painful choice: should the fleet ignominiously turn for home or should it proceed to real war? Most opted for the latter, but in a spirit of hesitant foreboding rather than patriotic joy.

As described in the last chapter, these arguments had already been reflected in war cabinet as gradually it was forced to confront strategic and tactical decisions for which task-force commanders needed approval. Those decisions – on rules of engagement, blockade and South Georgia – at least dealt with what Thatcher regarded as the main matter in hand, the impending battle. Yet war cabinet was also involved in what could seem a contradictory exercise, the search for peace. As April wore on, the dominant feature of this search became precisely the personal contest ministers had most feared: between the Prime Minister and her new Foreign Secretary, Francis Pym. The dragging-out of the Haig mission, to which Pym was strongly committed, became more and more irksome to Thatcher. Whitelaw found himself increasingly cast in the role of her 'interpreter' of the Foreign Office point of view. She became irritated by Pym's habit of adopting a strongly dovish stance in war cabinet, supported by his officials, but then guarding his political flank in Parliament by often sounding extraordinarily hawkish. 'She would respect him more if just sometimes he would communicate his true feelings to the backbenchers,' one minister said later. Thatcher was not above taking her revenge. ODSA always made a collective presentation to full cabinet each Tuesday. Once, the Prime Minister asked Pym to defend to this wider forum a controversial decision to which he had been most adamantly opposed in war cabinet.

Pym's Concorde flight to Washington to see Haig on Thursday, 22 April, was a last attempt at a marriage between Britain's 'immutable' principles and the terms of the previous weekend's Argentine package. British officials described it as a 'delousing operation'. The only concessions Pym was able to take with him were an offer that other flags might fly beside the British during the interim period and an acceptance that sovereignty might be open for discussion after an Argentine withdrawal. This could not be to any fixed deadline and there would be no 'creeping transfer of sovereignty'. There also had to be a recognition of local Falkland opinion in any deal.

Pym commenced an immediate four-hour session with Haig at

the State Department. It achieved little beyond convincing both men that they were still far from a feasible compromise; indeed, at times, both seemed fellow prisoners of British and Argentine intransigence. The following morning, Pym breakfasted with Reagan's national security adviser, William Clark, at the White House to emphasise Britain's urgent need of American support. It was the nearest that he was permitted to come to the President, whose continuing ignorance of the issue was a source of embarrassment to the State Department. At a final meeting at the British embassy, the mediators went over the ground again, seeing what possible flexibility there might be in the British position to make it worth one final offer to Buenos Aires.

Pym returned to London late on the Friday night, his 'shuttle diplomacy' immensely eased by Concorde. He told the following day's war cabinet that he felt they had squeezed all they could from negotiation and ought now to be ready to accept the terms which Haig would be sending next week. The essential feature of those terms would be an American presence on the islands as guarantee that any Argentine participation would not be overwhelming. The interests and wishes of the islanders would be safeguarded and a long interim period laid down. As Foreign Secretary, he felt such a deal would be in Britain's interests, both in avoiding war and to protect good relations with the rest of Latin America. He would recommend its acceptance.

Mrs Thatcher's reaction was hostile. Pym had returned in the midst of the South Georgia operation, then hanging by a thread. He was proposing concession and compromise with the very enemy against whom her boys (as she persisted in calling them) were pitting their courage. What appears especially to have upset her was the impression given by Pym to Haig that 'Britain might accept a settlement along these lines', and that Argentina might be told as much. A yawning gulf separated Prime Minister from Foreign Secretary.

*

Haig's final package – 'Haig Two' – was sent to both London and Buenos Aires on 27 April. It consisted merely of some subtle variants on the familiar themes: a phased joint withdrawal; American–British–Argentine supervision arrangements; Argentine participation in a 'traditional local administration' (a largely contradictory concept); and a longer-term negotiating framework 'taking into account the interests of both sides and the wishes of the inhabitants'. The interim period would be allowed to run up to a full five years. The junta rejected Haig's offer to take the package to Buenos Aires in person. In London the war cabinet briskly replied that it would not react until it had heard the junta's response.

The junta's decision-taking processes were now in ruins. In theory the supreme organ was the cabinet, headed by Galtieri and Costa Mendes, but behind it lay the intransigence of the navy. Admiral Anaya treated Costa Mendes with contempt and regarded Galtieri as a broken reed, hopelessly susceptible to American pressure. He was still smarting from the loss of South Georgia. Having refused to believe Washington's warning of British intentions, Anaya now accused the Americans of trickery and said the warning had been meant to 'confuse and disorientate' the Argentinians to help the British get their fleet into position. In fact, it is likely that the reinforcements landed by the *Santa Fe* at Grytviken had been sent as a result of precisely this American intelligence information passed to Buenos Aires in the vain hope of inducing concessions. Washington's reckless misreading of the Argentine character knew no bounds.

Anaya's lack of confidence in Argentine diplomacy was once more proved well founded. The one body on whom Costa Mendes had assumed he could rely for support was the Organization of American States (OAS). This group surely could not be nobbled by Britain and her friends. It was also backed by the 1947 Inter-American Treaty of Mutual Assistance (the Rio Treaty), under which nations in the Americas agreed to support each other against military threat from outside the continent. Buenos Aires had traditionally stood aloof from the organisation, displaying what other states felt was an ethnic European arrogance towards her mixed-race partners to her north. Now that Argentina needed OAS aid, the question was would they forgive and forget?

The OAS had been slow in responding to Argentina's request for an early meeting over the Falklands. When it gathered on 26 April, Costa Mendes immediately realised he would not get the two-thirds majority needed for joint action against Britain. He therefore opted for a resolution demanding the withdrawal of the task force, backed by his warning that British forces seemed about to land on 'Argentine territory'. He was unexpectedly assisted by an inept last-minute intervention by Haig, who until then had wisely left the OAS to sort out its own rivalries on this issue. Haig now pointedly attacked Argentina for her aggression, said the 1947 treaty had no application to the conflict and, in effect, told the OAS to keep out of a Washington peace effort. He was heard in stony silence. An OAS official said after Haig spoke, 'It was as if he could see the Nobel peace prize already within his grasp.'

Not until Wednesday, 28 April, after Haig Two had gone to Buenos Aires, did the OAS finally vote on a Falklands resolution. To Costa Mendes's dismay, no mention was made of a British withdrawal. A truce was advocated and, to make matters worse, both sides were recommended to honour UN Resolution 502. It was a wholly unexpected coup for Britain. The Argentine foreign minister was now running round Washington 'like a plucked chicken', in the felicitous words of one State Department official. He pleaded for more clarification from Haig on his new proposals (a not unreasonable request, given their vagueness) and for time for consultation. Apparently sharing Anaya's view that Haig had an overpowering interest in forestalling any war, he dedicated himself to playing for time. After yet more covert American pressure on Galtieri, through Schlaudemann in Buenos Aires, the junta finally decided against Haig Two. Costa Mendes was forced to admit that it 'falls short of meeting Argentine demands regarding . . . recognition of sovereignty and the form of a provisional administration'. In other words, no progress had been made on either of the central issues. The Argentine rejection spelled the death of Haig's shuttle.

Haig's failure was total and, for him, humiliating. His mediation had clearly been an attempt to imitate Henry Kissinger's Middle East peace shuttle in early 1974, but the parallel proved inappropriate in a number of respects. Unlike the Middle East, the Falklands conflict had not yet erupted into open hostilities. Domestic intransigence appeared high in both countries and there seemed no true yearning for any settlement which might avert bloodshed. Both were entrenched on matters of principle in which the US had no leverage, nor could Haig offer the inducements which oiled Kissinger's path back and forth between Cairo and Tel Aviv. The Argentinians afterwards described his pressure as crude and offensive to the junta's pride.

Haig was also inexperienced as a negotiator. Neither he nor his team were recognised Argentine experts: the most conversant member was Vernon Walters, who at least spoke Spanish and was said to boast a 'drinking friendship' with a number of senior officers. In addition, the distances involved were too great to maintain the momentum of wheeler-dealing. Nor were the ethnic characters of the two nations conducive to compromise. One of Kissinger's shuttle staff who was on the fringes of the Haig mission pointed out that Kissinger had been able to capitalise on the 'haggling instinct' of two adjacent Semitic peoples. No such tradition existed among Anglo-Saxons or Latins, let alone between them. The British could not see why they should make concessions on 'a matter of principle'. The Argentinians would not shift 'on a matter of pride'.

Haig showed immense personal resilience throughout the ordeal and impressed everyone with his genuine bafflement that two sensible nations could not sort out their differences. Yet frequently his guard dropped. The junta, he said on one occasion, were little more than 'a bunch of thugs'. His staff would long for a proper 'caudillo' system, a strong man in Buenos Aires who could at least deliver a decision. In another moment of despair, Tom Enders turned to Ambassador Schlaudemann and asked, 'What has become of our special relationship with the Argentinians?' Schlaudemann replied laconically, 'What special relationship?' A shared anti-communism – as Enders might have learned in South-East Asia – was not enough. The Americans had been unable either to comprehend the Falklands' place in the British political psyche, or grasp the limitations of military oligarchies in Latin America. It was a brave but sorry sub-plot to the Falklands war.

*

The coincidence of key moments in the Falklands negotiations with specific escalations in military activity has suggested to some that the British war cabinet was deliberately orchestrating either one or the other. There is no evidence for this, and war cabinet members strongly deny it. Indeed, most were appalled at how long-drawn-out both processes were becoming. Woodward's battle group was not finally assembled outside the MEZ until the middle of the fourth week after it had sailed. Nothing delayed the signal it received from Northwood: 'In all respects prepare for war by midnight, April 29th.'

It was not until Friday, the 30th, that a short discussion took place at a meeting of the National Security Council in Washington, after which Reagan accepted the Haig line that no further purpose would be served by refusing support for Britain. In his subsequent statement, Reagan continued to convey incomprehension of the importance of 'that little ice-cold bunch of land down there'. Nonetheless, he now imposed military and economic sanctions on Argentina (military supplies had in fact been denied since Carter's embargo) and offered 'matériel' aid to Britain. In Buenos Aires, Galtieri was shattered and told visitors, 'I feel much bitterness towards Reagan, who I thought was my friend.'

The British press were ecstatic. 'Yanks a Million,' cried the *Sun*. *The Times* responded with a more restrained 'A Friend Indeed'. A sigh of relief went up from Downing Street. The additional aid was more symbolic than real. Already, on Caspar Weinberger's orders, American tankers and transport planes had for some time been arriving secretly at Ascension. Now they could at least be acknowledged. Supplies included Sidewinder and Shrike air-to-air and air-to-surface missiles, back-up planes to release Victor tankers from Nato duties, fuel and ammunition. Perhaps the most critical American contribution was in the field of signals intelligence, radio communication and relay facilities. When the war ended, the British chiefs of staff were full of praise for the readiness with which the American chairman of the Joint Chiefs in Washington, General David Jones, responded to every request from London. On one occasion when Sir Terence Lewin felt compelled to telephone Jones personally to ask for urgent support to provide certain key communications channels for the British, the general simply said as Lewin began to speak, 'I know what you're going to ask for, and it's already done.' Whatever American political haverings took place over the South Atlantic war, US military support was unstinting, and vitally important. American electronic facilities in southern Chile were made available to Britain – and the Chileans themselves maintained close links with London throughout the war, through a continuous shuttle of military attachés between the two capitals. What America did not supply was long-range air early-warning aircraft, the famous AWACs. To have done so would have involved the US directly in the conflict, even though the lack of AWACs was the single most critical British deficiency of the war. America would hold Britain's coat, and even sew on some buttons, but the task force in the South Atlantic must fight its war alone.

9 » A WAR AT SEA

> Nelson's genius enabled him to measure truly the conse-
> quences of any decision. But that genius worked upon
> precise practical data ... He felt he knew what would
> happen in a fleet action. Jellicoe did not know. Nobody
> knew.
>
> Winston Churchill, *The World Crisis*, on Jutland

At 4.23 on the morning of Sunday, 1 May, following Britain's
decision to extend the maritime exclusion zone to a total exclusion zone, a single RAF Vulcan bomber of 101 Squadron, Strike
Command, attacked Port Stanley airfield. The elderly aircraft had

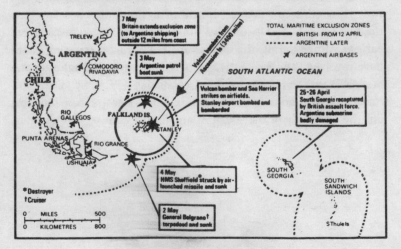

The Total Maritime Exclusion Zones

trained intensively for its role along with other bombers hastily converted from their nuclear role, using the range at Cape Wrath despite naturalists' protests about possible damage to nesting seabirds. The pilot, Flight Lieutenant Martin Withers, made an epic flight from Ascension Island which involved seventeen air-to-air refuelling operations outward and inbound. He made his final approach at low level to reduce the risk of radar detection, then climbed to 10,000 feet for the bomb run. Still 3 miles short of the coast, he released twenty-one 1,000-pound 'superfuse' iron bombs, and swung away homewards. One bomb fell on the runway, cratering the tarmac, while the remainder landed in a chain beyond it. The RAF had never been totally confident of closing the runway to short-takeoff Hercules transports and Pucara ground-attack aircraft, but they could render it unserviceable for high-performance jets if the surface had been extended to take them. Above all, they could force the Argentinians to accept that war was now upon them.

Woodward's battle group, some thirteen ships strong, entered the TEZ in darkness early that same day. The flight-deck crews aboard the carriers were already preparing the Sea Harriers for the next blow. *Invincible*, with her more modern radar and smaller air group, had been designated as air-defence ship, and was to concentrate on providing combat air patrols (CAPs) to fly standing cover over the fleet. The twelve Harriers on *Hermes* would take on the attack role. At first light, the entire strike force, led by Lieutenant Commander Andy Auld of 800 Squadron, took off from *Hermes*, assembled over the fleet, then turned in towards the Falklands coast. There had been much delicate balancing of possible fuel and bomb payloads. It was a measure of Woodward's confidence at this first encounter that he brought his carriers within 70 miles of the coast to fly off the aircraft.

The Harriers flew in low and fast, three aircraft detaching to attack the enemy's base at Goose Green, four making for Stanley's radar and anti-aircraft defences, the remainder for the runway and installations. 'The defences had been woken up by the Vulcan,' said Auld. 'As we came in, it looked as if we were watching a child's sparkler on Guy Fawkes' night.' Tracer arched towards them through the overcast sky as they roared over the airfield, released their bombs, and turned away. They saw no sign of missiles being fired against them, but back over the safety of the sea Auld checked his men: 'Gold Section, okay? Red Section? Blue Section?' One aircraft had been hit in the tail by a cannon shell. Auld detailed his wingman to fly close escort as they headed back towards the carriers, exhilarated by their own survival. They landed with perilously little fuel left, lifting exultant thumbs to the bridge as they opened the cockpits. As soon as the Harriers had been recovered, the carrier group turned away eastwards to open the range between the ships and the enemy, while the armourers set about refitting the aircraft with Sidewinder missiles. Woodward expected the enemy to respond immediately, if only as a matter of national pride.

Meanwhile, he had dispatched three ships – the destroyer *Glamorgan*, and the frigates *Arrow* and *Alacrity* – to commence a bombardment of reported Argentine positions around Port Stanley. Early that afternoon, with *Glamorgan* flying her enormous battle ensigns, they closed at high speed to within 12 miles of the low, misty coastline and began to shoot by the map, steaming slowly to and fro in a heavy sea. The quick 'crack-boom' of naval bombardment, to become so familiar in the weeks that followed, echoed dully across the sea. These actions were not a series of unrelated, dramatic incidents; they were operations in pursuit of a deliberate provocative strategy. The British credited the Argentinians with the will and the intelligence to launch an equally reasoned counter-offensive. From the moment that the task force entered the TEZ, its senior officers expected to meet a coordinated air and sea defence. 'We anticipated a surface engagement,' said one, 'and the sooner it was fought the better.'

At 1.25 p.m. the bombardment group had just completed firing off Port Stanley when four Mirage IIIs began closing fast from the west. In the operations rooms of ships throughout the task force, the little clusters of men hunched over their circular amber screens caught the flash UHF signal 'Heads Up West', and watched intently as the enemy aircraft moved towards the three ships of the bombardment group. The Harrier CAP began to lose height and gain speed to intercept them. The British pilots had enormous confidence in their own aircraft – they were taking Harriers very seriously long before anyone else did – but, in their discussions on the passage south, they had all agreed that the faster Mirage was the enemy they feared most. The Israelis had proved what it could do. If Mirages attempted to dogfight, the Harriers proposed to evade combat, using their remarkable VIF capability to accelerate, turn and decelerate in seconds for the three minutes or so before the Mirages would have exhausted their spare fuel capacity. Then, as the Mirages ran for home, it would be the Harriers who moved in for the kill.

The Mirages closed the bombardment group too fast for the ships' main armament to engage them. David Tinker wrote home from *Glamorgan*, 'The Royal Marines on the signal deck . . . strapped to the Oerlikon guns, very exposed, shouted to the Mirages as they went past, "Come here you buggers, let me get at you." . . . We engaged our gas turbines with a will, and sent up an enormous plume of smoke . . . It wasn't particularly noisy – a lot of wooshes and some dacca-dacca. We had all legged it into the hangar and lay flat on the deck, tin helmets on and fingers in ears; so we didn't see anything – but heard it all. First, the screams of "Aircraft, Aircraft" over the armament broadcast, bangs as we fired chaff, wooshes as all 16 chaff rockets were fired, then dacca-dacca from the aircraft, bang-bang as the bombs went off by the stern, lifting the screws right out of the water (we thought we'd been hit), then woosh-woosh as the rockets went past us . . .' A 1,000-pound bomb fell on each side of *Glamorgan*'s quarter deck. 'This caused us all to be very frightened,' remarked her captain drily. The destroyer suffered slight underwater damage. Meanwhile *Arrow* received superficial damage to her funnel and upperworks from cannon strikes, and a young seaman was wounded in the arm. Machine-gun fire from the direction of the shore damaged *Alacrity*'s helicopter as the three ships steamed away east at full speed. Meanwhile the Harriers achieved their first and most encouraging successes. The Mirages did not dogfight. As they pulled away, the British aircraft caught and destroyed two. A third, to their delight, was shot down by the Argentinians' own ground defences. It was an exhilarating afternoon for the ships' companies. In the operations rooms, men monitoring the enemy radio nets heard the pilots' Spanish chatter and watched the blips vanish from the radar screens as the Mirages exploded. Then the anti-submarine escort group – *Yarmouth* and *Brilliant* with a Sea King 'dipping' its sonar – found two enemy Canberra bombers approaching at high level, again from the west. Fearful of Exocets, they fired chaff. A few moments later, a Harrier brought down one Canberra. They saw the other turn for home.

As the afternoon light ebbed away, the British were surprised that no more enemy aircraft appeared. It had been a modest response to their challenge. Each side had been testing the defences of the other, and both were sobered by the encounter. 'We realised that they meant business,' said Captain Barrow of *Glamorgan*. 'They could drop bombs very accurately.' This was the first and last occasion on which the British attempted to shell the coast in daylight. *Glamorgan* returned to pursue her bombardment, to assure the enemy that the task group had not been deterred, at 8.40 that evening. One of the overwhelming lessons of the war both on land and at sea was that, even in the radar age, the night was still precious to those who were able to make use of it.

*

Now the focus of the battle shifted some 300 miles westwards, outside the limits of the TEZ and towards the Argentine coast. The British were expecting the Argentinians to come by air and by sea. While the ships' companies' thoughts were fixed on the Mirages firing over their heads, those of Admiral Woodward and his staff were with the Argentine fleet. The location and shadowing of its principal units had been the most vital preoccupation of the British command since the struggle began. In the weeks before the task force entered the exclusion zone, the question of how close to the Argentine coast British submarines might venture in search of the enemy's fleet had been a matter of some vexed debate between the war cabinet and the service chiefs. The Royal Navy wished to pinpoint the various surface threats as early as possible. If British submarines remained within the TEZ, there was a grave danger that enemy ships could approach with impunity within killing distance of the task force. The politicians seemed apprehensive that the presence of British submarines within a few miles of the Argentine mainland might provoke a disastrous incident before the government was diplomatically prepared. In the last week of April, the war cabinet at last relented. On 26 April, the rules of engagement were extended to include a 'defence area' around all units of the task force. *Spartan* remained in the exclusion zone. *Conqueror* was moved from her northern holding position to a station south-west of the Falklands, outside the exclusion zone. *Splendid* began to patrol to the north of her. At this stage, one of the primary tasks of the British SSNs was to detect and destroy the two Argentine 209 submarines. At least one of these was believed to be operational within the exclusion zone, and was causing much concern to Admiral Woodward and his staff, as well as to the war cabinet.

On 26 April, *Splendid* made a critical report to Northwood: she had sighted an Argentine task group composed of the enemy's two Type 42 destroyers together with Exocet frigates moving south along the coast at 10 knots. This was invaluable information, for it pinpointed one major threat. *Splendid* was ordered to continue shadowing the destroyer group. However, Northwood's central concerns were the location of the cruiser *General Belgrano*, and above all the carrier, the *Veinticinco de Mayo*. Twenty-four hours after *Splendid* located the destroyers, she was ordered to break off shadowing and move north in search of the carrier, while 'Conks', as the SSN staff at Northwood always referred to *Conqueror*, pursued the search in the south.

On the afternoon of 1 May, Commander Chris Wreford-Brown of *Conqueror* reported that he had sighted the *General Belgrano* and two escorting Exocet destroyers. Northwood's first reaction was disappointment that this was not the carrier group. Where, then, was this? Today there is still some doubt of the carrier's exact position at this time. It seems probable that she was at sea, steaming a considerable distance north of the cruiser group. There was a consultation by signal between Northwood and Admiral Woodward. The submarine force was under Admiral Fieldhouse's overall command, but naturally Woodward was kept closely in touch with all movement decisions concerning the SSNs. FOFI told Fieldhouse that he would like the *Belgrano* to be attacked.

The British Defence Secretary, John Nott, later argued that the old cruiser presented an immediate threat to Woodward's task force. The Argentinians admit that she was providing aircraft direction for their air force. Some naval officers suggest that criticism of the decision to attack the ship merely betrays 'wetness' or inability to grasp the realities of war. It may be years, if ever, before we know whether Admiral Anaya ever intended an early concerted surface attack which might have hurt the British, but which could have entirely destroyed the Argentine fleet in the process. What is incontrovertible is that the British strategic purpose was to defeat the enemy's air and sea forces before the amphibious landing force was committed. To achieve this, it was vital to seize the earliest opportunity to remove one or more major Argentine surface threats from the battlefield. 'You have got to start something like this by showing that you're bloody good and you're determined to win,' said a senior British commander forcefully. Sir Terence Lewin went to the war cabinet meeting at Chequers on the morning of Sunday, 2 May, to request permission under the rules of engagement to sink the *General Belgrano* some 40 miles south-west of the TEZ.

The cabinet discussion wound back over many previous debates about the rules of engagement (though significantly without Pym's presence on this occasion). What was the extent of the threat to the task force? Was it feasible to follow the cruiser into the total exclusion zone? Might conventional rather than wire-guided Tiger-fish torpedoes be used to cripple rather than sink her? Should the escorts be left unattacked so they could pick up survivors? It was acknowledged that, of the two big Argentine ships, the aircraft carrier would have made a preferable victim. But Lewin left ministers in no doubt of Northwood's collective view that the *Belgrano* should be put out of action at once. No minister demurred. The order was issued before lunch.

It was one of the critical decisions of the confrontation, a dramatic raising of the stakes in the South Atlantic by the Prime Minister. It is easy to understand the Royal Navy's enthusiasm for attacking the cruiser, for it would enable them to win an important victory, to make a decisive move towards securing command of the sea around the Falklands. But, both then and later, it seemed remarkable how readily Mrs Thatcher's cabinet assented to a step which caused Britain to inflict the first major loss of life of the Falklands war. Professor Lawrence Freedman wrote later that, while the attack on the *Belgrano* gave Britain 'an important military victory, yet it turned into a political defeat because of the premium that the international community put on the appearance of avoid-ing escalation. Any military action which is not self-evidently for defensive purposes, even if it is pre-emptive, becomes an outrage.'[*] On 2 May, Mrs Thatcher and her war cabinet steeled themselves to demonstrate decisively and bloodily to Argentina that the seizure of the Falklands would be met by whatever level of force proved necessary to repossess them.

The 13,645-ton cruiser had sailed from the port of Ushuaia on 26 April, carrying more than 1,000 men and escorted by her two destroyers. *Conqueror* attacked at 3 p.m. on the afternoon of 2 May,

[*] *Foreign Affairs*, Autumn 1982.

35 miles outside the TEZ, firing a pattern of Mk 8 torpedoes from around 2,000 yards. It is believed that she chose to use traditional torpedoes rather than the latest, sophisticated Tigerfish with which she was equipped because of doubts about Tigerfish's reliability. She then went deep to make her escape in the textbook manner. Her crew heard two heavy explosions as her torpedoes struck the cruiser, and soon afterwards further detonations and shockwaves as the escorts dropped depth charges, apparently at random and certainly not close enough to present a real risk to *Conqueror*. Twenty minutes after the attack, Commander Wreford-Brown moved cautiously to periscope depth 11 miles from the enemy. His first torpedo had struck the ship on the port bow. The second had hit her stern, killing or trapping more than 200 men, and destroying all the ship's power and communications systems.

Some naval experts later expressed surprise that the big cruiser so rapidly took on a list and began to sink after only two torpedo hits. There is speculation whether her watertight doors were closed, or whether effective damage control might have saved the ship. Whatever the truth, *Conqueror* saw her quarry listing steeply to port and already low in the water, with the crew scrambling desperately down the port side towards the big yellow liferafts. The *Belgrano*'s Captain, Hector Bonzo, gave the order to abandon ship. It was a stunning blow to the Argentine navy – the loss of one of its most prestigious units. Three admirals' sons were among the hundreds of men pushing their way to the upper decks from the rapidly flooding darkness below. Some carried their most cherished possessions – cassette players, photographs, family mementoes. The crew were not equipped with anti-flash protection. Burned men suffered terribly. They struggled in the oil and wreckage to free the boats and clamber aboard. Huddled into the overcrowded liferafts, the survivors talked, sang, prayed, for almost thirty hours before rescue came. The Argentine escorts appeared to have decided either to pursue *Conqueror* or make good their own escape rather than to pick up survivors. The sea state began to worsen dramatically, and a gale blew up. By the time the rescue was complete, 368 of the *Belgrano*'s crew were dead. Not until 1 p.m. London time the following day – after the news had been rumoured in Buenos Aires and printed in British papers – was *Conqueror* able to signal to London officially confirming that she had sunk the *Belgrano*.

The destruction of the cruiser, and initial reports of loss of life even more serious than the reality, caused as much shock among the task force as among the public around the world. Most officers and ratings expressed open satisfaction at the removal of a threat to their ships. In the crowded wardroom of *Invincible*, officers cheered and punched the air with their fists in exultation. But then reaction, reflection, set in. Almost all were privately shaken by the immensity of the human tragedy. 'I told my ship's company as matter-of-factly as I could,' said a British destroyer captain. 'There was a mixture of horror and disbelief. There certainly wasn't any pride.' More than a few men were bewildered by the government's decision to permit the sinking of the cruiser outside the TEZ. What was the purpose of declaring geographical limits within which enemy ships would be liable to attack, only to act outside them, even if Britain was within the letter of her legal rights? It is argued that, if *Conqueror* had not attacked immediately, *Belgrano* could have steamed through the shallow waters that reach out deep into the Atlantic in these regions, and given the submarine the slip. But it is difficult to believe that, if the British had delayed an attack until they had given warning of an extension of the TEZ, the task force would have been put at serious risk. Had it not been for the events which now swiftly followed, Britain's strong diplomatic position and the support for it from her allies could have been severely compromised by the *Belgrano* attack.

*

The following day, 3 May, began well for Woodward's battle group. Early in the afternoon, on station some 60 miles east of Port Stanley, *Coventry* picked up a surface radar contact, and reported to *Hermes*. A Sea King sent to investigate by the flagship was fired upon by two 700-ton Argentine patrol boats, *Alferez Sobral* and *Comodoro Somellera*. *Glasgow* and *Coventry* both launched their Lynxes, armed with the untried Sea Skua missile hastily provided to the task force as they sailed south from Ascension. Lieutenant Commander Alan Rich locked the Sea Spray radar onto his target, and fired his missile. The Sea Skua dropped away from the helicopter, ignited, and bored unerringly towards *Somellera*, which was still spewing up tracer. There was a blinding flash, an explosion, and the patrol craft began to sink. The second ship was severely damaged. The two helicopters turned back towards their parent destroyers. David Hart-Dyke, the captain of *Coventry*, ran up to the flight deck from his operations room to congratulate the returning crew. He found Alan Rich standing shaking uncontrollably, overwhelmed by the destructive power that he had unleashed. They were still very new to the brutality of war.

Tuesday, 4 May, began with another 4.30 a.m. Vulcan raid on Port Stanley, less successful than its predecessor. The bomber scored no hits on the runway. Later that morning, three Sea Harriers staged a further raid on Goose Green. The second aircraft over the target, flown by Lieutenant Nick Taylor, was hit by radar-controlled anti-aircraft fire from beyond the airfield, and dived into the ground. Taylor did not eject, and he became the first Harrier casualty of the war. Even a top-class aircraft could not fly low-level ground-attack missions against defended targets and escape unscathed. Five per cent of the task-force Harrier strength was gone.

Out among the ships, the crews were working defence watches, second-degree readiness. As so often at mid-morning, the surveillance radars were picking up false echoes suggesting incoming aircraft – anomalous propagation, it was called in the trade. Several ships had been discussing the problem on the UHF telephone between operations rooms. *Coventry* was chatting to *Sheffield*, who had taken over *Coventry*'s usual station at the south-west corner of the task force, then some 40 miles south of Port Stanley, because Hart-Dyke's ship was having technical problems with her 965 radar. There was a sudden silence. David Hart-Dyke turned to his air warfare officer beside him and said, 'Sheffield's got a communications problem. What a moment for it!' Then they heard an unidentified voice on the net declare flatly, 'Sheffield is hit.' It was 10 a.m. Hermes ordered Arrow and Yarmouth to move immediately to investigate, and signalled the silent Sheffield: 'Report your situation by any means.' A helicopter was tasked to fly to the scene. Glasgow was sent to take over radar-picket duty in the vital, vulnerable sector. More and more confusing signals began to flow. Yarmouth reported seeing a missile fly past her. Both frigates claimed to have sighted torpedo tracks. Glasgow's Lynx was launched, and dropped Mk 46 antisubmarine torpedoes, which immediately homed upon Yarmouth's and Arrow's towed anti-submarine decoys. The entire task force was called to action stations. Still there was total confusion about what had happened to Sheffield, except that she could be seen belching thick, black smoke. Had there been an enemy submarine attack? Or was there merely an internal explosion? Then Sheffield's Lynx landed aboard Hermes carrying the ship's operations officer and air warfare officer. They reported to Woodward on the disaster that had befallen her.

The weather was calm that morning, and visibility unusually good. Captain Sam Salt, a forty-two-year-old submariner whose father had died in wartime submarines, whose godfather was 'Red' Ryder, who won a VC at St Nazaire, was in his cabin. A short, balding figure popular throughout the navy, he had taken over command of Sheffield at Mombasa in January. Her ship's company had now been at sea five months, and completed 'thirty thousand miles of trouble-free motoring', as Salt liked to say proudly. They were suffering a little from the inevitable rundown of stores after so long at sea: beer and chocolate – the sailors' beloved 'nutty' – were gone, and they were rationed to potatoes only once every two days. But morale was high, for after so long together, the crew had grown to know each other very well indeed.

The deficiencies of the Type 42 destroyer were well known throughout the navy. At the beginning of the ships' building programme, for economy reasons they were reduced in size, losing 30 feet of length. The resulting hull shape was not happy in a heavy sea. More serious, like many modern British warships, the Type 42s had been compelled to sacrifice armament to keep their topweight at an acceptable level, and to preserve stability. Every captain wanted Sea Wolf for point defence, but the Type 42s carried only Sea Dart – with its unfortunate inability to engage low-level targets – for protection against air attack. At the start of the Falklands war, most of the British public still imagined destroyers and frigates supporting each other against air attack in the manner of Second World War escorts. As we have said, it was a critical feature of modern British warships that, while each possessed varying abilities to defend itself against air attack, most had no ability to defend other ships. Against an air attack, therefore, like the rest of the task force, *Sheffield* had to meet any threat from her own resources alone.

Lieutenant Commander Nick Batho, *Sheffield*'s air warfare officer, was directing the operations room when radar picked up a contact, apparently an incoming aircraft, approaching from the west. He informed the officer of the watch on the bridge, Lieutenant Peter Walpole. The missile director, a short, balding chief petty officer named Adamson, began typing into the keyboard of the ADAWs IV computer, seeking to point out a target. The British ships had been told to expect an air-launched Exocet to be fired from something like its maximum range of 45 miles, and from an aircraft flying at medium height. This radar contact was far closer and far lower. It could be a returning Harrier, or conceivably a Mirage or Skyhawk bombing sortie. On the bridge, Walpole suddenly saw smoke on the horizon. The British had been trained to expect a twenty-minute warning time between the detection of an incoming Russian aircraft, and the impact of any projectile that it unleashed. It was less than two and a half minutes after the operations room first detected the radar contact that Walpole and Lieutenant Brian Layshon, *Sheffield*'s Lynx pilot who chanced to be beside him on the bridge, realised simultaneously what was coming towards them: 'My God, it's a missile.'

Five seconds later, travelling at 680 m.p.h., the Exocet impacted in the hull amidships with 'a short, sharp, unimpressive bang', in Salt's words. There has since been speculation that only unused propellant in the missile detonated, but Salt and his men are convinced that the 363-pound warhead exploded. The missile had been released by one of a pair of French-built Super Etendard aircraft, from a squadron of fourteen in course of delivery to the Argentinians. Fired from pointblank range, around 6 miles, it detonated 8 feet above the waterline on Deck 2, in the vicinity of the forward engine room, causing a split in the hull some 10 by 4 feet. The blast effect tore watertight doors from bulkheads, and blew forward and aft up to the bridge. Ladders were torn from their mountings, equipment wrecked, and almost immediately thick black acrid smoke began to fill the lower decks.

Salt reached his bridge seconds after the explosion to find all power lost and the main broadcast system out of action. It was immediately clear that the lower decks must be evacuated to save men from the smoke. The casualties were mercifully light because the ship had remained at defence watches. If the crew had been sent to action stations, men would have been thronging the central passages when the missile struck. Most of those killed immediately were in the galley, preparing supper, or trapped in the computer room below the operations room. Damage-control teams at once began to try to establish smoke boundaries to stem the spread of the fire raging around the area of impact, but many of the watertight doors would no longer close. It was impossible to move between the forward and aft areas of the ship below decks. The heat was already intense. Most serious of all, the ship's water main had been fractured in the explosion, and they had no means of attacking the flames. As shocked and blackened men gathered on the upper decks, they sought to start the portable gas-turbine pump. The starting chain broke. They lowered feeble portable submersible pumps over the side, and even buckets. Salt escaped with difficulty from his choking bridge, for there were no rungs to climb down the outside of the bridge screen. Many men made their way up from below with the aid of respirators. There were only eight oxygen-breathing apparatuses on the ship. With the aid of these, some determined men began a struggle to work their way back below to fight the fire.

It was too hot, far too hot, and the smoke made visibility impossible. The men on the upper deck could feel the heat below their feet, see the ship's sides steaming. The forward superstructure was becoming unbelievably warm. *Arrow* was alongside now, her captain talking to Salt by walkie-talkie and discussing what she could do to help fight the fires, but it was already becoming hopeless. Three men were alongside in *Sheffield*'s Gemini inflatable, attempting to play water into the split in her hull. Salt was horrified for their safety when *Yarmouth* suddenly fired her anti-submarine mortars close by and announced the sighting of torpedo tracks. The presence of a submarine in the area was never confirmed, but the British, thrown off balance by *Sheffield*'s tragedy, were in no mood to take chances with doubtful sonar echoes. Salt glanced at his watch and wondered what had gone wrong with it. It seemed about twenty minutes since the missile exploded. Now he found that four hours had passed. Some forty casualties, most suffering from burns or choked by smoke, had been evacuated. The thick smoke still pouring from the hull had turned from black to white, and for a brief phase he and his men believed that they were winning the battle to save the ship. But the heat below was still appalling. An extraordinarily gallant petty officer who fought his way down into the ship was overcome by smoke, and never seen again. The fires were now within one compartment of the Sea Dart magazine. It was obvious that, whatever the crew risked, their ship would be unfit for any further action in the war.

As the frigates chased elusive submarine contacts, it appeared that the task force was still under direct threat. Salt made the bitter decision to abandon *Sheffield*. Commander Paul Bootherstone brought *Arrow* alongside, and men began to jump from ship to ship, while others were winched up into the hovering Sea Kings. At last, only a handful of men remained on the two tenable parts of the ship, the fo'c'sle and the flight deck. Salt, blackened from head to foot like his men, suddenly realised that he was also terribly cold and wet. With his first lieutenant, Mike Norman, and his marine engineer, Bob Rowley, he was winched into a Sea King, and flown away to *Hermes*, some 30 miles eastwards. Twenty-one men had died.

Sheffield drifted for three days before Salt reboarded her. On the morning of 9 May, she was taken in tow by *Yarmouth* in the hope of moving the hulk to South Georgia, and thence homewards. Early on the morning of 10 May, at the edge of the TEZ in a rising sea, she began to list sharply and then turned over and sank. 'Everybody has always said that modern warships are "one-hit ships",' said Sam Salt. 'Nobody had thought about the implications of a "one-hit ship" 8,000 miles from home. It's much worse than having a car crash – you lose everything. And of course you all keep saying, "What could I have done to prevent it?"'

*

It would be difficult to overstate the impact of *Sheffield*'s loss upon the British task force. Officers and men alike were appalled, shocked, subdued by the ease with which a single enemy aircraft firing a cheap – £300,000 – by no means ultra-modern sea-skimming missile had destroyed a British warship specifically designed and tasked for air defence. It was not even the fact of a lost ship that affected men so profoundly – most could accept that, in a war, there are bound to be casualties – it was the revelation of the fallibility of their own technology. There was an immediate, fierce discussion of the lessons learned. Why had *Sheffield* not fired her chaff? Because she had not believed she was facing a missile threat. In future, every ship facing even a possible missile would fire chaff. It remained a mystery how *Yarmouth* had escaped the AM39 Exocet fired by the second Super Etendard of the pair that attacked.

Sheffield had been unable to use her fire main once it was fractured because every ship had been ordered to keep its main united, to facilitate magazine flooding in an emergency. In future, all fire mains would be divided. Nothing could be done about the deadly inflammability of the ships: the plastic cable runs whose ignition had contributed to the clouds of toxic smoke that overcame *Sheffield*, the inadequate emergency pumps, the big passages running through the ship to provide access for machinery spares. There was no means of immediately providing the ships' crews with fire-retardant clothing to replace the man-made fibres which had proved frighteningly combustible. Men remembered and talked about the steel ships of the Second World War which took repeated hits without burning, the Fletcher class destroyer hit by five Kamikazes in 1945 which still did not catch fire. Smoke curtains could be erected at every possible interval throughout the ships of the rest of the fleet, horizontal passages could be kept permanently closed, and helicopters could fly far more frequent missile-decoy missions around their parent carriers, frigates, destroyers.

Yet what more could be done – except to take the war in more deadly earnest? 'We began to see that war is ghastly, that people do get killed. We suddenly felt hurt, and very, very angry with the Argentinians,' said a young principal weapons officer. Perhaps a part of the trouble with the entire British approach to the struggle in the South Atlantic before the destruction of *Sheffield* was that the men of the task force, and even those at home, felt so little animosity towards their enemy. If they did not hate Argentinians, it seemed difficult to believe that the Argentinians in their turn could hate Englishmen sufficiently to take great pains to kill them.

The truth about the loss of *Sheffield*, as almost every man in the fleet privately recognised, was that until that moment they had been living with the image, rather than the reality, of war. They were taking their task seriously, but they lacked that last ounce of tension, caution, readiness, that only imminent personal danger can provoke. Never again, after *Sheffield*, would the main task force operate so close inshore. Henceforth, Admiral Woodward was compelled to resolve an impossible dilemma: his purpose was to lure the Argentinians out to fight, yet neither strategically nor politically could he risk losing one of his aircraft carriers by moving within close range of the enemy.

'After *Sheffield* it became quite clear that any attempt to gain air superiority would risk the loss of the carriers,' said one of the task force's senior captains. 'It was a turning point in that it convinced Sandy Woodward that he had to keep his distance.' Woodward himself later confessed that, for three days after the loss of the destroyer, he was in a state of profound depression. When he was not in his operations room on *Hermes*, or talking on the secure telephone link to Admiral Hallifax, the chief of staff at Northwood, he spent many hours lying on his bunk turning over in his mind again and again the tactical options before him. He admitted to reading only three books in more than three months at sea. Unlike most of his men, he found it impossible to relax in front of a video screen for an hour or two in the evenings. Consciousness that he was 'a man hired to do a job' bore heavily upon him as he pondered how it was to be accomplished, how he and his fleet could solve the conundrum of defeating an air threat without in turn being destroyed by it. Even as he consulted with his captains by radio about the next moves, he sent a signal to all his ships: 'We shall lose more ships and more men. But we shall win.'

On 6 May, two Harriers flying CAP duties suddenly disappeared from the radar screen, and were assumed to have collided and crashed into sea. 15 per cent of the battle group's air cover had now been lost, and it was a matter of exasperation to the naval staff that the fact was announced to the world by the correspondents with the fleet, with the sanction of the Ministry of Defence. On 7 May, the total exclusion zone was extended to threaten any enemy warship at sea more than 12 miles from the Argentine coast. The British now had all the searoom that they needed for action, with *Spartan* and *Splendid* patrolling as close to the shore as they could reach, 'looking for custom'. But, after the sinking of the *General Belgrano*, never again did British submarines sight an enemy warship at sea. The SSNs undertook a new and critical function: lying off Argentina's air bases, and using electronic equipment, sonar and visual sighting to report the takeoff of aircraft sorties towards the Falklands.

*

The bulk of the task force now steamed its daily north–south 'racetrack' course well to the east of the islands. By night, ships closed in to bombard positions on the coastline. Whenever the weather permitted, Harriers strafed airfields and radar positions. They had now abandoned low-level direct attacks – the risk of attrition was too great. Instead, they 'toss bombed', releasing their weapons well short of the target, and turning away at maximum distance from the defences. They no longer expected to be able to close the runways to enemy aircraft, and at low level many of their bombs proved as reluctant to explode as those of the Argentinians later. Many sorties were flown merely to goad and tempt the enemy to respond. Harriers lingered over Port Stanley at 20,000 feet, above the ceiling of the enemy's Roland antiaircraft missiles. One pilot watched a missile burn towards him, then fall exhausted at 18,000 feet. The admiral was relieved of worry about the strain of intensive operations on his carriers. Often, sorties were impossible and the pilots merely took turns to sit in their cockpits for hours at a stretch on the flight deck, braced to meet an attack if the overcast suddenly cleared. For days, the enemy never came.

On 9 May, Woodward embarked on a new tactic. Apart from his Harriers, the weapons with the longest reach in his force were the two remaining Type 42 destroyers (*Coventry* and *Glasgow*) and their Sea Dart, effective up to 40 miles. Teamed with a Type 22 frigate (*Brilliant* or *Broadsword*) and its Sea Wolf to cover Sea Dart's critical blindness at low level, a Type 42 should be able to inflict crippling damage on any enemy air movement within range.

Coventry and *Broadsword* accordingly closed to within 12 miles of Port Stanley – the frigate's new 997/98 doppler radar was more effective than most of the British systems in overcoming 'clutter' and spotting targets close to land. Early that morning, the British ships detected an incoming Hercules transport, one of the nightly shuttle into Stanley which so dismayed the naval staff seeking to tighten the blockade. It was escorted by two Skyhawks. At maximum range, 38 miles, *Coventry* fired her Sea Dart. The missiles missed the Hercules, but one exploded beneath the two Skyhawks. At first the British believed that they had missed the targets altogether. Then they saw the Skyhawks disappear from the radar screen. The pilots almost certainly ejected. Shortly afterwards, *Coventry* again fired Sea Dart at a radar contact 13 miles distant. There was a vivid orange explosion as a Puma helicopter blew up. For the first time in the missile age, the Royal Navy had fired salvos in anger.

That morning of the 9th, a Harrier of 800 Squadron flown by Flight Lieutenant David Morgan sighted the 1,400-ton Argentine trawler *Narwhal*. A frigate had intercepted the Argentine ship hanging behind the British battle group ten days earlier, and had warned her to leave the area. Instead she remained, evidently gathering intelligence. Morgan asked for orders, and was directed to engage her. He bombed and strafed *Narwhal*, while a party of marines was hastily embarked in two helicopters, escorted by a third. A few minutes later, they boarded the damaged and drifting trawler. Some of her crew were already in a lifeboat, some were standing terrified with their hands up on deck, others were hiding below. Of the thirty Argentinians aboard, one was dead and twelve wounded. Among them, the British found an Argentine navy lieutenant commander, put aboard when the ship was commandeered for intelligence purposes at Mar Del Plata on 22 April. *Narwhal* sank under tow the following day.

On that day, the 10th, in Falkland Sound, *Alacrity* suddenly detected a ship and opened fire. Her first round provoked a huge explosion, presumably from fuel supplies. The 3,900-ton *Islas de los Estados* sank immediately. *Alacrity* continued her sweep of the sound, designed partly to harass the enemy and partly to discover what defences or mines might have been sited to cover its approaches.

Meanwhile, the two Type 42s were taking turns to operate inshore. On 12 May, *Glasgow* was operating with *Brilliant* in another '22–42 combo'. The destroyer was bombarding the shore in thick, low cloud which made effective spotting of her fall of shot difficult. Suddenly, four Skyhawks came in low towards the ships and broke into two pairs, one making for each British target. *Brilliant* launched her Sea Wolf. Two enemy aircraft blew up immediately. A third flew into the sea. The fourth vanished over the horizon. It was a triumph for the new system. But, an hour later, a second wave of attackers came in. They were too low for Sea Dart. Sea Wolf was switched on but, to the utter dismay of its aimers, the system 'reset' and refused to fire. As the Bofors and light machineguns on deck opened fire, three bombs fell away from the Skyhawks, hit the water and bounced over *Brilliant*. A fourth bomb hit *Glasgow* just above the waterline, smashed through her hull and fell out into the sea on the other side without exploding. The destroyer had had a miraculous escape, the first of many more such episodes to come, but she was now taking water. She was compelled to retire east for temporary repairs before returning home to England.

Despite *Brilliant*'s initial success with Sea Wolf, her crew had been given a foretaste of the problems to come. The system was designed to engage a single incoming target. Its computer was confused and thrown off balance by the approach of four aircraft simultaneously. Intensive fine-tuning of Sea Wolf by the ships' technical teams in the weeks that followed gradually improved its performance. But 'the war was still a first front-line trial for the missile', in the words of a British commander. The price of fallibility was that the second of Woodward's three Type 42 destroyers had been put out of action, for which the Argentinians could well afford to lose three Skyhawks. A third wave of attacking aircraft

later that afternoon was met by the Harrier CAP; they broke off
the approach and turned for home.

*

Every ship in the task force found its crews subject to sharp
fluctuations of morale throughout the war. The arrival of mail or a
success against enemy attack could set the messdecks buzzing with
excitement and pleasure, while a misfortune such as the crippling
of Glasgow made men restrained and taciturn for hours, sometimes
days. Men worried deeply about their families at home, and how
bad news might be affecting them. They cursed the broadcasters
and newspaper photographers when they believed that news and
pictures were being released in Britain which would cause fear or
pain. Captains found it worth going to great lengths to devise
special events and unexpected treats for their men. All the sailors
suffered greatly from the absence of their beloved fried potatoes.
After the loss of Sheffield, the deep friers in the galleys were
permanently switched off, an intolerable fire risk in a crisis. After
a bad week, one commanding officer found that the crew's spirits
revived dramatically when he allowed the friers to operate for a
day, and produce a vast supply of chips. The early actions of the
battle group had etched deep on every man's mind the vital
importance of being geared for instant action at any hour of day
or night. Throughout those weeks of tossing and rolling in the
heavy grey seas off East Falkland, it was not attacks that ate into
their energy and nerves so much as the threat of them. The sonar
teams switched every fifteen minutes so that the man on the set
was always listening acutely. Whales and freak sea conditions
created regular submarine alarms, accompanied by the firing of
depth charges, mortars, anti-submarine torpedoes. It now seems
almost certain that an Argentine submarine did indeed come close
to the task force at some point, and made an attack, unsuccessful
because of torpedo failure. 'The actual war part of it is not so much
frightening as tense,' wrote Lieutenant Tinker. 'In the first week,
when the fleet was closer inshore and continually under air threat,

some people were getting to their nerves' ends, especially those in the Operations Room, where the war is fought from . . .'

Closing in to bombard the coast or to land special-forces teams night after night was a great strain for the ships' companies. Steaming slowly offshore, under intermittent if inaccurate fire from the Argentinians' 105 mm and 155 mm guns, kept every man at action stations and deprived most of sleep through the hours of darkness. The smoke from the 4.5-inch guns drifted into the ships, while the noise of repeated explosions echoed dully below to men manning radar screens and control positions. Only the men in the machinery spaces were aware of nothing but the infernal roar of their engines. 'One felt very little emotion, firing at unseen men on the shore,' said a destroyer officer. 'It would have been different, we would have felt much more, if a ship had been the target.' Like so many Cinderellas, before dawn the bombarding ships hastened away to the safety of distant waters, and began the long, arduous routine of replenishing ammunition, usually by jackstay transfer from a store ship. Overlaid on this was the need to refuel at sea, usually every other day. Most ships suffered technical problems of one kind or another, accentuated by the devastating weather. It was one of the most closely guarded secrets of the war that *Invincible* steamed for some weeks on only one propeller – a smashed gearbox coupling had put the other out of action. The Type 22s' Sea Wolf tracking radar lacked the protective domes fitted to the Type 42s' systems, and the effects of salt and water proved severe. Most of the men on a modern warship are highly trained technicians, and the skills of all of them in the Falklands were pressed to the uttermost. 'One didn't depend on brilliant people to excel, but on the ordinary blokes to do what was expected of them,' said a frigate captain. As an achievement of seamanship, logistics, ship handling, the British campaign in the South Atlantic was a triumph for the Royal Navy: 'It proved that we train our people in the right way.'

*

Yet, by mid-May, as a strategic deployment to create the conditions for an amphibious landing, the operations of the task force had been a failure. On the 16th, two Harriers from *Hermes* bombed and strafed the Argentine supply ship *Rio Carcamia*, and attacked a second ship close to Fox Bay settlement on West Falkland at a cost of slight damage to one aircraft's tail. It was a typical day for the battle group, greeted with satisfaction by newspapers and broadcasters in Britain. But, that night, a Harrier pilot recorded, 'We are beginning to get the feeling that we could still be here in October.' More than two weeks after Woodward's force entered the TEZ, despite all the minor successes, the constant harassment of the enemy from the sea and from the air, the vast bulk of Argentina's sea and air forces remained resolutely at home. The winter weather promised to worsen and diplomatic pressure on Britain could only increase. Time was not on the side of the task force. Frigates had sailed the length of Falkland Sound firing on shore positions, consciously seeking to provoke the enemy's attention. Night after night, naval gunfire support officers hovered in Lynx helicopters off the coast, directing the fire of bombarding ships. The Type 42s had done their utmost to interdict enemy air movements until the price became too high.

The outcome of all this effort was the destruction of a handful of small ships, and the shooting down of at least seven and possibly nine enemy aircraft, in return for the loss of one of Britain's most modern air defence ships, the crippling of another, the loss of three Harriers and four Sea King helicopters by accident and enemy action. Asked afterwards why the Royal Navy was so terrifyingly vulnerable to air attack, devoid of active defence against sea-skimming missiles, a senior officer said simply, 'The Russians have no Exocet.' He added, 'This war has shown us how dangerous it is for our defences to become too scenario-orientated.' Woodward's force had inflicted a mere fraction of the damage that the Royal Navy had planned, hoped, counted upon achieving as a precondition of a British amphibious landing. Many land-force officers argued that the navy should have anticipated the danger that the enemy would refuse to fight on its terms. It seemed clear to many people even at the time that the Argentinians had everything to gain and nothing to lose by holding back their aircraft to await the only threat to their occupation that could not be ignored: an amphibious landing force.

What to do now? At Northwood, in Downing Street, on *Hermes*, options were once again being examined. Throughout this period, the war cabinet perceived remarkably few of the delicate naval equations being debated in the South Atlantic. They understood all too vividly the sinking of ships, but they knew nothing of '22–42 combos', or the difficulties of Sea Wolf in achieving solutions, or the niceties of positioning the carriers. At sea, there was a strong, bold faction within the fleet that favoured taking the entire task force west of the Falklands, presenting a challenge to the enemy that he could not refuse, and offering a chance of making the air blockade effective by ending the nightly Hercules shuttles. Woodward examined this notion very carefully before rejecting it. West of the Falklands, less than 300 miles from the Argentine mainland, the risk of further air-launched Exocet attacks seemed too great to tolerate, and that of devastating bombing attacks doubly so. The loss of a carrier would signal disaster. Sea Wolf and Sea Dart had indeed proved capable of shooting down enemy aircraft. But, on the basis of their performance to date, no responsible officer could hazard the safety of the fleet on their prospects of reliability. Both systems were dangerously vulnerable to saturation. The Harriers, effective as they were proving, were absurdly few in number.

One further option was forcefully urged by some members of the task force, both senior officers and rank and file: an attack by Vulcan bombers, or more plausibly by a team of saboteurs from the Special Air Service, on the enemy's mainland air bases. Argentina was believed to have taken delivery of only five of her order of fourteen Super Etendards capable of launching Exocets. If these, together with a substantial element of the Skyhawk and Mirage force, could be destroyed, the odds would shift dramatically in favour of the Royal Navy. It was the old 'gloves-off' argument that, at a more dramatic level, caused the Americans to consider invading North Vietnam at the height of the war in Indochina. Yet the difficulties of carrying out a bombing attack with any likelihood of success were overwhelming. And, despite the British government's resolute commitment to retaking the Falklands, there was an equally determined and persistent resolve to limit the conflict. At an early stage, the Attorney General had given his opinion to the war cabinet that any form of British attack on the mainland could be construed as falling outside the framework of Article 51 of the United Nations Charter, empowering Britain to act in her own self-defence. While British intelligence-gathering teams were deployed on the mainland in the course of the Falklands war – as the embarrassing landing of a Sea King in Chile on 16 May revealed to the world – at no point was an attack on the enemy's air bases authorised or undertaken. The British task force was obliged to meet the air threat on the Falklands battlefield and nowhere else.

Northwood was now compelled to acknowledge the failure of Woodward's force to achieve the stated preconditions for an amphibious landing. Thompson's men, still poised at Ascension Island, could not go ashore with air superiority already achieved. The enemy's air force remained intact, indeed was now perceived to be a far more deadly threat than when the task force first set sail. Yet it was politically unthinkable for the government to consider abandoning operations in the South Atlantic. A demonstration of force had failed to secure an Argentine withdrawal. Now it was decided, in effect, to double up on all the bets that had been placed hitherto. The government and the service chiefs cast aside the strategic rules for the conduct of amphibious warfare. They determined to embark upon a landing in the Falklands, and defy the Argentinians to do their worst on the day.

10 » CLEARING THE DECKS

But we steadfastly gazed on the face that was dead,
And we bitterly thought of the morrow.

Charles Wolfe, *The Burial of Sir John Moore*

The Monday after the sinking of the *Belgrano*, 2 May, was a bank holiday in Britain and Mrs Thatcher stayed over at Chequers. Not until the evening did John Nott hold a press conference to announce the attack on the *Belgrano*. As he was answering questions, news came that the cruiser had not only been hit but had sunk with heavy loss of life. With the rest of the war cabinet, Nott had assumed that conventional torpedoes would simply cripple the ship and force it out of action, while escorting frigates would pick up any casualties. Now he was visibly taken aback. This was not just enforcing an exclusion zone, it looked to the assembled pressmen like a quite disproportionate act of aggression. A tactical triumph was surely turning into a diplomatic disaster.

The gap which had separated the onward march of the war from the stately minuet of negotiation was never wider than now. Oblivious of events in the South Atlantic, Francis Pym had dined the previous evening, Sunday, with Sir Anthony Parsons and the UN Secretary-General Perez de Cuellar, in New York. With America at last on Britain's side and the fleet about to engage the enemy, the war cabinet had virtually left Pym to take the negotiating process wherever he chose. If the Americans could not get British administration restored on the Falklands, it was surely inconceivable that anyone else, let alone any Latin American, would succeed.

Mrs Thatcher was prepared to acknowledge that Britain should never be seen to be refusing peace and, under intense pressure from the opposition, conceded Pym's desire to try the UN route. Not for one minute did she believe it would succeed with Britain's demands intact.

A meticulous and reserved international civil servant, de Cuellar was still finding his feet as Secretary General. His vision of the UN was less grandiose and more realistic than that of his predecessors. He was aware of its limitations and of the damage it could do to its dwindling authority by rushing in where great powers feared to tread. A Falklands 'task force' had been established in his own office in the early days of the crisis under one of his assistants, the Pakistani Rafie Ahmed. De Cuellar had been insistent that Ahmed do no more than prepare a range of possible roles for the UN should anyone ask. Under no circumstances should the UN interfere when Haig was still pursuing his peace initiative: relations with Washington were bad enough as it was.

Now that Haig appeared to have failed, the Secretary General was coming out of his shell. For the benefit of Parsons and of his Argentine opposite number, Enrique Ros (supplanting Roca), de Cuellar jotted down what were modestly termed his 'ideas' on one sheet of paper. They were three: withdrawal, interim administration and long-term settlement – the same as Haig had brought with him to London a month before. However, the simplicity of this return to fundamentals was upset by Sunday's news shouted at the gathering diplomats by journalists outside the UN and relayed to them as they talked. It was of a rival peace initiative from de Cuellar's compatriot, President Belaunde Terry of Peru.

What had happened, that extraordinary first weekend in May, was that Haig had far from given up the ghost. Aware that any overt American role would now be counterproductive, he decided on a covert one. He donated his latest plan to Belaunde lock, stock and barrel. Peru had long been Argentina's closest Latin American friend, from a shared enmity towards Chile, and some of Haig's staff had argued that any hope for mediation would best be conducted through some such 'Latin cousin' rather than through Washington. Belaunde now sent his '7-point plan' to Buenos Aires. It was an ill-disguised version of Haig Two – 'Haig in a poncho' – with no extra ingredient beyond the offer of Latin American participation in the interim administration. De Cuellar in New York was embarrassed and annoyed. From now until the San Carlos landing three weeks later, each move in the Falklands peace negotiations was bedevilled by the conflicting ambitions of the various peacemakers.

War cabinet on Tuesday 4 May, followed by the weekly Falklands full cabinet, was dominated by a debate on how to limit the damage caused by the *Belgrano* sinking. Messages of concern were now pouring into London from friend and foe alike. Haig told a congressional committee that the sinking had 'contributed to continuing the dispute'. At the EEC, Italy and Ireland moved to have sanctions against Argentina lifted on their expiry on 17 May. At the UN there was a marked shift in sentiment away from Britain, with particular criticism of the sinking having taken place outside the declared exclusion zone. Argentina's public spokesman, Jorge Herrera Vegas, chosen for his command of English, came up with one of his many bons mots: 'Britain may not rule the waves, but she certainly waives the rules.' In Buenos Aires, Galtieri formally notified the Peruvian ambassador that, after the loss of his cruiser, he could not possibly recommend any concessions on Argentine sovereignty.

Argentine sources are keen to have it thought that the British sabotaged the Peruvian plan by their action. They argue that British bombing attacks on Port Stanley the previous day dramatically hardened opinion in Buenos Aires against concession, while Galtieri had apparently been ready to accept Belaunde's plan the very evening that news of the *Belgrano* was brought to him. Yet it is hard to believe that the junta, including Anaya, might have been on the brink of conceding a virtually identical peace formula to that so recently and comprehensively rejected from Haig. Indeed, it might equally be argued that Anaya was the junta member whose forces now had most to lose by continuing the conflict: his surface fleet came scurrying back to port. As it was, he encouraged the junta to reject Belaunde not once this week but twice, and then to reject de Cuellar as well. There is ample evidence that throughout the sea war Anaya thought he was going to win his campaign of attrition against the British fleet.

Ironically, it was in London that the *Belgrano* incident inspired new life into the search for peace. Pym's somewhat tired arguments about keeping world opinion on Britain's side suddenly seemed relevant again. As a result of Tuesday's war cabinet, Henderson in Washington was told to reopen the Peruvian proposals urgently with Haig: even hauling him back at Andrews Air Force Base from an evening flight to New York to do so. In London, so crushing an affirmation of Britain's superiority left many feeling uneasy – an illustration of how completely the public had been shielded from the true risks the fleet was now running. 'It's going a bit too easy for us,' a war cabinet member said at the time. 'We're looking like bullies.' Addressing the Commons, Pym felt constrained to say, 'We do not seek the military humiliation of Argentina.'

The idea of Argentina's military humiliation was no sooner stated than it seemed monstrously inappropriate. At 9 p.m. on the Tuesday evening, in the ponderous tones which became the defence ministry's hallmark, the acting chief public relations officer, Ian Macdonald, announced on television the loss of the destroyer *Sheffield* and of a Harrier over Goose Green. The ever-indecisive ministry promptly censored broadcasting lines from the task force which were reassuringly reporting that most of the crew were being rescued. Instead, Macdonald intoned, 'It is feared there have been a number of casualties but we have no details of them yet.'

As news filtered through to the Commons, MPs poured into the chamber to hear Nott announce the loss, a stunned Mrs Thatcher by his side. Only the far left seemed to take any grim pleasure from the news. The bragging and self-confidence of the campaign so far evaporated. Suddenly there was doubt on every side: so much so that Mrs Thatcher uncharacteristically ordered Lewin to go on television to allay public fear. Newspapers whose enthusiasm for the war had known no bounds now discovered its price. The *Daily Mail* brought out a black border round its front page. In Downing Street, the Prime Minister surprised her staff by the emotion with which she received the news. She had always told them the one thing she dreaded was to hear of the loss of a ship. Now it had happened, and she was visibly upset. At such moments throughout the war, she would retreat to her upstairs room and handwrite letters of condolence to the parents of service-men lost in action.

The impact of *Sheffield*'s loss was to reinforce rather than dampen the war cabinet's renewed enthusiasm for diplomacy. For the first time since 2 April, Thatcher felt the need of her full cabinet's support. It met in emergency session on Wednesday, 5 May, and heard a gloomy assessment of the military position. The fleet was clearly vulnerable to sea-skimmers and, although it was believed Argentina had only three Exocets left, no one could be sure. At least one enemy submarine was also thought to be at large in the vicinity of the fleet. Questions now started piling in on Lewin. What were our defences against Exocet? Why did they appear so inadequate? Why was the fleet so close to the islands? Should the carriers not withdraw? Again and again, that perennial question: was he sure he could achieve a landing? Calmly Lewin went through the list of risks, well concealing the trauma *Sheffield* had caused his service. The landing force aboard *Canberra* was still at Ascension. A number of options were still available. Woodward would of course be reviewing his strategy. He was sure the navy could achieve its aims. Suddenly, however, the politicians were looking for a way out: their confidence in the navy had begun to slip.

As on 2 April, Mrs Thatcher went round her full cabinet table, listening and ticking off names as she went. Pym's arguments, which before had been tedious obstacles on the path to glory, now

seemed to many a ray of hope. All talk was now of Peru. Was a
third-party interim administration acceptable? Could the Commons swallow only a vague reference to self-determination in the
longer term? Was a balanced withdrawal quite what they had
envisaged at the start? Thatcher's cabinet remained remarkably
united throughout the war. Unlike the war cabinet, it had little
raw material on which to base internal disagreement and certainly
little on which to base dissent from what was always a collective
presentation to it by the war cabinet. As at the start ministers had
been solid behind the task force, so now they wheeled round to
agree that the Belaunde plan be accepted in principle. Only two
ministers dissented, the Lord Chancellor, Lord Hailsham, and the
Environment Secretary, Michael Heseltine. Both felt the political
risk of concession far outweighed any military risk in proceeding.
Heseltine was a known aspirant to the future party leadership. Mrs
Thatcher was as suspicious of his motives in opposing her now as
she was of Pym's motives in opposing her in war cabinet.

In the Commons the following day, the Prime Minister
announced to the delight of the opposition that the government
had made a 'very constructive response' to the Peruvian proposals.
Of the parallel UN 'ideas' communicated to her in outline by
Parsons, she was more dismissive: 'If they are to be acceptable and
to command confidence, they must be precise as to the timing and
the sequence of verification of events.' Yet there was none of her
usual brusque rejection of help from the UN. Pym emphasised his
restored authority by showing sympathy to David Owen's and
Denis Healey's suggestion of UN trusteeship, a major British concession. It was, said Pym, 'a possibility and might in the end prove
highly suitable'. *Belgrano* and *Sheffield* had been sacrifices indeed in
the cause of peace. At last the Foreign Office's doves seemed to be
taking wing.

They were barely airborne when the junta shot them out of
the sky. *Sheffield* had sent its morale soaring. Its agents were out
scouring the world for black-market Exocets. Costa Mendes was
told to play for time. The Belaunde plan, he said, was too similar

to the Haig one. Argentina decided to switch her negotiating favours from Lima to the UN in New York, where she hoped she might eventually find more certain safeguards for her cause. Of all Costa Mendes's errors of judgement, this was the most disastrous. Had he picked up Belaunde that Thursday, he would have gained more than he could have dreamed possible in February and might just have saved his government's life. Pym was furious. Speaking in the Commons on Thursday evening, he said that, but for the junta, there could have been a 'ceasefire within hours'. All he could add, to groans from his backbenchers, was, 'if one phase of diplomatic effort has been brought to an end . . . another phase is already under way in New York'.

Ministers now began to recover some of their bravado. They assured themselves and friends that the acceptance of Belaunde had been a calculated gamble which had come off. It had been a cosmetic to show good faith in peace. Yet they could not conceal the fact that they had been severely shaken and that, by the end of the week, their war plan was looking awry. Two more Harriers had been lost. The submarine menace was still at large. There had been little sign as yet of the enemy air force, which remained intact and clearly dangerous. While ministers had always half feared the onset of peace and the recall of the fleet, they had also half assumed it would happen. Now hopes of peace seemed dead, and the price of victory was rising fast.

*

The final fortnight of the negotiating phase was the most frustrating. On 8 May at Chequers the war cabinet took the crucial decision of the war; to send the landing force south from Ascension, despite the demonstrable lack of sea or air superiority. The risks involved in this decision produced new and unpredictable tensions and alliances among the ministers responsible. For all the arguments between Nott and Pym over rules of engagement, the interests of defence and foreign affairs now moved closer together. Nott was beset with understandable worry as the task force moved beyond

Ascension. With a number of his senior staff, he knew that to turn it back after that point would be politically intolerable. Were it to go on, the risks in a landing were enormous. Even victory would present Britain's defences with severe logistical problems in the South Atlantic, the last thing Nott's delicate navy strategy required. Nott was a constant enthusiast for blockade rather than landing – though he appreciated his chiefs of staff's objections – and of any settlement which might internationalise the conflict and avert the need for a subsequent 'fortress' policy.

Often in a war crisis it is a politician's personality rather than his political stance which dictates his outlook. So now William Whitelaw found himself tending to be more bullish, concerned above all to support the military, haunted by the memory of Eden and Suez. Again and again he repeated, 'We must not leave our chaps with the job half done.' The Prime Minister likewise was relentless, convinced there was no alternative to going on, pushing Lewin for answers, sleepless yet apparently tireless, except for brief moments when she suddenly appeared drained of all energy.

Meanwhile, a negotiated solution was as elusive as ever. On 8 May, it had been clearly indicated that the landing date would have to be in the 18–22 May 'window', yet somehow the peace effort lost its urgency. The racing torrent of shuttle diplomacy, with its Concorde flights, its clattering telexes and 5-point plans, now emerged on to the flood plain of United Nations Plaza. Here Perez de Cuellar and the secretive Rafie Ahmed moved as if in slow motion. Ahmed, to a colleague, was 'the sort of diplomat to whom Heaven is an eternity of international talk and war never happens'. Communications which had taken hours now seemed to take days. 'Ideas for discussion' and 'awaited responses' took the place of proposal and counter-proposal. In Thatcher's view, a noble principle would die of thirst in such a place.

The de Cuellar initiative did not start well. The previous week it had false-started as a result of Peru's surprise proposals. Now it fell foul of Haig's anger. Washington felt that UN intervention had sabotaged the Peruvian plan. A State Department spokesman dismissed de Cuellar's ideas as 'amateurish' and the UN role as 'characteristically destructive'. Haig also saw behind it the work of his bête noire, Jeane Kirkpatrick, whose continued contacts with Galtieri's emissaries, such as Brigadier Miret from Buenos Aires, Mallea Gil from Washington and Enrique Ros in New York, rubbed salt in the wounds of his failed mission. On 11 May, Haig responded by secretly dispatching Vernon Walters back to Buenos Aires to see whether there might be room for yet more Washington diplomacy. Walters saw all the junta members and returned with the unsurprising message that they thought Haig ought to be leaning on Thatcher in the same way that he had previously tried to lean on them.

De Cuellar was again taken aback by this new Washington salient into the dispute, realising that Buenos Aires could now play two mediators off against each other. UN gossip was speculating about the nature of the coup Walters (an old CIA hand) was planning. In Britain the Tory press became convinced that the Foreign Office was once more about to cheat them of military success. Even the threatened cancellation of the Pope's long-awaited visit and Britain's possible exclusion from the World Cup did not dampen their ardour. Thatcher conceded Pym's argument that 'every avenue of negotiation' had to be tried, though she found it increasingly hard to see why. True, EEC sanctions were due for renewal, and Britain should not be seen to snub the UN Secretary General or risk having to use a Security Council veto before a landing. But the Argentine strategy was clearly to keep talking as long as possible to wear down the task force and Mrs Thatcher refused to play any part in that game. At one point, she went to bed inclined to accept one compromise and woke up adamant, convinced it would merely give ground to the enemy. Nor could she see anything but Foreign Office vacuity in Pym's references to 'our long-term relations with Latin America'.

This conflict of heart and head put Mrs Thatcher in the worst of moods. A stormy debate in the Commons on Thursday, 13 May, found her petulant and finally angry as her predecessor, Edward Heath, paid a series of pointed compliments to Pym for his peace efforts. Nothing better illustrated the strained relations between Prime Minister and Foreign Secretary than her glowering reaction to these remarks. Pym nonetheless ended the day worse off, after a grilling from the backbench 1922 Committee on the implications of the UN initiative. As so often before, Mrs Thatcher's line to her backbenchers had been kept in good repair by her ubiquitous parliamentary private secretary, Ian Gow. Hard-line Tory MPs knew they were speaking to her wishes in warning Pym off any revival of such concessions as were offered to Belaunde. He left the House that evening with more cries of 'No Surrender!' in his ears. It might almost have been Galtieri's army council meeting a month earlier.

Just as Britain was being driven by internal pressure towards a marginally tougher stance, Argentina's solid negotiating position showed a slight wobble. On Wednesday, the 12th, the pressure of Walters in Buenos Aires and de Cuellar and Ros in New York produced from the junta a private note offering what appeared to be a major concession: that a transfer of sovereignty to a fixed deadline would no longer be a precondition of settlement. Argentina, it said, would merely 'negotiate in search of a recognition of its sovereignty'. Argentine spokesmen in the US took their cue and appeared on morning television and at press conferences emphasising 'sovereignty is not a precondition'. How much weight should be attached to this is hard to judge. Roughly the same concession had been offered to Haig at the start of his mission and then been withdrawn. Besides, Argentina was now relying on the interim administration making any return to British rule inconceivable by permitting Buenos Aires to flood the islands with Argentine settlers. To add to the confusion, Galtieri swore at a public rally that 'the Argentine flag will never come down over the Malvinas' as part of any settlement. A huge opposition meeting that same week warned the junta that 'the recovery of the Malvinas was legitimate, but it was done by a government with dirty hands. If they try to

betray the people over the Malvinas, it will be a double deception.'
No one reading these words in New York or London could have
been under many illusions.

Thursday's embarrassments in the Commons finally exhausted
Thatcher's patience with diplomacy. Parsons in New York, the one
Foreign Office figure with whom she appeared to have established
a rapport, was arguing that the time had come to present Britain's
position coherently on paper. Thatcher promptly summoned both
him and Henderson back and girded the war cabinet for what she
intended to be Britain's last offer. On the Friday, Admiral Fieldhouse made his first presentation to the war cabinet of the dispositions of ships and men for Operation Sutton, the landing at San
Carlos, scheduled for the weekend of 21–22 May. Mrs Thatcher was
adamant that she could not have a leisurely UN peace initiative
meandering back and forth across the Atlantic just when the task
force was going in guns blazing. It had to be brought to a head in
a matter of days. Henderson and Parsons lunched with Acland at
the Garrick Club on Saturday, the 15th, to prepare for what was to
be the denouement of Britain's Falklands diplomacy.

The following day's war cabinet at Chequers is recalled by
participants variously as 'Mrs Thatcher's High Noon with the FO'
or merely 'a totally horrendous bull session'. The Prime Minister
had put in the first blow by telling the Scottish Tories at Perth on
the Friday, 'I should not be doing my duty if I did not warn you in
the simplest and clearest terms that . . . a negotiated settlement
may prove to be unobtainable.' From the start of the meeting,
Parsons had to struggle to concentrate her mind on the need at
least to clear decks for war in the most advantageous manner. It
was unquestionably Parsons's finest hour. Talkative, direct and
without the smoothness Mrs Thatcher finds so grating in diplomats, he sparred with her as few had dared. 'Prime Minister,' he
would interrupt, 'if I may finish what I was saying I think you
might agree with me.' He scrupulously avoided dangerous phrases
such as 'Britain's future good relations demand . . .' and used
instead such Thatcher favourites as 'Britain's interests require . . .'

Mrs Thatcher was so impressed that she later asked Parsons to join her Downing Street staff to keep guard on his old department – despite his being a long-standing Labour supporter.

Parsons's task at Chequers was to produce a package which would establish in de Cuellar's mind that Britain was still serious about negotiating a settlement. It had to be one which would not be politically disastrous for the government if accepted by Argentina, yet it should not seem intransigent if, as expected, it were rejected. It was, in other words, the final round of the diplomatic gamble which Mrs Thatcher had been pursuing in tandem with her military gamble. The proposals were hardly less concessionary than those accepted under the Peruvian plan, though by being more specific as to safeguards for British interests they seemed tougher. There was the offer of mutual withdrawal of forces, the timing and verification of which were laid down in meticulous detail. Rather than a returning British governor, there would be a UN administrator with his own staff. More stringent, the Falklands would for the interim period be governed 'in accordance with the laws and practices traditionally obtaining'. There would be just three observers from Britain and three from Argentina. Further negotiations would be 'without prejudice' and would be completed 'with a sense of urgency' by the end of the year; South Georgia would be excluded. Much of this was code for a 'recognisably British administration' and required a major compromise from Buenos Aires. That said, Britain had conceded titular sovereignty to the UN and a 'creeping loss of sovereignty' would have been certain in the longer term. Buenos Aires would certainly have received some reward for its aggression.

It was hard to see the Argentine leaders accepting such a package at this stage. The aggression which had so far won them so much imprisoned them into requiring so much more. The plan was taken back to New York by Parsons and handed to de Cuellar with a request for an urgent response from Argentina. The junta was now trapped by its own propaganda and decided to retreat to a hard line. Ros told de Cuellar that his government wanted all forces to withdraw to their 'normal bases'; the UN would have to have exclusive authority with no local or British involvement; there should be free access for Argentine nationals during the interim period; talks on sovereignty should be completed by the year end or the issue would revert to the full UN General Assembly, where Argentina felt sure of majority support.

This effective rejection of the British offer stimulated a frantic last-minute lobbying effort in New York. Ros was known to be personally dismayed at the junta's reaction. De Cuellar was appalled, realising that time had now run out on him. Mrs Kirkpatrick and her Spanish-speaking deputy, Jose Sorzano, saw a succession of Argentine emissaries – businessmen and diplomats as well as officers – in a bid to get them to accept. Sorzano told Miret and Mallea Gil to their faces that the British were going 'to kick the hell out of you'. They just bleakly denied it. Mrs Kirkpatrick was convinced a land war would spell catastrophe for US relations with South America. She feared Costa Mendes had been speaking for the whole continent when he had earlier told Haig direct, 'If there's war, it's all your fault.'

*

On Tuesday, 18 May, the chiefs of staff made their formal presentation of Operation Sutton to the war cabinet. In the words of one of those present, it was a 'classic of British military history'. Each service chief in turn described the part his forces were playing and, more important, gave his personal assessment of the risks ahead. It is interesting that the army and RAF forecast substantially greater losses of ships than the Royal Navy; indeed, Sir Edwin Bramall anticipated even more sinkings than eventually took place. But again Lewin's meticulous rehearsal paid dividends. Without underplaying the shortcomings of the campaign so far, especially in the matter of air cover, the chiefs conveyed full confidence in their ability to do what the government had asked of them. Later, the plan for the San Carlos landing was presented to the full cabinet; it was the first they had been told of it. No one now seriously believed anything could forestall the land war.

The following day, news of the Argentine response to the British proposals was received by the war cabinet with resignation rather than surprise. The order duly went from Northwood to Woodward aboard *Hermes* that he should proceed with Operation Sutton at his own discretion. From this point it would have taken a deliberate decision to abort the landing – indeed a sudden concession from Buenos Aires would have caused havoc to the task force. The war cabinet was also adamant that all concessions previously offered in the negotiations should be publicly withdrawn. Britain could not risk a ceasefire call in mid-operation on the basis of 'a little more give and take on one or two points'.

A white paper was prepared – described by officials as more 'red, white and blue' – to be published on the Thursday as the Prime Minister made a statement to Parliament. Her announcement of the failure of the peace process was greeted with either relief or disappointment, but virtually no opposition. On reading the white paper, Michael Foot paid her a genuine tribute. The government's case, he said, was 'fair and formidable'. By publicly withdrawing the various concessions made in it before her back-benchers even had time to examine them, Mrs Thatcher nipped in the bud any incipient rebellion from that quarter. The decks were now clear for war.

The Falklands white paper ended the peace process as far as any British compromise was concerned. It appeared to vindicate the Prime Minister's view that negotiation would never drive the Argentinians from the islands and that to offer concessions was a dangerous gamble. It put at risk the promises made when the task force sailed. It therefore jeopardised the political statement which the force represented. The white paper was also a vindication of the Foreign Office argument that Britain had to be seen to try. The proposals could not be called intransigent or deliberately designed to provoke an Argentine rejection. By sustaining the search for peace over six long weeks, Britain went into the land war with real advantages. Sanctions and embargoes against the enemy were intact (EEC sanctions were temporarily renewed on 17 May) and European support remained solid. Britain's massive retaliation appeared blessed with UN approval. Argentina was virtually without friends, and received little practical support even from her Latin American neighbours. Given the close balance of military advantage in the South Atlantic these were no small benefits. Diplomacy may have been powerless to stop war once the task force had sailed. It was by no means powerless in contributing to its eventual success.

11 » OPERATION SUTTON

An operation for a landing with a view to the repossession
of the Falkland Islands . . .

3 Commando Brigade orders, May 1982

In the first days of May, by helicopter and fast inflatable boat, parties from G Squadron SAS and the SBS began landing ashore on the Falklands to assess the strength, condition and deployment of the Argentine forces on the islands. 'I can tell you immediately what beaches are suitable for landing the brigade,' Brigadier Julian Thompson told the naval staff in mid-April, 'but until I know what enemy are on them, I can't tell you which one I would choose.' No plan for an amphibious landing could be formed until reconnaissance had taken place. This could not begin until the ships of Woodward's battle group were available to insert special forces teams. The huge 4,000-ton nuclear submarines – each as big as a Type 42 destroyer – drew too much water to move close inshore. Northwood had been slow to mobilise one of the smaller 'O' class patrol submarines ideally suited for special operations – *Onyx* did not reach the operational area until 28 May, after a month on passage. SAS proposals to insert patrols by high-altitude, low-opening parachute drop were rejected as too harzardous.

Before the naval Sea King helicopters from Yeovilton embarked on the carriers, 846 Squadron's CO, Lieutenant Commander Simon Thornewill, was telephoned by a friend at the Royal Aircraft Establishment at Farnborough. 'Would you like to take along a few sets of the new PNG?' he was asked. Yes, Thornewill would. In great haste, four helicopters were modified for the use of the most modern American passive night goggles. The pilots scraped in a few hours' training over Salisbury Plain. Now, at sea on *Hermes*, the PNG-equipped Sea Kings showed that their crews could fly in total darkness with exceptional accuracy. PNG was to be one of the decisive British weapons of the war. Early in May, the helicopters were sliding 20 feet above the sea and the coastline of the Falklands to land reconnaissance parties. The men plodded away across the hills, burdened by their huge packs, to select lying-up positions before dawn came. The six SBS teams concentrated chiefly on possible coastal landing sites. Seven four-man SAS patrols were deployed: three on West Falkland, one around Darwin, one above Bluff Cove, and three around Port Stanley, where it was already evident that the bulk of the enemy's forces were concentrated. 'We started out with a blank map of the Falklands,' said Julian Thompson, 'and fired special forces like a shotgun across the islands to see what they found.'

'The Falklands are everybody's playground now,' said an SAS officer laconically towards the end of the war. 'But in the beginning it was like landing on the other side of the moon. We knew nothing about what to expect.' Contrary to popular mythology, the British gained no intelligence of value from the Falklands population during the weeks of the Argentine occupation. Now, the British teams spent hours of daylight lying motionless – often freezing, always wet – in their meticulously camouflaged positions in the peat and tussock grass, watching the enemy going about their business around their trenches and gun positions. They formed an impression of an indolent, apathetic army careless of military routines, indifferent to their officers, suffering acutely from the weather. The Argentinians possessed small, elite special forces. But the line infantry were almost all conscripts, some retained in the army beyond their time of service to garrison the Falklands; many illiterate indians; some with only two to three months' training. They possessed fully automatic FN rifles which delivered more firepower than the British SLR; general-purpose machine-guns identical to those of the marines and paras; ample night-vision equipment superior to anything the task force carried; officers trained by the Americans, with much experience of counter-insurgency. But, above all, Major General Mario Menendez's army lacked the training and discipline in washing, changing clothes, keeping dry, looking after each other, which was second nature to the British. 'That sort of thing is not *macho*,' said a Royal Marine with great experience of Latin America. Yet it was vital to maintaining the condition and morale of men living on the barren hillsides of the Falklands. Already, before the British had even landed, the enemy's rank and file were unhappy and inadequately fed, unsure of why they were on the Malvinas, poorly equipped to remain there.

The Argentinians were patrolling half-heartedly on foot and by helicopter between the outlying settlements. They had placed a strong garrison at Darwin and Goose Green, together with substantial elements on Pebble Island, and at Fox Bay and Port Howard on West Falkland. The enemy's chief strength was overwhelmingly concentrated around Port Stanley. The deployments of the island's governor, General Menendez, were perfectly sound: the capital was the vital ground that he must hold, and he had begun to fortify the surrounding hill line. He could not hope to defend every possible landing site against the British. But, with his formidable helicopter lift of Chinooks, Pumas and Hueys, he could move his strategic reserve to mount a rapid counter-attack wherever the commando brigade came ashore.

*

The deployment of the principal Argentine forces was as follows:*

Around Port Stanley under General Joffre of 10 Brigade
3, 4, 6, 7, 25 Regiments (approximately 1,000 men each)
5th Marine Battalion (about 600 men)

---

* Incomplete, but based upon the best information available at time of publication.

3rd Artillery Battalion (30 × 105 mm, 4 × 155 mm guns)
An armoured car squadron with 12 Panhard vehicles
181 Military Police and Intelligence Company
601 Anti-Aircraft Battalion
A helicopter unit with 2 × Chinook, 9 × Huey UHIH,
    2 × Augusta 190a attack, 3 × Puma aircraft

At Goose Green
2, 12 Regiments (elements of)
Elements of 601 AA battalion
3 × 105 mm guns
Air force elements

On West Falkland under General Paral of 3 Brigade
8 Regiment
9 Engineer Company (at Fox Bay)
5 Regiment
9 Engineer Company (at Port Howard)
120 naval air personnel on Pebble Island

For the planning staffs at Northwood and on *Fearless*, there were three obvious options for an amphibious landing. First, to go to Steveley Bay on West Falkland, the most cautious choice in that it lay furthest from any possible Argentine ground response. Second, to secure a landing place on East Falkland, still at comfortable distance from the enemy: at a very early stage, San Carlos and Bluff Cove began to be considered in this context. Third – and in many ways most appealing – to land as close as possible to the main objective, Stanley. Once a direct assault on the capital had been rejected as impossibly hazardous, the nearest feasible landing site appeared to be in Berkeley Sound, to the north. The soldiers disliked the Steveley Bay alternative because it flouted every rule of warfare about the concentration of force against the main objective – 'like landing on Anglesey to attack Cardiff ', as Thompson expressed it acidly. Steveley Bay remained on the books principally because of Woodward's preoccupation with building an airstrip to relieve the pressure on his carriers, and because it still seemed possible that the war cabinet would sanction a landing only on West Falkland. San Carlos attracted some of the same objections – it seemed a very long way from Port Stanley, as the Chief of the General Staff Sir Edwin Bramall was among those to point out. The planners were deeply conscious of the need for a quick campaign if the landing force was ordered to go in. The weather and the huge logistic problems suggested that the condition of the commando brigade must deteriorate rapidly as the weeks went by.

Under the hot Ascension Island sun, the staff in *Fearless* wrestled with plans for a total seven possible landings in three alternative locations. It was a huge burden to impose upon a brigade staff, involving complexities and strategic dilemmas far above their normal military level. Each day, Thompson talked at length on the secure D Triple S phone to Northwood. Intelligence now estimated the total enemy strength on the islands at 10,000 plus. It had become clear that more British troops would be needed. Thompson was to get another battalion immediately – 2 Para – and 5 Infantry Brigade was to prepare to sail. Thompson's force should be capable of making the initial landing – which it was agreed must be at a point where there would be no immediate ground resistance. Then 5 Brigade would join them in the beach-head, and Major General Jeremy Moore would come down to assume command of the entire division. Moore decided to remain at Northwood for the time being, until an irrevocable decision had been taken to commit the landing force. *Fearless*'s sister ship *Intrepid* was being hastily recommissioned and sent to Ascension to reinforce the landing-craft strength and provide an additional helicopter platform. The 12,000-ton assault ships had been criticised in the past for requiring big crews – 600 strong – while being capable of carrying only limited numbers of troops for short periods. But they were the sole specially equipped command and assault platforms that the British possessed, with their huge floodable docks that became floating harbours for landing craft and small boats, their purpose-built amphibious operations rooms and flight decks. Without these ships, an armed landing on the Falklands would have been literally unthinkable.

Late in April, it became clear that, to allow the entire strengthened amphibious force to concentrate before a landing, the 'time window' for going ashore must be put back. It was now fixed between 19 May and 3 June. There was a moment of consternation about security on *Fearless* when, on the basis of these dates, the force's likely departure date from Ascension was posted among routine orders on the ship's notice board. Mail censorship was introduced forthwith. Meanwhile, 3 Commando Brigade disembarked units in rotation from *Canberra* and the landing ships for invaluable practice in landing-craft drill and live-weapon firing. On the vessels themselves, a huge 'crossdecking' operation was taking place. Stores were shuttled by helicopter from the overcrowded airfield, now handling more than three hundred air movements a day in place of its customary five a year. Vast quantities of equipment and ammunition were being shuffled between the ships in an attempt to make an inventory of all that had been loaded in such haste in England, and to ensure that henceforth supplies were 'tactically loaded', to emerge in the proper order after the assault landing. Simon Thornewill and his pilots became profoundly concerned that the intensive flying was eating away the helicopters' potential serviceability for the campaign. All 3 Commando Brigade's planning at this stage assumed that its battalions would leapfrog across the Falklands by air. Thompson later admitted that they had gravely underestimated the pressure on helicopters for shifting vital stores and ammunition. There would be precious little capacity to spare for moving men. He had asked Northwood to send more aircraft, more armour, more guns. But throughout the campaign the shortage of helicopters would be critical.

The amphibious planners worked by day and night in the crowded little steel caverns of *Fearless*, refining options. Major Roderick Macdonald, the sharp, imaginative engineer CO, worked out possible Argentine defensive plans based upon the methods that his own men would have used to cover the same positions. But this approach had its limitations.

'Why can't we land there?' the senior gunner, a fatherly ex-ranker named Mike Holroyd-Smith, asked a naval staff officer in surprise one day as they pored over a map.

'It's mined,' said the sailor simply.

'How do we know it's mined?' asked Holroyd-Smith.

'Well, we'd put mines there if we were defending it,' explained the sailor.

'On that basis,' said the gunner drily, 'we simply end up with everything mined.'

Hard intelligence from the islands was still arriving only in a trickle, not least because the SAS and SBS teams ashore – sometimes surviving twelve days at a stretch without resupply or personal contact with the ships – lacked facilities for 'burst transmission', the technology which enables an operator to draft a long message and then flash it across the ether in seconds. On the Falklands, the British teams were obliged to restrict their signals to brief, conventionally keyed reports to avoid the risk of radio location by the Argentinians' excellent modern interception equipment. There were also failures of liaison. Thompson's men were exasperated to discover that the RAF had established a highly secret intelligence cell ashore on Ascension Island, which was restricting everything that it learned for the use of its Vulcan crews. It was an example of an age-old problem.

It was also remarkable how little the amphibious planners were told about the deliberations at Northwood or the activities of the battle group. 'I think that Julian feels a little gloomy and pressured,' a marine CO wrote in his diary. 'We need a clear directive – either "Go and do it", or "Get back home".' All the landing-force officers craved clear instructions. Yet these could scarcely be provided as long as the political and diplomatic deadlock remained. There was an unexplained 'flap' at Ascension on 22 April, when Thompson was suddenly asked if his brigade could be ready to sail within six hours, or, failing that, the following morning. Training was cancelled, troops were hastily brought back from the shore, the ships prepared to move. That night, equally without explanation, they were stood down again. London had apparently considered, then rejected, a new means of increasing the diplomatic pressure. The 'flap' had one side effect that later proved significant: the scheduled test-firing of the Rapier ground-to-air missile launchers was cancelled. Any necessary fine-tuning or correction would have to take place after the landing on the Falklands. Yet the landing force and Admiral Woodward himself were placing an almost mystical faith in Rapier's ability to provide an umbrella against air attack within hours of the first troops reaching the shore.

The monotony of the routine in the Ascension anchorage was enlivened by a succession of false alarms. On 25 April, a 'flap' began about the possibility of an enemy submarine in the area. Each night thereafter, the principal units of the task force put to sea and passed the hours of darkness circling the island. A frigate was dispatched post-haste one morning to chase away an Argentine merchantman lurking in the area. A Russian spy ship hung off-shore for some days, and a procession of Soviet surveillance aircraft overflew the ships, causing serious concern about the possible passage of information to Buenos Aires – although, after the war, Argentine officers of all ranks vehemently denied that they had received any data from Moscow. On 27/28 April, 45 Commando spent a fiercely hot, irritating two days combing the barren moun-tainsides for a party of enemy saboteurs who were reported to have got ashore. The danger of sabotage at Ascension was a persistent source of concern to the British. At about the same time, at another British staging-post life was momentarily enlivened by a similar report on the Rock of Gibraltar.

On the ships at Ascension, the days passed in relentless physi-cal training, small-arms drill, equipment checks, lectures and videos about the Falklands and their people, sunbathing around the swimming pools and watching bloodthirsty evening films in the lounges. *Canberra* was a great deal more comfortable than most

troopships, but by the fourth week at sea she had come to seem a
dreary prison. Rumour ran rife. Every corner of the ship echoed to
the sounds of clashing breechblocks and shouted orders, jogging
feet shaking the deckheads. The main broadcast system gave forth
its metallic commands with maddening regularity: 'Hands to flying
stations! Hands to flying stations! No more gash to be ditched!'
Most of the comforts and entertainments of a cruise liner had been
stripped out before she left Southampton. Every hour, on the hour,
the lilting strains of 'Lilliburlero' drifted from beneath a hundred
cabin doors, signalling the latest World Service news bulletin with
its reports of the faltering progress of diplomacy, and the activities
of the battle group. They seemed a planet away. The brigade staff's
affection for Admiral Woodward was not increased by a signal
received as they struggled over the choice of landing sites: 'There
are 4,700 square miles of the Falklands and only 10,000 Argentinians, which works out at two per square mile,' declared *Hermes*
impatiently. 'What's your problem?'

Thompson's problem, pondering which had worn him to
exhaustion, was that as a junior brigadier he was carrying the
responsibility for an operation on which the entire hopes of Britain
rested. Failure would be absolute. There would be no second
chances. Yet he possessed diminishing confidence in the Royal
Navy's direction and judgement of the campaign. In the first days
of May it was becoming apparent that the air threat was not being
defeated by the battle group in the south. At no stage was Thompson formally told that the navy's promise of decisive air superiority
could not be fulfilled. He and his staff merely became progressively, grimly, aware of the situation. 'If the air threat had been
properly appreciated, I don't think this whole venture would ever
have been undertaken,' said one of them later. By 7 May, Northwood was impatient for the amphibious landing force to move
from Ascension. The five slower logistics landing ships had already
departed, on 30 April. Thompson urgently requested time for 2
Para, newly arrived on the ferry *Norland*, to practise disembarkation
into landing craft. He was granted a few more hours. On 8 May at

Chequers, the war cabinet ordered the amphibious task group
south from Ascension. At 2200 hours they sailed for the South
Atlantic. The final order for them to land was still more than ten
days distant. But, from the moment that they cast loose from
Ascension, few men in the ships doubted that they would now be
called upon to go ashore.

A prime choice for the assault location remained the north end
of Berkeley Sound, above Port Stanley. Several of the unit COs
were less than happy about this: the plan called for a complex
assault, overwhelmingly dependent on helicopters to secure the
high ground above the anchorage. If any mishap dislocated operations – above all, if the weather closed in on flying – the Argentinians would have a chance of seizing the hills and mounting a
formidable counter-attack within easy reach of their own bases.
Some officers were already convinced that this risk was acceptable,
because the Argentinians were too incompetent to move swiftly
against the British. If the Berkeley Sound plan succeeded, the
commando brigade would immediately be positioned within a
single bound of Port Stanley, with a chance of ending the war in
a week. Everything that the SAS had reported about the condition
and behaviour of the enemy suggested that 'after one good push,
they would fold'. The same arguments were advanced in support
of a landing further north, in the Cow Bay–Volunteer Bay area, for
which considerable detailed planning was also done.

The amphibious staffs had spent many hours discussing the
merits of a landing at San Carlos Bay, westwards on the opposite
side of the island. The long, narrow bay pushed two fingers inland.
One harboured the little settlement at Port San Carlos. In the other
lay the San Carlos settlement, and across the water the abandoned
sheep-carcase refrigeration plant at Ajax Bay. The objections to San
Carlos were that it was far from Port Stanley, and within easy
reach of the strong enemy garrison 13 miles southwards at the
adjoining settlements of Darwin–Goose Green. The beaches were
not ideal for landing large quantities of men and stores. There was
a danger that, since the bay was an obvious choice for a landing,

the Argentinians had mined the sea approaches. It was also over-looked by high ground, from which the enemy could bring down a devastating fire if they succeeded in deploying along it.

But the case for a protected anchorage, as far as possible from Argentine artillery, proved decisive. The naval staff had become deeply concerned by intelligence reports that Berkeley Sound and possibly Cow Bay were mined. Throughout the last week of April and the first week of May, the planners on *Fearless* had been passing on the progress of their deliberations to Northwood. In Britain, by late April, the chiefs of staff had become convinced that San Carlos was the right option. The army accepted the Royal Navy's argu-ments. But, presumably to preserve the freedom of debate on *Fearless*, they had not passed on their conclusions to Thompson and Clapp. On 8 May, Clapp at last signalled Northwood and asked for confirmation that they accepted the amphibious force view that San Carlos was the right choice, since it was becoming essential to 'go firm' on operational planning. Northwood concurred immedi-ately. It was to be San Carlos Bay, 50 miles east of Port Stanley on the opposite coast of East Falkland.

The SBS reported that there were no enemy whatever around San Carlos. It was visited occasionally by patrols, and there was an Argentine outpost overlooking the approach on Fanning Head. This would have to be 'taken out' before H-Hour. The SBS found no evidence of mines on the shore, nor could they see any mineclaying taking place at sea. The same high ground that threat-ened ships as they entered the anchorage would provide superb protection once they were safe inside it. Enemy aircraft would have only a few seconds in which to pick and aim for their target after crossing the ridge line. Rapier could be sited on the crests, at positions scientifically chosen by computers in Britain's chief radar research establishment at Malvern. It would be extremely difficult for an enemy submarine to penetrate San Carlos Water, and impossible for an Exocet missile to be used there. Both before and since the end of the war, there was a body of British service opinion which held that the landing force could have adopted a bolder approach and launched itself headlong against the enemy around Port Stanley. But this was an overwhelmingly political war. It was critical that casualties should be kept to a minimum if final victory was to seem worth the purchase. With hindsight, the choice of San Carlos Water as a landing site seems superbly judged. Admiral Fieldhouse, Commodore Clapp, Brigadier Thompson and his staff – especially Ewen Southby-Tailyour – contributed critically to victory by their shrewd assessment and final decision.

The war cabinet had already been informed of the landing plans. A formal presentation of the strategy for the San Carlos landing was made by Moore and Fieldhouse at Downing Street on 27 April. The options were displayed on maps. The Royal Marines' preference for Berkeley Sound was explained, as were the reasons for rejecting it in favour of San Carlos. Ministers asked what the service chiefs called 'the obvious questions', about the distance from the objective, about air cover and particularly about the danger of sending in *Canberra*. Each had been predicted and was crisply answered. The only lacuna in the presentation, it was later recalled, was the absence of any discussion of what the land forces would do once ashore. The intention remained at this stage for the sea war to have been won by the time San Carlos was reached. Operation Sutton was simply about getting land forces ashore. After that it was 'assumed they would simply go on and win'. War cabinet declared that it was immensely impressed with the presentation. The Prime Minister went out of her way to congratulate Lewin: 'Your chaps seem to have got your act together since last time.'

*

On 10 May, helicopters carried the unit COs of 3 Commando Brigade from the troopships to *Fearless* for an orders group. Some sixty naval, army and Royal Marine officers gathered in the wardroom to hear Thompson deliver his briefing. San Carlos was to be the place. The date remained unknown. The brigadier stressed that the decision about whether they should land at all still remained in the hands of the war cabinet. But they would now proceed towards a D-Day some time after 19 May until they were told to do otherwise. The two parachute battalions, together with 40 and 45 Commandos, would land first, while 42 Commando remained in reserve aboard *Canberra*. There were some raised eyebrows at the news that *Canberra* was to go all the way into the beaches with them. But not only did the huge ship contain important stores, she was also considered safer in San Carlos Water than offshore. There was still enormous faith in the combined ability of Rapier and the navy to protect the ships in anchorage, and it was impossible to crossdeck the brigade on to the assault ships until a few hours before the landing, because of the cramped conditions they would face. Besides, the staff had worked out that, even if the worst happened and *Canberra* sank in San Carlos, with her bottom on the seabed her upper decks would still be above the surface. Loss of life should be limited.

The task of the amphibious force would be to make a brigade landing. Thereafter, according to the directive from Northwood, they would exploit out of the beach-head only 'as far as is safe, sound and sensible', while they awaited the coming of 5 Infantry Brigade. This was to sail from Southampton aboard the liner *QE2* on 12 May.

There was intense debate during the weeks before the assault about how aggressively the British special forces ashore should act. Lieutenant Colonel Michael Rose, the brilliant and single-minded officer commanding 22nd SAS, threw out ideas like some strategic word-processing machine. He was forty-two, an Oxford PPE graduate, a stepson of the novelist John Masters, with the sort of hawkish good looks Hollywood might impose upon a CO of the SAS. A Coldstream Guardsman who had served with the SAS all over the world, Rose stalked the conference rooms of *Fearless*, fixing his piercing eye and outspoken comment upon every aspect of the planning. Like his SBS counterpart, the soldier was frustrated at having his headquarters in a steel cabin lashed to the superstructure of the command ship, while his men were operating with the battle group, from *Hermes* and a variety of frigates. However, the superb portable satellite communications of the SAS enabled him to talk freely each day both with his squadrons and with his base in Britain. At one stage, there was discussion of the possibility of sending disguised SAS men into Port Stanley, conceivably to raid the enemy's headquarters. But the risk of an embarrassing fiasco seemed to outweigh any military gain. The SAS were learning all they were likely to from the heights overlooking the town.

*

There was great concern about the threat presented by Argentine ground-attack aircraft when the British beach-head had been established. A substantial number of planes were believed to be based on the airstrip at Pebble Island, north of West Falkland. On the night of 11 May, an eight-man SAS team from D Squadron was landed on the mainland of West Falkland by PNG helicopter, together with canoes. The following day they lay up, waiting for darkness. But when it came, the weather conditions were too rough to launch their canoes. They lingered through another day, then paddled silently across the narrow strip of sea to Pebble Island, and passed the next day watching Argentine movements around the settlement and airfield from closely concealed positions. They confirmed the presence of a garrison of at least a hundred men, and a substantial number of enemy aircraft.

On the night of 14 May, the team marked a landing zone and guided in two Sea Kings from *Hermes* carrying forty-five men of D Squadron under Major Cedric Delves, together with Captain Chris Brown's naval gunfire support team from 148 Battery, 29 Commando Gunners. In recent years, naval gunfire support had seemed an increasingly redundant art. At the outbreak of the Falklands campaign, 148 Battery was within three months of dissolution by Ministry of Defence decree. Now, its skills were critical to every operation. Forward observers were all commando-trained special-forces officers. Chris Brown had already survived the landing on

South Georgia and an episode in which his helicopter force-landed on East Falkland after exchanging fire with an enemy warship. That night of 14 May, within a few minutes of landing on Pebble Island with D Squadron, he was calmly calling down fire on Argentine positions from the supporting naval frigates.

They got ashore late in fierce winds, and abandoned a plan for one troop to make contact with the civilians in the settlement. Instead, these men held the approaches against a possible Argentine counter-attack, while the remainder of the SAS moved rapidly among the enemy aircraft, placing demolition charges. The Argentinians, stationed among the shearing sheds half a mile down the gentle slope from the airfield, did not respond until the British began to withdraw. Then, as they moved towards the Sea Kings amidst the explosion of their charges and enemy ammunition, the Argentinians fired a remote-controlled charge which exploded close to them, showering the entire party with mud and slightly wounding two men. A half-hearted enemy counter-attack petered out when the British shot down the officer leading it. They reached the ships having totally destroyed eleven Argentine aircraft without losing a man, and retired at 29 knots in a Force 9 gale. It was a classic SAS operation, 'the kind of thing we have not had the chance to do since World War II', in the words of one of their officers. The morale of the landing force was much lifted by the Pebble Island raid – its success was evidence of what a well-handled British force could achieve against far larger numbers of the Argentinians.

*

At a meeting on *Fearless* 900 miles off Port Stanley, on 13 May, Julian Thompson had given the COs their final orders for Operation Sutton – 'operations related to the repossession of the Falklands . . .' The British officers were now as excited, expectant, for the most part as passionately confident and eager, as their men. 'I'm a lucky man,' Lieutenant Colonel Andrew Whitehead of 5 Commando wrote in his diary. 'Nothing like this has even been considered since Suez . . .' They were still vividly conscious of the air threat. Lieutenant Colonel Hew Pike of 3 Para wrote, 'The main worry at present is the vulnerability of the fleet to air attack, and it will be a great relief to everyone when this week is over, I think.' But there was little doubt in their minds that '3 Commando Brigade can hack it'. Whitehead wrote, 'I have never known the men so enthusiastic, motivated, and with such high morale.' In the cinema of *Canberra*, audiences of tense, fascinated young men crowded the seats, aisles and entrances to hear their intelligence officers outline the enemy's known deployments on the Falklands, flick through the now-familiar slides of his aircraft, tanks, guns.

A deep strand of sentimentality runs through all military life. On the passage south, the amphibious force had been troubled by no flicker of embarrassment about watching the commando forces band beat retreat on the flight deck of *Canberra*, perform a fervent 'Rule Britannia' not once but on many nights, play the *1812 Overture* aboard the freighter *Elk*, with orchestration from her Bofors guns, at the direction of the ship's delightfully picaresque captain. They were enormously proud of participating in this last, freakish fling of imperial adventure. Whatever the diplomats were saying in London and New York, the brigade now felt confident that it would receive the order to land. The skin of boredom and routine assumed after five weeks at sea fell quickly away. Men worked with intense concentration to prepare their equipment, camouflage their helmets, tape the metal frames of their packs, stockpile supplies of 'nutty'.

On 15 May, the civilians aboard the ships, including press correspondents, were sobered by the formal reading of the Declaration of Active Service, placing them under military discipline. Through the huge windows of *Canberra* – ruthlessly blacked out by night since Ascension Island – the marines looked out on an extraordinary panorama of nostalgia, a glimpse back through the time machine to The Cruel Sea. The vessels of the landing force ploughing zigzagging across the horizon, the silhouettes of the escorting frigates just visible between rain squalls. Even the big assault ships bounced spectacularly in the huge seas, although the landing force had now been so long afloat that few men were troubled by sickness. The promenade decks of *Canberra*, round which squads of men had run relentlessly for five, ten miles each day for five weeks of the passage, were now lashed by spray. The clumsy landing ships laden with vehicles, guns and stores wallowed like tired old roller-coasters. On the upper works of every vessel, gun crews manned Bofors, Oerlikons, GP machine-guns, Blowpipe missiles, huddled behind bulkheads in their heavy clothing and balaclavas and anti-flash capes. Sometimes during great passages of history, men are only aware of the significance of what they have seen when events have passed. But hundreds of men on the ships in the South Atlantic, from their admiral downwards, had begun to keep diaries. They knew from the moment that they passed Ascension Island that they were taking part in one of the great dramas of British postwar history. Most secretly nursed a corner of fear about what they were about to do. But they were part of a professional fighting force, perhaps the most highly trained and best-equipped that Britain had ever sent to war. Their arctic clothing and sleeping bags were the finest that money could buy, their rations scientifically selected for men fighting in extreme conditions, their weapons well proven, their units welded by years of working in concert. It is not surprising that the principal sensations among both officers and men were exhilaration at the chance to test their skills, and utter assurance in their own ability to defeat the enemy.

'Good luck, and may your God go with you,' said Lieutenant Colonel Malcolm Hunt as he ended his final briefing to the six hundred young men of his 40 Commando, sitting in a tight, earnest throng around his feet in the main lounge of *Canberra*. On the last Sunday morning before the landing, in the middle of the church service in the cinema the tannoy interrupted: 'Air attack threat, warning yellow! Air defence teams close up!' A few moments later, the bridge announced that there was air activity over the battle group, and details would be announced when they became available. The congregation continued with the singing of 'For Those In Peril On The Sea'. It was impossible not to be profoundly moved by the mood of the moment.

*

On 18 May, the amphibious force linked up with *Hermes*. Nothing was said in signal traffic of the navy's disappointment about the failure to win the air battle. Brigadier Thompson was told that Woodward was confident of the ships' ability to provide local air superiority over the beach-head. The Harriers would provide the strongest possible combat air patrols throughout the hours of daylight.

That day brought a critical reinforcement to the air strength: the container ship *Atlantic Conveyor* had brought with her from Britain a further twelve Harrier aircraft. These were now flown aboard the carriers. Four were RAF GR3 ground-attack aircraft, while the others were from the hastily constituted 809 Naval Sea Harrier Squadron, flown by pilots recalled from all over the world – Hugh Slade from Australia, Bill Covington from Arizona, Al Craig from Germany. They brought with them twenty-four much-needed extra maintenance crew. The following day, four further GR3s landed after one of the most remarkable single-seat air-refuelled flights in history, from Britain via Ascension. The total Harrier strength had now risen to thirty-five aircraft.

Woodward was stripping his own group of all the frigates that he could muster – seven in all – to provide naval gunfire support and air defence for the landing force during the critical last hours at sea and first ashore. The Type 22s, *Broadsword* and *Brilliant*, with their Sea Wolf systems, would obviously be vital. Captain Coward of *Brilliant* said that the missiles could only provide effective cover if the convoy was closed up very tightly indeed, to shoebox dimensions by the normal standards of fleet deployment. Then, said Woodward, in shoebox formation the convoy would sail.

There was one last major problem. It was unthinkable to send the entire brigade to San Carlos in *Canberra*. To spread the risk, the units must be dispersed between the ships. Even then, the chiefs of staff had warned the war cabinet, they must accept the chance of losing at least one, conceivably two, major units in the course of the approach and landing. The weather conditions in the South Atlantic made a vast crossdecking operation involving 1,800 men in the open sea seem inconceivable. Commodore Clapp's staff told Northwood that they believed the only possible method was to take all the ships either to South Georgia or into sheltered water some way south of East Falkland, transfer the troops, then put to sea once more for the final run to San Carlos. It was an alarming proposal. Northwood flatly vetoed it. Somehow, the men must be transferred on the open sea; they could not use up precious helicopter hours for the operation. On the morning of the 19th, to the consternation of the marines, they received a signal from *Fearless* warning them to be prepared to crossdeck by jackstay transfer – moving one man at a time by line between the ships. It seemed one of the more astonishing orders of the campaign, and it was fortunate that it proved unnecessary. A minor miracle took place that day. The South Atlantic relapsed into a mild swell. The assault ships launched their LCUs – the big landing craft capable of carrying a hundred men apiece. One by one, they came alongside the lower galley port doors of *Canberra*. Long files of marines laden with arms and equipment began to move through the liner's dining rooms; they leaped heavily between the ship and the landing craft as it pitched alongside, and waited patiently in the wind and spray until a full load was ready to bump half a mile across the water to one of the assault ships. One man missed the jump, and crashed into the sea between the liner and the LCU. For two terrifying minutes, hundreds of men lining the rails watched desperate efforts to save him from being crushed. Then he was hauled inboard, wet and shocked, but somehow none the worse. By late afternoon, the huge, difficult crossdecking operation had been successfully completed. The landing force was ready.

That day, Woodward received a signal from Fieldhouse informing him that he could give the commando brigade the order to land in the Falklands at his discretion. All that was now needed was the worst possible weather to mask the ships' approach to the islands. Forecasting for the task force was an uncertain exercise, principally dependent on the skills of the experts aboard the ships, since bulletins from Argentina had been cut off. Now, the 'met' men on *Hermes* told FOFI that there was a seventy per cent probability of 'a good clag' on the following day, the 20th. Thereafter, clearer weather seemed to be moving in behind. Like Eisenhower before D-Day, Woodward now bore the sole responsibility for a decision on which he knew that the hopes of his nation rested. Julian Thompson wanted an evening approach to Falkland Sound in order that his men might have the maximum possible hours of darkness in which to secure their objectives. But the navy were certain that the final approach by sea was the critical phase. After a debate between Commodore Clapp and Brigadier Thompson, a compromise was agreed. H-Hour was put back six hours, to provide that much extra darkness for the fleet. Then Woodward ordered them to sail that night for a landing in the early hours of Friday, 21 May.

Aboard the assault ships, the marines and paras crowded into messdecks and passages, storerooms and cabins. There was no room for movement or comfort, only for men to lie down surrounded by their equipment, cleaning weapons, writing letters, reading the incessant lurid war stories that had been their chosen cultural diet throughout the passage south. Young officers huddled in knots in the cabins, poring over maps and orders, and older men wondered for the thousandth time in history about the schoolboy faces going to war. What food the ships could provide for such vast numbers beyond their complement was issued to men queueing in relays with their mugs and mess tins, then returning to crowd back into their spaces. In the eerily lit tank decks marines worked on their vehicles, mounting machine-guns and lashing down canvases. Final briefings were held, at which for the first time officers saw air photographs of the airfield at Port Stanley, with its solitary Vulcan crater. There was acid comment

on the effectiveness of the air blockade, after all that they had
heard on World Service about the incessant Harrier and gunfire
attacks. That night, in a moderate sea, the eleven ships of the
convoy, together with their powerful escort, crossed into the total
exclusion zone. Men seized what sleep they could on cabin floors
and piled crates, lying beside their weapons. They lay down with
the knowledge of one bitter tragedy: a Sea King helicopter transferring a large party of SAS to the assault ship *Intrepid* had struck
an albatross, whose remains smashed into the engine, cutting all
power and causing it to crash into the sea. Twenty-two men,
including twenty SAS, drowned before they could be rescued. It
was the worst single disaster that the regiment had suffered since
1945. Most of the men who died had survived the helicopter
crashes on South Georgia and the brilliant raid on Pebble Island.
3 Commando Brigade were much saddened. Yet it is in the
nature of men at war quickly to transfer their thoughts from
the tragedy of those who have gone to the perils they themselves
have still to face.

*

Long before first light on 20 May, the ships' crews had risen,
breakfasted and gone to action stations. The Argentine air force
had not yet demonstrated its formidable striking power. It was
entirely evident, however, that the most hazardous phase of the
landing operation began now, in the daylight hours before they
approached San Carlos. They were seeking to keep the enemy in
ignorance of their destination until the last possible moment. Until
afternoon, their course lay south-west, towards Port Stanley itself.
Only when they were just short of the coast of East Falkland would
they turn sharply west, heading for the entrance to Falkland Sound
between the two islands.

First light revealed a thick grey mist. The forecasters had got it
right. Peering out into the murk that Thursday morning from the
bridge of *Fearless*, the helmeted and flash-caped Jeremy Larken kept
up a cool stream of orders to the convoy. '*Canberra* has been told

repeatedly not to ditch gash. Now she is doing it again,' he said firmly. 'Tell her not to.' Floating rubbish could be a deadly marker for an enemy ship or reconnaissance aircraft searching for their trail. Barely a mile ahead, 'the great white whale' lumbered through the seas on her appointed zigzag. There had been talk of painting her grey while she lay at Ascension, but there had seemed to be too little time and too little paint. Now it was too late, and she appeared to be an unmissable target for an attacking aircraft. All around her in the mist, the grey shapes of frigates and landing ships steered towards East Falkland, their speed of 11 knots geared to the pace of the slowest. 'Tell the gunners to keep their heads up,' said Larken, glancing out through the sandbagged bridge windows at the Bofors crews on the wings. 'They are very good chaps indeed, but at seventeen and a half one is liable to let one's concentration wander a little.' The hours slipped slowly by. There were warnings that the weather might clear at any moment. The most powerful tension was generated by the flat reports reaching the bridge at intervals through the intercom system: 'Two Sky-hawks have just taken off from Rio Gallegos, course so-and-so, speed so-and-so. Their estimated time of arrival in your area is so-and-so.' 'Four Mirages are steering east towards you, range a hundred and sixty miles, time of arrival so-and-so.' The British submarines and SAS intelligence teams covering movements from the main Argentine air bases maintained a constant stream of information. Enemy aircraft flitted to and fro across the fringes of the fleet radar screens all that day; by extraordinary good fortune, they never located or engaged the British ships.

It seemed incredible to most of the British captains that they had gone undetected. On the bridge of the frigate *Argonaut*, Captain Kit Layman looked out at the array of midshipmen, cooks, signallers manning his Bofors guns and seventeen Oerlikon and GP machine-guns: 'I couldn't believe that we were getting away with it. I kept wondering: Is it a trap? Will it be like the Japanese at Okinawa, letting us get right in close and then letting us have it?' Major General Moore had sent the landing force a good luck signal which some felt recalled unhappy precedents: 'The red and green berets did well together at Suez. I know they will do well again at San Carlos.' In the embarked force commander's cabin of *Fearless*, Julian Thompson sat idle at last, visibly strained to the limit by the tension of the occasion. He thought of the terrible vulnerability of all the floating targets around the ship, for instance *Elk*, with her 2,000 tons of ammunition. He was furious with himself that, having taken so much trouble to disperse his brigade, he had taken no thought for the fact that his entire staff was concentrated on *Fearless*. If they were lost, so was the direction of the brigade. But it was too late to do much about it now. His officers sympathised silently with his predicament but could do nothing to still his anxiety.

More than a hundred miles eastwards, Woodward and his carriers steamed their familiar 'racetrack' course. The admiral talked later about 'the struggle to take no counsel of one's own fears'. Many times during the war, he found himself wondering how the admirals of the Second World War stood the strain of years at a stretch exposed to the enemy at sea. At every stage of the campaign since the battle group sailed south from Gibraltar, the options available to the British had narrowed. Now, there were no more options. Unless Northwood, the war cabinet or the admiral himself exercised their right to order the landing force to turn back before 6 p.m. that evening, they were utterly committed to commencing a battle ashore. Once started, this must be won. Momentarily, in the deeper shadows of his mind, Woodward had asked himself the question: What would it be like to go home to England if I fail? But commanders on the edge of action cannot indulge notions of that sort. The landing must not fail.

Most of the troops never received a direct order to proceed – they merely realised that they had reached the point at which they were going ahead unless ordered to halt. Lieutenant Colonel 'H' Jones was with 2 Para on the ferry *Norland*. He asked the naval signaller to flash her neighbour, *Broadsword*:

'Have you received any orders?'

'Yes,' replied *Broadsword*. 'Haven't you?'

A few minutes later, the frigate closed alongside and fired a signal gun with the necessary brief message:

> TOP SECRET OPERATION SUTTON
> CTG 317.0 19N 190230Z May
> Ships pass to embarked forces
> 1. D-Day 21 May 82
> 2. H-Hour is 210639Z May 82
> 3. Break down and issue first line ammunition forthwith
> 4. Act immediately

Below decks, men were priming grenades, checking weapons, loading linked-belt ammunition, dozing or reading. As the light began to fade, they knew that they had survived the first great risk. When they had seen the power of the enemy's air force in the days that followed, they were deeply conscious of the blow that could have befallen them on 20 May. If the sun had broken through even for an hour, if the enemy had launched a series of sorties as determined as those that were to come the following day, something close to disaster could have overtaken the landing force. Sea Wolf and the ships' guns would have accounted for some aircraft. But many more would have broken through, just as they broke through on 21 May. The loss of one or more troop-carrying ships would have been a terrible political blow before the outset of the land campaign.

But this was a moment at which the British reaped the fruits of boldness, of happy ignorance of the powers of the enemy air force. As most men slept for a few hours on the assault ships, the confidence of their captains was steadily growing. 'The atmosphere seemed to be right,' said Jeremy Larken. 'The whole thing seemed to be working.' They might get away with it. At around 10 p.m., most of the ships served their troops with an action dinner – steak on *Canberra*, stew on some of the naval ships where conditions were desperately cramped. Then the men began to pull on their

Above: The men who gambled on a war: General Leopoldo Galtieri, Admiral Jorge Anaya, and Brigadier Basilio Lami Dozo. Argentina's three service chiefs and ruling junta *(Popperfoto)*

Below: A national humiliation: Royal Marines of Naval Party 8901 outside Goverment House after their surrender *(Camera Press)*

A TASK FORCE IS MOBILISED

Above: Royal Marines of 45 Commando parade before their departure for the South Atlantic *(Crown Copyright Reserved)*

Below: HMS *Hermes* sails from Portsmouth *(Camera Press)*

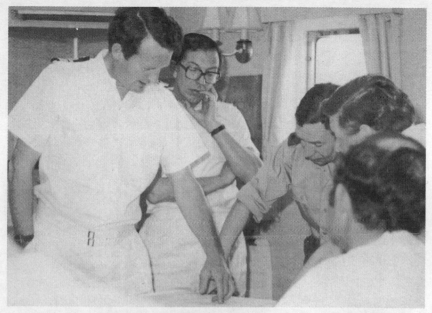

Above: Rear Admiral John 'Sandy' Woodward at a planning meeting with his staff aboad *Glamorgan* (*Crown Copyright Reserved*)

Below: The disastrous scene on the Fortuna Glacier after the crash of the two Wessex helicopters (*Crown Copyright Reserved*)

THE CRUEL SEA

Above: The assault ship *Intrepid* during one of the countless Replenishment-At-Sea operations *(Crown Copyright Reserved)*

Left: HMS *Conqueror* returns to Faslane from the South Atlantic, flying her Jolly Roger in recognition of the destruction of the *General Belgrano (The Times)*

THE FIRST TRAGEDIES
Above: The Argentine heavy cruiser *General Belgrano* on 2 May
(The Associated Press)

Below: The British destroyer *Sheffield* after being mortally hit on 4 May
(Crown Copyright Reserved)

PLANNERS AT SEA AND ASHORE

Above: At Northwood, Sir John Fieldhouse with *(right)* Major General Jeremy Moore, *(left)* his Chief of Staff Admiral Hallifax and Air Marshal Sir John Curtiss *(Camera Press)*

Below: Brigadier Thompson and the key planners of his 'R' Group. From the left: Ewen Southby-Tailyour, Roddy Macdonald, Viv Rowe, Gerry Wells-Cole, John Chester, Julian Thompson. Mike Holroyd-Smith is missing *(Crown Copyright Reserved)*

Above: Arguably the most critical moment of the war: on the bridge of *Fearless*, Captain Jeremy Larken *(left)* cons the amphibious force towards San Carlos through a thick mist on 20 May *(Max Hastings/Camera Press)*

Below left: Royal Marines raise the flag at San Carlos settlement. On the right is the local manager, Pat Short, the first Falklander to meet the landing force *(Camera Press)*. *Right*: The battle for San Carlos: a marine of 45 Commando digs in *(Lt Mark Duck, RM)*

Above: The last moments of *Antelope (Press Association)*

Below: Ardent's stern, wrecked by bombs *(Crown Copyright Reserved)*

Above: A typical San Carlos May morning: a Mirage 3 streaks over the remains of *Antelope*, while a bomb bursts and cannon strikes tear open the water *(Crown Copyright Reserved)*

Below left: Captain John Hamilton SAS. *Right*: Captain David Hart-Dyke of *Coventry (Crown Copyright Reserved)*

Above left: The adventurer who found his moment: Ewen Southby-Tailyour *(Crown Copyright Reserved)*. *Above right*: Captain Rod Bell, the Spanish-speaking Royal Marine who negotiated with the Argentinians *(Crown Copyright Reserved)*. *Below left*: Colonel Hew Pike of 3 Para *(Max Hastings/Camera Press)*. *Below right*: Captain Jeremy Larken of *Fearless* *(Crown Copyright Reserved)*

Above: Goose Green: medics at an aid post amidst the burning gorse
(Crown Copyright Reserved).

Below: The superb Sea Harriers' endurance over the battle area improved
dramatically when they began to refuel ashore at Port San Carlos
(Max Hastings/Camera Press)

Above: Colonal H's 'O' Group at Camilla Creek on the eve of battle *(2 Para)*

Below: The Argentinian surrender at Goose Green *(2 Para)*

Above: British 105mm gunners on Mount Kent, a picture taken by the author the morning after the dramatic seizure of the summit *(Max Hastings/Camera Press)*

Below left: COMMANDERS: Julian Thompson and Jeremy Moore at 3 Commando Brigade HQ on Mount Kent, a few minutes before a Skyhawk bombing raid on the position *(Camera Press)*. *Right*: READING AND WRITING: Mail had a critical impact on morale both at sea and ashore. Two marines of 45 Commando write their last notes home on the afternoon before their attack on the Two Sisters *(Camera Press)*

THE WINNING TEAM: The Prime Minister with the Lord Mayor of London, principal ministers, civil servants and service officers responsible for the direction of the Falklands war. Mrs Thatcher's Falklands Campaign Victory Dinner at No.10 Downing Street, 11 October 1982 *(Sport and General)*

1 Mr Bernard Ingham; 2 Capt. David Hart-Dyke; 3 Mr S.S. Holness; 4 Mr N.H. Nicholls; 5 Lt.-Col. M.I.E. Scott; 6 Cmdr. G. Middleton; 7 Mr Robin Fearn; 8 Mr D.H. Gillmore; 9 Mr J.M. Stewart; 10 Lt.-Col. D.P. de C. Morgan; 11 Capt. D.J. Scott-Masson; 12 Mr K.F. Slater; 13 Sir Brian Tovey; 14 Mr P.R.H. Wright;

15 Group Capt. J.S.B. Price; 16 Capt. J.F.T.G. Salt; 17 Col. H.M. Rose; 18 Capt D.M. Rundle; 19 Mr Ian Macdonald; 20 Major Chris Keeble; 21 Mr A.D.S. Goodall; 22 Mr C.F. Figures; 23 Capt. J.J. Black; 24 Mr R.T. Jackling; 25 Rev. David Cooper; 26 Fleet Chief Petty Officer M.G. Fellows; 27 Mr R.L. Facer; 28 Lt.-Col. A.F. Whitehead; 29 Mr P.J. Weston; 30 Lt.-Col. Hew Pike; 31 Lt.-Col. M.J. Holroyd-Smith; 32 Maj. J.J. Thomson; 33 Mr D.F. Whitwam; 34 Capt. P.J.G. Roberts; 35 Wing-Cmdr. P.T. Squire; 36 Mr John Coles; 37 Mr John Ure; 38 Lt.-Col. J.F. Rickett; 39 Sir Anthony Parsons; 40 Brig. M.J.A. Wilson; 41 Rear Admiral Sir John 'Sandy' Woodward; 42 Cdre. M.C. Clapp; 43 Admiral Sir John Fieldhouse; 44 Sir Ian Sinclair; 45 Field Marshal Sir Edwin Bramall; 46 Vice Admiral P.G.M. Herbert; 47 The Rt. Hon. Cecil Parkinson; 48 Mr M.D.M. Franklin; 49 The Rt. Hon. William Whitelaw; 50 Air Marshal Sir John Curtiss; 51 Admiral of the Fleet, Sir Terence Lewin; 52 Sir Robert Armstrong; 53 The Rt. Hon. Margaret Thatcher; 54 Air Chief Marshal Sir David Evans; 55 The Lord Mayor of London, Sir Christopher Lever; 56 Sir Frank Cooper; 57 The Rt. Hon. John Nott; 58 Vice Admiral D.W. Brown; 59 Sir Michael Havers; 60 Sir Antony Acland; 61 Admiral Henry Leach; 62 Capt. R. McQueen; 63 Air Chief Marshal Sir Michael Beetham; 64 Brigadier J.H.A. Thompson; 65 Maj.-Gen. Jeremy Moore; 66 Capt. L.E. Middleton; 67 Sir Nicholas Henderson.

VICTORY

Above: A ship of the Royal Navy enters Portsmouth Harbour on its return from the South Atlantic war *(Observer)*

Below: A rifle, a helmet and a jam jar of daffodils mark the spot where Sergeant Ian McKay fell on Mt. Longdon *(Daily Express)*

heavy web fighting order, to 'give the face a terrible aspect' with black camouflage cream; close their huge bergen rucksacks; pull on helmets. On the assault ships, guides led them company by company down through the jungle of passages, hatches and ladders to the tank decks. Sailors muttered, 'Give them hell, mate,' as marines and paras clambered clumsily past their posts. The tank decks were in near darkness, lit only by a dim red glow from the deckhead. A thin chain of red lights such as one might find on a Christmas tree marked the path through the darkened mass of Volvos and Land Rovers to the dock where the landing craft lay, ramps down. The men filed in, and sat down on the cold steel deck, waiting for the dock to flood.

In each of the assault ships, four LCUs and four smaller LCVPs were loaded with the men of the first wave – in all, two battalions and eight armoured vehicles of the Blues and Royals. There was a brief, frightening moment when an air-raid alert sounded. Packed crouched in the hulls of the landing craft, the blackened figures cursed silently at the prospect of being trapped in the dock under attack. Then the alert was cancelled. There was a surge of water under the landing craft as the dock flooded, the great stern ramp was lowered. Then they were bumping and backing out into Falkland Sound, at the mouth of San Carlos Water. A slight navigational error had brought the ships in behind schedule. Delay in transferring 2 Para from *Norland* to the LCUs much compounded their lateness. But, under the guidance of Ewen Southby-Tailyour, the little flotilla began to run in through the darkness, the silence around the ships broken only by the steady throb of the landing-craft engines, and the distant 'crack-boom' of the naval bombardment, diverting the enemy's attention by hitting positions on West Falkland and at Fanning Head. The mist had completely cleared, and the sky was brilliantly clear and starlit. It was bitterly cold, and most men shivered as they gazed wonderingly at the gun-flashes and the sharp shadows of the hills of East Falkland which had dominated their thoughts for so many weeks. They murmured quietly to each other, ate their inevitable 'nutty', and made themselves as comfortable as they could amid the cases of mortar bombs, bergens, ammunition and weapons laid beside each man.

In the south, a strong party from D Squadron SAS was already in action, laying down a furious barrage of machine-gun, mortar and Milan missile fire on the Argentine garrison at Darwin, where they arrived after a punishing forced march laden with extra ammunition – what one man later called 'the toughest yomp I have ever done with the SAS'. The Argentine commander at Goose Green subsequently admitted that his men thought they were being attacked by a force of battalion strength. *Glamorgan* was conducting another diversion, bombarding the area north of Berkeley Sound where the British had originally planned to land. It was the fiftieth birthday of her captain, Mike Barrow, who entered his operations room late that night at the end of his 126-gun salute to find all his men singing 'Happy Birthday To You'. Other diversionary operations were taking place at key points around East and West Falkland.

*

The first troops into action that morning were thirty-two Royal Marines of the Special Boat Squadron and an SAS team equipped with the superb new American 60 mm lightweight mortar, led by a young lieutenant and accompanied by a marine captain named Rod Bell. The son of a UN official, Bell had been brought up in Costa Rica and spoke perfect local Spanish. The British purpose was to force the surrender of the twenty-strong Argentine garrison at Fanning Head, covering the approach to San Carlos Water. Early that night, a Wessex III helicopter from *Antrim* swept Fanning Head with a thermal imager, which betrays the presence of life by registering body heat. The crew located the enemy positions and returned to *Antrim* to brief the SBS party.

At 11 p.m. the marines took off from the destroyer by helicopter for a landing zone within striking distance of Fanning Head. They were equipped with a remarkable array of special equipment, including 12-volt batteries to power a portable broadcast system. The Special Boat Squadron is the Royal Marines' own special operations force, less flamboyant than the Special Air Service, and trained chiefly for coastal operations as canoeists or frogmen, carrying out intelligence or sabotage missions. Like the SAS, they are immediately recognisable on a battlefield by their longer hair, idiosyncratic dress and webbing, and American automatic weapons. They pride themselves on being as tough as and more secretive than the SAS, although somewhere in their make-up is perhaps a trace of jealousy and more than a trace of rivalry with the better-known organisation. But in recent years the two have worked increasingly closely together, and most men in each will admit to great respect for the other.

Dropping out of their helicopters into the darkness, the heavily loaded marines in their balaclavas were carrying the formidable firepower of twelve GP machine-guns. They filed away across the hill for the 6-mile march to Fanning Head, led by an NCO carrying a thermal imager. They had no difficulty in reaching a ridge some 700 yards above the enemy position. A naval gunfire support officer began to call down salvos from *Antrim*, while the SBS machine-guns opened a devastating fire. They could see the Argentinians abandon their 106 mm recoilless rifle and scuttle for cover. Rod Bell and an SBS volunteer began a long, perilous crawl down the hill, dragging their loudhailer and batteries. 200 yards from the enemy, he began to call on them in Spanish to surrender. In the high wind, he quickly realised that his voice was quite inaudible. The SBS officer in command whispered urgently through the radio that he believed the enemy were mustering for a counter-attack. Bell and the other marine lay flat on the hillside while the British raiding party once again laid a furious barrage of fire over their heads, towards the enemy. The defenders halfheartedly replied. Then both sides settled to wait for the coming of dawn. Six Argentinians surrendered, and showed the British the way to three others who lay wounded. The remainder of the men in the outpost vanished. The enemy were all men of the 12th and 25th Regiments, from Darwin and Goose Green. They had been in position for three days without resupply, and had been killing sheep for food. One had lost some toes from frostbite. Several were wearing fragments of British equipment looted from the Royal Marine base at Moody Brook after the invasion of the islands. The Fanning Head position had been silenced, in mildly farcical fashion. The commanding officer of the SBS said later that he would never again attempt to mix the securing of a military objective with an attempt to gain a humanitarian propaganda coup by taking the enemy alive.

*

The first British troops of the main landing force waded ashore below San Carlos settlement a few minutes before 4 a.m. on Friday, 21 May. 2 Para was more than an hour late, and found the ramps of the landing craft going down 30 yards from the edge of the rocky gravel beach. They stumbled and splashed ashore, and began a long slog through the darkness, across a succession of streams and patches of marsh, to reach the summit of Sussex Mountain, the position that they were to seize and hold, protecting the approach from Goose Green. They met no enemy, and their advanced elements were on the objective soon after first light.

Only a few minutes after 2 Para's landing on the beach at the northern end of the settlement, a few hundred yards further north the first men of 40 Commando made their way ashore behind the Scorpions and Scimitars of the Blues and Royals, to be met by a shaggy band of filthy unshaven men – the SBS reception party who had been out on the hill for days. While A and B Companies cleared and secured open ground below and above the settlement, Charlie Company moved up the bluff from the beaches, to a two-storey white house, screened by gorse bushes, to seek out the local manager, Pat Short. Beside Lieutenant Paul Allen of 7 Troop strode Lieutenant John Thurman, a marine who had served a tour with the Falklands detachment and was engaged to the daughter of the governor, Rex Hunt. Thurman knocked on the door. Pat Short opened it and exclaimed, 'You're British!' In a few brief sentences, they established that there were no Argentinians in the area, but at once began to go through the standard house-clearing routine, two platoons advancing by bounds up the grassy avenue between the little groups of buildings, awakening the owners one by one, and apprising them of the situation. Most, like Pat Short himself, had been awakened by the noise of the approaching landing craft and naval bombardment. They had been expecting the British to arrive for days – Short had always believed that San Carlos was a likely landing site. There were some thirty people in the settlement – shepherds and farmworkers, as in most of the rural communities on the Falklands. In the understated fashion of most lonely island peoples, they showed little surprise at the extraordinary drama that had been thrust upon them. 'We knew somebody would turn up sooner or later,' said Mrs Monica May, offering coffee to her liberators, which seemed quite the wrong way around. It was difficult to take seriously tales of Argentine brutality when it emerged that the half-starved enemy soldiers who had passed through San Carlos on patrol had left the settlement stores and the houses' supplies intact. The marines left the Falklanders in their dressing gowns, clustered in little knots around the lamps on their kitchen tables, and moved rapidly along the hillside to take up their planned defensive positions covering the southern approach, towards Goose Green. Most men began to dig where they stood, in the first light of dawn, while a handful took up observation positions further out, on the high ground. On the flagpole beside Pat Short's house, men of C Company of 40 Commando raised the Union Jack at first light. The photographs of the moment had flashed around the world by nightfall.

Across the water, 45 Commando had occupied the abandoned refrigeration plant at Ajax Bay without incident, and were soon digging defensive positions on the hillside above. 3 Para, landing very late after the accumulated delays of the morning, boarded their landing craft from *Intrepid* and were soon on their way ashore further round the coast at Port San Carlos. With the coastline secure, the assault ships, *Canberra*, *Norland* and all their accompanying vessels moved inwards from Falkland Sound, to take up their anchorage positions in the heart of San Carlos Water. The British had overcome the greatest single hurdle of the Falklands campaign. By boldness, luck, superb planning and seamanship, they had established 3 Commando Brigade ashore without significant loss. After all that had gone wrong for the Royal Navy in the preceding weeks, they had now achieved a great feat of combined operations, proving that even a fleet that was a mere skeleton of the armadas which carried out the assaults of the Second World War could land a major amphibious force on a hostile coastline 8,000 miles from base. It was a fine achievement of modern war. It now remained to ensure that the British could stay there.

12 » SAN CARLOS

So all day long the noise of battle roll'd
Among the mountains by the winter sea.

Tennyson, *The Idylls of the King*

As Argentine descriptions since the war have it, a young army lieutenant in a position within sight of San Carlos was the first to call his headquarters on the morning of 21 May and report that he was watching two British ships unloading troops. The staff were disbelieving. A prewar naval study had concluded that San Carlos was an 'impossible' site for a successful landing. Through 20 May, as reports had come in to General Menendez's operations room of British ship movements, the suggestion that they were heading for San Carlos was dismissed as a diversion. It was the navy which decided to pursue the lieutenant's intercepted signal, and sent a Fleet Air Arm pilot in a solitary Aeromacchi to take a look. At about 10 a.m. the Argentinian spotted a British helicopter flying along a ridge above San Carlos, and swung in to attack it. Then, as he crossed the hilltop, he saw laid out before him what looked to him to be '. . . the entire English fleet . . .'

*

Such British warships as were not already closed up went to action stations an hour before dawn on 21 May. As the light grew, from their Bofors mountings and flight decks and bridges men gazed curiously at the low, brown and yellow hills rising from the shore; the anchorage, dominated by the huge white bulk of *Canberra*; the

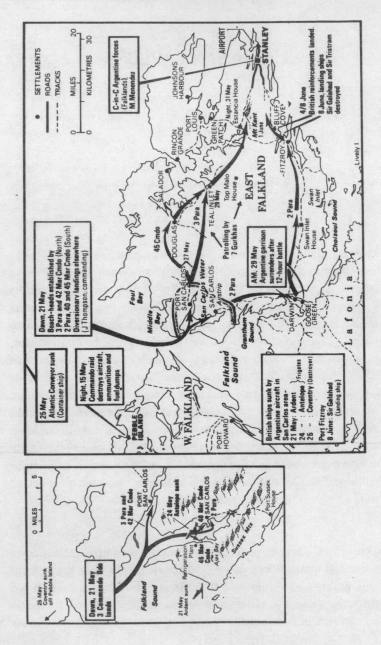

hundreds of marines and paratroopers clearly visible among the tussock grass, hacking at their trenches and defensive positions. Many of the civilian crew of *Canberra*, men and women, wandered on to the promenade decks and chatted excitedly in little knots beneath the lifeboats. Thousands of people seeing San Carlos for the first time decided that it looked very like Pembrokeshire or the north of Scotland, with its little clusters of white-walled, red-roofed houses beside the shore. 'Not unlike summer holidays in the Western Isles,' wrote an officer on *Broadsword*. 'Just like UK, isn't it?' mused a young marine captain of 40 Commando as he dug his trench with the incompetent assistance of Max Hastings.

A beautiful clear, crisp day was unfolding, with the sea steel-blue and only lightly choppy. On the flight decks of the assault ships, crews rapidly unlocked the rotors of the first Sea Kings, which roared away to begin the most urgent task of the day: transferring the twelve Rapier launchers with their generators, trackers and crews to the hilltop sites selected by the computer at Malvern. Landing craft started to shuttle between ship and shore, kicking up fierce bow wakes in their haste. High above, seldom visible to the naked eye, the Sea Harriers waited. 'We had no idea what to expect,' said Lieutenant Commander Andy Auld, the quiet, immensely experienced thirty-seven-year-old Scot who commanded 800 Squadron. Far below, vehicles to provide essential radio communications were already scrambling up the beaches. In San Carlos settlement, between the houses, the British army's beloved paraffin pressure-cookers were already roaring. Children from the settlements watched in awed fascination as the helicopters clattered overhead, and bewildered geese flew hither and thither in search of silence. In the kennels, the sheepdogs barked incessantly. The Falklanders, in their quiet way eager to give any help they could to the landing force, drove their tractors and trailers to and from the beaches and jetties carrying loads of bergens, ammunition, engineer equipment. Spasmodic explosions signalled only guns and mortars firing a few rounds to 'bed in'. As the sun came out, a glow of achievement, even contentment, overtook thousands of men both on the shore and at sea.

But the first mishap of the day was already in the making. 3 Para's landing at Port San Carlos had slipped badly behind schedule. They waded ashore in daylight at 7 a.m., fuming with impatience, to be met by an SBS reception party who reported that there were no enemy in the area. Moments later, the leading platoons spotted a large party of Argentinians, forty-two in all, retreating rapidly eastwards from the settlement. 3 Para's CO, Hew Pike, at once ordered his mortars and sustained-fire machine-gun platoon to engage them. Some desultory British fire followed. But the enemy was already too distant, and too obviously bent on flight, for Pike to consider sending riflemen in pursuit. Falklanders in the settlement reported that the troops had arrived from Fanning Head the previous day, and had been sleeping in the woolsheds. In their retreat they had abandoned much of their equipment, including clothing and decorations looted from Major Mike Norman's marines when Stanley fell seven weeks earlier.

Thus far, Pike had flashed only his landing signal 'Indian Hemp' to *Fearless*. Brigade should still have been awaiting his signal 'Lost Sheep' to announce the settlement cleared and secure. But, to the Paras' dismay, they now glimpsed a Sea King with an underslung load flying sedately around the hill towards the Argentinians. At this opening moment of the battle, there was a theory that armed light helicopters could usefully escort cargo aircraft. Two Gazelles were therefore accompanying the Sea King. Pike and his men were not linked to the helicopter radio net, and were unable to warn the pilots. Impotent, they watched the brief tragedy that followed. The big helicopter seemed to see the enemy first; it shed its load and ducked hastily below the horizon. Small-arms fire from the ground hit a Gazelle a few minutes later. It crashed into the sea just off Port San Carlos Jetty. The second Gazelle lifted rapidly forward, apparently in pursuit of the Argentinians. It too was hit within seconds, and crashed into the sea. The Argentinians enraged the British by firing upon the crews even as they struggled in the water. Three of the four men were killed. The fourth was badly wounded. The Argentinians made good their escape.

*

Now, for the first time, the enemy's air force made its appearance. Two pairs of Pucara ground-attack aircraft approached the long files of 2 Para, still struggling up Sussex Mountain, at around 1,000 feet. The first aircraft exploded abruptly. Among the equipment of the SAS party returning from their diversionary raid on Goose Green was the superb American Stinger ground-to-air hand-held missile. It was a Stinger that had destroyed the first Pucara, while a missile from the ships brought down the second. The following pair made one rocket pass from the east against 2 Para's B Company, and escaped without inflicting casualties. Meanwhile, a single Aeromacchi – almost certainly the first Fleet Air Arm reconnaissance aircraft flying from Port Stanley – attacked the RFA supply ship *Fort Austin* at the mouth of the anchorage. The bombs fell wide. *Fort Austin* retreated hastily to a safer haven, re-anchoring among the assault ships deep in the bay. But, that morning, all except two of the warships defending the amphibious landing force were deployed in Falkland Sound, west and north-west of San Carlos Water. The submarine threat still loomed large in the minds of Admiral Woodward and Commodore Clapp. Nor had they yet seen what the Argentine air force could do to ships in open water.

The anchorage suffered two air-raid warnings that failed to materialise. Then, two hours after first light, a second Aeromacchi came in over Fanning Head, heading for the Leander frigate *Argonaut* so low above the waves that the ship's flight commander momentarily believed that it had plunged into the sea. The aircraft loosed four rockets amidst a belated barrage of light automatic fire from the frigate, and broke away. The rockets missed. But cannon fire hit the master at arms in the chest, wounded two other sailors aft, and smashed a large hole in the ship's 965 surveillance radar array. Like so many crews that morning, the men of *Argonaut* were shocked by their first brutal contact with the enemy. 'It was such a beautiful day – bloody gorgeous,' said PO Taff Jones, a chatty Wiltshireman nineteen years in the Royal Navy, and now standing among the bren gunners on the open gun direction position above the bridge. 'We didn't see the Aeromacchi until it was right on us. Everybody was a bit shaken – seeing the wounded taken below and all that . . .' Captain Kit Layman, a tough, grey-haired forty-four-year-old whose father had served with the Royal Navy in both world wars, and whose grandfather was a veteran of Jutland and the Boxer Rebellion, was at his usual action station in the operations room, and knew little of the attack until it was over. 'It made me realise that this was no place to fight the battle – I had to be where I could see what was going on.' Layman, like most captains from that day forth, moved to his bridge and stayed there through all that followed.

And now the Argentine air force began in earnest. 'All hell was let loose,' wrote an officer on *Broadsword*. 'The air was filled with attacking aircraft, mainly Mirage and Skyhawk, and the battle raged for over six hours.' All along the shoreline, officers' whistle blasts and shouts of 'Take cover! Take cover!' sent men running to their guns and trenches. In the lounges of *Canberra*, 42 Commando lay prone on the decks among the crew while their machine-gunners and Blowpipe operators manned their weapons on the upper decks, flatly refusing to be relieved when their watch was up. As the first enemy aircraft raced 50 feet above the sea to attack, the Royal Navy began to fight its biggest action since the end of the Second World War.

Within an hour of the first waves of aircraft attacking, it became evident that it was the ships, not the men ashore, who were the targets. Marines and paras poured thousands of rounds of rifle and machine-gun fire into the sky from their positions. The Blues and Royals' Scimitars and Scorpions sought to engage passing aircraft from the hillside below San Carlos settlement. The SAS Stinger expert had died in the helicopter crash on 19 May, but the trooper who fired at the Pucara was so impressed by his own success that he now took up position on a headland and fired five more missiles at incoming Skyhawks, only to be dismayed by a succession of misses. Disappointment also came to the men manning the British army's principal infantry anti-aircraft weapon, the hand-held Blowpipe missile, of which dozens were fired in vain that day. Blowpipe was wholly ineffective against a crossing, rather than approaching, target.

But the landing force was merely the spectator of all that happened that day. It was the crews of the ships who fought the battle. They stood in their helmets and anti-flash capes, trousers tucked into their thick white stockings, manning Bofors guns and GPMGs, bren guns, rifles, even 66 mm anti-tank rocket launchers on the upper decks. Most were very young – the two seamen beside PO Jones on the *Argonaut*'s GDP were both seventeen, six months in the navy. Yet it was apparent from the start that the outcome of the struggle would depend largely on their efforts. In the operations rooms below decks, men hunched over radar screens controlling millions of pounds' worth of weapons technology, but radar detection was almost totally useless close inshore, surrounded by hills, against an enemy who became visible only seconds before attacking and was gone seconds later. Everything hung upon the physical skills and energy of the men on the decks firing their weapons. It was not merely the enemy's aircraft destroyed that mattered. The aim of the pilots was critically deflected by the tracer, missile trails, flares and exploding shells crowding the sky before and around them, sometimes with fatal results.

Antrim fired her Sea Slugs seconds before she was hit aft on the port side around her hangar by bombs and rockets. The bombs failed to explode, but one passed through her Sea Slug magazine, crippling all her anti-aircraft missile systems. Men on neighbouring ships watched fascinated as water spouts erupted around her. With increasing horror, they saw more bombs spilling into the water around *Norland*, the LSLs, worst of all, *Canberra*. It seemed impossible that the vast white target, her machine-guns almost constantly in action, could escape damage. Her senior naval officer, Captain

Chris Burne, won enormous respect that day for the unshakeable humour and courage with which he met the attacks and kept up a running commentary to the thousands of frightened men and women below decks. It was a performance in the great tradition of eccentric naval officers at moments of crisis.

The British were awed by the courage of the Argentine pilots, flying suicidally low to attack, then vanishing amid flushes of pursuing Sea Cat, Blowpipe, Rapier, racing across the sky behind them. Alone among the enemy's three services, the air force seemed highly motivated and utterly committed to the battle. 'We should have been able to work out that any nation which produces first-class Formula One racing drivers is also likely to turn out some pretty good pilots,' said *Arrow*'s doctor sardonically between attacks. *Brilliant* was hit by Mirages whose cannon shells sent shrapnel bouncing around the inside of her hangar, injuring several crewmen. More men manning rifles and machine-guns on the upper decks were wounded in a second attack on the starboard side. Ball, the missile aimer on the forward Sea Wolf system, at last gained a solution on an incoming Mirage on his television screen, and tracked his missile to explode beneath the aircraft's port wing, an astonishing feat of camera guidance. But Commodore Clapp and his staff on *Fearless* were coming unhappily to terms with the limitations of Sea Wolf. Close inshore, ground clutter was providing a fatal handicap to its tracking radar. 'We had not understood how badly clutter would affect Sea Wolf inshore,' admitted Clapp later. Everything would hinge upon the visually aimed weapons – and the Harriers.

*

Throughout the battles of the week that followed, many of the most vital actions were fought far out of sight of the British in the anchorage. Only seldom did they glimpse a Harrier diving in hot pursuit of enemy Skyhawks and Mirages, the Argentinians hastily jettisoning their bombs and flitting away over the hills. From the start, the British established three air patrol positions:

one north of the islands; a second over West Falkland; a third over the southern end of Falkland Sound. At first light each day, a pair of Harriers took station at each of these locations, to vector on to attacking aircraft either by visual sighting or by radar direction from one of the ships, most often *Brilliant* on the first day. Early on the morning of the 21st, the southern patrol had scored a sharp success by spotting and destroying a Chinook and a Puma helicopter with cannon fire. For the rest of the day, the British carriers were launching a pair of aircraft every twenty minutes, relieving each other on station, or launching probes far out to sea in search of possible Argentine surface ships moving to attack the beachhead.

In the first days, while they broke up and turned back several waves of Argentine aircraft out at sea, most of the Harrier kills were made against enemy aircraft leaving San Carlos after attacks. The CO of 899 Squadron and his senior pilot, Lieutenant Commander Mike Blissett, were chasing two Skyhawks out of the anchorage when suddenly they spotted a new wave approaching, and broke off to attack the more critical threat. They shot down four A4s. Two hours later, Lieutenant Clive Morell and Flight Lieutenant John Leery – who was to become one of the most successful pilots of the war – shot down one each, the first with a Sidewinder, the second at a range of 100 yards with cannon. The Harriers claimed one further aircraft that day, and sent surviving Argentine pilots homewards with a profound respect for the British fighter. Throughout the war, whenever a British pilot heard the hum in his headset – the 'aural tone' indicating that enemy aircraft were within his 'missile look angle' – its destruction was a near-certainty. He fired, and listened for the 'chirping' that showed his missile had locked on. Then he had only to watch the smoke trail of the AIM9L Sidewinder snake erratically across the sky, and the blinding ball of light as the Mirage or Skyhawk exploded. In every case in which a Sidewinder locked on, the enemy aircraft was destroyed. Of twenty-seven fired in the entire war, twenty-four hit their targets. The technology was working superbly. At high level, a Mirage could dramatically outperform a Sea Harrier, and the British pilots had great respect for the manoeuvrability of the Skyhawk. But the Argentinians' knowledge of British air defence, above all Sea Dart, drove them to come in low. There were never dogfights in the conventional sense, in which the Argentinians sought to engage in combat. They were too short of fuel for that. The Harriers' 'viffing' technique of sudden deceleration, of which so much was made during speculation in the press about air combat, was never relevant. There was merely a struggle between the intercepting Harrier, with its superb acceleration, and the enemy aircraft twisting and dodging to escape. As the Sidewinder fired, there was no shock, merely a soft 'whoosh'. If the enemy used his afterburner to increase his speed, he merely provided a brighter target for the homing missile and ensured his own collapse from lack of fuel before he reached home. Air combat, from beginning to end, was an entirely one-sided affair, the enemy's inability to dogfight perhaps flattering the performance of the Sea Harrier a little. 'Combat was exactly as we had imagined, as we had been briefed, as we had trained,' said Andy Auld. 'I felt as if I had done it all before except firing the missile – and except that all the normal peacetime restrictions on low flying had gone out of the window.'

The British faced a serious problem in locating attacking aircraft with sufficient speed. The submarines – reinforced by *Valiant* on 16 May – together with intelligence teams operating on the Argentine mainland, reported the enemy's takeoffs, and their aircraft could be tracked for most of their flight, flying at around 19,000 feet to conserve fuel. But, at least 50 miles from the Falklands, the Skyhawks and Mirages dipped to sea level – low enough to come home with wings streaked with salt – and vanished from British radar surveillance. This was where the fleet's lack of airborne early warning became critical. The Argentine aircraft only appeared as they weaved between the hills or swung among the inlets on their final approach, often seconds before they bombed. Again and again, the British failed to pick up an attack wave until the final moments. Again and again, with the Sea Harriers capable of remaining on station for only twenty minutes, enemy aircraft broke through while the CAP was engaged elsewhere. The air groups from *Hermes* and *Invincible* were doing all that could conceivably be asked of them; they performed better than any naval officer had thought possible. But they were few. That first day alone, they faced twelve separate incoming attacks involving a total of seventy-two aircraft. It is not remarkable that so many broke through, and were only intercepted on their home-ward runs.

*

Late on that morning of 21 May, the crippled *Antrim* steamed slowly into the shelter of San Carlos Water. *Fearless* directed *Argonaut* to take her place at the mouth of the bay. A Wessex carrying a naval doctor from *Canberra* closed in to take off *Argonaut*'s casualties from the first attack, and the frigate began to steam into the wind to enable the helicopter to winch men from her deck – it was too heavy to land. Suddenly, from the south, came a wave of Skyhawks. The Wessex sheared off and set down ashore. *Argonaut* fired her Sea Cat and at once hit a single aircraft, which crashed into Fanning Harbour. Then six Skyhawks released their bombs almost on top of them. Incredibly, these hit the water and bounced over the ship. Every man on the upper decks was deluged with water. The astounded Taff Jones watched a black object hurtling over his head – 'almost parted me hair'. He glimpsed a seventeen-year-old seaman who was caught emerging from the messdecks with a teapot and a handful of plastic mugs attempt simul-taneously to hurl himself up a ladder, rescue the teapot, and save a cascade of mugs failing around the deck. 'I shall remember that sight as long as I live,' said Captain Layman, watching from his bridge the pairs of Skyhawks coming in. In all, ten bombs fell in the sea around *Argonaut*, the massive splashes momentarily blind-ing the guns' crews. Two entered the ship. One penetrated the boiler room just above the waterline, struck the bulkhead, caused a boiler to explode, ruptured the steam pipes, and filled the machinery spaces with superheated steam. The ship had been at full speed. Now, she went dead in the water. Astonishingly, the ten men in her machinery spaces escaped alive. The second bomb hit forward below the waterline, passed through a fuel tank into the Sea Cat magazine and caused at least three missiles to explode without detonating itself. The two magazine handlers were killed instantly; the magazine flooded with escaping fuel oil. As the door of the Sea Cat hoist blew off just forward of the bridge, dense white smoke began to spew up from below. The ship was still heading for the shore, all steering gone, and the telegraph dead. Captain Layman sent a man forward to drop an anchor from the fo'c'sle, and began to receive his damage-control reports. 'It took longer than one might think to find out what had happened to the ship,' he said. There was a major fire forward in the messdeck above the magazine – bedding and aluminium lockers had ignited. One of the stokers, Hathaway, worked his way into the area with breathing apparatus, and within twenty minutes had controlled this fire. *Yarmouth*'s Wasp helicopter saw *Argonaut*'s plight, and on the pilot's initiative landed on the frigate's flight deck and began to take off wounded. The ship's auxiliary diesel generators were still supplying power to the key weapons systems, and they quickly rigged emergency leads to keep the forward Sea Cat operational. Layman signalled *Fearless*: 'We can float and fight, but not steam.' As the light began to fade, *Plymouth* moved out of San Carlos Bay and began to circle the crippled ship to protect her from further air attacks. When darkness came at last, *Plymouth* closed in and began to tow *Argonaut* into the relative safety of San Carlos, still nursing two unexploded bombs.

But, even as *Argonaut* was fighting to save herself, the last air attack of the day fell on *Ardent*, the 3,250-ton Type 21 frigate which had been carrying out naval gunfire support in the southernmost position of the naval screen. Two 1,000-pound bombs struck aft, severing all her vital systems and slashing her wide open for the next stick that followed, setting the entire after part of the ship on fire, killing twenty-four men and wounding thirty. Despite a gallant defence during which the NAAFI canteen manager continued to fire a GP machine-gun after all the main armament had been put out of action, there was never the slightest possibility of saving *Ardent*. Helicopters closed in around the ship and began pulling survivors from the water, evacuating the bulk of her 200 remaining men from the fo'c'sle where they had clustered in their 'once-only' survival suits. *Yarmouth* hastened to her side and completed the rescue with much of the ship already engulfed in flames and black smoke. Her captain, Commander Alan West, freely confessed to his own tears and those of some of his men as he gave the order to abandon her. But no ship of her size in any war could have hoped to survive punishment of that kind.

As darkness fell, wounded men were still being carried aboard *Canberra* and taken to the ship's operating theatres. 42 Commando had been sent ashore during the afternoon to join 3 Para around Port San Carlos. Although some stores remained aboard, the liner's role was now predominantly to provide medical support. Many of her crew had been exhilarated by her survival through the attacks of the day. But most were deeply shocked by an experience that they had never remotely envisaged when they sailed from Southampton. It is still not clear whether the Argentinians hoped to sink *Canberra* and missed – as it appeared to some of those on her decks – or whether, as the enemy's airmen claim, they had been specifically ordered to avoid her. In any event, she had had a fortunate day. Aboard *Fearless*, 3 Commando Brigade's staff were above all relieved that their own landing had been achieved without loss, and their build-up of stores and equipment had not attracted direct attack. This operation had begun slowly, because of the delay imposed on the helicopters by the need to seek cover below the horizon during air attacks. But there had been no evidence whatever of any attempt by Argentine ground forces to mount a counter-attack, or to concentrate men by helicopter for a thrust against the beach-head. Over 4,000 men were now ashore. The British were comforted, for any sound military commander must have been aware that the landing force would be at its most vulnerable during its first hours ashore. If General Menendez lacked the will or the means to exploit the military situation when the British were weakest, it seemed reasonable to hope that all the SAS reports about the indolence and incompetence of the enemy were justified.

It was clear that all the fears for the future of the task force must lie with the ships at sea, which had suffered such crippling damage to defend the beach-head. One frigate had been sunk, and four damaged. 'By the end of the day,' a senior marine officer wrote in his diary, 'the Argentinians had definitely cracked open the defence provided by our underarmed escorts. Had daylight lasted and had the enemy persisted with his attacks, he could have got in among our Landing Ships with possibly disastrous consequences.' A naval officer on *Fearless* said, 'Some people were very depressed that evening. Some of us had not appreciated until quite late on how much damage had been done to us. We thought we had given quite a good account of ourselves. Now we had to have a rethink.' Andy Auld and the other Harrier pilots on *Hermes* had done all that could have been asked of them, yet that night they were gloomily saying, 'We aren't shooting down enough.' The sheer weight of the Argentine air force had swamped the British defences. It was inevitable that the enemy would keep coming. What if their bombs began to explode?

That night, as Admiral Woodward talked by telephone to Commodore Clapp, and later took his usual hour-long nightly call to Admiral Hallifax, the chief of staff at Northwood, a number of important assessments and decisions were made. First, mercifully, the Argentinians had allowed themselves to be deflected from attacking the vital storeships and had gone instead for the escorts, probably because these were the first ships they saw in the few seconds left to them for target acquisition after crossing the hills. Woodward considered it a great tribute to the British missile systems, above all Sea Dart, that fear of them was forcing the enemy to fly so low that pilots had little aiming room and their bombs were not gaining sufficient time in flight to arm themselves. But it seemed vital to reduce the risk to the key supply ships by withdrawing all but two or three being immediately unloaded. It also seemed suicidal to keep warships out in Falkland Sound – they must all pull back into the shelter of San Carlos Bay itself.

Perhaps the most serious discussion concerned the performance of the Rapier missile batteries. At sea, immense faith had been placed in Rapier's ability to protect the landing force once it was established. Yet, after immense effort by the Sea Kings – shifting their ungainly loads as best they could between air attacks – Rapier had been established ashore only to discover that up to eight of its launchers were unserviceable at any one time on that first day. The long exposure to salt at sea had proved damaging to sensitive electronics. The difficulty of moving spare parts from the ships was acute. Unexpected snags were emerging, such as a tendency for the alloy pins retaining the missiles on their slides to snap, dumping the projectiles on the peat. It was almost a year since the operators had their last live-firing exercise, and it was taking time for them to refine the art of visual tracking on the battlefield, especially against targets passing below them. On 21 May, Rapier scored three hits, with ten missiles launched. But this was nowhere near providing the universal panacea against air attack that some optimists had expected. Admiral Woodward signalled testily from *Hermes*: 'I am sure that the Rapier detachments are doing all that they can. However, their performance yesterday was totally unsatisfactory. Put a bomb under them before they get one on top of them.' The message further exacerbated the land force's irritation with FOFI. It seemed an astonishing inversion of all the hopes of the task force that the admiral was now counting so heavily upon Rapier to defend his ships from air attack.

But the senior commanders of the task force – the Chief of Defence Staff in Whitehall, Sir John Fieldhouse at Northwood and Admiral Woodward on *Hermes* – retired to bed that night cheered by the conviction that, if the British had suffered a frightening day, the enemy had endured a far worse one. They estimated that the enemy had lost twenty aircraft. This claim was later reduced to sixteen, but no air force of its size could continue to accept such casualties on a daily basis. Frigates were one commodity with which the task force was plentifully supplied. The lost and damaged ships could be replaced in the line. Meanwhile, after the desperate tension of the past forty-eight hours, when the entire future of the operation hung in the balance, the great triumph of the landing had been secured. From now on, it was a matter of keeping their nerve and pressing on. 'I never thought we should lose,' said Julian Thompson, 'because I knew the political will was there.' But it was a time of acute tension.

While the commanders debated the tactics of the morrow, on the crippled ships men worked through the night to repair the damage. *Argonaut* was being towed into the anchorage behind *Plymouth*, with her crew labouring below decks to pump out her flooded spaces and get her machinery back into action. Suddenly, without warning, her lighting and all auxiliary power failed. An extraordinary silence fell upon the ship. With difficulty she completed her tow and dropped an anchor. Working by torchlight, engine-room staff examined her diesels. It was revealed that one bomb had fractured a fuel tank, the sea had spilled in, and the auxiliary engines had become polluted with salt. Patiently, a team led by Fleet Chief Artificer Uren began to strip down and clean them. Others worked on temporary repairs to the holes in the ship's side, 'stuffing them with mattresses and other good World War II stuff like that,' as Kit Layman said cheerfully. Without the constant hum of generators and ventilators with which they lived by day and night every moment of their lives, 'people went around whispering as if they were in a cathedral. It was a bit of a low point. Everybody was absolutely whacked after being at action stations for seventy-two hours.' The diving officer, a young sub-lieutenant named Peter Morgan, undertook the appalling task of lowering himself into the forward magazine flooded with diesel oil where lay the bodies of the magazine handlers – and the unexploded bomb that had killed them. Thirty minutes later he surfaced, to report that it lay directly above several live Sea Cat missiles.

Auxiliary power was restored to the ship just before first light. The crew were exhausted, and acutely aware that their most dangerous problems were still unresolved. Layman considered that *Argonaut* still lay too far out in the anchorage – 'we knew that they would be coming again' – and requested a tow deeper into the bay. After a prolonged delay at last three landing craft commanded by a breezy Ewen Southby-Taily our appeared alongside. With Layman directing operations by waving his arms from the top of his bridge, the LCUs pulled *Argonaut* slowly up the channel, until she dropped anchor between the assault ships. Shortly afterwards, a matter-of-fact pair of Royal Engineers clambered up the ship's side and asked to be taken to the bombs. Warrant Officer John Phillips and Staff Sergeant Jim Prescott set to work with their rocket wrench, and within an hour had set off a controlled explosion to defuse the weapon in the boiler room. 'Sounds all right,' they said, as the ship's company waited tensely for the outcome on the upper decks. The bomb aft indeed proved safe to remove. The forward bomb, however, was impossibly situated for the bomb-disposal men to work upon. The only hope was for the ship to patch the external hole below the waterline, pump out the magazine, then extricate the weapon as it lay. The captain thanked the engineers, who moved on to other business as routinely as they had arrived. *Argonaut* embarked upon a saga that continued all that week, repairing her damage, while on the decks above her gun crews manned their weapons through all the attacks that followed. As Layman had informed CoMAW, she could not steam. But the tough old steel ship could 'float and fight'. She was called upon to work very hard to do both.

*

That Saturday morning was again bright and clear. In the anchorage, the men stood by their weapons, waiting expectantly while the shuttle of helicopters and landing craft continued, listening intently for the tannoy call 'Air-raid warning red'. A Sea Harrier from *Hermes* spotted the wake of an enemy patrol craft to the south, attacked with cannon and watched the desperate crew run themselves aground on the shore. Two C-130s made a run over West Falkland escorted by six Mirages, but the British were unable to engage them. As the day wore on, the tension began to relax. Thick cloud lay over the Argentine home bases. It also seemed evident that they were licking their wounds after the formidable pounding of the previous day. The British, trying a new tactic reflecting their persistent faith in Sea Wolf and Sea Dart, had posted a '22–42 Combo' of *Broadsword* and *Coventry* as 'a major missile trap', in the admiral's words, out to the north-west. They were seeking to catch Skyhawks and Mirages at long range. Sea Wolf could provide protection against low-level attack. But that Saturday the two ships waited in vain. As darkness fell, the Argentinians had failed to appear.

Under cover of night the British began some vital redeployments. *Glamorgan* steamed in to take the place of the damaged *Antrim* in the escort screen. To the vast relief of most of those at sea and ashore, *Brilliant* escorted out of the bay the Great White Whale *Canberra* and a string of supply ships. There were protests from some commanding officers that stores remained aboard the liner, but none of these were vital. The loss of *Canberra*, or even serious damage to her, would be a disastrous blow to British prestige, out of all proportion to the military advantage of keeping her in San Carlos. The surgical-support teams were now established ashore, in the disused refrigeration plant at Ajax Bay. Commodore Clapp and Admiral Woodward had agreed to reduce to an absolute minimum the unloading of store ships in the anchorage during daylight. This was a serious blow to 3 Commando Brigade, all of whose planning was based upon the assumption that the brigade's logistics support would remain afloat, readily available in San Carlos. Instead, the build-up began of a vast brigade maintenance area at Ajax Bay, into which stores were shuttled as quickly as they could be landed by mexefloat pontoon. Each night, a convoy of supply ships sailed into the anchorage and offloaded for a few hours, only to set forth again long before dawn for the safety of the open sea, east beyond the battle group. It was a procedure which drastically delayed the build-up ashore, and caused deep dismay among the staff of 3 Commando Brigade, who felt that once again the Royal Navy had imposed a critical decision upon them with little consultation. But the navy's arguments are very easy to understand, and the naval staff considered that the land force compounded the problems greatly by indecision about their own needs and priorities.

*

For a brief moment on Sunday morning, yet another bright and beautiful day, some of the men in the anchorage began to believe that the enemy's air force had abandoned its offensive. The day began well for the British. Harriers caught one Huey and two Puma helicopters, destroying all three, *Antelope*'s Lynx crippled an enemy freighter with a Sea Skua missile. *Brilliant* and *Yarmouth* trapped and forced aground the Argentine supply ship *Monsunen*. Then the Skyhawks and Mirages resumed their attacks on the warships. 'All were frightening,' wrote an officer on *Broadsword*, 'but some seemed comical in retrospect. Sea Cat chased three Mirages, and just when some seemed to be gaining, they ran out of steam and fell in the water like something from a *Tom and Jerry* cartoon. Other missiles and bofors fire hit the hillside in pursuit of one jet, scattering a herd of cows who left a trail of dust . . .' 45 Commando, dug in above Ajax Bay, cursed the gunners whose overshoots hammered in around the marine positions.

It was lunchtime when *Antelope*'s Lynx, returning from a check on the ship she had attacked that morning and had now found sinking, suddenly spotted four Skyhawks moving north up Falkland Sound. They disappeared behind Fanning Head and split into two pairs. The first came in low from the east as the ship's guns opened fire; they seemed to flinch from the barrage and turned away. *Antelope*'s pursuing Sea Cat smashed into one aircraft. At that

moment, the other Skyhawks attacked from the north. The first
aircraft screamed over *Antelope* and made for *Broadsword*. A bomb
hit the big frigate aft. Again it failed to explode. The second aircraft
met *Antelope*'s barrage as it approached. Hit in the wing by 20 mm
Oerlikon fire it almost plunged into the side of the ship, pulled up
sharply and smashed into the after mast at 400 m.p.h. The men
on deck heard a sharp crack. The Skyhawk disintegrated, and its
ruins fell into the sea on the port side. Simultaneously, the ship
reeled under the impact of an incoming bomb, which penetrated
aft on the starboard side. A few moments later, yet another
Skyhawk closed on the port quarter and hit *Antelope* with a second
1,000-pounder below the bridge, once again failing to explode, but
ploughing into the petty officers' mess, where it killed a steward
and wounded two sickberth attendants.

Antelope manoeuvred successfully to dodge the next wave of
attacks, then closed in on *Broadsword* to seek shelter while she
examined her own damage. At 2.30 p.m. she limped up San Carlos
Water alongside the crippled *Argonaut*, and prepared to deal with
her bombs. Staff Sergeant Prescott and Warrant Officer Phillips
flew to tackle the second frigate's difficulties. Most of the ship's
company were evacuated to the fo'c'sle, leaving only skeleton
crews manning the armament. For more than an hour, they
wrestled with the bomb delivered by the first Skyhawk. The crew
shivered in the icy northerly wind, and eventually were ordered to
move aft, to the shelter of the flight deck. A broadcast from the
bridge announced that the bomb-disposal team would try a new
method of defusing the bomb. Prescott and Phillips detonated a
small charge, then walked forward to inspect the results. As they
approached, the bomb exploded. Prescott seemed to be hit by a
door blown free by blast, which killed him immediately. Phillips
suffered a badly injured arm, but escaped to the upper decks with
two of *Antelope*'s crew who had accompanied the soldiers. Fire-
fighting teams were already at work. A huge blaze was spreading
outwards from the heart of the ship, billowing smoke and cascad-
ing sparks in the breeze. With great courage, every landing-craft

coxswain in the anchorage closed in on the crippled ship and began to take off survivors. The captain, Nick Tobin, was rescued by an LCVP which closed in forward, where he had scrambled down with four others who had remained alongside him on the bridge. A few minutes after the evacuation was completed, the anchorage was shaken by a series of explosions in the magazines which produced some of the most dramatic photographs of the war taken from neighbouring ships, their crews watching sombrely in the darkness. The next morning, her back broken, the frigate settled slowly into the water, her bow and stern disappearing last, leaving only a handful of life rafts and sailors' caps bobbing silently on the water. It was a spectacle that thousands of men ashore and afloat had witnessed from beginning to end. They had never seen a ship sink before. It was an experience that drove into each of them how bitter and how costly the struggle for the Falklands had now become.

'This was the time that we were at our lowest ebb,' said the principal weapons officer of a destroyer. 'We wondered how long we could keep going. We put on a brave front for the sailors, but we were deeply shaken by the speed and futility of the ship's going down. There seemed a possibility of stalemate. How much more of this could we take?' From *Hermes*, Admiral Woodward conducted an urgent tactical discussion with his captains, by secure telephone. Seven enemy aircraft were believed to have been destroyed that day, but still it was not enough. Captain Black of *Invincible* and Captain Coward of *Brilliant* urged the admiral to bring his carriers closer inshore, perhaps to within 50 miles, to increase the Harriers' endurance on CAP. Four pairs of aircraft could be kept on station instead of two or three. For the rest of the war, the location of the carriers would be a deeply vexed issue within the task force, with many naval and marine officers in San Carlos arguing that they should have operated at much shorter range. Woodward pondered the issue very carefully indeed. He remained totally convinced that the safety of *Hermes* and *Invincible* must be his first priority. If one or both carriers were lost, disaster faced the fleet. The Argentinians had now given far too convincing evidence of their determination and striking power to increase the risk to the battle group. David Hart-Dyke of *Coventry* proposed taking his ship much further west towards the Argentine mainland, to give Sea Dart a real chance against the incoming enemy aircraft. No, said Woodward, this risk also was too serious. If anything went wrong, the destroyer would be too far from possible rescue. The '22–42 Combo' would be deployed once again north of West Falkland.

On 24 May, *Broadsword* and *Coventry* lay on station, yet in vain. The waves of enemy aircraft that swept towards San Carlos gave them no chance of firing. *Coventry* did achieve a solution against a patrolling enemy Boeing 707 reconnaissance aircraft. But, to her crew's disappointment, the Sea Dart flash doors refused to open. By the time they had been forced into motion with a hammer, the aircraft was out of range.

At 9.15 a.m. on the 24th, Skyhawks hit the landing ships *Sir Galahad* and *Sir Lancelot* with one and two bombs respectively. None of the three exploded. The ships were half unloaded, and no vital stores remained aboard them, but their loss would have severely affected the flexibility of the landing force. The largely civilian crews evacuated them, with indecent haste in the view of some naval officers. But they could be salvaged if and when their bombs had been dealt with. It was another sharp shock to the men deployed around the bay.

This was the day, however, on which the defenders at last began to believe that they were gaining the measure of the air attacks. Rapier, after its initial difficulties, was coming of age. Its triumphant crews, perched behind their camouflaged trackers high on the hilltops, claimed three enemy aircraft. *Fearless*'s Bofors claimed two more, the Harriers a final three out of only twelve which attacked. Andy Auld and Lieutenant David Smith were vectored by *Broadsword* onto a formation of four Mirage Vs approaching north of Pebble Island. When the Mirages spotted the Harriers, as usual they jettisoned their bombs and fuel tanks and wheeled for home. The British fighters dived to gain vital speed against the faster Argentine jets – like almost every engagement of the war, this one took place below 500 feet. Auld manoeuvred hard behind the fleeing aircraft until he heard his 'aural tone' and fired two missiles. He was turning to try for a gun kill on a third aircraft, and had just radioed to Smith, 'I can't reach this one, what about you?' when Smith's Sidewinder flashed past his shoulder. Two of the enemy aircraft exploded, the third fell out of the sky after losing its tail and part of a fin. Auld called to *Broadsword*'s radar operator to check his screen: 'Check your six o'clock – we have just splashed three Mirages.' 'Super,' *Broadsword* radioed back. 'That makes eight today so far.' 'Well, that's it for today,' called Smith. 'We might as well go home.' Auld thought, 'Yes, he could just be right, because they can't go on taking this rate of loss much longer.'

The pilots were tired, appallingly tired, after six hours a day in their cockpits. 'Dear Harrier Pilot,' wrote a lady in Scunthorpe who sent a fruit cake to the *Hermes* air group, 'I hope you are still alive to read this . . .' They had lost not a single aircraft in air-to-air combat, but the previous night a pilot had plunged into the sea five miles ahead of the carrier during a night launch. Four aircraft in all were lost in accidents, against three from ground fire. When the pilots climbed from their aircraft at nightfall, they were often too exhausted even to hear the commander's evening broadcast on the events of the day. They lived in their own private world of alerts, takeoffs, patrols, landings, with an occasional can of beer if they were not rostered for night alert, and otherwise only sleep and morning briefings two hours before dawn, followed by take off again. 'You tended to switch off the bad things, because you couldn't let thinking about them affect your flying,' said Lieutenant Commander David Braithwaite, flying with 809 Squadron from *Invincible*. 'One was conscious only of being cold, and of being tired. Initially everybody was a bit frightened, but then even that wears off. That's when you've got to be careful.' The maintenance crews achieved an astonishing 80 per cent serviceability, even with each Harrier averaging six ninety-minute sorties a day. The British possessed only a handful of pilots, but among them were some of the most experienced fliers in the Fleet Air Arm. These men tended to become the highest scorers, the most effective in combat, partly because of their ability and partly also – as Andy Auld admitted wryly – 'because we learned to know when and where there was likely to be something happening, and the senior pilots made sure that they took those patrols'.

*

Throughout the war, the Argentinians were immensely hampered by the poor coordination of their own forces. The responsible air force commander, Brigadier Ernesto Crespo, was not officially informed by the navy or army of the British landing at San Carlos on 21 May until 10 a.m., two hours after the other services became aware of it. He dispatched his early sorties that day on his own initiative, based upon sketchy reports of some form of British operation taking place in the bay. Rear Admiral Juan Jose Lombardo, based in Porto Belgrano, was intended to exercise the same sort of overall direction of Argentine land, sea and air operations around the Falklands as Sir John Fieldhouse was providing for the British. But, as the war situation worsened, inter-service cooperation deteriorated. The army and air force became increasingly reluctant to accept direction of the war effort from a naval officer, when the navy's ships lay impotent in their ports. The navy appears to have mounted its Super Etendard and other air strikes against the British fleet without consulting or informing the air force of its operations. The navy claimed after the war that it was an obsession with prestige targets that persuaded the air force pilots to attack British warships rather than the much more important transports, although the air force in turn blames the poor intelligence it was receiving, and the need to attack the first visible target after coming in sight of San Carlos.

The greatest tactical fear of the British – that the Argentinians might begin sending escorts with their bombing aircraft – never materialised. Even a handful of escorts deflecting the Harriers'

attention might have made a marked impact upon the enemy
sortie rate against San Carlos. But the Argentinians, with only two
Hercules C-130 tanker aircraft, had no resources to spare for escort
duties. Their air force commanders, appalled by their losses, were
already bringing aircraft home away from their own bases, to
prevent them from understanding the full scale of the losses. Some
aircraft with fuel cells damaged by small arms were staggering
back only by flying the last miles coupled to a tanker aircraft. After
the war, Argentine sources claimed that only eighty-one of the air
force's 223 combat aircraft possessed the range and air-to-air refuelling capacity to fly against San Carlos from the mainland – the
Mirage IIIs, Mirage Vs, Canberras and certain marks of Skyhawk.
Of these aircraft, they admitted the loss of 41 per cent of the
first-line fighters, thirty-four aircraft, significantly fewer than
the British claimed. In addition, Aeromacchi and Pucara aircraft
were still operating from Port Stanley and Goose Green. It was a
measure of the ineffectiveness of the British air blockade that,
between 1 May and 14 June, the Argentinians flew 435 tons of
cargo to the Falklands, and claim to have evacuated 264 wounded
men. The strike aircraft operating from the mainland claim to
have planned 505 combat sorties during this period, of which 445
were attempted, and 302 completed. The Argentinians made no
secret of their dismay at the ferocity of the British defences around
the anchorage and, as the days went by, the Harriers turned back
more and more waves before they even approached the islands.
The determination of the enemy's pilots seemed to be visibly
ebbing away. Although the British were not aware of it at the time,
the tide of battle was turning.

*

In the anchorage, the British situation was causing deep concern.
While the enemy's air attacks continued, the logistics build-up was
progressing with painful slowness. One of the most important and
most painful lessons of the war is that even the most realistic
peacetime exercises do not test logistics to the full, do not reveal

men's utter vulnerability to supply problems on the battlefield. Moving ships only in darkness was drastically reducing the expected flow of stores. The 'floating logistics concept' agreed at Ascension Island had been abandoned in the face of the air threat. Ships containing urgently needed equipment were discovered to be far out at sea, and could be brought in with the night convoy only after complex signal discussion with the battle group. The navy was dismayed to discover, for instance, that the vital Rapier generators ran on petrol, and there was a chronic fuel shortage in the anchorage. The difficulties were once again provoking tensions between *Hermes* and the commando brigade. Many naval officers were demanding privately or openly to know what the landing force was doing. Why had it not moved from the bridgehead? Why was the navy expected to endure daily punishment while the campaign ashore did not advance?

Each day, Thompson passed long stretches at the satellite terminal at Ajax Bay. After waiting sometimes hours for a connection, he talked to Northwood. Every call brought the same questions. What was he doing? When would he move? Thompson had understood that he was merely to defend the bridgehead until Major General Moore and 5 Brigade arrived. But new imperatives were rapidly taking over. Overwhelming public attention in Britain was focused upon the air–sea battle in which the Royal Navy was suffering so badly. The war cabinet and Northwood were becoming increasingly impatient for evidence of British movement, British achievement, to justify the lost ships and lives. They also considered it essential to establish British dominance over the Argentinians without delay. 'Unfair pressure from UK,' a brigade staff officer wrote in his diary on the 25th. 'They don't appreciate the pressure of the air threat and tend to dismiss it. The navy's argument is that they have suffered enough and it's now our turn.' Thompson explained patiently to Northwood each day that his helicopters were totally committed moving rations, casualties, ammunition, guns. There were insufficient movement assets to put even a single battalion on the road to Port Stanley. 'Yet I am convinced that we shall be ordered to press on regardless,' wrote the staff officer. Nor were Northwood alone in their concern. Many marines and paras were weary of lingering idle around the anchorage, watching others fight a battle of attrition, the very battle that Woodward had hoped to win before the landing force came ashore. 'It seemed to me that we ought to get on and get into contact with the enemy,' said a marine CO. 'It was a bad thing psychologically not to be in contact – bad to leave the Argentinians entirely alone except for a few Harrier strikes.'

At his brigade headquarters in the gorse beside the San Carlos settlement manager's house, where children played among the camouflaged tents and parked Volvos, Thompson called his COs to an 'O' Group on the 24th. As they sipped soup from thermoses, he urged them to curb their natural impatience. The offloading of the ships must progress further before helicopters would be available to move men. For the time being, SBS and SAS reconnaissance operations were to have priority on available helicopters – it was critical to know more about enemy deployments. Meanwhile, he told his officers: Look east, prepare for the move towards Port Stanley. The SAS would reinforce the vital high ground of Mount Kent as soon as possible, and major units would follow them. Nothing was said about Goose Green. Unhappy but totally aware of their brigadier's predicament, the COs dispersed to their helicopters and returned to their units, debating what they could find for their men to do to keep them busy.

*

It was a strange battle, that week in San Carlos Water, concentrated both in time and space so that it developed a routine of its own. In each twenty-four hours, there were sixteen of darkness, during which the men ashore could do little but sleep and talk. The rigorous blackout made it impossible to cook, read or work. In Port San Carlos, many of the landing force had moved into the settlement buildings and were living in relative comfort. But for the men at Ajax Bay, San Carlos settlement and on Sussex

Mountain, there were no refinements. They slept in the bitter cold and damp of their trenches, with only spasmodic chances of a night in a shearing shed to dry their clothing. At dawn each day, after the ritual of 'Stand to', when men manned their weapons until the light had cleared, the smoke of hundreds of tiny hexamine cookers curled over the company positions as men brewed their tea and oatmeal with apple flakes. Each unit dispatched patrols and manned observation positions overlooking its own area by day and night. One afternoon, 40 Commando captured an Argentine naval lieutenant commander among rocks high above San Carlos. It seemed almost certain that he had been providing intelligence for the air striking force. Such an incident was a welcome break in the usual monotony of digging to improve positions, manning the radio nets, moving rations and ammunition. 'It was comical in a way, after the first day when we realised they weren't going for us,' said a twenty-year-old from Nottingham named Kevin Priestley, of 45 Commando. 'When the attacks came in, we shouted to each other, and sometimes you'd get the whole commando jumping with excitement. We'd look at our watches and say, "Time for the aerobatics to start."' News picked up on the net or from World Service was passed eagerly from man to man by word of mouth between positions. An occasional bottle of whisky or carton of cigarettes 'rassed' from one of the storeships was deeply prized. No man much minded the discomfort and cold in themselves; the growing frustration and boredom grew from the feeling that the landing force, through all these days, was only an impotent spectator of the great drama unfolding below in the anchorage and offshore. They cheered passionately as enemy aircraft exploded, and cursed aloud when they saw ships struck. They fired their rifles and machine-guns and Blowpipes whenever an attacker came within miles, to the dismay of the logistics staff, desperate to husband ammunition.

Until the very end of the war, most men continued to feel a sense of fantasy about events: the spectacle of a British warship burning before their eyes was too close to television war films and too far from anything that they themselves had ever experienced to seem real. Only once throughout the air battle did the men around San Carlos face direct attack. At last light one evening, without warning, two Skyhawks burst over San Carlos settlement at very low level. In slow motion, men watched in horror as parachute-retarded bombs floated gently down towards 40 Commando's position. Yet only two men were killed by direct hits, and three wounded, demonstrating the effectiveness of deeply dug entrenchments and the weakness of bombs in the soft Falklands peat.

Meanwhile, across the water at Ajax Bay, three more Skyhawks dropped twelve bombs on the brigade maintenance area, killing six men, wounding twenty-seven, and starting a major fire in 45 Commando's heavy-weapons ammunition dump. For hours in the darkness, men laboured to move the wounded from beneath wreckage to the main dressing station, which itself harboured two unexploded bombs, while mortar and Milan rounds burst into the bay, and small-arms ammunition crackled and popped through the night. Brigadier Thompson visited the area, profoundly alarmed. The entire brigade's operations had been planned on the assumption of keeping its logistics afloat. The air assault had forced them instead to create huge dumps at Ajax Bay. But these now seemed appallingly vulnerable to attack. Where else could they go? Thompson asked himself desperately. The answer was nowhere. It was fortunate for the land force that the enemy never attacked Ajax again after inflicting that one, deadly fright.

It was a paradox that, for the ships' crews, life for many hours in each twenty-four seemed incomparably more comfortable and secure than for those ashore. Drinking gin in a warm wardroom amongst a throng of officers before an invariably excellent Royal Naval dinner, men talked earnestly about the events of the day and weighed the odds for the morrow. In the privacy of their cabins, exhausted captains interviewed a seemingly endless procession of department chiefs about their machinery, ammunition, supply states. Could they put to sea tomorrow night for a replenishment-at-sea operation and still be back on station in time for dawn action stations? What news was there of Able Seaman Smith or Jones, lying wounded at Ajax Bay or aboard the hospital ship *Uganda*? Could something be done to strengthen the port Bofors mounting or was it more urgent to deal with the troublesome condenser aft, where kelp was clogging the intakes? Senior officers afloat had far less sleep than their counterparts ashore, because lights blazed and men worked as steadily through the hours of darkness as those of daylight. At intervals through the night, even those in their bunks were awakened by the steamhammer 'clang!' against the hull as 'scare charges' were exploded in the water to deter enemy frogmen. The crews operated at defence watches – six hours on and six off – for the entire war, with action stations routines in addition. The signals staffs were among the most overstrained of all. On the command ship *Fearless* well over 100,000 signals – a million copies in all – were passed before the war ended. One officer calculated that there had been over 5,000 calls to the bridge in the same period.

Long before dawn, men woke and breakfasted so that every chair and loose fitting could be lashed down, all galley operations shut down before action stations. On many ships, once action stations had become a routine, the crew was roused by a calm tannoy pipe rather than a dramatic hooter. A pipe wore less hardly on the nerves. Even in darkness, most men scarcely bothered to remove their white anti-flash capes, but relaxed and ate with them pushed down on their necks. At dawn, they merely pulled them over their heads and donned their gloves. Then the captains made a routine daily broadcast to their ships' companies. 'Good morning,' Jeremy Larken of *Fearless* began a characteristic report. All over the ship, more than a thousand men, many of whom never saw the light of natural day, strained to catch his voice over the hum of vents and air conditioners, the roar of machinery and the constant traffic of transmissions, telephones, hurrying figures. 'It's quite a murky day, although not as murky as we should like to see it. I wanted to warn both the ship's company and our visitors what a tremendous amount of noise a bomb makes when it explodes in the water. It's liable to make the ventilation system go "splutter putt", caulking fall from the deckheads and so on. I'm simply lining you up so that, if you hear a very big bang, you needn't feel the world is coming to an end . . .'

In the wardroom, a crowd of pilots clustered around the loudspeaker. The second officer of an evacuated LSL tinkled tune-lessly for a moment at the piano. Captain Larken moved on to describe the deployments for the day: '. . . *Broadsword* is leading the band, with *Plymouth* as goalkeeper. Rapier is in good form and bright eyed, so let us all hope for a good day . . .'

As the dawn came up over the battlefield, a yellow dinghy drifted alone over the last resting place of *Antelope*. The upper-works of every warship resembled sets for some cinema epic of the Battle of the Atlantic, with young men muffled in gauntlets, balaclavas and helmets huddled behind sheet steel and sandbags over their machine-guns. 'Everybody moans about modern youth,' said the captain of *Arrow* one morning. 'They should come and see some of these lads.' He pointed to his seventeen- and eighteen-year-old Oerlikon gunners on the bridge wings. They were only proving for the thousandth time in history that even the very young, when they find great responsibilities thrust upon them, almost invariably respond marvellously well. At this moment in British history, it cheered many men very deeply to see the teenagers performing their duty so finely. Among the younger men, as always it was loyalty to their comrades and to their ships and units that dominated their thoughts and behaviour in action.

'I think morale is becoming better rather than worse,' said the surgeon lieutenant on *Arrow* on the morning of the 25th. 'People are becoming angry, getting more aggressive towards the enemy.' A fleet chief petty officer, at his action station in damage control, said, 'It's all been theory since 1945. Now it's the real thing, and mistakes will be made, lessons learned, the same as last time. The lads were a bit shaken up by the losses. It's not the ships – they can be replaced. It's the men.' Then the first red alert of the day was sounded, and the captain broadcast to the ship's company: 'Remember, lads, when they come, give them hell.' War is full of clichés, because only clichés can match the drama of the moment.

*

25 May is Argentina's National Day. The British knew from the beginning that the enemy would exert himself to the utmost to do justice to the occasion. But, as the waves of enemy aircraft came in, the defences responded with formidable effect. Two Mirages being chased from Falkland Sound by Harriers were shot down by Sea Dart missiles fired from *Coventry*, lying forward on picket with *Broadsword*. *Coventry* later shot down a third aircraft, Rapier claimed one, and *Yarmouth* another. The morale of the men in the anchorage soared.

Now the Argentinians delivered one of the most crippling double blows of the entire campaign. At 2 p.m. at her usual station north of Pebble Island, the crew of *Coventry* were in high spirits after the destruction of three enemy aircraft, a satisfying achievement for Sea Dart. Her captain, the elegant and energetic David Hart-Dyke, debated whether to move from the area after his success to avoid the risk of being targeted for direct attack, but decided against doing so. He and his men were elated by the morning's kills, and were looking for more. An air-raid warning came through, and he sent the crew to action stations once again. *Coventry*, with the escorting *Broadsword* half a mile astern, was running at 12 knots on her Tyne cruising engines, and beginning to work up to high speed. For a brief moment Sea Dart achieved a solution on the attackers, only to lose it again. 'Where the hell are they, then?' asked Hart-Dyke, on his high seat in the operations room, peering intently at the radar screen in front of him. 'I can't see them.' Then two Skyhawks streaked from the contours of Pebble Island and came at deck level for the ships. Every automatic weapon on the destroyer was in action as the Skyhawks opened fire with cannon. The aircraft seemed to flinch from *Coventry*'s fire, and swung aside towards *Broadsword*.

On the frigate, Sea Wolf was switched on. Its computer examined the two approaching targets, almost indistinguishably close together, sought to decide which to attack, and found the decision electronically too difficult. The missile system switched itself off. *Broadsword*'s crew flattened themselves on her deck, while her guns kept firing. In an agony of expectation, they waited for the inevitable bomb. Then there was a loud 'Clang!' aft. A single bomb had entered the starboard side of the ship and bounced out through the flight deck, destroying the Lynx helicopter but failing to explode.

Sea Wolf now gained a solution on the second pair of Skyhawks closing in. But, to the aimer's dismay, as he prepared to fire, *Coventry* swung across *Broadsword*'s bow. Hart-Dyke had ordered a sharp starboard turn to present the smallest possible target to the incoming aircraft, and was expecting *Broadsword* to manoeuvre to avoid him. Sea Wolf was unable to fire.

Sea Dart achieved a solution, fired, and missed. *Coventry*'s 4.5 gun was firing continuously, and all her automatic weapons that would bear were in action. The Skyhawks bombed fine on the destroyer's port bow. Of the four 1,000-pound bombs that fell, one landed astern and the others smashed into the port side, tore deep into the ship and exploded, wounding her mortally. Hart-Dyke recovered from a brief moment of unconsciousness to find himself surrounded by black smoke and wreckage. One bomb had exploded immediately aft and below the operations room, killing nine men in the forward engine room immediately, and causing havoc in the areas above. 'All I could see around me were people on fire, like candles burning,' said Hart-Dyke. His own face was badly burned, and flesh was hanging loose from his hands. For a moment he sought in vain for an escape route through the port side, only to find it completely vanished. He found himself behind a queue of men stumbling in search of an exit. He thought of his home, his children, his wife. Then he staggered through the starboard door and up a twisted, ruined ladder to his bridge. There were flames and thick smoke everywhere. He somehow made his

way out on to the port bridge wing, and fell on his hands and
knees to breathe more easily. He asked if the main broadcast was
still operational. It was not. He ordered his warfare officer, Lieutenant Commander O'Connell, 'Get the ship moving fast to the east.'
'Aye, aye, sir,' said the obedient O'Connell. He vanished to follow
his captain's bidding, when Hart-Dyke achieved a moment of
clarity and thought: That's a ridiculous order. The ship was already
listing heavily to port, and all power had gone.

With difficulty, the captain clambered up the starboard side
and saw his men already abandoning ship, helping each other to
put on 'once-only' suits, quietly making their way into the liferafts.
There was no shouting, no screaming. Hart-Dyke walked down the
steeply tilting side of his ship and stepped into the water. During
the passage south, a petty officer had approached him one day and
offered him a card bearing a prayer of St Joseph that he assured
the captain would bring him safely home again if only he carried
it. Now, blackened and burned, he was pulled over the side of a
liferaft by the same Petty Officer Burke, who declared with satisfaction, 'You see, sir, it works.' But, to their dismay, they found the
raft being sucked against the ship, brushing against the 4.5 gun,
its barrel still hot, and finally puncturing itself against the tip of a
Sea Dart missile on the launcher. Hart-Dyke found himself back in
the water, while many men scrambled on to the hull of the
destroyer and clung to its sinking upperworks. Then helicopters
began to appear overhead. Every available Sea King and Wessex
had been vectored to *Coventry*'s position from San Carlos. Some
crewmen were soon winching themselves into the water to rescue
wounded men. One aircraft landed on *Coventry*'s red-hot hull to
pick up men. Some of Hart-Dyke's men helped him aboard a
Wessex, which landed him on *Broadsword*. There were 283 survivors in all. Nineteen men had died. In the bath of the captain's
cabin aboard the frigate – the comfort, even luxury of the 22s'
living accommodation was a standing naval joke – Hart-Dyke
suddenly realised how desperately cold he was. His feet were blue.
The frigate's crew stripped and bathed all the survivors before they

were transferred to the supply ship *Fort Austin* for eventual repatriation to Britain. The ships in the San Carlos anchorage seemed
to be carrying many survivors that week, too many. The loss
of *Coventry*, the third of the Type 42 air-defence ships to be put
out of action, was a bitter blow, not least because of the further
doubts that it cast upon the efficiency of the fleet's missile systems.
The cold was creating intense difficulty for the aimers, who found
themselves unable to track missiles whose tail glow was obscured
by a cloud of condensation. Both Sea Dart and Sea Wolf were
achieving kills. But they seemed unable to provide decisively
effective protection for themselves, far less for the task force. And
the Argentinians had still not finished for the day.

*

Admiral Woodward had always believed that the Argentinians
would choose this occasion to launch a renewed Exocet attack on
the carrier task group, and he was perfectly correct. The Argentinians rightly judged that the weight of British defensive power
around the battle group was concentrated on its western flank,
closest to the mainland. On 25 May, when two Super Etendards of
the second attack squadron took off from Rio Gallegos searching
for the vital targets – *Invincible* and *Hermes* – they flew north,
refuelling in mid-air from other Etendards. This was a vital
mission, for the aircraft carried two of only three air-launched
Exocets remaining to the Argentinians. It seems that their desperate efforts to purchase more missiles in the course of the war
failed; they were even unable to find extra fuel drop-tanks, of
which they were chronically short. 110 miles north-north-east of
the Falklands the Etendards turned south. They rapidly located the
battle group on radar, 70 miles northeast of the islands.

The enemy was still more than 30 miles to the north when the
Type 21 frigate *Ambuscade* detected an attack on her 992 radar, and
immediately alerted the fleet. The fate of one missile has never
been determined, but several men on *Ambuscade*'s bridge saw
the smoke trail of a second Exocet boring in, the red glow of its

exhaust clearly visible. The ship opened fire with its 4.5 gun, Oerlikons, GPMGs. Above all, every British warship fired chaff radar decoy. A Lynx helicopter is also believed to have been operating an active decoy. But the 13,000-ton container ship *Atlantic Conveyor*, perhaps 2 miles to starboard of *Ambuscade*, possessed no chaff. The missile veered sharply in mid-air from a course towards the warships – including *Invincible* – and struck *Conveyor* below the superstructure on the port side. After the explosion, a huge fire quickly took hold. *Ambuscade* lowered her sea boat, and with three other frigates closed in to begin taking off survivors. The container ship's vital cargo of Harriers had been transferred to the carriers a week earlier. But she also carried ten Wessex and four giant Chinook helicopters, together with the tentage for the entire landing force. One Chinook's rotors were bolted into place and by exceptional good fortune the aircraft was already airborne. *Conveyor* was scheduled to enter San Carlos with the night's convoy to fly off the remainder. But, within an hour of the Exocet strike, the ship's helicopters, upon which all the British plans for their breakout from the beach-head hinged, were blazing ruins. Scores of sailors and RAF technicians leaped overboard into their liferafts. One of the last to leave the ship was the master, a splendidly colourful veteran seaman named Ian North, the much-loved bearded 'Captain Birdseye'. He swam to one liferaft in his orange 'once-only' suit, and found it already overcrowded. He disappeared into the failing light, swimming towards the next, and was never seen again. Eleven other men died. The loss of the Chinooks, capable of lifting eighty men each, was a crippling blow to British strategic plans for the campaign, another bitter shock for the Royal Navy. Thenceforth, Woodward's carriers were seldom closer than 200 miles to San Carlos. The Harriers' CAP endurance had been shortened yet again.

It was only with hindsight – and of no comfort to the fleet that night – that Woodward and his crews could perceive 25 May as the turning point of the war at sea. From then on, with the sole exception of 8 June, the Argentine air force made only brief hit-

and-run raids upon the British ships. One third of its fighter strength had been destroyed, and many of its best pilots lost. Like the German invaders of Crete in 1941, who were on the verge of abandoning their attack until they suddenly realised that it was the British who were broken and retreating, the task force slowly perceived that, however grievous its own wounds, those that it had inflicted on the enemy were even more crippling. The British had accepted their share of both good and ill fortune: on the day of their approach to San Carlos, the weather gave them a priceless advantage. In the week that followed, however, it was extraordinarily clear for the South Atlantic in winter. The enemy's pilots benefited accordingly. If those vital first days had been heavily overcast, the British might have achieved their victory in the Falklands at a fraction of its eventual cost. But they also enjoyed the luck of the enemy's bombs failing to explode. It was perfectly true that it was the threat of Sea Dart that caused the pilots to fly too low. But only a very modest improvement in Argentina's technical capability would have been needed to fuse their bombs so that they exploded on impact. The Argentinians were furious to learn later that the bombs' American manufacturers had a manual on such improvements which was denied them under the US embargo; they regarded such information as normal after-sales service.

The British won the battle for San Carlos – which was the decisive struggle of the war, the last moment at which the entire campaign might have foundered – thanks to the courage of their captains and crews, and overwhelmingly to the achievements of the Sea Harriers. The Harriers accounted for thirty-one – and the most reliable thirty-one – of the total 109 enemy aircraft claimed destroyed at the end of the war. In addition, the Harriers made an enormous contribution by breaking up and turning back enemy attacks before they had been pressed home. It is difficult, however, to regard the armament with which the Royal Navy sought to defend their own ships as anything but inadequate. Sea Dart claimed eight kills, Sea Wolf five and Sea Cat six by the end of the war. Yet the failures and inadequacies of each system were directly responsible for the crippling of *Glasgow* and the loss of *Coventry*, and indirectly for many other losses. No defensive system in war can be perfect, but that with which the British sailed into battle in the South Atlantic was almost fatally fallible. 'We have moved too quickly and too completely into the missile age,' as a senior captain said ruefully after the battle of San Carlos. It had been a very, very close-run thing.

While the events of that week opened a further gap in the relationship between the men in San Carlos Water and Admiral Woodward – dispatching his abrasive signals from the distant operations room of *Hermes* – it is difficult for his critics to fault his handling of resources. The technical shortcomings of the Royal Navy were no responsibility of Admiral Woodward. In the situation in which he found himself by 25 May, his decision to refuse any hazard to his carriers may be unromantic, but was clearly correct. The hostility and scepticism that he generated were caused by the gulf between his earlier bombastic confidence and his later caution in action, together with his knack of upsetting those who did not know him well. At the end of the day, however, it was his task force that successfully asserted their command of the sea around the Falklands in the face of the Argentine navy and air force. For this, he is richly entitled to his share of the credit, of which so much also goes to his men. It was only the ship designers of the Royal Navy who, for all the excuses made for them by the heads of their service, can have derived little satisfaction from the battle for San Carlos.

*

But all these reflections are the product of hindsight. On 25 May, in San Carlos, far from basking in a victory, the British were nursing a deep sense of dismay. Above all, that day signalled the collapse of London's patience with the slow progress of the build-up in the beach-head.

To those who admired Brigadier Julian Thompson and his

conduct of operations in the Falklands, it would come as a shock
when the war was over to learn that a faction in London – both
politicians and service chiefs – spoke less than warmly of him.
They appeared to believe that, from 21 to 25 May, he allowed his
forces to idle in the beach-head while desperate pressures were
mounting on the British from outside. First, the government was
increasingly alarmed by the risk that the United Nations would
abruptly make an irresistible demand for a ceasefire, which would
leave the British controlling only their beach-head around San
Carlos. While the directors of the war were unanimous in explain-
ing this later, at the time they told neither Thompson nor Woodward of the reasons for their sudden urge for movement. Second,
and equally critical, was the imperative of public expectation
following the task force's continuing losses. Some British commanders, including Woodward, spoke warmly after the war about
the lack of 'back-seat driving' during the campaign. Yet Thompson
was exposed to relentless pressure to move from the moment of
the landing at San Carlos. Once again, it may be argued that a
relatively junior officer was being asked to accept huge responsibilities: in this case, for possible disaster to the land force that could
follow a decision to move too soon. Throughout the campaign, if
there were important British weaknesses, they were in the area
of command and control, of communication and understanding
between the disparate elements of the task force at sea and ashore.
For all the marvels of modern technology there were remarkable
lapses of liaison. Inter-service confidence, both in Britain and the
South Atlantic, became very strained indeed. Important intelligence in the possession of the Chiefs of Staff in London never
reached Thompson in the South Atlantic. If the chiefs of staff in
London had always expected 3 Commando Brigade to advance
from the beach-head immediately after landing, none of those at
San Carlos seemed aware of their intention until after the event.
Claims in London that Jeremy Moore had always emphasised the
importance of fighting a quick battle to establish ascendancy over
the enemy may be well founded, but the realities on the spot made

this immensely difficult. Contrary to the Whitehall view, there is no reason to suppose that, had Moore been at San Carlos from 21 to 25 May, he could have done any more or any better with the resources at his disposal. One chief of staff described this period later as 'the worst of the war – waiting desperately for us to do something'. Yet there is no senior officer who served ashore in the first days after landing who believes that Thompson could have moved before he did.

The world now knows that the Argentinians never counterattacked the beach-head, never attacked the advancing British march across East Falklands, never even sent fighting patrols to dislocate operations at San Carlos. But all these risks were very real at the time. Indeed they would have been automatic initiatives for any energetic and competent army. There was also serious concern about the Argentinians' Pucara ground-attack aircraft. Thompson would not have been forgiven had he suffered a serious setback because he underestimated the enemy's power to cause him mischief, as other officers were to do two weeks later when *Galahad* anchored at Fitzroy. So serious were his supply problems in that first week that, at one point, the main dressing room station was down to a day's supply of anaesthetics, and brigade was having immense difficulty maintaining the flow of rations to the units around the anchorage. There is no doubt that part of the problem stemmed from poor organisation of helicopter movements, which was still in the hands of a grossly overstretched naval staff. Much more to blame was the fact that a small force at the end of an immensely long line of communication was waging a war with a dangerous minimum of equipment and resources. But, in the wake of the Royal Navy's disturbing losses in the first days following the landing, there was a period of acute agitation at Northwood and in Whitehall. Under enormous public and diplomatic pressure, Thompson's difficulties were forgotten. The government strove to produce some evidence of British success.

Thompson was at his headquarters working on revised and much more modest plans for an advance without the three Chinook helicopters, each with the lifting power of five Sea Kings, that had been lost on *Atlantic Conveyor*. Suddenly he found himself summoned to the satellite terminal at Ajax Bay. It was Northwood who now told the brigadier exactly what he was to do. The command in Britain considered it essential that the landing force should engage the Argentinians at the first opportunity. The obvious choice was to send a force to Goose Green, the enemy base only 13 miles south of San Carlos. Thompson said that he regarded Goose Green as strategically irrelevant: once Stanley fell, Goose Green must go also, which was scarcely true the other way around. He had planned to leave a small force masking any possible Argentine sally from Goose Green, which anyway seemed unlikely from the enemy's performance to date, and concentrate on moving forward to Mount Kent, the vital ground for a push on Stanley. He could press on towards Kent with part of his force, by all means, said General Dick Trant – now Fieldhouse's deputy at Northwood, with General Moore incommunicado aboard *QE2* – but to Goose Green a British force must go. Indeed, in a ruthless conversation between Northwood and San Carlos, it was suggested if Thompson remained reluctant to march his force immediately, another commander would be found who was not.

After four days of almost unbroken bad news, London needed a tangible victory. If ever there was a politicians' battle, then Goose Green was to be it. At no notice, Thompson summoned his commanding officers. 2 Para was to carry out a 'raid' on Darwin–Goose Green. Meanwhile, 45 Commando and 3 Para were to begin the breakout from the beach-head on foot – 'yomping', in marine parlance. Since the lack of helicopters made it impossible to fly men towards Port Stanley, they would walk – across the frost-baked peat and marshes of East Falkland in winter. The unit commanders were astonished. One at least refused to believe that it could be done. It was the nemesis of all their hopes for a swift helicopter leapfrog across the island. There was a deep fear that the units that marched would exhaust themselves long before they had even reached a battlefield.

Hew Pike had committed 3 Para to a programme of intensive patrolling when he heard on the 24th that there was unlikely to be a rapid breakout. Now, his unit was caught off balance, with many men wet and tired. But they took great pride in their claims to be able to accomplish anything. At 1 p.m. on the afternoon of 27 May, 3 Para set out for Teal Inlet, bearing their enormous loads, and setting a cracking pace across the rolling, broken country.

'We have to fight and win three victories,' Lieutenant Colonel Andrew Whitehead of 45 Commando wrote in his diary. 'Against the enemy; against the appalling terrain and weather; and against our own logistic inadequacies.' Then, at first light of 27 May, his men boarded landing craft to be taken up San Carlos Water to Port San Carlos. There, carrying an average of 120 pounds a man, the marines began their historic march across the island. While they were doing so, 2 Para went to Goose Green.

13 » GOOSE GREEN

The concept of massed parachute drops into battle was obsolete within a generation of its inception in the Second World War. Yet, in every army in the world today, paratroops remain elite formations. They possess a glamour, an aggressive self-confidence and toughness that earn some suspicion and jealousy from other units. In the British army, 'the maroon machine' – the Parachute Regiment – has never been universally popular. Its critics argue that maintaining parachute formations is uneconomic when they are never likely to jump into battle. Some accuse the regiment of adopting a reckless, bull-headed approach to battle, and recall 'Bloody Sunday' in Londonderry as a case study in mishandled peacekeeping. In 1974, the sceptics were successful in bringing about the disbandment of 16 Para Brigade, the regiment's all-arms formation. Some hoped that this would be followed by the dissolution of the unit's three fighting battalions.* But the public and political power of the image of the red beret is enormous. Even in peacetime soldiering, most senior officers are conscious of the value of a unit which, when it is needed, is needed very

---

* A British infantry battalion is composed of some six hundred men, normally organised into a headquarters company and four rifle companies – A, B, C, D. Each company – around ninety strong – is made up of three thirty-man platoons and a headquarters. Each platoon divides into three eight-man rifle sections and a headquarters. In addition, there is a support company composed of anti-tank, mortar and sustained-fire machine-gun platoons. A battalion is commanded by a lieutenant colonel, with majors leading the companies, lieutenants leading the platoons, corporals or lance corporals leading sections. A Royal Marine commando possesses one fewer rifle company, and marine ranks are more senior than their army equivalents: thus companies are commanded by captains.

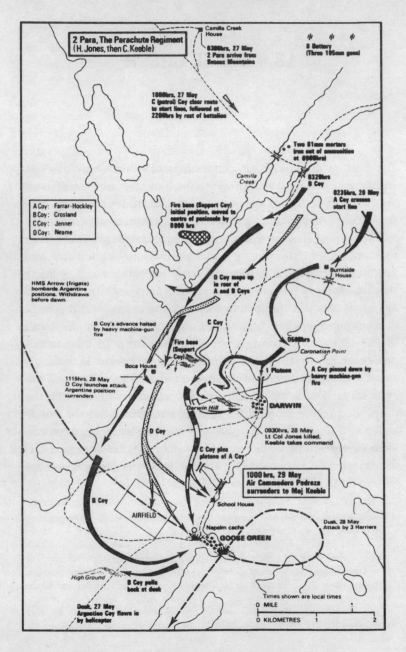

2 Para, The Parachute Regiment
(H. Jones, then C. Keeble)

Camilla Creek
House

0300hrs, 27 May
2 Para arrive from
Sussex Mountains

B Battery
(Three 105mm guns)

1000hrs, 27 May
C (patrol) Coy clear route
to start lines, followed at
2200hrs by rest of battalion

Two 81mm mortars
(run out of ammunition
at 0900hrs)

Camilla
Creek

0320hrs
B Coy

0235hrs, 28 May
A Coy crosses
start line

A Coy: Farrar-Hockley
B Coy: Crosland
C Coy: Jenner
D Coy: Neame

Fire base (Support Coy)
initial position, moved to
centre of peninsula by
0800 hrs

HMS Arrow (frigate)
bombards Argentine
positions. Withdraws
before dawn

B Coy mops up
in rear of
A and B Coys

Burntside
House

B Coy's advance halted
by heavy machine-gun
fire

C Coy

0500hrs

Coronation Point

Boca House

Fire base
(Support
Coy)

1 Platoon

A Coy pinned down by
heavy machine-gun
fire

1115hrs, 28 May
D Coy launches attack.
Argentine position
surrenders

B

DARWIN

Darwin Hill

D Coy

0930hrs, 28 May
Lt Col Jones killed.
Keeble takes command

C Coy pins
platoon of A Coy

1000 hrs, 29 May
Air Commodore Pedroza
surrenders to Maj Keeble

B Coy

School House

AIRFIELD

Napalm cache

Dusk, 28 May
Attack by 3 Harriers

GOOSE GREEN

High Ground

B Coy pulls
back at dusk

Dusk, 27 May
Argentine Coy flown in
by helicopter

Times shown are local times

0   MILE   1

0 KILOMETRES   1   2

badly indeed: to attempt the impossible. On Sunday, 4 April, 2 Para's hockey team had been fighting out the final of the inter-regimental cup when the man who brought out the oranges at half-time told the officers of the team tersely, '"O" Group at four o'clock.'

They had gone back to win the match. Early that evening, some thirty-five expectant young men gathered in the battalion training office at Aldershot to be addressed by their commanding officer. Lieutenant Colonel Herbert Jones, universally known as 'H', had driven headlong home from holiday in France at the first news of the crisis. The unit was on the point of embarking for a six-month tour in Belize. Now, the order that they all craved so passionately had come: they were warned to stand by for the Falklands task force.

The men who began to prepare for war that night, like their counterparts of 3 Para already at sea, were among the most dedicated fighting soldiers in the British army. Many of the company commanders of both battalions, such as Major John Crosland of B Company, had served in the SAS, and seen action in Dhofar. Dair Farrar-Hockley, the thirty-five-year-old officer commanding A Company, with his jutting chin and passionate commitment to the army, was the son of the colonel commandant of the regiment, married to the daughter of another general. Chris Keeble, toweringly tall and silver-haired, second in command of the battalion, joined the Royal Anglians from Douai School in 1963, and transferred to the paras in 1971. He found them 'far more professional than most infantry units. In an ordinary infantry battalion, there is an undefined limit about what you can do. The philosophy of the Parachute Regiment is that there is nothing you cannot do. I find that very attractive. There are no limits.'

2 Para used their last days before embarkation to organise a hasty battalion exercise, and to begin an intensive programme of preparation for battle. H Jones's fascination with the business of war had always gone beyond professional duty. 'He had grown up with the philosophy of soldiering,' in Chris Keeble's words. The

son of a prosperous West Country landowning family and the brother of a naval officer, H joined the Devon and Dorset Regiment after Eton, and transferred to the paras in 1980. At the age of forty-two there was still a boyish passion about him, a quick temper, a charm and devastating grin that could light up his face without warning. 'He was intolerant in some ways – he wouldn't suffer fools,' said Keeble. 'But he had a habit of being right. He was a real leader.'

Jones was a passionate believer in a balanced battalion with specialists and equipment for the widest possible range of tasks, while Keeble emphasised that the critical factor for a unit on the battlefield is 'its power to generate violence'. They doubled 2 Para's complement of machine-guns and procured a dozen American M79 grenade launchers. Both before and after they embarked on the ferry *Norland*, the men worked obsessively to improve their medical training and procedures for handling casualties. Dr Steve Hughes, the unit's medical officer, had been in the army only eighteen months, but had made a special study of casualty statistics, of the commonest cases of wounds. Men practised exchanging specialist skills. They established a complete alternative tactical headquarters with which Keeble could assume immediate command on the battlefield if Jones was hit. They spent £120 from unit funds to buy privately a plastic human arm on which they practised identifying veins and attaching drips as they sailed south.

'All the time we had this terrible preoccupation that we might miss the show,' said Keeble. H had flown ahead to join the amphibious task group already at Ascension. As *Norland* steamed south, the paras daily pleaded with her captain to move faster, demanded to know why they could not take a more direct course. When they learned of the tortuous debate within the high command about possible landing sites, they were impatient of schemes for going ashore as far away as possible from the enemy: 'Why can't we just go in and banjo the bastards?' They did not expect that their own regiment would take a prominent part in the

campaign: 'The whole flavour was that it was to be a commando
benefit. We were just happy to have caught up.'

*

In the first days after the San Carlos landing, 2 Para suffered acute
frustration and discomfort on Sussex Mountain. The cold and wet
– far more fierce than on the shoreline – might have been tolerable
if the battalion had been active. But they were forbidden to patrol
forward towards Darwin because D Squadron of the SAS was
operating in that sector.

The most that could be said was that, in Keeble's words, 'it was
a useful learning time'. They watched the air battles and occasionally poured fire at Argentine Skyhawks and Mirages streaking past
them towards the anchorage. They cooked their rations and took
turns to dry clothes and boots. But B Company had already lost
seven men to trench foot, and the others were little better off.
'We were slowly deteriorating,' said Keeble. 'H's natural impatience
was beginning to turn to real concern. While the Argentinians
hacked at the ships, the landing force remained immobile. One
afternoon around the fourth day, H declared flatly, "We are not
winning. We are losing."'

On the morning of 23 May, 2 Para received a warning order
from 3 Commando Brigade: the battalion, less approximately one
company which would continue to hold Sussex Mountain, was to
march that night to carry out 'a large-scale raid' upon the Argentine positions at Darwin and Goose Green. For all their eagerness
to be gone from Sussex, H and his officers were less than happy
about this plan. To attack strongly prepared enemy positions
from the obvious direction – the north – with only minimal support seemed hazardous, to put it mildly. Could the unit, or at
least elements of it, land by sea or air from the south? No, replied
brigade briefly. There were no helicopters for them to do so, and it
was not navigationally feasible to bring in landing craft. On the
afternoon of 24 May, D company led off the long march to secure

Camilla Creek House, 11 miles down the route, for the remainder of the battalion. At 7 p.m., Chris Keeble and the men who were to remain on Sussex watched unhappily as the remainder of 2 Para began to file out from their positions in the failing light. Then, minutes later, a signal came from brigade. The poor flying weather made it impossible to move up their supporting artillery in time for the attack. The raid was cancelled. D Company began their long march back up the mountain, while the others slipped wretchedly back into their trenches. 'I've waited twenty years for this,' said H savagely, 'and now some f—ing marine's cancelled it.'

It was already past midday on the afternoon of 26 May when Jones was summoned to another urgent 'O' Group at brigade. 2 Para was to go to Goose Green after all. In the intervening forty-eight hours, Brigadier Thompson had made a renewed attempt to convince Northwood by satellite telephone that the southern isthmus could be masked while his forces made the decisive push towards Stanley. He failed. 3 Commando Brigade was ordered by General Trant to proceed with the move on Goose Green, Some senior officers in England later affected surprise that Brigadier Thompson had not sent two battalions to do the job, but this seems wisdom after the event. The best intelligence available in San Carlos suggested that the Argentinians had only a weak battalion defending the settlement. Moving even one British unit with fire support to Goose Green was an immensely difficult – and, to Thompson, strategically irrelevant – exercise. At the afternoon 'O' Group at San Carlos, it was decided that, this time, the whole of 2 Para – some 450 fighting men – would march. It was to be a battalion attack, but Thompson still intended to withdraw the unit when it was complete. He needed men too badly for his main offensive to leave a battalion in the south. 2 Para would be supported by only half a battery of artillery – three 105 mm guns, all that could be lifted to a firing position at Camilla Creek House with the helicopters available. Mike Holroyd-Smith, the senior gunner, hinted to H that it might assist Julian Thompson's efforts to avoid undertaking the Goose Green attack if 2 Para insisted on more gun support. That would at least mean delay. 'I'm not delaying anything,' said H briefly.

Keeble did pass a request for some Scorpion and Scimitar light tanks to support the operation. But petrol for them was acutely short and, more important, the staff doubted that they could cover the ground. The same arguments prevented the dispatch of any 'BVs' – Volvo tracked vehicles – to move the battalion's heavy weapons. The mortar platoon could not conceivably man-pack all eight of their tubes together with ammunition. It was decided to take only two mortars, the remaining men carrying bombs. However, the navy was making available gunfire support from the frigate *Arrow* – alone providing the equivalent of a full battery of 105 mms in firepower. Harrier strikes would be available from first light on the 28th. There would be no time for H to issue formal orders to his men before leaving Sussex Mountain. This would have to be done during the next day's lay-up at Camilla Creek House. Meanwhile, the most urgent priority was to gain up-to-date intelligence about the enemy positions covering Darwin. The colonel would pass the last hours before the battalion marched aboard the assault ship *Intrepid*, debriefing the SAS patrols who had been operating above the Darwin–Goose Green peninsula since the week before the landing.

H walked out of the brigade command post among the gorse below San Carlos settlement with the brigade major, John Chester. 'Colonel, I'm sorry you've been f—d about so much,' said Chester. 'John, life's too short to worry about things like that,' answered H, and walked away to his helicopter.

2 Para began to move from Sussex Mountain at 8 p.m. that night, D Company once again taking the lead. The men had abandoned their packs and wore only fighting order. But they were burdened with forty-eight hours' worth of arctic rations and an immense weight of extra ammunition and equipment, which bore especially hard on support company and the medical teams. The engineer reconnaissance troop of 59 Squadron, who had been flown to Sussex in time to join the battalion, carried all manner of

borrowed and scrounged equipment. Their own still lay aboard the landing ship *Sir Lancelot*, evacuated with an unexploded bomb aboard.

The long files stumbled and cursed quietly through the darkness and the unyielding rocks and tussock grass, squelching through streams and patches of bog. 'But it was a good night,' said Dair Farrar-Hockley. 'We felt we were doing something.' 2 Para gave little thought to the strategic merits of attacking Goose Green. They knew only that at last they had a task that enabled them to move from Sussex. Two hours short of Camilla Creek, sporadic enemy shells began to fall to the east of the column. From the craters on the track beneath their feet, they knew that the Argentinians had shelled that too during the night, but mercifully the fire continued to fall well wide of them as they marched. The men were terribly tired, and they suffered one serious loss: the forward air controller, a fifty-four-year-old RAF squadron leader whom they believed should never have been asked to undertake such a mission, dropped out utterly exhausted. His role was taken over by the anti-tank platoon commander, Captain Peter Ketley.

Around 3 a.m., they saw D Company's red torch signal. Camilla Creek House was secure. H ordered the entire battalion, except for the men manning a defensive screen, to take shelter in the buildings for the remainder of the night. Four hundred men lay down in dense exhausted huddles in every room and passage of the abandoned house and its surrounding sheds to gain what rest they could for what was left of the night, dozing and shivering without sleeping bags or blankets.

Three hours later, dawn revealed that the battalion's refuge lay in a fortunate hollow, invisible on all sides to any enemy more than 500 yards distant. A few men expressed concern that the unit was so tightly massed, but H was confident of their safety and security from view. He was happy to use the buildings to shelter his men through the day, and to give them the best possible chance to march to their battle that night dry and as rested as possible. It was at this moment that men listening to the BBC's

World Service news bulletin heard its London defence correspondent's statement that 2 Para was within 5 miles of Darwin (see
next chapter). The battalion, and above all its colonel, were first
shocked and then enraged. Jones at once ordered the battalion to
deploy and dig in across a widely dispersed defensive area, to meet
the enemy air or artillery attack that seemed inevitable. To Robert
Fox, the BBC correspondent accompanying the unit, H made his
later famous threat to sue the Secretary of State for Defence if any
of his men died in the forthcoming battle. It is known that the
Argentine garrison at Darwin–Goose Green was reinforced in the
early hours of 28 May by the helicopter transfer of elements of
General Menendez's strategic reserve from Mount Kent area. Brigadier Thompson and 2 Para are convinced that the BBC report that
morning directly influenced the battle they fought next day. The
Argentinians were waiting for them.

C Company discovered the alertness of the enemy as soon as
they attempted to move forward to reconnoitre. They were fired
on, and abandoned the attempt. About noon, the TAC team south
of Camilla Creek House spotted a blue Land Rover advancing up
the track towards them. They allowed the vehicle to close on their
position, then jumped it. After a brief exchange of fire, they closed
in to take prisoner its three Argentine occupants, two of them
wounded, before they could use their radio. One proved to be the
officer commanding the enemy's reconnaissance platoon. The Darwin garrison, he revealed, was substantially stronger than the weak
battalion brigade had expected, and they were braced for an attack.
'What the hell have the SAS been doing down here?' demanded H
furiously, if unreasonably. D Squadron had withdrawn before the
latest surge of enemy reinforcements.

Around 4 p.m., in sombre but confident mood, 2 Para's officers
crouched in a half-circle around their colonel as he gave his orders
for the battle. H described the plan as 'a six-phase night-day,
silent-noisy battalion attack to capture Darwin and Goose Green'.
C Company – Patrol Company – would reconnoitre the last 4 miles
to the start line and secure it. A and B Companies would then

advance south through the Argentine positions, taking the eastern
and western sides of the isthmus respectively. D Company would
pass through B in the second phase, and then in turn be passed
again by B for the attack on Boca House. They aimed to dispose of
all the enemy's outer positions in darkness, leaving only the settlements themselves to be seized in daylight, to minimise the risks to
the civilian population. Lieutenant John Thurman of the Royal
Marines provided a detailed description of the ground they had to
cross. There were no dramatic references to the opportunity before
them, for they were not necessary. 2 Para, to their own astonishment, had been called upon to fight the first set-piece battle of the
Falklands campaign, indeed the British army's first action against
a major enemy since Korea. From the moment that each officer
and man joined the regiment, he was imbued with the memory of
Bruneval, Merville, John Frost's stand against the bridge at Arn-
hem. Each generation of parachute soldiers inherits an eagerness
to demonstrate that its men can match these feats. It is difficult
not to be moved by the vision of 2 Para, led by their colonel with
his passionate determination to show what the battalion could do,
setting forth from Camilla Creek House that night against an
enemy forewarned and forearmed.

'I've never been involved in anything like this,' Robert Fox of
the BBC confessed to H.

'Neither have I,' answered the soldier.

H had a few moments in which to brief the artillery gun
position officer, Lieutenant Mark Waring, as three 105 mm guns
of 8 Battery, 29 Regiment, were shuttled through the darkness
beneath helicopters of 846 Squadron, and dumped on the soggy
peat. Only twelve Sea King lifts were available to move the gun
section and ammunition – an immensely delicate night-flying
operation. In response to the reports of Argentine reinforcements,
Waring had been able to bring in 320 rounds a gun. Only minutes
before the airlift from San Carlos began, he was compelled to
replace one gunner wounded in the arm during a brief Skyhawk
attack. In the valley where the guns were now being dug in, the

men worked all night strengthening defences, laying camouflage nets and preparing ammunition. Much would depend on the gunners when dawn broke.

At 6 p.m., C Company began to advance towards the start line in intermittent rain. For the next three hours, they probed cautiously down the track, led by engineers of 59 Squadron who bore some of the most hazardous and least enviable responsibilities in the land force throughout the war. They worked waist-deep in streams in the darkness to ensure that three bridges between Camilla Creek and the start line were clear of mines, then lay shivering with the infantry as they waited for the assault companies to reach them. The remainder of the battalion moved at 10 p.m., after checking their weapons and receiving platoon and company orders in the freezing grass. The quick, comforting crumps of the naval gunfire support echoed across the night as they advanced. Some Argentine harassing fire searched towards their line of march, but well wide of the companies. At 2.35 a.m., A Company crossed the start line in the classic infantry formation, two platoons forward and one back. Dair Farrar-Hockley's men advanced rapidly and silently on their first objective, Burntside House. They were still 500 yards short when the enemy dug in around it opened fire. The paras replied with a fierce deluge of GPMG, then closed in down the hill to clear the house with small arms and grenades. The enemy had fled, leaving two dead. Inside, lying terrified on the floor, were four British civilians, two of them elderly women. Once again the soldiers cursed their intelligence. They had been assured that Burntside House was solely occupied by Argentinians, and had raked it ruthlessly with machine-gun fire. Mercifully, the only casualty was a dog which lost a tooth.

'Then we waited for the bright and fascinating tracer criss-crossing the sky to our right front to cease,' wrote Lieutenant Clive Livingstone, commanding the engineer detachment. 'All the time we were trying to avoid the by now uncomfortable rate of indirect fire about us. Rain began to pour down, adding to our discomfort.' B Company, starting to move forty-five minutes after

A, encountered an enemy machine-gun post almost immediately after crossing the start line, which Corporal Margerison's section dispatched with automatic fire and grenades. Then John Crosland's men began a long phase of what the battalion called 'gutter fighting' – working steadily south by compass bearing, clearing line after line of enemy positions. It was a section commanders' battle, demanding rapid, ruthless, courageous initiative from small groups of men. 2 Para did it superbly well. Yet already, two hours after the battle had begun, problems were becoming apparent. 'It was going brilliantly, but very slowly,' in Chris Keeble's words. They suffered a serious blow when they learned that, out in the sound, *Arrow*'s 4.5-inch gun had jammed, and they lost critical firepower for a time. The guns and mortars were already concerned about their own expenditure of ammunition. The rifle companies had left behind their 2-inch mortars – 'a mistake I would never make again,' said Dair Farrar-Hockley – and depended for illumination chiefly on their meagre stocks of hand-held Shermulley flares. Early in the action, a big gorse hedge in the midst of the battlefield caught fire and blazed brightly for hours, but the choking smoke added to the paras' difficulties.

While B Company was meeting constant opposition, by 5.30 A Company had advanced to its second objective, Coronation Point overlooking Darwin, without meeting resistance. Dair Farrar-Hockley reported by radio to the colonel and asked to press on. H, several hundred yards further back on the track running down the central spine of the isthmus, seemed sceptical that they could have got as far as they claimed. For more than thirty minutes, as the precious darkness ebbed away, A Company remained motionless until H had worked forward to join the company commander. Then, at last, he ordered the advance to continue. The battalion had now been in action for five hours with scarcely a single casualty. The only hitch in the plan was that some Argentine positions unseen by B Company as they advanced had begun firing from the rear, and D Company were committed to clearing these instead of passing through B. But 'we were all confident that we

could have breakfast in the town, our last objective,' said Clive
Livingstone. Morale was very high, even among some of the men
who had been without sleep for three nights.

Now, as dawn broke, the balance of the battle began to swing
dramatically away from the British. They were caught on open
ground where the only shelter lay in the contours, facing a thoroughly well-prepared enemy. Intelligence had reported specifically
that the Argentine positions lacked overhead protection. In reality,
their trenches were strongly roofed, and all the reports of a
demoralised and unmotivated garrison seemed confounded. 'All
this rubbish about them not wanting to fight,' said Keeble wither-
ingly. 'They were fighting hard.' An astonishing weight of artillery
and mortar fire was being directed against all the para companies
deployed down the isthmus. As A Company began to move again
across the open ground, leaving 3 platoon covering the enemy
positions in Darwin itself, Dair Farrar-Hockley spotted movement
on the hill before them. He shouted, 'Ambush! Take cover!' just as
the Argentine machine-guns opened fire. 2 Platoon, in the lead,
were able to seize shelter in the gorse. 1 Platoon, behind, was
caught in the open and found itself immediately in serious trouble.
Corporal Melia of the engineers was killed instantly. 'A massive
volume of medium machine-gun fire was unleashed on us from
a range of about 400 metres,' wrote Livingstone. 'The light now
rapidly appearing enabled the enemy to identify targets and bring
down very effective fire. Although this too would work for us, the
weight of fire we could produce was not in proportion to the
massive response it brought. We stopped firing – our main concern
was to move away whenever pauses occurred in the attention
being paid to us. The two platoons were not able to suppress the
trenches which were giving us so much trouble. We took about
45 minutes to extract ourselves by use of smoke and pauses in
firing . . .'

A Company estimated that they were facing around a hundred
enemy, including substantial numbers of snipers and machine-
guns. Even a conscript enemy could feel formidable firing with

unlimited quantities of ammunition from well-prepared positions, while the paras were suffering severely from the limited supply of ammunition inevitable among an attacking infantry force. Farrar-Hockley made a brief attempt to move 1 Platoon into position for a flank attack. But the company was under intense fire. Private Tuffen, just seventeen, was hit in the head and kept conscious by his mates for four and a half hours to save him from lapsing into a coma. Private Worrall was wounded. Corporals Abols and Prior ran out to drag him into cover, and were halfway back under fierce machine-gun fire when Prior was hit. Corporal Hardman now dashed to join Abols. Together they brought Prior to within a few feet of safety before a further bullet hit him in the head. They took his body to the safety of the gully, and went out yet again, to bring in Worrall. It was one among many superb efforts by 2 Para's junior NCOs that day.

John Crosland of B Company said laconically, 'Up to first light, we were definitely winning. After first light, it was dawning on people that we were doing the grovelling.' The overwhelming problem was to maintain momentum, to avoid being pinned where they lay. It requires a great effort of will to rise from the ground and move under heavy fire, the more so when others who have attempted it lie wounded or dead. They were constantly deluged with mud and peat from exploding shells and mortar bombs. Most men found little time for emotion or thought. Their minds were dominated by the need to survive, and to keep going. Some threw away their sub-machine guns to pick up Argentine rifles with greater range and hitting power. In the rear, a shuttle of light helicopters had begun to bring up more ammunition from San Carlos. The problem was to move it forward to the rifle companies, and get wounded men back.

While A Company suffered to the east, towards the western shore Crosland's B had begun a long, bitter battle to reach the Argentine positions behind the ruined Boca House. These had been sited to meet a possible British landing from the sea, but they proved equally formidable against the landward attack. Crosland had left his 5 Platoon to provide covering fire from high ground while he advanced with 4 and 6. Yet it was 5 which began to suffer severely from Argentine machine-gunners. When at last they started to pull back over the ridgeline into dead ground, they lost three wounded. Private Illingworth had already dragged back one of these men, and was on his way to recover a second when he was shot dead by a sniper. Four men from Crosland's lead platoon successfully crawled onto the spine of the ridge above Boca House, but were instantly pinned down. 'We were outranged,' said the major. 'We just couldn't get across the open ground to get at their machine-guns, and after five hours of fighting, ammunition was critical.' Bob Ash, an artillery forward observer, met a request for a fire mission with an unhappy shrug: 'We just haven't got the rounds.' Mortar ammunition had run out altogether. Behind A and B Companies, D was still mopping up Argentine positions by-passed during the night, securing dazed and confused enemy soldiers wandering among the scrub and gorse. Unceasingly, enemy mortar and gunfire searched up and down the ridge through every company back to the British gunline.

The guns were in action even as they were bracketed by Argentine shells. 'The section fired almost continuously,' wrote Mark Waring, 'and cartridge cases and salvage began to pile up inside the camouflage nets in proportions we had never experienced. It was becoming increasingly difficult to keep all three guns in action. The soft ground caused the trails to bury themselves almost to the layers' seats.' Harriers from the fleet had been unable to take off because of fog at sea, but two Argentine Pucara began an attack on the British gunline soon after dawn. The defending Blowpipe team released their missiles as one aircraft closed. It turned away to fire its rockets harmlessly into the valley west of the guns. The second aircraft disappeared. But, while the guns struggled to remain in action, at sea *Arrow* was compelled to retire. She had continued to provide support for two hours after first light, long after she was intended to retire to the safety of the San Carlos anchorage. But now, at last, she was ordered to go. There would be no more naval gunfire support for 2 Para.

At 8.30 that morning, the battalion's position was unenviable. Not one of its rifle companies seemed able to break through the open ground and end the noisy, bloody deadlock that the Argentinians had imposed. Conventional tactical manoeuvres had become impossible. Men lay and crouched the length of the isthmus. Some crawled among the dead and wounded, relieving them of spare ammunition. In C Company, a few became resigned to their predicament, and began to brew tea under mortar fire. Colonel H lay beside Dair Farrar-Hockley, impatiently seeking to improve the accuracy of the artillery support, deflected by the high wind gusting across the hillside. 'Dair,' said the colonel, 'you have got to take that ledge.' Farrar-Hockley began to move forward with some sixteen men including his second in command, Chris Dent. Unknown to him, the battalion adjutant David Wood joined the rear of the party as they started up the hill. Dent was shot at once and rolled back, dead. Corporal Hardman and Captain Wood were killed a few moments later. Lance Corporal Toole, lying beside Farrar-Hockley, said flatly, 'Sir, if you don't get out of here now, you aren't going to.' They crawled back whence they had come.

A little way below, they met Tony Rice, the artillery battery commander. 'For God sake come quickly,' he said. 'The colonel's gone round the corner on his own.' H Jones had pinpointed a machine-gun that he believed he could take out. Clutching his Sterling sub-machine gun, followed by Sergeant Norman and Lance Corporal Beresford, he began a dash up a gully towards it. Seconds later, he was hit in the back of the neck by a bullet fired from higher up the hill behind him, which plunged through his body. He fell mortally wounded. In the space of a few minutes, the battle for Darwin Hill had cost the lives of the commanding officer, Captain Dent, the adjutant David Wood and nine other men.

Yet even as H lay hit, the turning point of A Company's action came. Machine-gun and 66 mm rocket fire was silencing the enemy trenches one by one. Corporal Abols fired one 66 direct into a bunker mouth, and was rewarded by a sharp explosion and then silence. The first white flags began to appear. A Company was still under mortar and artillery fire, but the centres of resistance had crumbled. Then Farrar-Hockley's sergeant major said to him, 'Sir, I think the CO's dying.' Morphine, field dressings and the drip in H's arm were useless. Farrar-Hockley saw his eyelids flicker, but no other movement. He knelt, holding the colonel's hand until it was obvious that he was dead. Then, speaking cautiously to avoid alerting the entire battalion to the bad news, he said on the radio to Chris Keeble, 'I think you'd better get up here at once.' A Company, with three of its own men and three from attached units dead and twelve wounded, now deployed around the captured positions amidst twenty dead Argentinians and seventy-six prisoners, of whom thirty-nine were wounded.

The moment news reached battalion headquarters that H was hit, a request had been passed to 'teeny-weeny airways' – the marine air squadron at San Carlos – for a Scout casevac helicopter. The first call was rejected, but a second shortly afterwards, more urgently phrased, was accepted. A Scout was approaching the Darwin area a few minutes later as a Pucara strike came in. The enemy aircraft dived steeply, firing at the helicopter. There was a sudden ball of smoke, and the remains of the Scout crashed to the ground. Lieutenant Richard Nunn, brother of the officer commanding the marine company in South Georgia, and brother-in-law of David Constance, the marine liaison officer with 2 Para who had cleared an Argentine trench behind B Company a few minutes earlier, was killed instantly.

Chris Keeble was meanwhile pressing forward down the isthmus to take over command of the battalion. He made a rapid assessment of the state of the battle. A Company, it was clear, had 'gone firm' on their objective and need not be a source of immediate worry. But B Company was still locked in head-on confrontation with the Argentine positions behind Boca House. It was essential to start an outflanking move, to restore the momentum of the battle. Before the colonel was killed, he had ordered support company's Milan and machine-gun teams to move round from their initial position, down the spine of the isthmus to provide direct support for B Company. At last, they had reached a position from which they could engage the Argentine strongpoints at a range of 1,500 yards. They began to fire the formidable Milan missile rounds with dramatic effect. Keeble now consulted with John Crosland, and ordered D Company to bypass B along the shoreline, moving behind the shelter of the protective lip alongside the sea itself. They advanced rapidly, completely concealed from the enemy around Boca House. At last, the British were able to bring a massive concentration of fire down on the enemy. Covered by Support and B Companies, at 11 a.m. D rose from the shore and scrambled up the hillside, saturating the Argentinians with GPMG fire. Cluster by cluster, the enemy began to emerge from their bunkers to surrender, exhausted and shocked. There were ninety-seven in all.

Keeble now spoke to Dair Farrar-Hockley, and ordered his company to press on towards Goose Green itself, in support of C Company. Impossible, said the major. Casualties had depleted their ranks too severely. Darwin Hill had to be held against possible counter-attack. He could offer only one platoon. C Company, with Farrar-Hockley's 3 Platoon, began to make their way round the hill. A patrol was dispatched into Darwin settlement itself, from which the civilians had fled. They cleared the area of its few defenders with small arms and grenades.

2 Para had fought its way doggedly and superbly through to its first objectives, and cracked the outer shell of Argentine resistance. Yet they were still confronting the formidable defences of Goose Green itself, its approaches and airfield. Keeble ordered C Company to push forward down the eastern coast, while D and B Companies swung across the isthmus from the west. Clive Livingstone described the 'terrifying combination of artillery, mortar, machine-gun and anti-aircraft airburst fire' into which C Company advanced towards the lonely landmark of Goose Green schoolhouse. 'Little

or no cover was available. It was hard to believe that this weight of fire could be maintained for long. It was.' Perhaps the most deadly weapons facing the British at this stage were Argentine air force radar-controlled 35 mm antiaircraft guns, firing from the eastern tip of Goose Green settlement against the paras working slowly towards them. Whenever men began to move beyond the ridge crest overlooking the Argentinians, an overwhelming barrage of fire fell upon them. Chris Keeble was on the high ground when the entire gorse line erupted under enemy cannon strikes. He thought calmly: I'm going to die now. As he scrambled across the ground, his smock became entangled in a cattle fence, from which it took several moments to extricate himself. He found himself temporarily unable to make contact with his rifle companies: 'I remember thinking, I'm losing control. It was not that I was frightened, it was simply that I was the boss, the 2 i.c., trying to maintain the momentum of the attack.' It was a very bad two minutes.

While B Company swung around the airfield in a wide hook to approach Goose Green from the south-west, C and D Companies linked for a combined assault on the schoolhouse. The Argentine defenders fought back fiercely until a white flag suddenly appeared from an enemy position. One of D's subalterns, Jim Barry, moved forward to accept the surrender. He was instantly shot dead. It was almost certainly a mishap in the fog of war rather than a deliberate act of treachery, but the infuriated paras unleashed 66 mm rockets, Carl Gustav rounds and machine-gun fire into the building. It was quickly ablaze. No enemy survivors emerged.

2 Para was now closing the ring around Goose Green. Keeble brought up his mortars to a new position behind Darwin Hill. The enemy's 20 mm anti-aircraft guns on the airfield had been silenced. But, as D Company reorganised after the assault on the schoolhouse, two Skyhawks closed in to bomb, narrowly missing their positions. A few minutes later, two Pucara attacked with napalm and rocket fire. The blazing jelly exploded wide of D Company. As the first Pucara pulled out, a Royal Marine Blowpipe operator with

great courage leaped to his feet, put the clumsy tube to his shoulder and fired. The Pucara crashed. An engineer section was drenched with aviation fuel from the ruptured tank of one aircraft. By a miracle, it failed to ignite. But Sapper Plant found himself unable to stop shaking for several minutes after taking a bullet through his combat smock. Small-arms fire from B and D Companies brought down the second Pucara.

When Keeble, still under fire on the gorse line, heard aircraft again, he thought simply of more Pucara: 'That's all we need.' Then he heard the naval gunfire support officer say, 'We've got the Harriers!' Three British aircraft swung in to deliver a superb, surgically accurate cluster-bomb attack on the enemy's radar-controlled cannon and gun positions. The area around the enemy positions exploded, devastated. Suddenly, the sun came out. At that moment, the paras now believe, the Argentinians at last understood that they were within sight of defeat. An hour before last light, their fire began to slacken. They were not yet crushed, but they were surrounded. As the light began to fade, the weary British troops found themselves faced by yet another serious threat. An Argentine Chinook and six Huey helicopters landed south of Goose Green, obviously to disgorge reinforcements. Keeble at once called down artillery fire on the area, and ordered B Company to move southwards and deploy to block a possible attack. To their relief, none came. The Argentinians trickled away into the hills, to be rounded up in the days that followed by 2 Para and the Gurkhas.

Now, for the first time that day, Keeble had time to take stock of his own position. He and his men had won a famous victory, yet they still confronted a formidable defensive position. He commanded a desperately tired battalion which had taken substantial casualties, and which, despite the trickle of ammunition arriving by Gazelle, was still close to exhausting its firepower. The second in command of B Company lay on the hillside, within reach of death unless he could be evacuated urgently. There was a similar case in the regimental aid post, where Steve Hughes had been labouring devotedly all day. The battalion was encumbered by scores of prisoners, many of them wounded. If the British were to be obliged to mount a frontal assault down the hillside towards Goose Green that night or the following morning, they could still suffer terribly from the minefield and defensive positions.

Keeble began by ordering the rifle companies to pull back into the dead ground, off the ridgeline overlooking Goose Green. Men lay on the hillsides among their weapons, in silence or talking with the quiet of absolute weariness. It was desperately cold, and soon they began to shiver, for their bergens and clothing were still at San Carlos. They gathered the wounded and such of the dead as they could reach, above all the body of their colonel.

Keeble talked to brigade by radio. First, he asked for reinforcements. Julian Thompson immediately agreed to dispatch J Company from 42 Commando, to take up position covering the southern approach to Goose Green. Then Keeble asked whether, if it was absolutely necessary, the settlement could be destroyed. Yes, replied Thompson. Keeble set out his shopping list for further operations: three more guns, ammunition for them to a total of 2,000 rounds, the battalion's six unused mortars and bombs for them, the Cymbeline mortar-locating radar. Two BV vehicles would bring down more small-arms ammunition for the rifle companies. A Wessex helicopter was dispatched for casualty evacuation, which rashly circled over Goose Green before departing, drawing heavy Argentine fire. Captain John Greenhalgh, an outstandingly courageous and skilful helicopter pilot, flew his Scout to the paras' forward position in total darkness, and was talked down onto a green torch beacon to evacuate a cargo of freezing wounded men. It would normally be the job of the adjutant to organise the recovery of the wounded, but Dave Woods was dead. RSM Simpson took over, dealing with the battalion group's seventeen dead and thirty-five wounded.

While his men worked to repair the losses of the day, Keeble explained his own plan to the brigadier. If the battalion had to fight for Goose Green, so be it. But he fervently hoped that they would not. They had fought the Argentinians to a standstill that day, and now encircled them. However precarious the predicament of 2 Para, that of the enemy was worse. It remained only to convince their commanders of that. Keeble asked that guns and Harriers should be prepared for a devastating demonstration of British firepower at 9 a.m. the next day, two hours after first light. Meanwhile, said the major, he proposed to summon the enemy to surrender. If his plan succeeded, he could save the lives of scores of men, perhaps those of all 112 civilians, the local population interned in the community centre at Goose Green.

It was an eerie, restless night on the isthmus. Most men slept as best they could without sleeping bags in the piercing cold. Some took shelter in what seemed welcoming shellholes, and discovered only at dawn that these were mine craters where stray cows had killed themselves, still surrounded by acres of hidden explosive. HQ Company moved the Argentine prisoners in among the burning gorse to keep them warm. Rod Bell, the marine interpreter, was fascinated by the sight of the clustered enemy saying their prayers in the darkness, lit by the flames of the gorse, led by a young second lieutenant shot in the leg and with a shrapnel wound in the eye. Some knelt, others clutched rosaries. Both sides seemed conscious that they were the survivors of a devastating experience. 'Fire only if you yourselves are being attacked,' Keeble ordered his men that night. The darkness passed in uneasy silence.

At first light the next day, 30 May, Keeble began to put his plan into effect. At his bidding, Rod Bell had chosen two prisoners, senior NCOs. These men were taken to the height of the ridgeline and presented with a white flag and a letter drafted by Bell in Spanish on Keeble's orders. It informed the Argentine commander that his position was besieged, and that it seemed humane and essential to arrange for the safe delivery of the civilians in Goose Green. It suggested that the time had come to surrender or accept defeat.

The prisoners walked away towards their own lines watched by the distant paras. Almost immediately, they returned. Their commander had agreed to a meeting. Major Keeble, Brigade Liaison Officer Major Hector Gullen, Rod Bell, Major Tony Rice, artillery battery commander, put aside their personal weapons and walked to a little hut beside the flagpole on the airfield with Robert Fox and David Norris, the two British correspondents accompanying 2 Para. There, at 8.30 a.m., they met Air Commodore Wilson Pedroza and an Argentine naval officer. Agreement was quickly reached about the release of the civilians. Then the delicate question was broached of a possible Argentine surrender. If there was to be anything of that sort, said Pedroza, a dapper, impeccably turned-out officer in sharp contrast to the filthy, battle-stained British officers before him, it must be done with honour. 'They can do whatever they like if they surrender,' said Keeble tersely to Bell. At last, Pedroza declared that he must consult with his own high command. He disappeared back into Goose Green. Later in captivity he told Max Hastings that, when he signalled General Menendez, he was reluctantly given discretion to act as he thought necessary.

The British expected some eighty Argentinians to march out to surrender. Instead, to their astonishment, they watched a contingent of more than 150 men moving out from Goose Green to form up in a hollow square around Pedroza, just beyond D Company's perimeter. The Argentinian made a brief patriotic speech. He called on his men to sing their national anthem. Then, as they threw down their weapons, Keeble walked forward to take the commander's pistol, noticing as he did so that all the men mustered around him wore air-force uniform. Where were the rest of the army contingent? At that moment, the astounded British saw a great column of men emerging from Goose Green, marching towards them in three ranks. More than 900 Argentine troops commanded by Lieutenant Colonel Italo Pioggi laid down their arms before D Company. 2 Para had brought about the collapse of an enemy force more than treble its own strength. They buried 50 Argentinian dead and took 1,200 prisoners of war. It was an extraordinary triumph, its conclusion a great tribute to Major

Keeble's handling of a desperate situation. Brigadier Thompson recommended that Keeble should be confirmed in command of the battalion, and many of 2 Para were saddened that the service machine in Britain saw fit to ignore Thompson's signal and fly out a new commanding officer, Lieutenant Colonel David Chaundler.

When the men at San Carlos heard of the manner of Colonel Jones's death, all those who knew him agreed that it was characteristic. His action was a classically romantic, heroic gesture, the deed of a man to whom Goose Green represented the climax of a lifetime as a soldier, and who could not watch his men do that which he would not do himself. Some officers suggested that H's dash up Darwin Hill was irresponsible, the renunciation of his vital task of commanding his battalion on the battlefield. Major Keeble later pointed out that, at the moment the colonel made his move, 2 Para's essential problem was that it had lost the ability to manoeuvre tactically in the face of the overwhelming enemy fire. The vital task was to break the deadlock. At that moment, H, with his tactical headquarters team, represented precious firing, fighting power on Darwin Hill. He was determined to make use of it. 'He was simply doing what he wanted his battalion to do,' in Keeble's words. His lonely charge was an act in the British army's great tradition of battalion leadership on the battlefield. This warm, impulsive, utterly dedicated soldier became a national hero with his death and the award of his posthumous Victoria Cross. It is impossible to believe that, if he were to begin it all again, H would have chosen to do it any other way. Major Keeble received the DSO, Dair Farrar-Hockley and John Crosland the MC at the head of a long list of the battalion's decorations for Goose Green.

In all, 2 Para lost seventeen men killed and thirty-five wounded – a bitter price, yet a remarkably small one for a battle of such length and ferocity. Had they been made aware of the full strength of the defences, had they been able to complete their assault in darkness with much stronger fire support, it might have been possible to fight their way through to Goose Green more quickly, and at lower cost. After the war, senior officers in London com-

bined to express their astonishment that more men were not
sent with 2 Para, that some sort of helicopter-lifted attack was not
mounted simultaneously from the rear to divide the defence's
attention. 3 Commando Brigade's ignorance of the enemy strength
at Goose Green was the result of yet another liaison failure
between London and San Carlos. Intelligence Staff at the Ministry
of Defence were in possession of General Menendez's full order
of battle, by courtesy of sigint. Yet details had never been passed
to Thompson's team. This could have proved a tragic omission. A
British defeat or stalemate at Goose Green was entirely possible
but for the quality of 2 Para. The real measure of the battalion's
achievement was that, with 450 men, discovering only on the
battlefield that they faced an enemy four times their own strength,
they persisted and at last prevailed.

The paras now enjoyed their euphoric moment of victory. They
were overwhelmed by the relief of being spared another battle.
Keeble led his men into the settlement, and knocked on the door
of the first house, where he found the settlement manager, Eric
Goss, with his wife. 'Would you like a cup of tea?' asked Mrs Goss.
The British moved on to meet the rest of the civilian population,
pouring out of the church hall where they had been confined.
They fell on the paras, hugging and kissing men in the great surge
of relief to be alive and safe. In the last hours before the surrender,
the Argentinians had savagely vandalised houses and looted property. Keeble was seized by regret that he had treated the enemy
with honour. The paras were struck by the fact that they had
captured only one enemy officer on the battlefield. Most of them,
it seemed, had stayed as far to the rear as possible throughout the
struggle.

The settlement was strewn with vast quantities of abandoned
ordnance: rockets lashed to a children's slide, napalm tanks, artillery ammunition, mortar bombs, cannon shells. Cattle wandered
untended in the surrounding minefields. There was a vast clearing-
up operation to be undertaken. Keeble consulted with brigade, and
Thompson in turn with London. The logistics problems and the

disposal of the prisoners alone made it difficult for 2 Para to fulfil brigade's original intention of withdrawing from Goose Green now that it was secure. Less openly expressed, but perhaps more important, was the feeling that, after 2 Para had fought a major action to win Goose Green, it would seem politically extraordinary immediately to abandon it. The battalion, it was agreed, would remain upon the battlefield that it had conquered, resting, re-arming, and clearing the debris. The operation that 3 Commando Brigade conceived as a 'major raid' ended as one of the decisive actions of the war. The Argentinians had been given a devastating demonstration of Britain's absolute will to achieve victory at whatever cost in blood and treasure.

14 » THE POLITICS OF THE LAND WAR

One only jumps from a smaller conflict to a larger stalemate at greater expense.

Omar Bradley during the Korean War

'We're going to move and move fast!' said the Chief of the Defence Staff, Sir Terence Lewin, in a rare public comment on 22 May, the day after the San Carlos landing. As with all statements from Whitehall over the following week, it was a pious hope rather than a firm prediction. Ostensibly the landing bred a new unity in the war cabinet. The initiative now lay clearly with the operational commanders. Ministers' sphere of decision was reduced as peace negotiations went into suspense. They could only watch, listen and wait. Yet they proved to be bad bystanders. The landing had itself been a phenomenal success. Not a single marine commando's life had been lost going ashore. But, as with the original, equally successful, mobilisation of the task force, Lewin wondered whether success was not a worse drug to administer to politicians than failure. 'They became high on it,' he said later. Then came the battle of San Carlos and a sequence of naval reverses which seemed at times to threaten the whole operation. Lewin suddenly found his politicians plunged into gloom.

'War cabinets that week were the worst of the whole war,' one minister recalled later. 'We simply could not understand what the hell was going on down there. We were losing a ship a day and nothing on land was moving.' Parliament was still in session and thirsting for news of the operation by the minute. Ministers were

under constant public pressure. Lewin was on the phone to Fieldhouse and Fieldhouse to Thompson almost continuously. As after
the sinking of *Sheffield*, a shiver of tension crept into relations
between politicians and the military. Whitelaw declared he was
'lying awake at night with visions of Suez'. Nott would wail to his
colleagues that the chiefs of staff were 'still talking about their
bridgehead; they seem to have no objective but to build a bridgehead'. The limitations of Operation Sutton were suddenly apparent
– it was a plan for a landing, not a land campaign. Again Lewin
found himself fending off questions: Why were the air attacks
getting through? Why was it so necessary to await 5 Brigade? Was
Thompson not too junior an officer for so onerous a task? Why
was it taking Moore so long to get down there? 'That's what
happens when you leave everything to the navy,' said one minister.
'They're hopeless on land.' Confidence in Thompson began to
crumble fast; war cabinet was shielded totally from his difficulties
with Woodward and seemed unaware of the revised objective
given to him at Ascension, simply to secure a beach-head and await
5 Brigade. Increasingly, Major General Moore seemed the white
hope of the politicians. He, surely, would galvanise San Carlos and
move out towards Stanley. When it was learned that Moore was a
prisoner aboard QE2, unable to reach East Falkland before the end
of the month, ministers were shocked. Lewin was chided that it
might have been quicker by gondola.

This pressure was reflected in conflicting leaks from the war
cabinet as the post-landing week progressed. On the first Sunday,
ministers indicated to Lewin their desire to 'push forward as fast
as possible out of the bridgehead'. Downing Street duly briefed the
press that an attack on Port Stanley was expected 'in a matter of
days'. On Monday, 23 May, Nott responded to this overt pressure
on his commanders by declaring an opposite line: 'There can be
no question of pressing the force commander to move forward
prematurely,' he told the Commons. After 25 May, when task force
ship losses had risen to five, Thatcher was herself repeating this
identical phrase to a meeting of Tory women. Yet, as the weeks

wore on, impatience grew on all sides. MPs, journalists and particularly broadcasters trying to fill avidly watched programmes had been led to expect early action. They now indulged in intense speculation. The BBC's *Newsnight* programme became a nightly seminar at which defence experts, some of them recently retired from units actually in the Falklands, plotted possible moves with maps and models. Yet why was nothing happening? A Cabinet Office official recalled that, 'at this time the war cabinet seemed close to panic – ministers were desperate not to back-seat drive but unable to contain their frustration at what they seemed to feel was Thompson's inaction'.

The breakout from the beach-head north towards Teal Inlet and Port Stanley and south towards Goose Green was debated at war cabinet on the Wednesday morning and lobby correspondents were told to 'expect news shortly of advances by British land forces'. This they dutifully reported. The trouble, as Sir Frank Cooper later reflected, was that there were only two places where such a breakout might occur. Since Goose Green seemed the most likely, the news was as good as out. The following morning, 27 May, the BBC radio correspondent Christopher Lee had it confirmed by a senior member of the operations staff, who told him the attack was already in progress and he could not see why it should be secret. The Prime Minister was going to announce it that afternoon in the Commons. It was duly broadcast on the 1 p.m. news and was picked up round the world. Thatcher told the Commons that 'the British forces have begun to move forward from their San Carlos bridgehead'. No one who had been following the week's news could have been in any doubt of its direction.

At the time, 2 Para were still trekking towards their nighttime bivouac at Camilla Creek. Ministry of Defence officials, desperate lest the news alert the Argentinians to rush reinforcements south, now had the difficult task of putting the cat back in the bag. It proved impossible. By evening, all media were assuming that Goose Green was the destination and this was broadcast that night on the BBC Overseas Service, to be received on the Falklands.

Once again the British military and political machine had demonstrated its inability to maintain the confidentiality of its decisions in the course of a highly political war. As Sir Henry Leach put it, 'None of us had any experience of modern war with modern media technology.' Yet the Goose Green affair was really the result of political impatience. Like Buenos Aires before its original invasion, British politicians needed news of some success after the losses of 25 May too badly to heed the caution they so often counselled on others. With the press showing not an ounce of self-restraint, it was a poor showing for the home front. The Goose Green victory was in fact not announced until 10 p.m. on Friday. Parliament departed for the Whitsun recess temporarily sated with success.

*

With Goose Green under her belt, the Prime Minister felt once more the heat of international pressure. The UN had begun an immediate Security Council debate on news of Britain's landing the week before. Parsons had fended off a variety of ceasefire calls, put together desultorily by a number of states, including Panama, Japan and Ireland. Eventually a resolution (505) was agreed and passed the following Wednesday (the 26th): it did not order a ceasefire but merely urged the parties to cooperate with the Secretary General 'with a view to ending the present hostilities'. The resolution also asked the Secretary General to renew his efforts for peace, 'bearing in mind the approach outlined in his statement of May 21st'. This phrase had originally begun, 'in accordance with the approach . . .' but this had been contested by Parsons as it implied Britain's concession of UN administration, since withdrawn. London wanted no hint that Britain might be forced to reopen her pre-landing compromises. It was Uganda who came up with the 'bearing in mind' formula, and the council voted unanimously for the resolution. It gave de Cuellar just seven days to negotiate a ceasefire, a time limit to which he strongly objected. 'The Security Council is tying my hands,' he said.

The task force's second week on the Falklands opened with

renewed calls for Britain to show restraint – or 'magnanimity in victory' as Alexander Haig put it. It coincided with the arrival in London of Pope John Paul and a series of impassioned pontifical pleas for peace: 'The scale and horror of modern warfare,' he told a congregation in the war-scarred city of Coventry, 'make it totally unacceptable as a means of settling differences between nations.' The Pope's visit was an intense relief from the news of battle and produced an effusion of joy from Britain's Catholic community. It seemed eerily distant from the matter in hand, yet it added to the sense that Britain had made her point and nothing could be served by further bloodshed.

Now, as throughout the conflict, British propaganda's coy presentation of the war as a series of half-secret triumphs served Britain's interest badly. To the war cabinet and to the Argentinians, the struggle remained finely balanced. To the commanders on the ground and at Northwood, the concept of British magnanimity seemed wholly inappropriate to a battle they were by no means certain of winning. Yet popular and world sentiment was that 'it is only a matter of time: and a confounded long time at that'.

On Tuesday, 1 June, the war cabinet met to discuss once again the options for a negotiated settlement. Later that week, the Prime Minister was departing for the western summit at Versailles, at which Britain would be under intense pressure to initiate a peaceful ending to the conflict. A Foreign Office blueprint, prepared by Palliser's team, had examined the various possibilities for an interim administration and constitutional options for a long-term settlement. Once again, the Foreign Office bandwagon was on the road to 'internationalise' the dispute. Diplomatic lines were put out to Washington to press Haig and Reagan to lean on the Prime Minister at Versailles. It was even agreed to commission Lord Shackleton to dust off and revise his 1975 report on the islands' economy.

In Argentina, the war party was at last looking rattled. Members of the junta had not been seen in public for days. The air force, reeling after the initial losses over San Carlos on the first day of the British landing, was subjected to bitter public criticism for permitting British forces to build up their bridgehead unmolested. Each day, official propaganda seeking to convince the nation that Argentina was winning was looking more thin. After Goose Green, this policy was adjusted to prepare people for bad news rather than good. At the same time, the junta commenced a new and desperate diplomatic offensive. Brigadier Miret and Admiral Moya, the junta's diplomatic 'monitors', left Buenos Aires again for New York, where they were joined by General Mallea Gil from Washington, taking with them a major Argentine concession. Argentina would now be ready to accept a version of the final British peace plan – in effect, she would be ready to withdraw 150 miles – in return for UN trusteeship. Miret was also and most significantly empowered by a military directive to negotiate a solution with de Cuellar without recourse to Buenos Aires for approval. The junta had by now all but discarded Costa Mendes. Again the focus for much of their activity became the UN and the offices of Kirkpatrick and Sorzano. And again the Argentinians found themselves embroiled in the internecine strife of US foreign policy.

A series of exchanges between Haig and Kirkpatrick the previous week had been leaked to *Newsweek* magazine. The UN ambassador had accused Haig of having 'a boy's club view of gang loyalty' with London, and his department of being 'Brits in American clothes'. She added, 'Why not just disband the State Department and have the British Foreign Office make our policy?' For good measure Haig replied (the conversation has never been denied) that Mrs Kirkpatrick was 'mentally and emotionally incapable of thinking clear on this issue because of her close links with the Latins'. The State Department's dismay at the New York activity, which had a possible Security Council ceasefire call as its aim, was the more heartfelt since Haig was piecing together yet another peace plan for Reagan to take with him to the Versailles summit at the end of the week. As a contribution to this, Kirkpatrick had seen Reagan for forty minutes on 31 May and pleaded with him to stop Britain causing a bloodbath at Port Stanley. It would, she said, wreck Washington's Latin American relations for years. Above all, she did not want the US to have to side with Britain in vetoing a ceasefire call at the end of the week. Not for the first time, Britain was faced with two competing peace initiatives from across the Atlantic.

The first was a Security Council resolution sponsored by Spain and Panama, to be voted on Friday, 4 June. It called on both sides to 'cease fire immediately' and on the Secretary General to initiate the implementation of Resolutions 502 and 505 'in their entirety'. This proved too much for Britain. In Parsons's words, 'there is no direct and inseparable link' between ceasefire and Argentine withdrawal; there was thus too much scope for stalling. More important, the reference to 505 revived the concept of UN administration borrowed from the British white paper but since disowned by Britain. Parsons would accordingly cast a veto. The significance of Britain's rejection was overwhelmed, however, by the astonishing behaviour of the American delegation. Despite pressure from Kirkpatrick and Enders up to the last minute – that a British veto would be enough, and there was no need for them to court trouble by supporting it – Kirkpatrick was instructed by Haig to reinforce the British veto. At the last minute Stoessel in Washington suddenly conceded the strength of Kirkpatrick's argument. Haig gave approval in Paris where the Versailles meeting was beginning. He had to reach Pym to tell him. Then he had to return to Stoessel, and so back to Kirkpatrick.

This cumbersome process was not completed until after the US veto had been cast. Kirkpatrick then found herself passed a note from Washington telling her to announce she would have abstained had communication reached her in time. This she then did. It was the worst of both worlds. The US had contrived to please no one and offend everyone. Kirkpatrick's crisp remark to reporters was, 'You don't understand it? I don't understand it either.' To make American misery complete, no one appeared to have told Reagan before he sat down next to Mrs Thatcher at

Versailles the following lunchtime. She stayed tight-lipped as a posse of reporters descended on Reagan to ask for an explanation of the 'flip-flop'. Plainly ignorant of what they meant, he lamely replied, 'You've caught me a long way away from there.'

The second initiative was Reagan's 'five-point plan', formally presented to Thatcher at Versailles on 3 June. Evolved by the State Department in collaboration with the Foreign Office in London, this was yet another attempt to shift the Falklands crisis into an international context. Its aim was to involve third-party nations in a peacekeeping operation following an Anglo-Argentine withdrawal. Links had already been established with Jamaica, Brazil and possibly other Latin American states. Haig had assured the British that under such circumstances the US might be ready to take part: a crucial safeguard against 'creeping Argentine sovereignty' in London's eyes.

Talk of peace reopened many of the old wounds within the war cabinet. After the fall of Goose Green and the arrival of General Moore with the reinforcements of 5 Brigade, ministers assumed that Port Stanley would now fall to a quick punch. Yet again the land forces seemed bogged down by the logistical problem of moving men and ammunition across East Falkland. As positions were built up round Stanley, Lewin was able to take consolation only in the fact that, with Moore on the ground, ministers could not complain to him of the inadequate seniority of his commander. The chiefs of staff now inundated war cabinet with tactical briefings on why taking a heavily defended town without civilian casualties and with minimal military ones would be a long and painstaking operation. 'I think ministers were a bit ashamed of the way they behaved after San Carlos,' said one official. A war cabinet minister admitted, 'We were learning from experience: we wanted a quick victory, but this time we were more ready to defer to military advice.'

In this context, the new moves towards a peaceful settlement never had a chance. Certainly, departmental interest in averting a battle for Port Stanley was substantial: both the Foreign Office and the Ministry of Defence, together with the chiefs of staff, were acutely conscious of the heavy losses which might be incurred in such a battle, and the damage it would do to any long-term hopes for a settlement of the Falklands issue. The military victory which had seemed the only route out of the Falklands tunnel now seemed likely to prolong it. To ministers such as Nott and Pym, anything appeared preferable to a permanent British garrison and continuing harassment from the Argentine mainland. If Britain had been prepared to accept a UN administrator before the land war, how much better to accept one now, to avert further loss of life?

The American military historian, Fred Ikle (who happened to be assistant secretary at the Pentagon during the Falklands war), has noted that the moment of impending victory or defeat is often the most irrational in any conflict.* The about-to-be-vanquished bids its troops to prefer 'death with honour' to the shame of a negotiated defeat (the order usually going out from the security of HQ). The about-to-be-victorious argues that the 'blood of our war dead' demands that no quarter be given to the enemy and any previous compromises be withdrawn. This applies in a limited war as much as in a global one. By refusing to negotiate during battle, Omar Bradley commented during the Korean war, 'one would only jump from a smaller conflict to a larger deadlock at greater expense'. In uncanny re-enactment of this scenario, General Galtieri now ordered his troops on the Falklands to 'fight to the last man'. Port Stanley, he said, would only be a battle in a longer war. Meanwhile, Cecil Parkinson went on British television on 6 June to declare that there had been an 'enormous change of mood in Britain since the landing'. There would now, he said, be 'no place for the Argentinians in those islands or in the future administration of them'. Any question of shared sovereignty was out of the question. 'We have to be prepared to hold on to what we have repossessed.' Or, in the words of a colour sergeant on the Falklands, much quoted in the British press, 'If they're worth fighting

---

* *Every War Must End*, Columbia, 1971.

for, they must be worth keeping.' This progressive hardening in Britain's position as the land war continued was to cost her another week of agony and death. It finally prevented any lasting solution to the Falklands dispute emerging as part of the fruits of victory.

15 » TRIUMPH ON KENT, TRAGEDY AT FITZROY

'Amphibious warfare is not a battle on the European plain.'

A Royal Marine at Fitzroy

2 Para's victory at Goose Green enormously lifted the spirits of the land force. After days of lingering, they had achieved a solid success, asserted to the Argentinians their absolute determination to reconquer the Falklands at whatever cost in effort and blood. However, the battle also dispelled some British hopes that a mere military demonstration would provoke the enemy to collapse. A pattern had been set for the rest of the war: in every position, the Argentine defenders had to be pushed persistently and hard before they began to crumble. There was no longer any enthusiasm in the British command for a precipitate, unsupported rush against the positions around Port Stanley. Brigadier Thompson and his staff considered it essential that every attacking battalion should be supported by guns with the maximum possible reserve of ammunition – probably around 500 rounds a gun. The battle for Goose Green would have been incomparably easier for 2 Para had they possessed more support. That mistake would not be made again. But a Sea King helicopter could carry only 60 rounds of gun ammunition in a single lift. To move four six-gun batteries of artillery and their ammunition across East Falkland for the battle against the enemy's main positions would be a huge task. Indeed, it became the principal logistic problem for the remainder

of the war, vastly increased when 5 Brigade arrived on the battle-field.

All the plans made before the loss of *Atlantic Conveyor* and its heavy-lift Chinook helicopters had become meaningless. The prospect before 3 Commando Brigade was of a continued foot march across East Falkland, towards the chain of hills surrounding Port Stanley. 45 Commando, which left San Carlos with 3 Para on 27 May, had plodded doggedly over the hills and across countless streams and marshes towards Douglas settlement. At 10 p.m. that night the marines 'sank exhausted into sleep' after covering more than 13 miles across terrible terrain at a cost of fifteen men injured with sprained ankles, strained muscles and suchlike. After a night on the hills in freezing rain, when the sodden men prepared to move the next morning, Colonel Whitehead was determined that they should reach shelter by nightfall. They abandoned their huge bergens and set off in fighting order, still burdened heavily enough by their weapons and ammunition. Perhaps the most encouraging discovery of the march was that their Volvo tracked vehicles – the 'BVs' as they were always known – could cover the ground astonishingly well. There were only a handful with each unit, but they sufficed to carry the heavy weapons, much of the wireless equipment and stragglers recovered on the line of advance. Similarly, the Scorpion and Scimitar armoured reconnaissance vehicles which had been sent with the two marching units coped superbly with the going. Thenceforth, the tanks covered staggering distances across the island, accompanying any battalion that had need of them.

The men marched in long files, 10 yards apart so that a moving commando stretched across 3 miles of East Falkland. Even if they managed to dry their feet during the night, each morning within a few minutes they had squelched through a marsh in the darkness, waded a stream or merely endured a torrential rain shower. Their canvas webbing stiffened and shrank on their shoulders, their hair hung matted on their skulls, the strain of stumbling across the hillside with grenades, weapons and linked-belt ammunition across their chests was etched into each face long before evening. They talked mostly in obscene monosyllables about the f—ing rain, the f—ing choppers that never came for them, the f—ing Argies and the f—ing Falklands.

The bare hills lacked the richness of wildlife that adds so much to the Highlands of Scotland. There were the geese, the occasional sheep or herd of cattle cantering away from the sound of helicopters. There were occasional enchanting rivers that are said to hold some of the finest seatrout in the world – a young para tickled a 5-pound fish one morning. There were occasional wonderful glimpses of empty coastline, each creek and hillside with its lyrical local name – Rincon de los Indios, Horse Paddocks, Halfway Cove, Letterbox Hill. Deep in their hearts, the men drew great pride from the feeling that no infantry in the world could so readily achieve what they were doing, if they could do it at all. But the cold, the long shivering nights, the struggle to move again after 'taking ten' each hour did not make for happiness. Each day, their NCOs were compelled to push them a little harder to discourage straggling, and each day more men found their blisters or tendons or ankles intolerable, 'although it's all guts really', as the RSM of 45 Commando remarked laconically. The worst thing – unlike any exercise they had ever endured – was that they had no hint of when it might end. It may now seem obvious that the Argentinians would not attack their line of march, would not endure a siege when the battle finally came. It did not seem so then.

45 Commando reached the little hamlet of Douglas to find the delighted local Falklanders alone. A party of the enemy had left the previous day. Whitehead was moved by his men's extraordinary performance – 'the commando looked so very impressive – my heart was leaping with pride in them'. But after days nursing permanently soaked and frozen feet, they needed thirty-six hours in which to recover. On the morning of 30 May, they began to march again, accompanied by a local tractor and trailer carrying part of their heavy equipment. Shortly after 8 p.m. that night, they reached their initial objective, the green-roofed settlement at Teal

Inlet, an estuary dug deep into the north-east of East Falkland. 3 Para, who had marched from San Carlos at the customary furious pace in which the Parachute Regiment takes such pride, had been there before them, arriving late on the night of the 29th and leaving once more at last light on the 30th. On the night of 31 May, after an epic march which exhausted even Hew Pike's fit men, 3 Para secured Estancia House, a lonely cluster of farm buildings within sight of the lower slopes of Mount Kent.

That night also, one of the most important advances of the war was achieved. D Squadron of the SAS had been patrolling the upper slopes of Mount Kent since early May, and had been established in strength there since 27 May. They met and destroyed several enemy patrols, and now reported that the summit seemed lightly held by the enemy, if at all. Brigadier Thompson and his staff struggled urgently to get together sufficient helicopters to lift a substantial British force on to the mountain before the Argentinians awoke to its critical importance, and defended it in strength. If the enemy held the high ground, 3 Commando Brigade would be able to achieve nothing on the hills overlooked by them, and would be dangerously vulnerable to observed artillery fire.

On the night of 30 May, an operation to fly marines on to the mountain had been frustrated by a fierce whiteout, which forced the leading Sea Kings to turn back to San Carlos. Late on the afternoon of 31 May, the helicopters embarked the leading elements of K Company, 42 Commando, together with Lieutenant Colonel Nick Vaux and Lieutenant Colonel Michael Rose of the SAS. Given the risk of enemy air interception in the failing light, in order to land the first wave before darkness had fallen, Lieutenant Commander Simon Thornewill and the other superb PNG pilots began a remarkable contour-flying dash 40 miles across East Falkland. They were attacking into the unknown, far beyond any other British positions, and at this stage it seemed impossible that the enemy would fail to respond to such a deadly challenge to his safety. The two helicopters in the first wave were desperately overloaded. When the men had clambered aboard, mortar rounds,

Blowpipe missiles and heavy equipment were pushed in on top of them until all movement or hope of quick escape in an emergency was gone. The young marines, their blackened faces unsmiling, were certain they would face a battle on landing. The ground rushed by 20 feet below, as the Sea King lifted and dipped with the hills, sending cattle and sheep fleeing in all directions across the empty wasteland. For those who savour the ironic clichés of war, Max Hastings shouted to Colonel Rose above the roar of the helicopter that it seemed impossible that the Argentinians could fail to start shelling the landing zone after the first lift. Rose shrugged and grinned: 'Who dares wins.'

The two helicopters set down behind a ridgeline 2 miles below the summit of the mountain, and men fought their way through the mounds of equipment to tumble out into the tussock grass. To their alarm and bewilderment, they immediately saw a firefight in progress less than a mile northwards, with tracer carving the sky in the dusk and occasional fierce explosions. The marines hastily took cover beneath the huge grey rocks that dominate all the hills of East Falkland, scrambling over the boulder falls, dragging their cases of mortar rounds and bergens. Then the firing died away, and out of the darkness loomed the mild, imperturbable figure of Major Cedric Delves of D Squadron, South Georgia, Pebble Island and various other South Atlantic addresses. 'No problem, boss,' he told Rose. 'There was an Argie patrol up there, but we've malleted one lot and we'll sort out the others in the morning.' Rose, Nick Vaux and commando headquarters established a bivouac a few hundred yards from the landing site. K Company, under Captain Peter Babbington, went through the motions of carrying out a company night attack on the summit of Mount Kent, to discover to their enormous relief that it was untenanted. Two hours after the initial landing, the one surviving British Chinook helicopter brought in three 105 mm guns and 300 rounds of ammunition. On its return to San Carlos, the low-flying helicopter misjudged its height and struck a lake. The pilot made an instant recovery, regained altitude, and made a successful landing at San Carlos. But the Chinook was too severely damaged to fly again that night. No more gun ammunition could be brought in. K Company were alone until they could be reinforced.

It was appallingly cold on the hilltop, even behind the ridge-line and out of the wind. The men brewed hot chocolate on their flickering hexamine cookers and ate their rations. Then, those fortunate enough to have sleeping bags – who did not include Vaux's riflemen – settled down to snatch what rest they could. There was nothing useful to be done through the sixteen hours of darkness, and no soldier could sleep for that long. Long before dawn, almost every man on the hillside was awake, shivering silently behind his rock, praying for daylight and a reason to begin to move, to shake off the layer of ice and snow crusting sleeping bags, clothing, equipment. At first light, Vaux and Rose climbed 2 miles to join K Company on the summit, taking with them a Blowpipe troop to support the defenders against the enemy air attack that seemed inevitable. On the crest of the hill, in the patchy snow and undying wind, they stood and gazed down on the distant blur of Moody Brook, the former Royal Marine base 12 miles to the south-east. It was an enormously exhilarating moment. If the enemy was unable or unwilling to mount a counter-attack against the seizure of Mount Kent, it seemed unlikely that he possessed the initiative to do anything but wait for the British to fall upon his main positions. At Rose's urging, the gunner forward observers called down a few salvos on Moody Brook, believed to be an Argentine base camp. There was too little ammunition to open a major bombardment. But the Argentinians must now know that the British had established decisive strategic dominance over them.

At Vaux's headquarters below, a mildly amused young Royal Marine guarded four unhappy Argentine prisoners who had been seized by the SAS after a brief firefight. These men, it transpired, were from the enemy's special forces, the best that he could pit against the British. They looked as dejected and eager for escape from the war as the prisoners taken at Goose Green. That night,

Thornewill's Sea Kings began to bring in the rest of 42 Commando, to secure the adjoining ridgeline of Mount Challenger, which also proved unoccupied. A week earlier, the enemy's strategic reserve had been based in the valley below, but had been flown out to Darwin and Goose Green to reinforce the garrison when it became apparent that the British were moving against the settlements. Vaux's men found abandoned Argentine positions and equipment. They were thankful to be spared the need to face their former inhabitants. It was enough to have to contend only with the elements on Mount Kent.

3 Para now held Mount Estancia and Mount Vernet, north-east of Kent, while the SAS were firmly established on the Murrell Heights north of Stanley harbour. On 4 June, 45 Commando reached a position on the rear slopes of Mount Kent, having marched every yard of the distance from San Carlos. The key fighting elements of 3 Commando Brigade were thus positioned on the north axis of advance against Port Stanley, impatient to begin the battle before their men deteriorated in the chronic cold and wet. The story of the remainder of the Falklands war is above all of a struggle against weather and logistics, to enable the British land force to embark on its final offensive. After the brilliant weather that had served the enemy's air force so well in the week following the landing, now day after day British flying operations were crippled or completely halted by mist, snow, rain and gales that whipped the sea in San Carlos Bay into white horses, filled trenches with inches of water that froze to create a skin of ice by night, and made the old Passchendaele misery of trench foot a desperate problem for the soldiers of 1982. It was at the beginning of this difficult and frustrating phase of the war that Major General Jeremy Moore landed to take over command of the British land force, and 5 Infantry Brigade arrived at San Carlos Bay.

*

'If it had not been for *Galahad*, 5 Brigade would have come home smelling of roses,' said a senior land-force officer when the campaign was over. Yet, for the British public and for many men fighting in the Falklands, the saga of the lost landing ship at Fitzroy and the fifty-one men who died aboard her and nearby on 8 June dominates every other memory of 5 Brigade's war. In military terms, it is wrong that it should be so. In a struggle on the scale of war in the South Atlantic, it is astonishing that Fitzroy was the only really bloody setback that the British suffered. Yet it is human nature to focus upon this as the only British misfortune that cannot readily be dismissed as the chance of war. At Fitzroy, Britain suffered a glimpse of what might have happened on a much more terrible scale if the enemy air force had reached the landing convoy before it entered San Carlos Water on 21 May, if their bombs had exploded in larger numbers during the battle for the anchorage, if any of the sunken ships had been less fortunate in losing so few men killed.

5 Infantry Brigade, commanded by a stylish forty-seven-year-old Light Infantryman named Tony Wilson, who had won the Military Cross and OBE in Northern Ireland, was officially designated as Britain's 'out-of-area' force, earmarked for operations outside north-west Europe. It comprised 2 Para, 3 Para and the 1st/7th Duke of Edinburgh's Own Gurkha Rifles. Formed in January 1982, its first experience of working together was an exercise in Norfolk named Green Lanyard. This ended well enough, but not surprisingly some officers felt that it revealed the lack of team experience of the brigade staff. On 2 April, the Ministry of Defence telephoned 5 Brigade's barracks at Aldershot to warn Brigadier Wilson of the Falklands crisis, and of the possibility that some of his men would be needed. Later that day, he learned that 3 Para was being transferred to 3 Commando Brigade, and a few days later that he was also losing 2 Para. In their place, he received 1st Battalion Welsh Guards and 2nd Scots Guards. After much political agonising and consultation with the Nepalese government, it was agreed that the Gurkhas should remain part of the formation if it was to go to war. Wilson was told that 5 Brigade in its new form might well be ordered to the South Atlantic, and was offered a full-scale

brigade exercise to knit the formation together and enable the men to stretch their legs in good time before going to sea. Wilson selected the Sennybridge training area in the Brecon Beacons for Exercise Welsh Falcon, because it most resembled the Falklands. On 22 April, the brigade began two weeks of battalion attacks, intensive live firing, helicopter movements with Puma helicopters, and practice amphibious assaults which were considered by some of those involved to be something less than a total success, and which raised serious fears among some senior officers.

From the beginning, it never seemed that the Ministry of Defence took the prospect of 5 Brigade going to war very seriously. When the staff asked MoD for vital bergen rucksacks, they were at first told that there were none; then, that there might be eighty; and only after Welsh Falcon that £80,000 would be found to provide them for the entire force. They received 2,000 sets of arctic trousers, but only 1,000 smocks. When they asked for rubber overboots, they were told that these were obsolete. They were refused ammunition for M79 grenade launchers on the grounds that these were special-forces equipment. The only tracked vehicles they were offered were elderly Sno-tracs. The normal allocation of artillery for a brigade going into battle is three batteries. Wilson was given one. Before 5 Brigade finally sailed on QE2 on 12 May, the clothing deficiencies had been solved only after the unofficial intervention of a Guards officer's father in the House of Lords. Wilson's formation lacked a self-contained logistics regiment, air squadron, or full complement of vehicles or guns. Senior officers of the brigade were convinced that the Ministry of Defence simply did not expect them to have to fight. On 12 May in London, a full-scale land battle in the Falklands still seemed very far off.

They sailed amidst emotional scenes at the dockside, to enjoy two weeks of magnificent food and wine aboard QE2 on a passage far less austere than that of 3 Commando Brigade. Even the war cabinet found something faintly bizarre about dispatching men to war on the greatest luxury liner in the world. The brigade was accompanied by Major General Jeremy Moore and his eighty-strong staff, who boarded the ship at Ascension Island. Units were warned that they could be out of England for up to six months. They were given no formal orders, for as yet no plan existed. They spent much of the passage being intensively briefed about the Falklands in the same manner as 3 Commando Brigade, and hanging on World Service bulletins in the wake of the San Carlos landings. The ship had been provided with a vastly expensive Scot Satellite communications system for the benefit of the land-force commander, but this worked only erratically, giving Moore 'one of the worst weeks of my life' as the great drama unfolded on East Falkland while he lacked any means to influence it.

Some of those on QE2 were still uneasy about the inexperience of 5 Brigade's staff, and much more so about the breach of an official promise that they would have the chance to restow vehicles and equipment before arriving in the Falklands. Much useful material was out of their reach and would remain so. 5 Brigade's headquarters' tent never reached the shore of East Falkland throughout the campaign, and sailed home to England again when the war was over without even being unpacked. There were also officers who asked in bewilderment, 'What possessed the Ministry of Defence to send two public-duties battalions to the South Atlantic?' Both Guards battalions joined 5 Brigade from prolonged tours of ceremonial duties, during which their infantry training was obviously less intensive than that of a marine or parachute battalion. The Welsh Guards had completed an exercise in Kenya the previous winter. Like all Guards units, these two could be accounted among the finest in the army. But, however enthusiastic and efficient their officers and men, they could scarcely be as mentally and physically attuned to a campaign in the Falklands as 3 Commando Brigade. They were trained to fight from armoured personnel carriers. 'We are not bergen soldiers,' as one of their officers said. In the firm opinion of many of 5 Brigade, the Ministry of Defence sent the Guards because they were expecting them to serve as a garrison, not to have to fight. A very senior officer at the Ministry of Defence confirmed after the war that, when they were dispatched from Britain, 5 Brigade was considered a reserve for 3 Commando Brigade, not a force of matching capabilities.

On 28 May, at South Georgia, the brigade transferred to *Canberra* and *Norland* for its final passage – this was as far as the war cabinet was willing to risk *QE2*. There had been some discussion of sending 5 Brigade to open a new beach-head in the north-east of East Falkland, but it was concluded that there were insufficient Rapier launchers available to give effective protection to a second anchorage. Moore, Wilson and elements of their staffs embarked on the destroyer *Antrim*, and hastened ahead of the main body to San Carlos Water, where they boarded the command ship *Fearless* on 30 May. Moore later said that he wished he had adopted the course followed by the new CO of 2 Para and other personnel needed urgently in the Falklands, who parachuted into the sea from a Hercules – although that would have been no mean undertaking even for a fit man of fifty-three. As it was, Moore had to gather into his hands very quickly the strands of an immensely complex situation. One of the most decorated soldiers of the Royal Marines with an MC and Bar won in the Far East as a young fighting officer, Moore was also immensely popular among his corps, a bright, cheerful man with an infectious grin and great natural authority. He had never been considered an intellectual soldier, a strategic thinker, but he possessed as much experience of battle, and of amphibious operations, as any general in the British forces.

Both during and since the war, Moore gained much respect among the high command and the war cabinet at home. When difficulties began to develop in the South Atlantic and relations between Admiral Woodward and Brigadier Thompson were clearly less than smooth, the chiefs of staff were eager to get Moore on to the scene as rapidly as possible. Senior officers at home asserted later that, once he arrived at San Carlos, difficulties seemed to slip away, and the path of command relations appeared to become far more straightforward. They had criticised Julian Thompson's delay in beginning the breakout from the beach-head, yet they now seemed perfectly resigned to the two-week pause between Goose Green and the battle for Port Stanley. Moore, they were confident, knew what he was doing. He himself cannily reinforced this feeling by dispatching a long, cheerful nightly signal to London throughout the war, which created an impression of constant activity for the encouragement of Northwood and the war cabinet even when in reality little was taking place.

Thompson was relieved by his major general's arrival, for it spared him his unhappy twice-daily pilgrimages to the satellite terminal at Ajax Bay, to be cross-questioned by Northwood and urged to make more speed. Now, he could address himself simply to fighting the war, and escape the problems of command and control, arguing with the navy about ship movements, grappling with the huge logistics difficulties. Thompson's achievement before Moore arrived – in getting the landing force ashore, controlling it through the first ten days and securing Mount Kent – had been substantial. The major general also arrived at the right time to profit from the growing battle experience of Northwood and the war cabinet at home, who were coming to terms with the pace of war, and slowly beginning to understand the difficulties with which the land force was struggling.

The land force now comprised some 9,000 men. The first decision that Moore had to make was whether to use 5 Brigade to support 3 Brigade's push upon Port Stanley from the north and west, or to open up a new axis of advance in the south. On *Antrim* during the passage from South Georgia, Brigadier Wilson made no secret of his eagerness to press on from the south. To one marine staff officer, he seemed 'obsessed with the fear that Julian Thompson would win the war before his men could do anything'. But it was natural, even admirable, that a commander given the chance of taking his brigade to war should be anxious for it to play a full part on the battlefield. The major general agreed to give Wilson the chance he wanted.

It was agreed between Moore and his brigadier that 2 Para, resting and restoring some semblance of normality at Goose Green, should be placed under Wilson's command. His entire brigade would then begin to open up a southern axis of advance towards Port Stanley via Fitzroy and Bluff Cove, adjoining settlements 36 miles east of Goose Green. Helicopters would be made available to move the brigade at least from San Carlos to Goose Green. 'It seems a good plan,' wrote a senior staff officer who had been at San Carlos from the beginning, 'but I have doubts whether it takes sufficient account of the shortage of helicopter assets.' Within hours of Wilson's arrival at San Carlos, it became evident that these fears were well-founded. When Moore had been fully briefed about the position of Thompson's men, strung out between Teal Inlet and Mount Kent, it became vividly apparent that, if 3 Commando Brigade was to maintain itself with rations and equipment at the end of a long and tenuous line of communication – to say nothing of building up supporting guns and ammunition to defend itself against possible counterattack and prepare for an advance on Port Stanley – it would need every heavy helicopter available to the landing force. Wilson, not surprisingly, was dismayed. But Moore had little hesitation in accepting that Thompson must have all the aircraft to support his men – operating in deep discomfort in the field – and to exploit the great opportunity on Mount Kent. Every effort would be made to transfer 3 Brigade's stores maintenance area from Ajax Bay to Teal, where a landing ship could bring in supplies under the protection of Rapier anti-aircraft missiles. But, until these things had been done, Wilson would have no means of moving his men from San Carlos.

The Gurkhas started to come ashore from *Canberra* on 1 June, and set off immediately to march to Goose Green. The tough little soldiers so much beloved by the British public were out of their element in the South Atlantic winter, and had suffered severely from sea sickness. But they made no difficulty about the 'yomp' to Goose Green. Wilson himself flew by Gazelle to Goose Green to meet for the first time the men of 2 Para, still under the temporary command of Major Chris Keeble. Some paras harboured a suspicion of Wilson for his habit of wearing a red beret (and green

Wellington boots) in the field. Although he was indeed jump-qualified, the Parachute Regiment cherishes a belief that only its own members, rather than Light Infantrymen who happen to be controlling its battalions, should have the privilege of wearing the 'cherry beret'. More than that, perhaps, they felt themselves to be veterans of the Falklands war, while the Brigadier was a newcomer. They were appalled by Wilson's first proposal to get his brigade moving: he suggested that 2 Para should provide a screen on the high ground while the newly arrived infantry marched along the coast to Bluff Cove. The paras considered that this plan grossly under-estimated the difficulties of marching men across the Falklands. Wilson believed that, by leapfrogging his battalions, it was perfectly feasible.

Chris Keeble came up with another idea. Brooke Hardcastle, the local Falkland Island Company manager, had suggested that the civilian telephone link might be open between Swan Inlet House, a few miles up the coast, and Fitzroy settlement. Why not try a telephone call to discover the situation in the east? Wilson agreed immediately. Five light helicopters were assembled for a piratical little expedition. Bearing a dozen men commanded by Major John Crosland, the former SAS trooper commanding B Company, they took off at 2 p.m. that afternoon for Swan Inlet. After firing a salvo of Matra rockets into the empty hillside to cover their landing, they assaulted the house to find it unoccupied but for an abandoned Argentine jacket. Smashing a window to break in, Colour Sergeant Morris wound the telephone handle twice, the correct signal for a call to Fitzroy, Almost 30 miles east, a teenage girl answered, and eventually fetched her father, Ron Binney, the local manager.

'This is the British army,' announced Morris. 'Can you speak freely?'

'Yes,' said Binney.

'Are there any Argentinians near you?'

'No – they just blew up the bridge to Bluff Cove and left.'

'Fine,' said Morris, 'we'll be with you shortly.'

At Goose Green, Chris Keeble had completed his battalion's handover to the Gurkhas. The paras were still terribly tired after their battle, but eager to seize the chance to give the war a dramatic leap forward. On the return of Crosland and his men with the news that Fitzroy was open for the taking, Wilson commandeered the only surviving Chinook. At 4 p.m., as last light approached, Chris Keeble crammed most of his A Company – seventy-eight men – into its huge hold, and waved them away eastwards. The battalion's indefatigable Scout helicopter pilot, Captain John Greenhalgh, had already landed a reconnaissance party to confirm that the coast was clear. A Company spilled out of the Chinook onto the high ground above Bluff Cove settlement. That evening, a second Chinook lift brought in seventy-eight men of B Company. It was the thirteenth birthday of a small refugee from Port Stanley who was staying in the settlement. He had begged to be allowed to stay up late to see the British army, who he was certain were coming. He was not disappointed. A patrol from A Company advanced into the settlement and confirmed that there was no enemy in the area. Then they deployed to cover the approaches, and began to dig in.

It was one of those bold strokes that can win wars, a feat of decision and imagination by Wilson and 2 Para. Or was it? Major General Moore's staff at San Carlos were appalled and exasperated when they learned of a huge risk taken without their knowledge. 'Grossly irresponsible,' one commented in his diary. 2 Para was exposed to enemy counter-attack or bombardment miles beyond the range of British fire support. The staff on *Fearless* laboured until far into the night to organise the movement of guns and supplies to cover the battalion. It had been their intention – although 5 Brigade was unaware of it – to use the precious Chinook, which had been bringing Argentine prisoners back from Goose Green, to shuttle 5 Brigade's main headquarters and communications vehicles southwards. They believed that the brigade's first priority should be to establish secure command and control of its units, and Wilson's staff were anyway desperately short of communications equipment.

The dash for Bluff Cove also seemed designed to force a strategic decision upon the British command. It was well known that many of 5 Brigade were bitter about the favoured treatment apparently being given to 3 Commando Brigade in the allocation of helicopters and resources. Major General Moore had declared firmly that the attack on Port Stanley would be a two-brigade affair in which everybody would have a role. But 5 Brigade still feared passionately that the Royal Marines would somehow push them aside, and mount their own offensive while the Guards and Gurkhas were still struggling to make their painful way towards Bluff Cove without helicopters. 2 Para's move pre-empted any decisions about how and when the brigade advanced. Wilson told a correspondent, 'I've grabbed my land in this great jump forward. Now I want to consolidate it.'

Wilson could claim that he had saved his brigade from the possibility of heavy fighting and long delays on the road to Fitzroy, if the enemy had moved men forward to oppose his advance by land. But for the week that now followed, most of the energies of Moore's staff and of the Royal Navy were devoted to the problems of 5 Brigade. Somehow its scattered elements had to be enabled to concentrate behind 2 Para's exposed positions.

The Gurkhas began to sweep Lafonia for Argentine stragglers left behind by the Goose Green battle, and took responsibility for securing that area. Meanwhile, the two Guards battalions had landed at San Carlos on 2 June. They took over the soggy trenches left behind by 3 Commando Brigade. But, to the dismay of Julian Thompson, Moore ordered 40 Commando to remain in reserve around San Carlos while both Guards battalions marched with Wilson. For 40 Commando – now deployed around the entire anchorage – to hand over to one of 5 Brigade's units would waste time. The landing-force staff was also alarmed at this time by intelligence reports that the Argentinians on the mainland were considering a dramatic 'spoiling move' against the British beach-head, perhaps by paratroop assault. Moore wanted the strongest possible force available to meet any threat to his rear area. As a Royal Marine himself, the general was also at pains to dispel any suspicion that the campaign was being conducted as a 'benefit match' for his Corps, with the green beret undertaking none of the less glamorous tasks.

On the afternoon of 3 June, the Welsh Guards began an attempt to march to Goose Green. They walked for twelve hours before 5 Brigade agreed with their CO that the exercise should be abandoned. The Guardsmen were far too heavily laden. Their handful of Sno-tracs were breaking down every few miles. It was evidently uneconomic to exhaust the battalion merely to get them to Goose Green. Back the Guards marched over Sussex Mountain. The news of their misfortunes aroused exasperation, even contempt, among 3 Commando Brigade, waiting impatiently in the mountains to begin the next move towards Stanley. 'We have got to wait for 5 Brigade to get its act together,' they were told. Now they learned that the Guardsmen – anyway the object of the usual regimental rivalry – had failed to perform even a modest 'yomp' to Goose Green. Yet, not only were these men fresh from public duties, they had also missed the invaluable six-day acclimatisation period from which 3 Commando Brigade profited after coming ashore. The Guards lacked the priceless Volvo tracked vehicles; and also, perhaps, the sense of being directed by an efficient, experienced brigade staff such as that of 3 Brigade.

If 5 Brigade could not be given helicopters and could not march, how were they to get to Fitzroy? The only conceivable answer was by sea. There began the immensely complex series of amphibious operations which culminated in tragedy. On the night of 5 June, the Scots Guards embarked aboard the assault ship *Intrepid* and sailed through the darkness out of San Carlos, round the coast of Lafonia. At a pre-arranged location at Lively Island some miles offshore, *Intrepid* launched the passengers from her dock in four landing craft, under the command of the doughty

Major Ewen Southby-Tailyour. It was an appalling night. The weather began to worsen soon after the landing craft were released. Their radar became unserviceable. Even in passive night goggles, Southby-Tailyour found it difficult to judge his course. Suddenly starshell burst overhead and, to the consternation of the bedraggled Guardsmen, a salvo of gunfire landed in the water nearby. After some confused lamp signalling, Southby-Tailyour persuaded a British frigate to desist from shelling them, but the flotilla had been badly alarmed. The winds were now gusting up to 70 knots, and the LCUs were making only 2 knots through the water. 'It was the worst night of my life,' said Southby-Tailyour later. They had left Intrepid shortly after midnight. At dawn, after seven hours at sea, they struggled ashore at Bluff Cove. The exhausted Guardsmen made their way from the beach to the positions of 2 Para, where Lieutenant Colonel David Chaundler had now taken over from Chris Keeble in command. The Guards had already identified four exposure cases in their ranks. They had no orders, and found no one at Bluff Cove to give them any. The paras themselves had received only two days' rations in five days, and were hungry and cold. Chaundler was appalled by the spectacle of the demoralised, soaking Guardsmen. One of his officers wondered aloud, 'How the hell are we ever going to see this through to the end if we do things like this?' The senior Scots Guards officer felt unable to make any decision about the battalion deployment until his commanding officer arrived from Darwin. At last, after much delay, it was agreed that the Guards would take over the positions established by 2 Para, while Chaundler's men retired to the shearing sheds at Fitzroy to begin drying themselves out.

Intrepid, meanwhile, had returned at her full 20 knots to San Carlos to reach the relative safety of the anchorage before first light. The navy was deeply concerned about intelligence reports of an Exocet missile launcher based ashore. Northwood had also entered the debate about the southern axis. A staff officer wrote in his diary, 'Mrs Thatcher is under pressure to get Stanley. Every day that Stanley is not taken is another country lost to world opinion.

We can't risk losing another ship or the Cabinet may be unable to resist pressure for a ceasefire.' Northwood's extraordinary proposal was that the men of 5 Brigade should be brought ashore at Teal Inlet, on the northern side of the mountains, where LSLs had been unloading stores under the safety of Rapier cover since 2 June. The Guards could then march to the southern flank. 'Too many people in England are using too small scale maps of this island,' said an officer on *Fearless* acidly. With deep reluctance, the navy agreed to make one more attempt to complete the offloading of 5 Brigade from an assault ship. On the afternoon of 6 June, the Welsh Guards were embarked on *Fearless*, along with two of her LCUs. They were to rendezvous late that night off Fitzroy with *Intrepid*'s four landing craft, brought out from the shore by Southby-Tailyour. *Fearless* lingered at sea as late as she dared that night, waiting for the landing craft from Fitzroy, with whom she had no means of communicating. Southby-Tailyour and his crews had met appalling weather. It was impossible for them to put to sea. At last, with the danger of daylight approaching, *Fearless* offloaded two companies of Guardsmen into her own two remaining LCUs, and watched them move astern out of the dock, and away towards the shore. Then the assault ship turned back to San Carlos, with more than 300 men still in her tank decks.

The navy had now had enough. In signal consultation between Commodore Clapp, Admiral Woodward and Northwood, it was decided that it was too dangerous to expose an assault ship again without a large escort. In which case, interrupted Northwood, we shall not sail an assault ship again. In modern terms, these were capital ships. The risking of them had now become an intensely political issue in London. After further debate, Northwood reported a decision: the government could not face the possibility of losing *Fearless* or *Intrepid*, but they were willing to hazard the smaller, less prestigious 5,700-ton landing ships. All further movement in the open sea must be by LSL. Yet the LSLs were ships of the Royal Fleet Auxiliary, largely crewed by civilians and armed only with Bofors guns.

The night that the first elements of the Welsh Guards reached Bluff Cove, the landing ship *Sir Tristram* also arrived, unannounced, with an enormous load of artillery ammunition. Ewen Southby-Tailyour and other marines running the beach party ashore were astonished that the navy was willing to allow the ship to remain inshore through the daylight hours when there was no effective local air defence. 'Where are the naval ships protecting the offload? Same old answer, I'm afraid,' a marine wrote in his diary. It was now tacitly conceded by the navy that the power of one or even two frigates to protect another ship against air attack was vastly outweighed by the risk that the escorts would merely become additional targets. It is also important to see events at Fitzroy in the context of operations elsewhere. The weight of enemy air attack had diminished in the past few days to nuisance proportions. The last serious attempt to bomb shipping, on 6 June, had been a half-hearted sortie by two Lear jets. One was destroyed by a Sea Dart from *Exeter*; the other turned tail and fled. Under immense pressure to move supplies, the navy had been unloading at Teal Inlet for almost a week without interference. They had even risked bringing the ammunition ship *Elk* into San Carlos during daylight without attracting bomb attack. In a situation teeming with calculated risks, the dispatch of landing ships to Fitzroy seemed merely one more.

What was much more serious at Fitzroy, however, was the complete absence of communications between ship and shore, and between the naval command at San Carlos and 5 Brigade's tactical HQ in the garages on the jetty. There was never any suggestion that the thousand or more infantry ashore should be asked to provide some air defence for the ships unloading – which could well have been done with automatic weapons and Blowpipe missiles. The most effective means of communication then existing within 5 Brigade's scattered elements was personal visit by helicopter. It was in an attempt to improve this situation that, at 4 a.m. on 8 June, Ewen Southby-Tailyour was awakened from a borrowed bunk on *Tristram* and asked by a 5 Brigade staff officer to send a landing craft urgently to Goose Green to bring back the vehicles and vital signals equipment of 5 Brigade main headquarters. He ordered *Foxtrot 4*, under the command of Colour Sergeant Johnston of the marines, to sail to Goose Green with the commandeered coaster *Monsoonun*, load Main HQ, and return under cover of night. There was now one LCU and a mexefloat pontoon in the little bay. The marines ordered these to continue offloading ammunition from *Tristram*.

At 7 a.m., to their astonishment, they saw a second landing ship round the point into the bay and drop anchor. The previous afternoon, following the decision to hazard no more assault ships moving troops, Prince of Wales's Company, 3 Company, the mortar platoon and support echelon of the Welsh Guards had been transferred aboard *Galahad* to sail to Fitzroy. At the last moment, 16 Field Ambulance was also ordered aboard. By the time the medical teams had been loaded, their departure was four hours behind schedule. The ship's master suggested to the senior officers that they should go to bed: 'We're not going anywhere tonight.' He then signalled *Fearless* to report that, since he could no longer expect to reach Fitzroy and offload in darkness, he assumed that his sailing was postponed until the following night. Fifteen minutes after being urged to go to bed, the senior army officers aboard learned that there had been a change of plan. *Fearless* had ordered that they should sail immediately.

Not a single man at Fitzroy or Bluff Cove the following morning had an inkling of *Galahad*'s coming. Brigadier Wilson himself said later that he knew that the remainder of the Guards were on passage but, when they failed to arrive during darkness, he assumed that their sailing had been postponed. There was no direct discussion between 5 Brigade's tactical headquarters and *Fearless* about the troops' movement. Wilson himself left Darwin by helicopter that morning with his brigade major, Brendan Lamb, for a conference with Major General Moore, unaware of the situation. His senior gunnery officer was in temporary command at Fitzroy.

The sequence of events aboard *Galahad* during the five hours that followed have the slow-motion inevitability of classical tragedy. There may have been a sense of purpose and efficency aboard the landing ship, but there was certainly none of urgency or crisis. The troops aboard had not been present in San Carlos during the first week of devastating air attack. They had never seen what the Argentine air force could do. During the preceding few days, even aboard *Fearless*, there is no doubt that a subconscious feeling had grown that 'the air problem is hacked'. The Welsh Guards were under orders to join the rest of their battalion at Bluff Cove. The LSL could not get up the narrow channel direct to the beach there. Since the bridge linking the two neighbouring settlements had been blown, if the troops now came ashore at Fitzroy, they faced a circuitous 12-mile march to their destination. To the Guards who boarded the LSL from the shore, their senior officer seemed determined that his men should not be 'mucked about any more' after all their movements and counter-movements of the past few days. He wanted landing craft to be brought out to the ship in which they could be sailed direct to Bluff. Ewen Southby-Tailyour, who was horrified by the spectacle of the LSLs lying unprotected in the bay in broad daylight, commandeered the landing craft half loaded with ammunition from *Tristram*, and steered hastily across the water to *Galahad*. With Major Tony Todd of the Royal Corps of Transport, he urged the Welsh Guards officers to put as many of their men as possible aboard, and move ashore. They declined. There is a military regulation that men and ammunition do not travel in the same boat. 'I'm not putting my men in with a mixed load,' said one. 'And anyway we don't want to be at Fitzroy. We want to be at Bluff Cove.' After a prolonged and sometimes heated discussion in which the marine pressed the urgency of disembarking the troops, Southby-Tailyour returned ashore and went in search of 5 Brigade's staff, to explain the situation. The first staff officer he met was frankly disbelieving that there were men aboard the LSL at all. 'They've all got off,' he said. Southby-Tailyour disillusioned him. The staff officer set off to hasten the disembarkation of the Rapier launchers that were intended to provide the area's critical defence against air attack. Wilson had asked for Rapier as soon as he put 2 Para into the settlement. But, like so much else, the missiles had proved impossible to produce for 5 Brigade at short notice. Major Barney Ross-Smith of 5 Brigade HQ now ordered the landing craft to go alongside *Galahad* and begin to bring off the Welsh Guards. But, unknown to him, the CO of 16 Field Ambulance aboard the landing ship had discussed the situation with the senior Welsh Guards officer. The medical officer, a Colonel, said that, since the field ambulance wanted to be ashore at Fitzroy – which the Guards did not – and since they had a difficult and urgent task in setting up a dressing station ashore, it seemed important to unload their stores first. The mexefloat pontoon and the LCU began shipping medical supplies. The Guards lingered in the ship's cafeteria watching a video, gathered their equipment, or stood by the ship's rail gazing out beyond the flat desolate shoreline of the little bay, to the mountains rising into the distance.

Barney Ross-Smith had just returned to 5 Brigade HQ when a radio message arrived from Bob Edwards, the marine beachmaster, to report that the ramp of the LCU had jammed in the upright position, and that, rather than disembark the Guards from the lowered ramp of *Galahad*, it was now necessary to bring the landing craft alongside the ship, and move the men to clamber down the side.

It was now 1.10 p.m. Four aircraft streaked across the sky. 2 Para were zeroing their weapons a little way down the shore. A few Scots Guardsmen began to fire on the aircraft from their positions, until a shout from a senior officer ordered them to halt: 'They're Harriers!' Some men on the landing ships heard an urgent shout to 'Get down!' Then the two Mirages and two Skyhawks were on them, and their world exploded. Corporal Mike Price of the Welsh Guards heard the cry to lie flat, but was too astonished to move, until: 'The next I knew, I was on fire, like.' Johnny Strutt, a charming, boyish-looking subaltern of twenty-two, was hurled into the air by the explosion of the first bomb amidships, and woke 'to find myself lying covered by a great mound of stuff. Then I was helped up, and somebody led me towards a boat.' A large consignment of petrol for the Rapier generators was aboard *Galahad*. This ignited immediately, inflicting terrible burns on scores of Welsh Guardsmen assembling to board the landing craft. The horror was compounded by the ignition of white phosphorus bombs carried by the mortar platoon. Many of those who died were still in the cafeteria but, within seconds of the first bomb landing, the whole of the centre of the ship was burning furiously. Men saw their own skin and flesh fry and melt before their eyes as if in slow motion, watched others fighting to douse flames in their hair and to rip off their own burning clothing. Then they began to stagger towards the ship's side and help each other in a shocked stupor towards the liferafts that were already bursting open on the water. A few hundred yards across the water, the engineering officer of *Sir Tristram* had just warned his mainly Chinese staff that an air attack might be imminent when the whole ship was lifted by the explosion of a bomb, and the Bofors guns on her upper deck began to hammer at the fading attackers. With great courage, several officers and men fought their way through a tangle of wreckage to the lower decks to shut off machinery, while others launched the ship's boats, and hastened across the water to *Galahad*, whose predicament was clearly far more desperate than their own.

Hugh Clark, the CO of a helicopter squadron who chanced to be at Fitzroy, immediately took off and called on the radio net for every available British helicopter to make for the scene. Within minutes of the attack, aircraft were winching men from *Galahad* and from liferafts, hovering low over the water to use the down draught of their rotors to push survivors' boats away from the ship towards the shore. As great gusts of flame and black smoke spewed into the sky from the bowels of the landing ship, the men of 2 Para dashed to the shore, and began pulling survivors from the rafts and helping casualties to medical aid. All that afternoon

and evening, a tragic procession of blackened, dazed, terribly
wounded men was brought aboard the assault ships in San Carlos
Bay to be lodged in the ships' messdecks, or landed directly at the
main dressing station at Ajax Bay.

*

Even as the rescue operation was being mounted at Fitzroy, urgent
efforts were being made to save the frigate *Plymouth*, which had
also been heavily attacked that afternoon. It is still uncertain
whether the Argentine air force deliberately conceived the attack
on the frigate as a diversion to distract attention from their
imminent attack on Bluff Cove, but it undoubtedly had that effect
on the British Harrier CAP. *Plymouth* was warned to break off her
bombardment of Mount Rosalie on West Falkland before an imminent air attack, expected at 1.30. But it was some minutes short of
that time when five Mirage Vs raced towards her up Falkland
Sound, turned and attacked from the port quarter. To the men on
the ship's bridge, *Plymouth* seemed agonisingly slow to answer the
call for full speed. A Sea Cat struck the leading Mirage, and an
Oerlikon gunner hit the second, but the ship was hit by four
1,000-pound bombs of the ten that were dropped. One hit a depth
charge which exploded, caused major damage and started a fire.
One passed through the funnel. The others passed two feet above
the heads of a horrified group of men caught on the upper deck
manning an anti-submarine mortar. Bleeding smoke, *Plymouth*
limped into San Carlos Water and set about controlling her fires
and patching her holes, in which she was eventually successful.
The Harrier CAP which had been covering Fitzroy all that morning
had been drawn off to meet the attack on *Plymouth*, only minutes
before the Skyhawks struck *Galahad*.

Fitzroy suffered two further ineffectual enemy air attacks that
afternoon, which were met by a hail of small-arms fire from
the troops ashore. One pair of aircraft seemed to flinch from the
weight of the defences and turned away without bombing. It is
believed to have been these which were flying low westwards in

the direction of Goose Green when, just south of Johnson Island, they met *Foxtrot 4* returning from the settlement with the vehicles of 5 Brigade headquarters. Despite Southby-Tailyour's order not to sail back in daylight, Colour Sergeant Johnston had put to sea. 'I've been shot up once by the navy when we tried to move at night,' he said. 'I'm not going to risk that again.' The Argentinians attacked the landing craft with bombs and canon, scoring a direct hit on the stern control position. Colour Sergeant Johnston and five of his crew were killed. Late that afternoon, a desperate signal was picked up from the drifting hulk of *Foxtrot 4* – their craft had been smashed open and they were sinking. They were able to call for help only by using the radio in one of the brigade Land Rovers. The coaster *Monsoonun* hurried to her aid and took off the survivors. She attempted to take the remains of the LCU and its precious signals vehicles in tow, but *Foxtrot 4* quickly sank. The only consolation for the tragedies of the day was that the Harrier CAP caught one wave of Argentine aircraft on their way back from Fitzroy. Flight Lieutenant David Morgan destroyed two aircraft, Lieutenant David Smith a third, and a fourth was seen to crash later.

Thirty-three Welsh Guardsmen, seven men of the Royal Navy and eleven other seamen and soldiers were killed, together with forty-six injured by the air attacks. Even the unwounded survivors had lost all their clothing and equipment, without which they could not conceivably fight ashore. And they were much shaken by their experience. They were sent to San Carlos to recover, while two companies of 40 Commando were flown forward to Bluff Cove to bring the Welsh Guards back to battalion strength for the British offensive. It was a prolonged, painful business. Yet it caused no delay to the launching of the British offensive, which had been scheduled that morning to begin on 11 June. In that respect, the loss of *Galahad* was a far less serious blow than that of *Atlantic Conveyor*.

The Fitzroy tragedy must be seen in the context of a campaign that generally went brilliantly well for the British. Among many calculated risks, this was one which went wrong. The view of the

Royal Navy was expressed by a senior officer on *Fearless* that night: 'We must accept full responsibility for hazarding the landing ships at Fitzroy. We cannot accept responsibility for the fact that there was anybody still aboard *Galahad* when she was attacked.' The naval staff reproached themselves chiefly for failing to impress on the troops aboard *Galahad* the importance of disembarking rapidly after dawn. 'We were accustomed to working with Royal Marines who understood the imperatives of amphibious warfare,' one officer said. A marine who was a shocked spectator at Fitzroy wrote, 'There is an assumption that amphibiosity is a mystique created by marines for their own salvation. But amphibious warfare is not a battle on the north European plain.'

*

To London, the debacle at Fitzroy came as a disaster. It immediately plunged the war cabinet into precisely the argument it least liked, over information policy. Moore was signalling Northwood that the Argentinians believed he had lost 900 men and thus the whole momentum of his advance. It was operationally vital that they continue to believe this as long as possible. Fieldhouse accordingly told Lewin that he wanted Bluff Cove casualties 'talked up' as far as possible, despite the anguish it would cause to service families.

The Ministry of Defence valiantly responded with briefings that casualties had been heavy and 'might delay the expected British assault on Port Stanley'. Again, the return of the House of Commons to the fray of war from the Whitsun recess complicated the implementation of information policy enormously. Surrounded by gossip and speculation, Nott had to maintain his stance two days, even three days, after the disaster by lamely stating that to announce casualties 'could be of assistance to the enemy and put our men at greater risk'. As, two weeks earlier, he admitted he had been wrong not to reveal the identity of the ship lost when *Coventry* had sunk (or at least had been wrongly persuaded, against his own opinion, by Fieldhouse), this statement rang untrue. Nott then dented Moore's intention by adding that 'the task force commander's plans have not been prejudiced by these attacks'. The Fitzroy casualty list – which Nott had clearly been right to keep secret – was not finally released until after the assault on Port Stanley had commenced.

In every campaign of every significant war, mishaps incomparably more culpable and more bloody have taken place, which have passed without notice. But the *Galahad* episode reminded ministers and service chiefs of the hazards of fighting a war under the public glare. The difficulty of persuading the civilian public at home to accept the horrific realities of war caused Sir Robin Day to ask, in a lecture some years ago, whether in the post-Vietnam age any western democracy with a free press and television can hope to sustain national support for any war, however necessary. Who could forget the television image of a survivor being rushed from *Galahad* on a stretcher, the stump of one missing leg projecting bloodily into the sky? Fortunately for the government, the war in the Falklands was brief, and the graphic pictures of *Galahad* reached London only after it had ended. But it was the presumed difficulty of persuading the public at home to accept such images, as much as the issue of security, which underlay the navy's bitter resistance to the Prime Minister's decision to allow correspondents and cameramen to accompany the task force. War correspondents can be an enormous asset in helping to maintain the national commitment by their dispatches from the front. Yet when setbacks occur on the battlefield, neither reporters nor generals will ever find the demands of the media easy to reconcile with the presumed national interest.

Some officers have argued since the war that 5 Brigade should never have been committed to opening up a new axis of advance when transport resources were so limited. But once they had begun to do so, their difficulties were not unique. The fundamental cause of the tragedy at Fitzroy was Northwood's refusal to continue moving the Welsh Guards by purpose-built assault ships, and the decision instead to commit them to an LSL, effectively a civilian-run ship. The muddles and problems that beset 5 Brigade occurred in many other places at many other times during the campaign: the disappearance of the Harrier CAP, requested by 5 Brigade and on station until late on the morning of 8 June, minutes before the air attack; the lack of naval escort; the failure of a red air-raid warning to reach the men on *Galahad*; the delay in setting up Rapier; the collapse of schedules; the breakdown of liaison. It was the coincidence of all these things that proved fatal on 8 June. The most difficult failure to excuse is that of communication – the ignorance of so many senior officers about what troops were where and when. One of the British commanders responsible for 5 Brigade's operations said afterwards, 'You must understand – we were looking east at that point, towards the enemy in Stanley against whom we were about to advance. We really weren't worrying so much about what was going on behind us.' It was a breach of the vital rules of security in war.

'Yes, yes,' said Napoleon as he heard the merits of an officer being eulogised, 'but is he lucky?' Tony Wilson was not lucky. He attempted to do his utmost with a formation that, from the beginning, lacked many of the critical advantages of 3 Commando Brigade – months of relevant training, the chance of practice landing-craft drills, to acclimatise themselves before making a major move. They possessed an inexperienced brigade staff with inadequate command and communications equipment, no specialised vehicles, a formation whose units scarcely knew each other. When all their difficulties and misfortunes in the Falklands are added together, it becomes remarkable that the men of 5 Brigade contributed so effectively to the battle for Port Stanley that was launched only three days after the *Galahad* tragedy.

16 » THE BATTLE FOR THE MOUNTAINS

John Bull, at seasons, in a panic fright,
Cries out for troops for all the world to fight.
The House of Jaw responds with long debates,
And votes a huge increase of Estimates.
The British Army, when the talk is o'er,
Remains inadequate as 'twas before.
No stronger force has John his Fleet behind,
But pays his money, and has eased his mind.

Punch, 1871

From the day that 3 Commando Brigade landed at San Carlos, the British always planned for a rapid campaign. They aimed to achieve victory by mid-June. The worsening winter weather, the increasing difficulty in keeping ships operational on the gun line, the political and diplomatic pressures, the interminable logistics problems: all bore down upon the land force. 'There was a real fear that we might be gazing at each other for months around Port Stanley,' in Hew Pike's words. It is very easy when a war is over to suggest that the enemy's collapse was inevitable. In early June, looking down towards Stanley from Mount Kent, Mount Challenger, Mount Estancia, the task facing the two British brigades seemed daunting. Thirty-three enemy company groups had been identified in a garrison totalling 8,400 men provided with heavy guns and ample ammunition, dug into positions on the hills that they had been fortifying for six weeks. The British possession of Mount Kent prevented the enemy from using it to dominate the marine advance, but did nothing to diminish the task of assaulting the defending hill line covering Stanley: Mounts Harriet and Longdon, Two Sisters, Tumbledown, Sapper Hill. Each one was covered by minefields, defended by infantry with recoilless rifles and heavy machine-guns, supported by thirty 105 mm and four 155 mm guns.

The campaign thus far demonstrated that the Argentine command had no grasp of the principles of strategy: their air force had failed to mount effective ground attacks, as the British had feared. Their army had failed to defend key features, to interdict the British advance, to harass or counter-attack positions that the marines or paras had occupied. General Menendez perhaps lacked confidence in the ability of his conscript soldiers to do any of these things. Even more, the Argentinians' passive conduct of the campaign suggested that, when confronted with the devastating shock of a British military response that they had never reckoned with, they pinned all their hopes upon holding their ground and seeking diplomatic, rather than military, deliverance. Menendez and his superiors retained the view that he had made Port Stanley virtually impregnable. Miret in New York assured Sorzano that they could stalemate the British in the hills round the capital for months. The Argentine fleet would meanwhile take to sea to harass British supply lines. Lami Dozo telephoned Enders in Washington only two days before the battle for Port Stanley to assure him that British shipping losses were so great as to prevent an all-out assault. He told him that Menendez could hold out for two months at least and Argentina would win the war. Enders reflected that 'anyone who thinks that will think anything'.

Yet, at Goose Green, the enemy had proved that, if there was one skill his soldiers possessed, it was the ability doggedly to defend prepared positions. On ground that they knew, plentifully supplied with night-vision equipment, weapons and ammunition, it seemed likely that they would be formidably difficult to dislodge. 'We don't really know what sort of fight they will make of it,' an officer of 3 Para wrote home on 9 June. 'We rather hope they will see the writing on the wall and see discretion is the better part of valour. But I have told my chaps that we can't expect the Argies to leg it everywhere.'

In fact, the Argentinians' problem was not their tactical position, let alone their logistics. It was morale on the ground. Among the troops on the mountains it was worse than the British ever dared to imagine. 'Until the 1st of May no one had really believed that we were going to fight,' said a soldier of the 7th Regiment. 'But, when the English started attacking, everyone started getting more worried. Some of our boys complained about the weapons they had. They were told that they had enough ammunition for two or three days, but when the time came to fight they ran out in two or three hours . . .' Guillermo, another soldier of the 7th Regiment posted on Wireless Ridge, said that he did not even know until after the war where he was. 'No one really told us where we were going . . . We weren't prepared psychologically. I felt like a machine. In my company we all had secondary education at least, but in A, B and C companies, who were the ones most in the front line, there were boys with whom I talked who didn't even know what the Malvinas were.'

Guillermo described the growing shortage of food among the men, as the Argentinians' ability to fly helicopter resupply sorties dwindled. He and his comrades walked the 3 miles to Port Stanley on several nights in order to loot depots. Those who were further from the capital lacked even that opportunity. 'Every time we heard the Hercules transports land at the airfield, our spirits rose. We expected more food to come. But then afterwards we couldn't understand what was happening because nothing ever reached us.'

For a brief period, the British cherished the hope that the Argentinians would accept that their fate was sealed, with two British brigades around them on the high ground, and capitulate. One night, Mike Rose of the SAS, accompanied by a captured Argentine officer and Captain Rod Bell, the marine interpreter, flew to try to get a telephone connection to Port Stanley through the civilian circuit from Estancia House. The line was down. But, the following day, Bell began to broadcast on the radio circuit kept open by the Falklanders, under Argentine supervision, for the purpose of supplying medical aid to the settlements. He gained contact with Dr Alison Bleaney, acting senior medical officer of Stanley Hospital, and urged any Argentinian who might be listening to talk to the British, for humanitarian reasons, to protect the interests of the civilian population. There was no immediate response from the enemy, but Rose and Bell were certain that the Argentinians were listening. They began to transmit daily in the same persistent, persuasive terms, demanding that the enemy answer in the name of humanity and decency. It was do-it-yourself psychological warfare.

One of many deficiencies revealed by the campaign was the lack of a PsyWar unit at the disposal of the Ministry of Defence. Even more astonishing, Bell – who had been co-opted as interpreter from his usual job as adjutant of the commando brigade's headquarters and signals squadron – was almost the only Spanish speaker available to the force. Julian Thompson's request for a team from the army intelligence centre at Ashford had been refused, since there were strict orders from London that any questioning of prisoners was to be carried out with kid gloves. A fluent Spanish-speaking Royal Naval officer who sailed from Britain on *Fearless* was sent home from Ascension when his superiors belatedly discovered that he had not been positively vetted. For the remainder of the war, all British hopes of negotiation with the Argentinians rested on the transmissions of Rose and Bell, based upon Bell's knowledge of the Latin American character, and Rose's experience and training in handling sieges, such as that of the Iranian embassy in London.

The silence on the medical circuit made it evident that the Argentinians had no immediate interest in surrender. A senior enemy naval officer, Captain Melbourne Hussey, was listening and reporting to General Menendez. But Menendez had no intention of yielding until honour had been satisfied. The British would have to fight, and many of their commanders were convinced that Port Stanley would be in ruins before General Menendez conceded defeat. In their sangars and trenches among the rock falls and tussock grass of the mountains, the marines and paras shivered and waited impatiently for their offensive to begin. Each day, when the weather conditions were tolerable, the tireless Sea Kings shuttled to and fro across the hills, guns and ammunition pallets swinging beneath their bellies, building up the huge stocks of ammunition that Moore and Thompson were certain were necessary to saturate the enemy positions as the infantry went in. And, each day, more men were reported suffering from exposure, diarrhoea, trench foot, caused by the endless wind, rain, snow and cold on the hilltops. Some officers argued that 3 Commando Brigade could have abandoned the high ground until they were ready to attack, leaving only observation posts on the summits. But that would have demanded yet more 'yomping' to and fro for tired men, and the comforts available in the valleys behind the crests seemed too marginal to justify the effort. So they sat it out, for seven, eight, nine days, while 5 Brigade reorganised and prepared itself around Bluff Cove. 'If it had been an exercise, I would have brought my men down from Kent on the third day,' said Nick Vaux of 42 Commando. Somehow they survived, and even seemed to come to terms with the misery of the elements. The weather throughout the winter was cold, sometimes very cold. But it was never as bad – as literally intolerable – as the experts and planners had feared before the landing. A 3 Commando Brigade officer wrote to his wife, in the sort of words in which many hundreds of men were writing to their wives, 'It shouldn't be too long, and I promise you I shan't take needless risks. I think of you all so much and I love you all so dearly. Darling, I know what it must be like, always waiting for news and being so much at the mercy of events, but I know you have the character and the courage to win through the difficult time and keep the family together. I so long to be back with you and I shall value our life together as never before after this. One takes so much for granted . . .'

Above all, in those days, it was critical for them to reconnoitre and patrol, to pinpoint the positions of the enemy. There was a report that caused much concern at Moore's headquarters, that the Argentinians were reinforcing on West Falkland. SAS and SBS teams were put ashore to investigate. On 10 June, Captain John Hamilton, a Green Howards officer serving with 22nd SAS who had led the landing on the Fortuna Glacier, was leading a patrol on the hills above Port Howard. Two miles north of the settlement, he himself moved forward with a signaller for a closer look at the Argentine positions. A stocky, boyish-looking figure with immense mountaineering experience, Hamilton was described as 'a classic SAS officer'. He had been at Pebble Island, the diversionary attack at Darwin on 21 May, Mount Kent. Now, at dawn on the hill above Port Howard, he and his signaller found themselves trapped by an Argentine force sweeping down behind them. Surrounded, they shot it out until Hamilton was hit in the back. 'You carry on, and I'll cover your back,' he told the signaller, and kept firing until he was killed. The signaller was later captured when he ran out of ammunition. Hamilton was awarded a posthumous Military Cross.

A patrol from G Squadron SAS commandeered a civilian yacht at Bluff Cove, had its engine repaired by army engineers, and sailed east along the coast in broad daylight. Finally, they beached their craft within 2 miles of the Argentine positions on Mount Tumbledown. An enemy helicopter flew overhead without opening fire, and the bewildered Argentinians took no offensive action against the SAS party for two days, during which G Squadron called down artillery fire onto the back of Tumbledown. Throughout the last weeks of the war, an SAS 'rapid reaction force' was based aboard the LSL *Sir Lancelot* at San Carlos, moving out as men were needed anywhere in the islands.

Less celebrated than the SAS or SBS, the marines' Mountain and Arctic Warfare cadre, a twenty-strong specialist group of officers and NCOs, supported by a further twenty of their students, carried out intensive patrolling and observation operations well forward of the British positions. During the advance across the island, a MAW team commanded by Captain Rod Boswell attacked a party of sixteen Argentinians of the elite 602 Commando

Company of the enemy's special forces, who had taken refuge in a lonely building named Top Malo House. After a fierce, brief battle, they took nine prisoners, the remainder having been killed or burned when the house caught fire.

Each night, at a less dramatic and yet equally heroic level, patrols moved out from the British positions on the mountains of East Falkland to probe the minefields and defences of the enemy. The thin files of blackened men – usually one section of engineers and another of riflemen commanded by a junior officer or NCO – marched silently across the hillside until they approached possible minefields or positions. 'The going proved extremely difficult,' wrote Sergeant Halkett of the commando engineers after an operation to explore assault routes for 42 Commando. 'Our feet were continually submerged. After about 1½ kilometres we came across a single low strand of barbed wire. After having a look I informed the officer commanding that this was an enemy mine- field . . . While Corporal Fairbairn and myself were doing this, we saw fires burning on the lower slopes of the hill 200–300 metres away. These were quite plainly the enemy. I could not understand why the enemy did not open fire. It was a clear, moonlit night almost as bright as day, and there we were right out in the open with virtually no cover . . . Corporal Fairbairn and myself then went into the minefield to try and find out the density and type of mines, using our bayonets as prodders . . . Total length of patrol 20 kilometres, approximate duration 16 hours.'

The flat phrases conceal the utter exhaustion of the men, the strain of probing minefields within shouting distance of the enemy, seeking samples to bring back for technical examination. On a patrol on the same sector of the front two days later, a marine lost a foot in a minefield and had to be carried back up the mountain by his comrades, fully conscious because in the extreme cold morphia failed to anaesthetise him. On 6 June, a patrol of 45 Commando led by Lieutenant Chris Fox had been lying up undetected for half the day on Two Sisters when a twenty-strong party of Argentinians stumbled on their position. In a fierce firefight, the British killed twelve and wounded three, before making good their withdrawal. When men returned at first light from such experiences, there was no warmth or shelter in which to recover: only the chance to lie huddled in a sleeping bag beneath a bivouac improvised from ponchos, stirring some mess of dried chicken supreme or beef and mashed potato powder on the flickering heat of a hexamine cooker. Piece by piece, the British built up their picture of the Argentine defences and began to plan their routes around the minefields to reach them. But without effective air reconnaissance – for the Harriers lacked the high-altitude cameras to take useful pictures – and without satellite photographs, tactical intelligence was obtained largely by men's courage and persistence, on foot in the mountains.

For Major General Moore, the dilemma remained: by what route and with what force should his brigades attempt the breakthrough? All his officers agreed that, once the British began to move, it was critical to maintain momentum, to keep passing fresh battalions through to exploit each success, denying the Argentinians any chance to regroup. Moore's second in command, Brigadier John Waters, was one of those who favoured attacking on the southern axis, towards Mount Harriet and Mount Tumbledown, leaving Two Sisters and Mount Longdon untouched. Once these were outflanked, they must collapse. But, to maintain the flow of supplies forward and casualties back once the battle began, Brigadier Julian Thompson was convinced that the British must hold a variety of air and ground routes, and must attack on a wide front, from Mount Longdon across to Mount Harriet. It was Thompson's view that prevailed. The plan that Moore had agreed on 8 June, at the meeting aboard *Fearless* a few hours before *Galahad* was hit, called for 3 Commando Brigade to open the offensive on Mount Longdon, Two Sisters and Mount Harriet, with 2 Para in reserve. The following night, the Scots Guards, the Welsh Guards and the Gurkhas would pass through to attack Mount Tumbledown and Mount William. Then it would be 3 Commando Brigade's turn once more, and so on until the enemy had collapsed.

The worst casualty of the *Atlantic Conveyor* disaster was strategic flexibility. It is mobility that provides flexibility on the battlefield, and the loss of the Chinooks was irreplaceable, even when a trickle of new Wessex helicopters and pilots began to come ashore. Helicopter organisation was one of the least satisfactory aspects of the British campaign. A tiny naval staff attempted to direct the movements of several squadrons of transport helicopters, and inevitably there was confusion and wasted effort. There were cases of helicopters sitting idle on RFA ships because the helicopter staff were simply unaware that they existed. The pilots flew to exhaustion – often nine or ten hours a day without leaving their cockpits, eating and drinking whatever could be pushed through their windows as they refuelled. Maintenance crews in the little tented forward bases established ashore worked on the aircraft at night, by torchlight, and achieved miracles in maintaining better than 90 per cent availability throughout the campaign. Pilots somehow endured the strain of lifting artillery while constantly searching the horizon for enemy aircraft. They sought to fly as much as possible below the skyline to conceal themselves, and became expert at seeking instant cover in folds in the ground under air attack. But the facts remained unalterable: there were too few of them. If the British offensive bogged down, the land force lacked the lift capability to switch flanks, or suddenly to move an extra gun battery to cover a new sector. Every helicopter that the force possessed would be fully occupied flying forward the ammunition and supplies to keep the offensive moving.

Admiral Woodward was becoming urgently concerned about the diminishing number of ships that he could provide for naval gunfire support. From a maximum of twenty-six warships in the last days of May, his total available battleworthy units had declined sharply. He warned Major General Moore that, each night after the opening of the battle, the number of guns that he could put into the line must diminish. *Argonaut* was finally relieved of her unexploded bombs after the senior clearance diver, Lieutenant Commander Brian Dutton, had worked for a week deep in her hull, finally guiding the fully fused bomb with his own hands as it was delicately winched over the side. The frigate survived a further near disaster when she began to go astern to abandon her unwelcome charge on the bottom and found that its cable had entangled itself in her screw: every revolution was hoisting the bomb back inboard. Sub-Lieutenant Peter Morgan dived to clear it. *Argonaut* was at last free to sail out to the repair ship *Stena Seaspread*, which was performing an extraordinary procession of patching-up operations on warships in the open sea east of the Falklands. The saving of *Argonaut* was one of the Royal Navy's epic achievements of the war. But almost every ship of the task force was by now suffering wear and tear. On 30 May, the battle group had survived yet another air-launched Exocet attack, when *Avenger* achieved the remarkable feat of shooting down the missile with its 4.5-inch gun. 'Forty-five seconds warning this time,' wrote David Tinker from *Glamorgan*, 'and we got into positions (bows towards missile) and fired chaff . . . The attacks are not particularly frightening, they are over so quickly. It is an odd feeling being attacked: a mixture of "Goodbye, cruel world" as you lie there with tin helmet on, braced for it; and a feeling that "They must be mad. Don't they know it's very unsafe shooting things at other people?" The best thing to do is to have a few wets before an attack. I'd had a drink before the Exocet attack and the pulse rate stayed very normal, although when "Brace, brace, brace" came over the broadcast I did think to myself "Expletive deleted". They had it worse in the Ops Room where they could see it coming towards us – the Ops Officer said his heart almost pounded itself out of its rib cage. Poor man: ignorance is bliss on these occasions.' Yet this was to prove the Argentinians' last air-launched Exocet strike of the war. The tanker *British Wye* survived an extraordinary attack that day, when she received a near-miss from bombs rolled out of an Argentine Hercules transport. The enemy was becoming desperate.

*

On the morning of 11 June, on hillsides along the entire range held by the British, 3 Commando Brigade's commanding officers briefed their men for the battle. Most had created models of the terrain, using ponchos artistically arranged on the ground, marked with string and tape to show their unit routes. Around each CO, in a circle, crouched his officers, hunched against the cold, listening intently as he outlined the mortar- and artillery-support plan, timings, phases. 'This is the decisive battle of the war,' said Nick Vaux of 42 Commando with quiet emphasis. 'Surprise and absolute silence are vital. If necessary, you must go through that old business of making every man jump up and down before he starts, to check that nothing rattles. Persistent coughers must be left behind. If you find yourself in a minefield remember that you *must* go on. Men must not stop for their oppos, however great the temptation. They *must* go through and finish the attack, or it will cost more lives in the end.'

As he talked, on the snow-dusted hillside around him men gathered their weapons and equipment for the helicopter lift forward to the positions from which the commando would march. 'The enemy are well dug in in very strong positions,' Vaux finished. 'But I believe that, once we get in among them, they will crack pretty quickly. We want to end up with Argies running all the way back across those hills to Port Stanley to show the others what is coming to them.' After the experience of Goose Green, it was evident that, in night operations, the quality and training of the British told heavily against their opponents. Thompson's men would attack by night, and seek to secure their objectives before dawn.

All that long, cold afternoon, men stood and stamped their feet and chattered and drank tea and gazed through binoculars at that strange, alien country which seemed like the other side of the moon – the enemy positions they would assault that night. Then, in the twilight, the long files of heavily burdened figures moved forward, each conscious of thousands of others doing likewise along the length of the British line. The British guns had been harassing the enemy positions intermittently for several nights. Now, they began to pound in earnest, not all at once or from the same position, but in sudden blasts of noise and fear from many directions – not least from the sea, where four frigates steamed slowly back and forth on the gunline. The Argentinians answered hesitantly, ineffectually, throwing up spouts of dirty smoke well wide of the British advance. In the deepening darkness, nervous defenders began to call for starshell. The flares burst over the marching men, causing them to freeze where they stood or crouched. It seemed impossible that they could not be seen. Yet, when the flares died, silence returned. Whispered word was passed back down the line from the guides who had marked the route at such hazard: 'Keep right on the track of the man in front. From here on, this is the only swept path through the minefields.' And so they marched on, through the frozen, empty mountains.

Vaux's 42 Commando was to attack Mount Harriet, a steep, lonely crest at the southern extremity of the hill line. His patrols had explored a long circuitous route to launch the rifle companies into their attack from the Argentine rear. It seemed a perilous march, for the entire approach lay across open ground on which it seemed impossible that the Argentinians could fail to see the British if they made proper use of their night-vision equipment. Yet Vaux's plan succeeded brilliantly. There were exasperating delays on the march as one company lost its way, and the other could not make contact with the Welsh Guards who were securing the start line. But Vaux refused to be worried or hurried. 'We will maintain one tactical bound between companies moving across the open,' he insisted firmly into the radio. At last, late but unscathed, his men were in position. With a massive naval and artillery bombardment in progress, they began to scale the hill. They were within 100 yards of the summit when the Argentinians at last detected them and opened fire. Captain Peter Babbington's K Company took on the Argentinians dug into the rocks with 66 and 84 mm rockets and GPMG fire, leapfrogging forward in the wake of the explosions, clearing bunkers with small arms and grenades. Between the explosions, the hillside echoed with British shouts of 'Sixty-six!' and 'Grenade!' to warn their oppos as they fired. Many of the enemy fled before the marines overran them. But, as Babbington's men closed in, enemy artillery fire began to fall among them, wounding four men in his company head-quarters. One NCO was killed storming a bunker. Corporal Larry Watts stormed an enemy position with grenades, then rounded a rock to find himself suddenly confronted by a rifle barrel. Shot in the neck, he seized the gun and sought to thrust it aside, only to be hit again, in the heart. Corporal Newland sat talking into his radio, continuing to direct his section's attack even after being shot in both legs. As L Company began to work round the face of the hill towards the commando's second objective, K Company had already taken more than seventy prisoners and secured the summit of Mount Harriet for the loss of only one man. It was a remarkable feat of arms, all the more so since Brigadier Thompson had been convinced that Harriet would prove the most difficult of his brigade's objectives.

45 Commando were also very late crossing the start line at Murrell Bridge for their attack on Two Sisters, after making slow progress over the difficult ground in darkness. X Company, making for the southern peak, seized their first objective without difficulty, but were then pinned down by intense machine-gun fire attacking their second. They lay under mortar and recoilless-rifle fire until men succeeded in blasting the Argentine positions with three 66 mm rockets, two of which hit their targets. While X Company continued with a conventional fire and manoeuvre assault, Y and Z began to claw their way up the hill. Z stormed an enemy strongpoint shouting their 'Zulu!' warcry without losing a man, but two of the three troop commanders of Y Company were wounded by mortar fire, and an engineer was killed. There is no greater test of even highly trained troops than to ask them to continue an attack under heavy fire in darkness – 'the tendency towards inertia is greater by night than by day,' in Andrew White-head's words. But, urged on by the colonel and supported by

intensive artillery and naval gunfire, 45 fought their way towards
the summit. 'There was inevitably a period of uncertainty which I
spent trying to sort out in my own mind where everybody was,' as
the CO said. 'But the weight of fire that two rifle companies can
bring to bear is formidable.' 45 was 3 Brigade's Scottish commando, and many of the men on the hillside were from north of
the border. 'A lot of the time I felt very detached from it all,' said
Lance Corporal Stuart Bain, a section commander in Y Company
from Elgin. 'People were frightened before it began rather than
while it was going on.' As happened in every battle in the war, the
first layer of Argentine resistance was tough to crack. But once
45 had broken through, they were able to advance steadily, wearing down the enemy at each point with their fire. Many of the
defenders trickled away into the darkness before the marines could
reach them. Corporal Harry Siddall was astonished by the way that
the night battle proved a business of sound rather than spectacle:
'It wasn't anything like the movies. I'd expected big balls of flame,
yet there were just big bangs. I saw shrapnel bouncing off the
rocks, and it seemed like some sort of natural phenomenon.'

Siddall, a thirty-one-year-old Yorkshireman, advanced over a
crest with a gunner beside him, some distance ahead of his section.
Suddenly, they found themselves face to face with four Argentinians. The gunner bombardier fell back down the hill cursing
repetitively in his fear, 'F—ing hell! F—ing hell!' Siddall tossed a
grenade which killed one of the enemy and wounded another.
Then his section scrambled up behind him, and they pressed on.
Many Argentinians lay motionless in their sleeping bags, waiting
only for a suitable moment to be taken prisoner.

After the war had ended, many Argentinian soldiers were
bitterly critical of the lack of leadership their officers provided on
the battlefield. The rumours current among the British about the
enemy's extraordinary brutality to his own men proved to have
been true. Attempts to go absent without leave were punished by
beatings or forcing the offender to sit for hours with his naked
feet in the freezing water on the mountainside. Many officers

withdrew from front-line positions at the opening of the battle. Some men were evacuated suffering from self-inflicted wounds. On the night of the British attack on the mountains, as an Argentine stretcher-bearer named Juan Carlos said afterwards, 'When some of the soldiers found themselves alone, in the middle of the night, in the total darkness, and they looked for the support of their superiors, they couldn't find them. So they too retreated. It was only logical. If the professionals had gone, what were mere conscripts expected to do?'

Harry Siddall, like many men that night, became an instant war veteran: 'You very quickly found that you could tell whose guns were firing from where. I felt neither hatred nor friendliness towards the Argentinians. I simply thought about the job in hand, and they happened to be in the way of getting that job done.' Two and a quarter hours after the firefight began, although 45 Commando was still exposed to constant shelling from the Argentine artillery, they had seized the summits of Two Sisters, and pulled back from the crest line to await the coming of dawn. Andrew Whitehead looked in wonderment at the strength of the positions the enemy had abandoned. 'With 120 men,' he said, 'I could have died of old age holding these hills.'

The most serious casualties of the battle for Two Sisters were inflicted many miles from the mountain. The County class destroyer *Glamorgan* was providing naval gunfire support for 45 Commando. At 2.35 a.m., Captain Mike Barrow had just ordered his ship to break off the bombardment and begun to steam away towards the battle group when the men of the land force saw a streak of light break away from the shore and race out to sea across the darkness. Eighteen miles from the shore, the men in *Glamorgan* thought at first that one of the enemy's desultory 155 mm shells had been fired at them. Then the navigating officer, Ian Inskip, said, 'I think a missile is on the way.' Jillings, the Sea Cat director-aimer, instantly fired. Chaff was belatedly blown into the sky. Barrow turned his ship stern on, and was making 24 knots when the Exocet – its launcher having been dismounted from a frigate and established on a trailer ashore – plunged through *Glamorgan*'s upper deck abreast of the hangar and smashed into the galley below. The watchers on East Falkland, including 42 Commando on the face of Mount Harriet, saw a great ball of flame as the missile exploded, followed seconds later by another explosion as the ship's Wessex helicopter blew up, killing six of the nine men in the hangar instantly, including Lieutenant David Tinker. 'It doesn't feel that you are very far away,' he had written to his wife a few days earlier . . . 'For all I know, Portsmouth is just over the horizon. It's not very different down here, as it is at home, although I can't imagine it is summer somehow . . . I'm looking forward to when I can put my dreams into practice . . .' The ship shuddered, and Barrow immediately reduced speed to 10 knots lest *Glamorgan* had suffered serious structural damage. A fierce fire was raging in the area of the explosion, and six men in the galley preparing breakfast were dead. Barrow felt grateful, however, that this crisis had been thrust upon his ship now, with his crew seasoned by six weeks of war, rather than on 1 May when the shock would have been incomparably greater, For two and a half hours, his men fought the fires before they could be controlled. Two of the ship's four turbines were stopped by the blast effect. A chief petty officer in the hangar lay trapped by wreckage, half underwater for almost three hours, until he could be reached. But he, and the ship, survived. Gradually they were able to correct the heavy list caused by the vast quantities of water poured into the flames. Thirteen men had been killed and many more burned or wounded, but the strong old ship was soon able to kick up to 24 knots, steam to a rendezvous with *Stena Seaspread* and make repairs sufficient to enable her to continue in action until ordered home.

While *Glamorgan* was fighting for her life afloat, ashore 3 Para were fighting the most costly land action of the war, for the last of 3 Commando Brigade's objectives, Mount Longdon. A little past 9 p.m., after an exhausting four-hour march, Hew Pike's men were moving up the lower slopes of Longdon when a corporal of B Company stepped on a mine, shattering his leg and provoking the first barrage of fire from the Argentinians. Instead of the company they had expected to meet, 3 Para faced a battalion of the enemy's 7th Regiment, supported by snipers equipped with superb night-vision equipment. A Company, working along the ridge north of Longdon, secured its objective but then became pinned down by heavy and accurate fire – 'Holding on uncomfortably,' as Hew Pike put it. B Company, commanded by a tough, stocky little ex-SAS man named Mike Argue, began to advance on the summit itself. A hundred feet below it, they began a bitter fight from position to position, meeting fierce resistance from mortars, machine-guns, snipers, recoilless rifles. The battle dissolved into a series of section actions by small groups of British soldiers, working forward up the hill using 84 mm and 66 mm rockets to blow open the enemy's positions. Lieutenant Andrew Bickerdike, commanding Argue's 4 Platoon, fell, shot in the leg. One of his men, Corporal Bailey, charged the bunker 50 yards ahead, from which he had been fired upon, but fell across it, shot in the legs and stomach. Bickerdike's platoon sergeant, Ian McKay, hastily regrouped the men, then leaped to his feet and charged forward, working in above the bunker to lob in two grenades before he fell dead. For his outstanding courage, he was later awarded a posthumous Victoria Cross.

Pike had brought up his support company to provide the maximum firepower behind B company's advance, but the Milan groups soon found themselves under intense enemy fire. One three-man missile team was wiped out by a direct hit from a recoilless rifle. Men found themselves being hit more than once by the same sniper, a terrifying tribute to the accuracy of the Argentinians' fire. The British forward artillery observer, Captain Willie McCracken, called down fire within yards of his own position. Hew Pike later remarked that the nearest shells to fall around him that night were British, yet the British gunners fired with such precision that not one of his men was killed by them. A section of 5 Platoon found itself under heavy machine-gun fire. Two men, Gough and Gray, charged the enemy position with grenades and bayonets, capturing one survivor.

B Company paused to regroup for a renewed attempt to clear the last enemy positions, with some snipers still firing on them from behind as well as in front. Argue's 4 Platoon was reduced to twelve men out of twenty-five, and the others had suffered as severely. In all, the company had already lost thirteen men killed and twenty-seven wounded. They pushed forward again, but it was simply too tough a nut for them to crack, after hours of heavy fighting and casualties. Hew Pike – by now commanding from alongside Major Argue – ordered B Company to halt while A moved round to pass through their positions, and more artillery support was called in. Only as the first shadows of dawn broke on the hillside did the firing begin to ebb away. The battalion saw through its own exhaustion that resistance was fading. 'I shall never forget the sight that morning, of A Company advancing through a thick mist with bayonets fixed,' said Pike. Many of the last Argentine defenders were killed with the bayonet. The battle for Mount Longdon and shellfire during the day that followed cost 3 Para twenty-three men killed and forty-seven wounded. A steady procession of stretcher-bearers stumbled heavily back off the hillside to the forward dressing station with their tragic burdens. 'The 2 docs fought to save their lives,' Sergeant Hopper of 3 Para wrote in his diary. 'They lost the battle for one of them. This was particularly harrowing as the soldier had only been on Longdon for a few minutes when a shell exploded and a piece of shrapnel severed the artery in his thigh. While the doctor fought to staunch the bleeding and get a drip going, all we could do was stand holding a poncho over them while the snow fell, and listen to the soldier crying out to us.' 'I suppose it was as fine a feat of arms as 3 Para has ever undertaken,' an officer of the battalion wrote home after Longdon. 'But what a cost, and such good people lost, so terribly young, mostly . . .' It was inevitable that the men who had fought should be saddened by the casualties. In reality, the cost had been astonishingly small.

45 Commando's battle had cost four killed and eight wounded, while 42 lost only one killed and thirteen wounded. 'We have been

incredibly lucky,' said Nick Vaux, as he stood with his headquarters group surrounded by the abandoned Argentine weapons, clothing and supplies on the summit of Harriet. As the early morning mist cleared away to reveal the valley and the approaches to Tumbledown dotted with fleeing enemy soldiers, the gunners called down airburst shells in their path. Marines and paras herded the straggling, desolate groups of prisoners to be taken away to the rear. Helicopters shuttled to and fro across the hills evacuating wounded.

The greatest disappointment, that morning of 12 June, was that 3 Commando Brigade was unable to push further forward. 42 and 45 Commandos had been briefed to seize their objectives, and thereafter 'to exploit forward to Tumbledown', if this was possible. But, after the delays of the night, there was no more darkness left in which they could do so. Forward of Harriet and Two Sisters lay two miles of open ground across which the British must advance before reaching their next objective, the steep mountainside of Tumbledown honeycombed with bunkers. When Julian Thompson consulted with his battalion commanders before dawn, he had no hesitation in ordering them to 'go firm' on their positions. Had they continued their advance, daylight would have come before they had even begun an attack on Tumbledown. The consequences could have been disastrous. 3 Para, who suffered throughout 12 June from artillery fire directed by enemy observers overlooking Pike's positions from Tumbledown, were impatient of the marines' failure to push forward during the night. It is probably true that the Royal Marines' approach to war is slower and steadier than that of the paras. But, if 3 Commando Brigade had attempted to push through to Tumbledown that morning, they would almost certainly have suffered casualties far more severe than those of 3 Para, or the units which subsequently delivered a night attack against it. The next phase would be left for 5 Brigade.

There was one more remarkable little action in the early hours of that morning: while the British were still securing their hill positions, a single Wessex helicopter slid low over the ridge north of Port Stanley harbour, and approached the town. British observation teams had reported seeing large gatherings of Argentine vehicles outside the town hall each morning, obviously attending a regular conference. With astonishing gallantry, an antisubmarine Wessex pilot had accepted an SBS proposal to fly unsupported against Stanley and attempt to strike direct at the enemy's orders group. He fired one missile which missed its target and blew a large hole in the roof of Port Stanley police station. His second struck a line of telegraph wires beside the road, and dived into the harbour. Then he turned away to escape, as every gun in the area opened fire. It was a source of great pleasure to the British that, while the Wessex pilot came home intact, the Argentinians shot down one of their own helicopters approaching over the harbour.

*

The British plan, emphasising the importance of maintaining momentum, called for 5 Brigade to move forward during the afternoon of 12 June and launch a night attack against Tumbledown and Mount William. But by early afternoon, helicopters had still not arrived to move the Scots Guards to their assembly area below Mount Harriet, behind Goat Ridge. Brigadier Tony Wilson reported to Major General Moore's headquarters that he considered it essential to delay his attack for twenty-four hours. His request provoked some irritation and derision from the men of 3 Commando Brigade. Yet it seemed reasonable that, when the Royal Marines had had more than a week to reconnoitre their objectives before their attack, 5 Brigade should have a few hours. Moore agreed to Wilson's request. The Scots Guards moved forward to their assembly area on the morning of 13 June and, amidst sporadic shelling, their officers studied the positions that they were to attack that night.

The first troops into action on 13 June were thirty men of the headquarters company of the Scots Guards, commanded by Major Hon. Richard Bethell, a thirty-two-year-old former SAS officer who had sought his commanding officer's permission for a more active

role than he could otherwise have expected in the night's operations. Bethell, supported by a troop of the Blues and Royals, was
to conduct a diversionary attack on Argentine positions south-east
of Mount Harriet. He had already been involved in various event-
ful Scots Guards patrol and observation operations during which
his Land Rover survived hitting a landmine, and the battalion's
reconnaissance platoon was compelled to withdraw from Port
Harriet House under heavy mortar fire, taking several casualties.

At 8.30 p.m., the Guards' party had still encountered no enemy
after advancing some distance. Suddenly, one of the Blues and
Royals' Scorpions struck a mine, which blew it into the air and
caused severe damage, without wounding the crew. The remaining
vehicles halted where they stood, while Bethell's group moved
forward. They spotted a cluster of enemy sangars. As they closed
in without seeing movement, it seemed obvious that these were
abandoned. At last, Bethell stood in the middle of the position with
Drill Sergeant Danny White, debating where the enemy had gone.
Suddenly, four feet away, they heard snoring. An Argentinian
opened fire, the British replied, and the entire position exploded
into life. Bethell and his men began to fight their way through
eleven enemy trenches one by one, with grenades and small arms.
Two Scots Guards had been killed and four wounded in the first
exchange. Bethell armed himself with a bren gun seized from a
dead soldier. The action continued for more than two hours. His
requests for direct support from the Blues and Royals could not
be met, since they felt unable to advance further through the
minefield.

At last, the enemy positions fell silent. Bethell decided that he
had contributed all that could possibly be expected of a diversionary attack. His party included four pipers who served as medical
orderlies, and he was lying by an Argentine trench discussing with
one of these how the wounded were to be carried back, when a
scene beyond the imagination of Hollywood took place. An appallingly wounded enemy soldier dragged himself over the parapet of

his trench and tossed a grenade at Bethell's feet. Bethell shot him down with the bren gun before the grenade exploded, riddling his legs with shrapnel and wounding the piper in the lung. The party now began to withdraw under mortar and artillery fire, carrying their casualties. A few minutes later, they found themselves once more in a minefield. Two men, one of them a physical training instructor, lost feet, blown off even as they were carrying wounded men themselves. There were two other casualties. In desperation, Bethell used his torch to search for a path among the mines. The battered group of Guardsmen made their way slowly back to the Blues and Royals' position, somehow carrying their wounded.

Meanwhile, the main body of the Scots Guards had launched their attack. At 9 p.m., G Company crossed the start line in the cold, clear darkness, meeting occasional flurries of snow. They reached their objective without opposition. But, as Left Flank Company passed through G to approach the main heights of Tumbledown, they met fierce enemy machine-gun fire. Within a few minutes, Argentine snipers using night sights had killed three Guardsmen and wounded two more. The usual British formula of replying with 66 and 84 mm rocket fire seemed to have little impact on the enemy positions among the rocks. The Scots Guards could hear some of the Argentinians shouting and even singing as they fought. These were the best troops General Menendez could put into the field, the 5th Marines, ninety-two strong, supported by mortars and ten sustained-fire machine-guns. As the night wore on and the fierce firefight continued, they showed no sign of crumbling, and their main positions held firm. At 2.30 a.m., after a brief bombardment, Major John Kiszeley, commanding Left Flank Company, personally led a charge on the forward enemy position. 'Are you with me, 15 Platoon?' cried Kiszeley, as he advanced through the darkness. There was only silence. 'Come on, 15 Platoon, are you with me?' he shouted again. 'Aye, sir, I'm with you,' shouted a voice. Then came another: 'Aye, sir, I'm f—ing with you as well.' Headed by their company commander, Left Flank Company

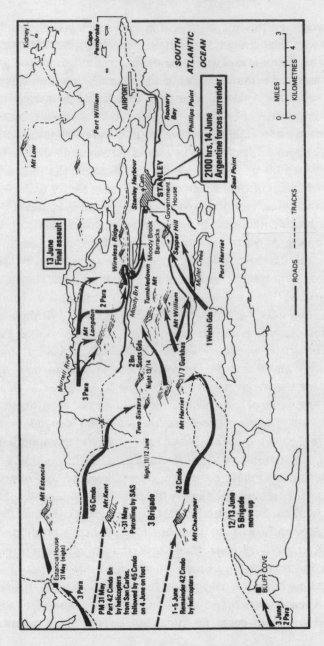

charged on up the hill. Kiszeley himself killed three men, one of them with his bayonet. An incoming bullet passed through his pouch and bayonet scabbard before lodging in his compass.

Just seven men of the Guards' 15 Platoon reached the summit of Tumbledown after the bitter battle up its forward slopes. Three of them, including the platoon commander, were immediately shot down by machine-gun fire. Four Guardsmen remained unwounded on the crest until reinforcements scrambled up to support them. Left Flank Company lost seven killed and twenty-one wounded to gain its objectives. At 6 a.m., when Right Flank Company began the third phase of the battalion's attack, they met immediate machine-gun and sniper fire which wounded four men including a platoon commander. The Guards reached the last of the enemy positions on Tumbledown only after a further six hours of struggle inch by inch up the rocks, using phosphorus grenades and automatic weapons to force the enemy from his bunkers. The battalion had lost a total of nine men killed and forty-three wounded to capture one of the most strongly defended Argentine positions of the war. Whatever the difficulties and disappointments of 5 Brigade in the preceding fortnight, the seizure of Tumbledown was an achievement that none of 3 Commando Brigade's battalions could claim to have eclipsed.

*

Even as the Guards were fighting for Tumbledown, an equally dramatic series of actions had begun at the northern end of the British line. As 5 Brigade pushed forward in the south, 2 Para was to seize Wireless Ridge, as a start line from which 3 Para could launch the next phase of the British assault on the night of 14 June. The SAS proposed to distract attention from David Chaundler's attack on Wireless Ridge by launching their own diversionary attack with the assistance of Captain Chris Baxter, commanding the Royal Marines' Rigid Raider Squadron. Hitherto, Baxter's fast assault boats' role in the war had been confined to running a water-taxi service in San Carlos Bay. He was eager to contribute more directly to the battle.

On the night of 12 June, four Rigid Raiders landed on Kidney Island, north-east of Wireless Ridge. They lay up through the day and set off on the night of 13 June for a fast run round the coast to attack enemy positions on the eastern end of Wireless Ridge. En route they embarked twenty men of the Boat Troop of D Squadron SAS which had carried out the raid at Pebble Island, together with an SBS team. The aim of the operation was to create the noisiest possible diversion from 2 Para's activities to the west. The raiding party was supported by sixty men of D and G Squadrons, who gave close covering fire with mortar, Milan and GPMGs from the northern shore of the harbour inlet. As they hit their beach, the enemy opened overwhelming fire with anti-aircraft cannon. All four Rigid Raiding craft were hit and damaged, and the assault party had to conduct a fighting withdrawal into dead ground. An Argentine hospital ship immediately switched on her searchlights and illuminated the area. Before the party could reach cover, two SAS and one SBS had been wounded. It was a noisy, flamboyant operation that irritated some land-force officers who believed that it smacked of piracy more than warfare, and came close to ending in disaster. But it must have contributed materially to the Argentine conviction that they were now under simultaneous, converging attack on three fronts.

2 Para, meanwhile, back under the control of 3 Commando Brigade, were ready to mount their assault on Wireless Ridge on the night of 12 June, when they learned that 5 Brigade's twenty-four-hour delay had caused the postponement of all operations. Late on the afternoon of the 13th, both the battalion and the headquarters of 3 Commando Brigade came under air attack by Skyhawks in one of the last Argentine air-force interventions in the war. But they suffered no casualties, and 2 Para moved off on schedule towards their start line. H-Hour was to be at 8.30 p.m. Chaundler's men faced the task of seizing four objectives, defended by the Argentine 7th Regiment, with elements of the enemy's 1st Parachute Regiment. The battalion had learned an enormous amount from their experience at Goose Green. For Wireless Ridge,

they proposed to put that experience to good effect. They had discovered the need for every spare man to be available to bring forward ammunition and evacuate wounded. On the 13th, a party of thirty-five was detailed for these tasks.

Above all, 2 Para had impressed themselves with the value of overwhelming firepower. For Wireless Ridge, in addition to two batteries of guns with plentiful ammunition, a frigate for naval gunfire support, the sustained-fire machine-gun platoon on the start line, they would take forward a troop of the Blues and Royals' Scorpions and Scimitars, with their formidable 76 mm guns, Rarden cannon, and superb night-vision sights. Whereas most of the British night-vision equipment suffered from 'bloom out', which caused it to become temporarily useless after a bright explosion or flash, the tanks' second-generation equipment provided an almost perfect, continuous view of the battlefield. David Chaundler, the new battalion CO, felt very conscious of his status as the outsider now called upon to take 2 Para into battle. His confidence was not increased by the sudden arrival at his headquarters of a map captured from the Argentinians fifteen minutes before H-Hour. It showed a minefield lying in the midst of A and B Companies' axes of advance. 'Too late for that,' he shrugged, and moved forward with his tactical headquarters.

From the moment that D Company moved forward to assault the first Argentine position, a devastating volume of fire descended upon the enemy. 6,000 rounds of artillery ammunition were unleashed on the Argentine positions in the last twelve hours of the fighting. The ridge was lit by continuous flashes from the Blues and Royals' guns, the explosion of ammunition in enemy positions, the bursting shells of the 105s and naval guns. It seemed that nothing could persevere in the face of such fire, and very few Argentinians attempted to. D Company secured their objective virtually without resistance. A and B swept forward – through the alleged minefield – without serious difficulty. Whenever Argentine machine-gunners attempted to respond, overwhelming fire was poured down upon them. 'This is how an all-arms battle should be fought,' said Chris Keeble, watching with satisfaction from his Tac 2 position. David Chaundler called the battle 'a standard Salisbury Plain four-phase night attack with all the trimmings. We decided to make this a noisy attack rather than a silent one because second-rate troops do not like being shelled.' D Company finally swept round eastwards to seize the forward slope of the ridge. Chaundler suffered a moment's concern when he learned that the Scots Guards were in difficulty on Tumbledown – his own men would be dangerously exposed at dawn if the enemy still held the mountain overlooking them. But, a few minutes before first light, he heard that the Guards had gained their objectives. In their positions on the ridge among abandoned Argentine weapons and equipment, the shaggy, filthy, unshaven but wholly triumphant men of 2 Para began to brew up and make themselves as comfortable as the gusting snow showers permitted. In their mood that morning, they could have marched to London. 'One more push ought to do it, eh?' said one of A Company's NCOs. As Max Hastings typed a dispatch beneath a flapping poncho in a peat hag in the midst of A Company's position, a cheeky nineteen-year-old private named Bernie Bernard pushed his head underneath and demanded a cigar, which no mere correspondent could have been cheeky enough to refuse him. Bernard groped for it in a crevice in the rocks: 'If I can find my way up here in the dark and get through Goose Green, I can find a cigar in the rocks,' he declared airily. 'Go on – tell them which unit did it.' Every para was proudly convinced that only his regiment could have done as they had done from San Carlos to Wireless Ridge.

Then, quite suddenly, word began to come through the radio net: 'The Argies are legging it – they're running everywhere.' Men ran shouting the news to each other, pulling on equipment as the companies were readied to move in five minutes. Along the length of the British line, officers and soldiers watched in fascination through their binoculars the astonishing spectacle of Argentine soldiers fleeing across the hillsides towards Stanley. Brigadier Tony

Wilson, standing on Mount Harriet, turned to his senior gunner: 'Bloody hell, they're starting to break.'

In the first glimmerings of dawn, 2 Para's D Company found themselves looking down on the old Royal Marine barracks at Moody Brook, ruined by shellfire and bombing. Beyond it, 3 miles eastwards across the water, lay the roofs of Port Stanley. Spasmodic Argentine shelling was still coming in between the positions of 2 Para and 3 Para. Suddenly, D saw approaching up the rocky hillside some forty of the enemy paratroopers. The Argentinians were making the only counter-attack of the war. The paras were momentarily alarmed, for their own ammunition was almost exhausted. They hastily fixed bayonets and prepared grenades, while the gunner forward observation officer called down artillery support. A few moments' heavy firing was enough for the Argentinians. They trickled away across the valley, to join scores of others now hastening eastwards. David Chaundler had been disturbed by the first reports of the counter-attack. Finding that he could not raise Phil Neame, the company commander, by radio, he moved forward to look for himself. As soon as he saw the scene below – the approach to Stanley open for the taking – he called Julian Thompson. The brigadier ordered Chaundler to do nothing until he himself arrived. When Thompson climbed from his helicopter below the ridgeline, he walked forward in some dismay at the sight of Chaundler standing fully exposed on the skyline, and hastily pulled him back into cover. 'It's okay, Julian,' said the para cheerfully. 'It's all over.' Within a few moments, Thompson had approved an immediate advance by Chaundler's battalion. There was still a risk that, given time, the enemy could regroup. On the ridge above Moody Brook, the colonel held a hasty 'O' Group, ordering his B Company to advance to secure the opposite hillside, the Blues and Royals' tanks to provide a firebase from the rockline where they stood, and Dair Farrar-Hockley's A Company to advance with all speed down the road to Port Stanley.

Suddenly, the pent-up fears and resentments of weeks on the

mountains had exploded in the ranks of Menendez's army. 'Everything was in terrible disorder,' said a young private of the 3rd Infantry Regiment named Santiago. 'Nobody really knew what the orders were, whether we should go on fighting or not. Many junior officers were disoriented because we had lost the OC of our company and we couldn't find him anywhere . . . We were all very nervous after all we had lived through. Our platoon commander told us to take up positions in the houses: "Don't be afraid of anyone. Go into the house, and if a kelper resists, shoot him."' In reality, of course, the men did nothing of the kind. As they straggled back through Port Stanley, Santiago described how young conscripts broke down and cried when they saw 'depots stashed with food and clothes which had never got to us'.

It was an extraordinary moment, a transition from war to victory within the space of an hour. The Gurkhas and Welsh Guards advancing on Mount William and Sapper Hill met spasmodic shelling, but no significant resistance, and swept forward to secure objectives for which the British had expected to fight a bloody battle. Hew Pike of 3 Para was giving his orders for his battalion's attack towards Moody Brook that night when he learned on the radio that Farrar-Hockley and his men were already past the ruined barracks and dashing for Stanley.

*

The paras marched east along the battered little road which led to the capital sustained only by the euphoria of the moment, for they were utterly exhausted. Their path was strewn with the wreckage of defeat – Argentine clothing, a litter of loose ammunition everywhere, abandoned vehicles and guns on the hillside above. Smoke gusted across the road from burning buildings. The sound of intermittent firing still drifted over the hill from the south, where the Gurkhas and Welsh Guards were closing in. There was no sign of life ahead in the little bungalows encircled by paling fences, which marked the outskirts of Port Stanley. There was a brief pause when men at the point of A Company reported that they believed they could see a moving Panhard armoured car. A para with a 66 mm rocket launcher was hastily brought forward. Then the advance continued. A small ship began to move across the harbour. They saw that it carried a white flag. A message came through the radio to halt and await the arrival of David Chaundler. A few minutes later, having exchanged their helmets for red berets, headed by their colonel and Chris Keeble, 2 Para began to stride triumphantly into the outskirts of Port Stanley.

The episode that followed has no place in the history of the war, nor among the achievements of the British land force. Max Hastings quotes his dispatch that day as a curiosity of journalism, not of the battle for the Falklands.

The battalion's officers had advanced perhaps two hundred yards beyond their halting place when a new signal was brought to the colonel's attention. No British soldier was to advance beyond the racecourse, pending negotiations. There was a bitter mutter of disappointment. Where was the race-course? Beside us now. There was a brief chorus about Nelson-ian blind eyes, rapidly stifled. The colonel ordered A Company to turn aside on to the racecourse. Suddenly, the tiredness of the men seeped through. They clattered on to the little wooden grandstand and sat down, still draped in weapons and machine-guns, to cheer one of their number as he clambered out onto the roof and, after some technical difficulties, tore down the Argentine flag and raised that of 2 Para. At their urging, I took a group photograph of this memorable gathering of desperadoes on the stepped benches. Then, inevitably, men began to brew up and to distribute a few cases of Argen-tine cigarettes they found in the starter's hut, first booty of the battle.

I wandered down to the road. It stretched empty ahead, the cathedral clearly visible perhaps half a mile away. It was simply too good a chance to miss. Pulling off my web equipment and camouflaged jacket, I handed them up to the commander of one of the Blues and Royals' Scimitars, now parked in the middle of the road and adorned with a large Union Jack. Then, with a civilian anorak and a walking stick that I had been clutching since we landed at San Carlos, I set off towards the town, looking as harmless as I could contrive. 'And where do you think you're going?' demanded a parachute NCO in the traditional voice of NCOs confronted with prospective criminals. 'I am a civilian,' I said firmly, and walked on unhindered. Just round the bend in the road stood a large building fronted with a conservatory that I suddenly realised from memories of photographs was Government House. Its approaches were studded with bunkers, whether occupied or otherwise I could not see. Feeling fairly foolish, I stopped, grinned towards them, raised my hands in the air, and waited to see what happened. Nothing moved. Still grinning and nodding at any possible spectres within, I turned back on to the road and strode towards the cathedral, hands in the air. A group of Argentine soldiers appeared by the roadside. I walked past them with what I hoped was a careless 'Good morning'. They stared curiously, but did nothing. Then, ahead of me, I saw a group of obviously civilian figures emerging from a large, official-looking building. I shouted to them: 'Are you British?' and they shouted back, 'Yes.' Fear ebbed away, and I walked to meet them. After a few moments' conversation, they pointed me towards the Argentine colonel on the steps of the administration block. I introduced myself to him quite untruthfully as the correspondent of *The Times* newspaper, the only British newspaper that it seemed possible he would have heard of. We talked civilly enough for a few minutes. He kept saying that most of my questions could only be answered after four o'clock, when the British general was due to meet General Menendez. Could I meanwhile go and talk to the British civilians? I asked. Of course, he said. I walked away towards that well-known Stanley hostelry, the Upland Goose, down a road filled with file upon file of Argentine soldiers, obviously assembling to surrender. They looked utterly cowed, totally drained of hostility. Yet I did not dare to photograph their wounded, straggling between comrades. It was only when I saw officers peering curiously at me from their vehicles that I realised that my efforts to look civilian were defeated by my face, still blackened with camouflage cream.

Walking into the hotel was the fulfilment of a dream, a fantasy that had filled all our thoughts for almost three months. 'We never doubted for a moment that the British would come,' said the proprietor, Desmond King. 'We have just been waiting for the moment.' It was like liberating an English suburban golf club.

A few minutes after Max Hastings walked into the Upland Goose, a much more serious drama unfolded a few hundred yards westwards. Each morning of the offensive, from the transmitting room of *Fearless*, Rod Bell and Colonel Rose had been intensifying the pitch of their broadcasts on the medical radio circuit. Early on that Monday morning, 14 June, Dr Alison Bleaney had visited the Argentine Captain Melbourne Hussey and begged him to respond to the British appeals. 'The position of the Argentine forces is now hopeless,' broadcast Bell that morning, 'you are surrounded by British forces on all sides . . . If you fail to respond to this message and there is unnecessary bloodshed in Port Stanley, the world will judge you accordingly.' Hussey listened to the British noon broadcast. But, despite Alison Bleaney's desperate pleas, he refused to answer until he had consulted with his superiors. At 1 p.m., he returned to the little room in John Street and broadcast a simple message to the British: General Menendez would talk. Late that afternoon, a single Gazelle helicopter bearing Bell, Rose and a signaller clattered over Port Stanley, a white parachute trailing from its belly. The British landed some distance from their intended arrival point. In a moment of mild farce, the delegation was obliged to scramble through a succession of hedges and ditches to reach the Argentinians. As they passed the hospital, Rose spotted a girl looking out from the hospital balcony. 'You Alison?' he called. She nodded. 'You did a great job!'

The negotiations with Menendez in Government House were

cool and formal, but it was immediately apparent that the Argentinian had no intention of continuing the fight. There was a brief dispute over the future of West Falkland: Menendez said that he had no power to surrender its garrison. Unknown to the Argentinians, the British had privately, reluctantly, decided that, if the governor was willing only to capitulate on East Falkland, they would accept these terms and pursue further operations against West Falkland. But, when pressed by Rose, Menendez gave way. West Falkland would surrender also. At every stage, Rose was able to confirm details of the negotiations direct with London. With the help of his remarkable portable satellite communication link, the British government monitored the talks minute by minute. There was a brief intervention from London at one point, when Rose had been discussing with the Argentinians whether their troops might return home in both British and Argentine ships. No Argentine ships, said London decisively. Such a gesture might diminish the force of the enemy's surrender. Finally, the terms of the capitulation were agreed. Menendez cried a little before shaking hands with Bell and Rose. Then they began the long wait for Major General Moore to arrive to sign the document, hampered by temporarily impossible flying conditions. At last, the weather cleared. At 9 p.m. on the evening of Monday, 14 June, the British and Argentine commanders put their signature to the document that ended the war in the Falklands, with the surrender of all Argentine forces on the islands.

*

The last war cabinet before the assault on Port Stanley had met on Friday, 11 June, and was given no indication of the impending denouement. The timing of the assault was left wholly to General Moore's judgement. Ministers were committed to hanging on grimly for the military to do their job – despite mutterings through clenched teeth about the traditional, methodical slowness of the infantry. The meeting thus heard a catalogue of logistic facts of life: the build-up of artillery ammunition, the problems of

5 Brigade regrouping after Bluff Cove, the risk of a return of the enemy air force. When, on Saturday morning, news came in that the assault had begun, Mrs Thatcher and John Nott drove at once to Northwood to monitor events in the operations room there. The swiftness of the assault and the rapidity with which it was pushed home came to ministers as a total surprise. By Monday morning, it was clear that total victory was at hand. The most important issue seemed to be how best to announce it. Of that there was no doubt. The Falklands crisis had begun in the House of Commons and many of its most dramatic political moments had taken place there. It was in the chamber that victory should be declared. All news from the South Atlantic was to be put under embargo until then.

Throughout Monday afternoon, MPs – indeed the whole nation – were thus kept on tenterhooks as the Prime Minister waited for news of the surrender negotiations. When finally she rose from her seat at 10.15 p.m., many expected her to do no more than announce a further advance. The drama was thus all the greater when she related that, in the course of that day, 'Our forces reached the outskirts of Port Stanley. Large numbers of Argentine soldiers threw down their weapons. They are reported to be flying white flags over Port Stanley.'

The House of Commons, so often the scene of synthetic emotion, now gave way to relief and joy. Initially it was Mrs Thatcher's Conservative supporters who led the cheering. But Michael Foot made the occasion complete with unstinted praise. 'I can well understand the anxieties and pressures that must have been upon her during these weeks,' he said, 'and I can understand that at this moment those pressures and anxieties may be relieved.' He gave a theatrical pause, then added, 'And I congratulate her.' Always a deft reader of the mood of the House, Foot gave the cue for rejoicing to be bipartisan, national and heartfelt. It was Thatcher's most intense moment of personal triumph since she had entered the Commons as Prime Minister almost exactly three years before. Congratulations poured in from all sides. In Downing

Street and the Foreign Office, telexes clattered into life to express the relief and pleasure of allies overseas (relief in many cases more strongly expressed than pleasure). As Mrs Thatcher returned home to Downing Street that night, her face drawn with exhaustion but unable to conceal her elation, a crowd gave a hearty rendering of 'Rule Britannia' on her doorstep.

*

As the men of the land force tramped the last miles towards Port Stanley, most British soldiers were still stunned by the suddenness of their victory. Countless thousands of enemy troops remained around Port Stanley who had scarcely fired a shot. The victors gazed in astonishment at the huge stockpiles of weapons, ammunition and equipment that the Argentinians could have used against them. When the first British officers drove up the windswept road to Stanley airfield and beheld regiment upon regiment of infantry, Exocets on trailers, radar-controlled antiaircraft weapons, missiles, artillery, shells, they could scarcely credit the conduct of Menendez. 'We thought that at least he would make us push him out of Stanley, then surrender when he had lost the capital,' said one. As men sought houses in which to shelter and wandered the streets like tourists gawping at the wonders of Paris or Rome rather than the neat little bungalows of a colonial town, they could not bring themselves to behave like victors. Colonel Tom Seccombe, deputy commander of 3 Brigade, was walking with two colleagues down the street when they met two Argentine officers. They held a stilted conversation with them, and it was only when they had parted that the British turned to each other and wondered vaguely whether they should have disarmed them or taken them prisoner. The dominant, overwhelming emotion in the minds of the land force was relief: relief that there need not be another bloody battle, relief that they had survived, relief that they could leave this barren, unyielding landscape and go home. 'I wanted to cry tears of joy,' Sergeant Hopper of 3 Para wrote in his diary. 'The padre and I celebrated by shaking each other's hands.'

'We almost ran into Stanley,' Hew Pike wrote to his family in England, 'down the moorland to be greeted with scenes of destruction, chaos, shambles. It is such a merciful relief that it now seems to be over. I am so terribly sad about the people we lost. The Duke of Wellington was indeed right about "the melancholy nature of victory".'

In the last hours before their surrender, humiliated and dejected Argentine soldiers looted, wrecked and fouled some civilian homes in Port Stanley. Yet some British soldiers behaved almost equally badly in the first days of victory. Sadly, it is part of the nature of war. Many of the tales of a fascist Argentine army behaving monstrously throughout their occupation of the Falklands were ill founded. There were incidents in which officers struck civilians; in which troops looted civilian property; in which the authorities commandeered Falklanders' vehicles, homes, stores. Yet, by the standards of most occupying armies, the Argentines' behaviour was very moderate. When the British reconquered Stanley, they found that the civilians still possessed ample stocks of food and alcohol. There had been no systematic pillaging in the capital, and only isolated occurrences in outlying villages. This is all the more remarkable when the plight of some of the Argentine soldiers is considered – cold, far from home, in conditions entirely unfamiliar, often hungry. The enemy appeared to possess adequate stocks of food, but to have had immense difficulty distributing it to men on the hills and in distant settlements. Even the British, incomparably more efficient, found logistics an overwhelming problem.

The Argentine occupiers of the Falklands appear to have embarked on a policy of conciliation, however heavy-handedly it was executed. When a small party of SBS landed on Pebble Island on 15 June to accept the surrender of the local garrison, they found that the two dozen local inhabitants had been confined to the manager's house since the SAS raid on 15 May. But the Falklanders seemed to feel no hatred for their jailers, and even insisted that one young Argentine soldier whom they had befriended should have lunch with them before he was taken with the others to imprisonment in the shearing sheds. 'I want to tell you,' said the earnest young Jorge in broad Californian, 'that these people have been like a family to me. I want to come back here without my uniform.' A cheerful red-headed Falklander in her mid-thirties, Arina Bernstein, wagged her finger at him. 'But don't you come planting your little flag here again, Jorge.' The Argentinian continued, 'Maybe some of the things that we were taught about the Malvinas when we were so high were not right. Three-quarters of us did not want to come here. When we heard that you were on Mount Kent, we knew that we could not win. It was just that, in the beginning, nobody in Argentina ever believed that you would really send such a force to capture the Malvinas . . .'

For the listening British soldiers, his passionate protestations of good intention came three months too late. Gazing down on the vast columns of dejected Argentinians queuing to throw down their arms on Stanley airfield, few of the British doubted that they had not been eager to fight. The entire conduct of the campaign by General Menendez suggested a passive, reluctant defending force. Partly, they had been conditioned by American training to rely heavily on motor transport and material resources to wage war, and were totally at a loss when, lacking these things, they found the British willing to fight without them. Much more than mere strategic difficulties, there is no doubt that Menendez and his forces never recovered from the shock of discovering that the British were proposing to wage total war against them for the recovery of the islands.

In the days following the surrender, as 11,313 Argentinian prisoners were herded to the jetties to be loaded aboard British ships for repatriation, the British began the massive task of clearing up: exploring the vast, recklessly haphazard minefields laid everywhere around the Argentine positions; restoring water and power to Port Stanley; cleaning up houses; recovering abandoned vehicles; finding shelter for more than 7,000 men. Suddenly San Carlos, which had been the hub of the British campaign, found itself a backwater. The ships of the amphibious force sailed round the island to lie off Port Stanley, where Sturdee's battle cruisers had lain at anchor before their battle against Von Spee almost seventy years earlier.

The Falklanders' spontaneous enthusiasm for their deliverance seemed to die very quickly, and very understandably. It was replaced by a bleak realisation that their lives and their community had been transformed for ever. Instead of Argentine vehicles throwing mud up and down the street, there were now British ones. Instead of a vast alien army of Argentinians camped all around them, there was now a scarcely less alien British army. This is the nature of most liberations, yet none the less saddening for that. Just as many Falklanders made clear their impatience to be left alone once more, so the British did not conceal their burning anxiety to be gone from the islands, to go home to enjoy their triumph among their own people. They had done what they came to do. By the end of June, most of the men who fought had sailed. Gone too were many of the ships of Woodward's battle group, to be replaced by other men and other ships, with the thankless task of holding those barren, unlovely islands for Britain, without the prospect of the glory.

17 » AFTERMATH

Any civilian who attempts to write a military history is of
necessity guilty of an act of presumption.

Sir John Fortescue, *History of The British Army*

On Monday, 26 July 1982, a service of thanksgiving for Britain's
victory in the Falklands was held in St Paul's Cathedral, attended
by the Royal Family, the Prime Minister and many of the army,
naval and royal marine officers who fought in the South Atlantic.
It was said that Mrs Thatcher was displeased that the Archbishop
of Canterbury's sermon failed to strike a sufficiently triumphal
note. If that is so, she could find no similar fault with the victory
parade held on 12 October, Columbus Day, when she stood beside
the Lord Mayor of London on the saluting base as contingents of
the three services marched through the City of London, cheered
by thousands of spectators, on their way to a luncheon in their
honour at the Guildhall. The evening before she had held a dinner
at Downing Street for all the leading personalities of the war (see
photo section). That summer and autumn, it sometimes seemed
that there was a continuous celebration of the Falklands campaign,
with vast crowds flocking to Southampton, Portsmouth, Plymouth,
to welcome home each ship; every town and village competing to
do honour to its local heroes. The Prime Minister professed to find
joyous evidence of a 'Falklands spirit' in every corner of British
life, deterring strikers and repelling left-wing agitators, impressing
the Russians and earning the envy of our American allies, so
mindful of their own recent military catastrophes.

There is an element of truth in all these assertions. The Falklands war indeed provided an impressive demonstration of British will and military efficiency. It gave the British people a warm glow to feel that here, at last, was an honourable and romantic success for the nation. Yet from the beginning, even as the war was being fought, it was remarkable how many servicemen in the South Atlantic and civilians at home perceived an underlying absurdity in a struggle so far from home for a leftover of empire. This is not to suggest that they opposed the war. Once President Galtieri had been allowed to do what he did, most of Britain agreed the government had to respond as it did. The British public's resilience in the face of bad news and casualties proved far higher than many people – and many politicians – would have predicted. But *triunfalismo* as they call it in Buenos Aires – triumphalism – is a sensation which sits more easily on the nations of Latin America than on Britain. There were not a few service officers who were reluctant to take part in a succession of victory parades. It seemed somehow faintly unEnglish to make much public display of what was simply a job well done, and made necessary by a huge political and diplomatic failure. Most of the men who fought in the South Atlantic came home conscious that the way of life of the Falklands had been destroyed for ever by the war, and doubtful about government proposals to spend countless millions of pounds to create a new, artificial economy merely to justify the struggle.

This battle by land and sea for a cluster of South Atlantic islands fascinated the world. It was a freak of history. Most of the popular celebrations of victory were spurred by enthusiasm for the achievements of the men who fought, rather than for the cause. Very few of the conclusions that can be drawn from the Falklands experience have a wider application than to this conflict, at this moment of history, under this British government. But under the headings below, we have sought to draw up a provisional balance sheet for the war in the South Atlantic, 1982.

The British Campaign

The struggle for the Falklands was essentially a small colonial war midway in kind between a counter-insurgency operation and the armoured warfare seen in Europe in 1944–45. It cost Britain 255 men killed and 777 wounded, some of them maimed for life: three times the British casualties during the EOKA campaign in Cyprus, one third the number of British killed in Korea, and a hundred fewer than those killed in Ulster since 1969. Argentina's exact losses remain unknown, but Buenos Aires announced a provisional total of 652 men dead and missing in the war. The British task force lost 6 ships sunk and 10 others more or less badly damaged. Of 28 Harriers and 8 RAF Harrier GR3s deployed, 4 Sea Harriers were lost in accidents, 2 Sea Harriers and 3 GR3s were shot down by ground fire. The British have claimed the destruction or seizure of 109 Argentine aircraft. Of these, the 31 attributed to the Harriers and 30 destroyed on the ground or captured seem clearly confirmed. Of the remainder, Rapier claimed 9, Sea Dart 8, Sea Wolf 5, Sea Cat 6. The victims included 31 Skyhawks, 26 Mirages, 23 Pucara, 18 helicopters, 1 Canberra and a C-130. The true total is probably somewhere approaching the British claims, although never in the history of air warfare have all claimed kills been confirmed in final statistics. The Harriers flew some 1,650 sorties for a loss rate of .55 per cent, as against the 4–5 per cent that was considered acceptable in the Second World War. The cost to the British taxpayer of the operation itself was put by the government at £700 million plus £900 million for lost ships and planes. An unofficial estimate put the total cost of regaining and holding the Falklands at £2 billion over four years.

It is clear from our research that no detailed and realistic assessment was made of how the British would actually defeat the Argentinians in a full-scale South Atlantic war before the task force set sail. The nearest the Royal Navy appears to have come was a rough calculation of the strategic balance of ships and weapons on each side. The reason for this appears to have been that, at the start, no one envisaged war. As it was, the risk of a British disaster at sea – for instance, the loss of a carrier – was very real indeed. Had the expedition been merely a single operation in a wider war, the odds would not have seemed unreasonable. Sooner or later Britain was almost certain to win. But, as the nation's only throw, a huge commitment of national prestige and residual power, the dangers were enormous.

Since the war ended, senior naval officers have firmly declared that they did weigh the odds before the task force sailed, and were not surprised by the eventual losses. Yet private estimates in the Ministry of Defence suggested that no more than two or three ships would be sunk – the chief casualties anticipated were among the Harriers, with a 50 per cent predicted attrition rate. There is overwhelming evidence that the navy was deeply shocked by the sinking of the *Sheffield* and by the fallibility of naval weapons systems revealed in the first weeks of the campaign. The power of the Argentine air force was greatly underestimated. In dispatching Admiral Woodward's battle group, the service chiefs (at least the navy ones) convinced themselves that the Argentinians were not a major enemy, and that therefore conventional calculations about air and sea threats could be cast aside.

After the failure of the Royal Navy's attempt to gain air superiority before the arrival of the amphibious force, the government and service chiefs committed themselves to an even greater gamble, that of sending in the landing force regardless. The navy's capabilities for resisting air attack inshore were even more limited than in the open sea. But, by 8 May, when the crucial decision was taken at Chequers, the government and its commanders were committed politically, and could not conceivably have sailed the force home again empty-handed. In the event, the brilliant choice of San Carlos as a landing site was just enough – matched by the power of the Harriers, the Rapier missile, and other British weapons systems – to hold the tactical balance against the enemy's air force.

Rear Admiral Woodward did all that could be achieved with

the force at his command. He was the one man who, like Jellicoe, could have 'lost the war in an afternoon' by suffering a disaster to his carriers. The lack of point defence on the ships, of airborne early warning and powerful air cover, was not his fault. He earned hostility from many officers of the land force, and even from some naval officers, for the manner in which he directed operations rather than for the substance of his decisions. The Royal Navy's habit of acting first and informing other services later, rather than working in close consultation, created substantial problems. But it was the contrast between Woodward's early ebullient confidence and the later, bloody reality that seemed most painful to some of those under his command. Once battle had been joined, the officers and men of the Royal Navy showed that they had lost nothing of the courage, superb seamanship anghting skill that their service has demonstrated throughout its history.

The logistics of the South Atlantic war, the mobilising of scores of ships and 28,000 men to fight and support an operation 8,000 miles from home, were astonishing and played a major part in convincing the war cabinet that the navy could also meet its military objectives. 30,000 tons of stores, provisions and ammunition were shipped from Portsmouth and Devonport alone. Twenty-one Royal Fleet Auxiliary ships and 54 merchant ships chartered or requisitioned from 33 companies sailed in support of the 51 warships which worked with the task force at various times. An air-to-air refuelling system was designed and fitted to RAF Nimrods, Hercules and Harriers in less than a month. By the standards of total war between European nations, the deployment in the South Atlantic was small business. But, as an achievement by the British services in 1982, it was remarkable, and a tribute to the direction of Sir Henry Leach and Sir John Fieldhouse at Northwood.

The Royal Navy argues that its tactics quickly conquered the Exocet-missile threat: after the mishap to *Sheffield*, every other air-launched attack on a warship was frustrated. *Atlantic Conveyor* was lost because she lacked chaff, and *Glamorgan* was hit by a land-launched Exocet, against which effective response was difficult.

The probable truth is that, if more Exocets had been launched against the British, most would have been avoided but some would have got through. Defence against sea-skimming missiles remains uncertain and unreliable. The navy may justly claim that, in making their calculations about the risks of sending a battle group, they took account of the fact that the Argentinians were known to possess only five AM39 Exocets. It is no more relevant to ask what might have happened to the task force if the enemy had been able to buy another twenty Exocets, as they sought to do, than to ask if Woodward would have been sent had the Argentine air force possessed fifty Phantoms. They did not. This was part of the strategic equation from the beginning.

The Royal Navy will not be dramatically recast as a result of the lessons learned in the Falklands, since it is so unlikely that a similar campaign will be fought again. Point defence on ships will be improved, and more money may be made available to refine Sea Wolf and Sea Dart, although the latter is approaching obsolescence. The navy will take steps to reduce the quantities of inflammable material in its ships, although too much has been made of the threat posed by aluminium superstructures. Ship designers have been forcefully reminded that it is essential to distribute vital installations – computers, communications and command centres, damage control resources – as widely as possible within a ship, rather than to centralise them at a single vulnerable point. Ships as small as *Ardent* and *Antelope* would have sunk after suffering the damage that they did regardless of any design changes in their structures. No ship in history has possessed all the weapons and capabilities desired of it. British ships were for many years designed for war against the Soviet Union. In his post-Falklands statements, John Nott remained unrepentant about this implication of his 1981 navy review – although he was compelled to reprieve *Invincible* from sale to the Australians.

Once the land force was ashore, the Royal Marines and men of the Parachute Regiment did everything that had been expected of them, and more. The war proved that British military training is good, and re-emphasised the case for elite infantry forces, trained and equipped for exceptional exertions on the battlefield. A Pentagon assessment made even before the war was over said, 'The British operation vindicates totally the concept of a professional standing army without conscripts and with an elite officer class. It also vindicates the establishment of specialist corps of highly trained and prepared units ready for instant deployment.' Battlefield weapons and equipment, with the exception of the Blowpipe missile and Cymbeline mortar-locating radar, performed well. The Royal Artillery and Royal Engineers provided superb support for the infantry – indeed, the gunners' contribution to most of the battles of the war was decisive. Most of the problems of the campaign stemmed from lack of quantity. The land force fought all the way on shoestring resources. Peacetime exercises do not test an army's logistics as thoroughly as its tactics. The organisation and support of the land force were not as finely tuned as its teeth elements, though that is no reflection on the thousands of men who laboured by day and night on the lines of communication.

A senior officer said after the war that it had proved that 'the things we did on the basis of well-tried and proven formations worked, and the *ad hoc* arrangements turned out much less happily'. Joint-service liaison and staff work left much to be desired. From beginning to end, 5 Brigade were the victims of 'ad hoccery'. It seems less surprising that the *Galahad* disaster occurred than that something much worse did not happen on the southern flank. Many men of the land force said that the Falklands experience was not a good omen for a war in north-west Europe, where British plans depend heavily on reinforcements rushed to the continent from Britain. It was 3 Commando Brigade, the thoroughly practised formation led by men of great experience in working together, who were the stars of the campaign. There was little that the brigade would have done differently with hindsight, except perhaps to carry less luggage and more firepower.

The attack on Goose Green reflected haste and underestimation of the enemy by those who set it in motion, redeemed only by the brilliant performance of 2 Para. With the possible exception of South Georgia, the battle was the one instance in the campaign of 'back-seat driving' from London. The politicians and service chiefs, deeply alarmed by the losses in San Carlos, demanded urgent action from the land force for political as well as military reasons. After the event, their reasoning and their decision may well have seemed justified. But this episode was a classic demonstration of the risks and complications which can set in when a military operation is being conducted to serve an urgent political purpose. Command and control proved less than perfect throughout the war. Despite the miracles of modern communications technology, there were significant misunderstandings and failures of liaison between both commanders afloat and ashore and between the services. There is much scope for improving joint-service liaison, although it can be argued that this went astonishingly well at short notice, compared with the years before combined operations were satisfactorily established in the Second World War.

Major General Jeremy Moore proved a good front-line commander, constantly visiting his units, encouraging his officers, never allowing his nerve or purpose to be seen to weaken. But he arrived on the battlefield when the most difficult days and decisions were over, and his divisional staff found great difficulty in grasping the reins at such a late stage, when they themselves had been brought together at very short notice. It may well have been a strategic error to open up the southern axis with 5 Brigade, creating massive demands on strained transport resources, rather than merely using Brigadier Wilson's battalions as a reserve for 3 Commando Brigade. The overwhelming burden of the land war fell upon Brigadier Julian Thompson and his brigade staff, whose achievement it is hard to overstate. Thompson found the long weeks at sea – lacking a firm directive and faced with political and service liaison issues of a kind that few officers of his rank are asked to undertake – very difficult indeed. Once he was ashore in command of his brigade, he was in his element. 'The brigadier is splendid – so straightforward and philosophical,' one of his commanding officers wrote home. 3 Commando Brigade, and the country, were lucky to have Thompson.

The accident of history which had made the Royal Marines a specialist arctic-warfare force, trained in Norway, contributed decisively to victory in the Falklands. While Argentina's conscripts, mostly shipped from the country's arid northern region, suffered terribly in the alien Falklands landscape, the marines possessed precisely the training and equipment to prosper in it. They won the land campaign as cheaply and as quickly as was reasonably possible with their resources. There was probably no moment at which the Argentinians could have defeated them, but a less competent British force could have become bogged down in a disastrous stalemate in the mountains. This was the best outcome which the government in Buenos Aires aspired to, once the British beach-head was secure. It would be wrong to pretend that, even at Goose Green or on Mount Longdon, the enemy offered the kind of resistance that might have been expected from a better-motivated, better-trained European force. Although the paras' battle losses were severe by the standards of limited conflicts, they would have been considered very light for an action in north-west Europe in 1944. The chief enemies the British forces had to contend with were Argentine air power, supply difficulties and the weather.

The Falklands campaign was fought with remarkable respect for decency on both sides. There were unhappy incidents such as the shooting of the Gazelle crews in the water at San Carlos and the killing of Lieutenant Barry under a white flag at Goose Green, but these appear to have been the unauthorised doings of peasant soldiers. The Argentine high command seemed anxious to conduct the war within its own understanding of honour. It is hard to make much of the discovery of napalm stocks at Goose Green, when the British were using the equally horrifying white phosphorus. Moore's men were meticulous in offering kid-glove treatment to prisoners, all of whom they repatriated without any serious attempt at interrogation, either during the war or after it ended. The result is that many questions about the Argentinians' behaviour may never be answered.

Beyond the failure of intelligence that made it possible for the Argentinians to launch their invasion, few British campaigns in the past century have been fought with a lower level of military data about the enemy. No satellite photographs and no good air-reconnaissance photographs were available. Signals intelligence made a valuable contribution, but the British fought the war knowing astonishingly little about the organisation, abilities and personalities of the Argentine army. This reflects very poorly not only on the Secret Intelligence Service, but on the level of information available from military attachés in Latin America. In intelligence as in so much else, Britain was reminded of the cost of being overwhelmingly 'scenario orientated' to the confrontation in north-west Europe. 'The motto of the Falklands war is: "You never know",' one of the British commanders declared after it had ended. For the hundredth time in her history, Britain was reminded that there is always an unexpected military threat for which defence planning must be flexible enough to provide.

This was a campaign mirroring a host of others that British forces have conducted throughout their history: launched with high hopes, considerable muddle and inadequate resources; redeemed and finally carried through to victory by remarkable service efficiency, some outstanding weapons systems (which did extra duty for those that failed), and the quality and courage of the men who fought the battles by land, sea and air. An officer said when it was all over, 'We re-learned a lot of old lessons. We talk a great deal about what went wrong. What is really remarkable is how much went right.' The government and the service chiefs were richly entitled to claim their triumph for judging correctly that they could launch and win their great gamble. It is a matter of personal taste whether the risk of disaster should be a foreword or a mere footnote to the task force's history.

The Argentine Campaign

Argentina's advance intelligence assessments were as poor as those of Britain. Just as the nation's diplomats misjudged Thatcher's willingness to meet force with force in defence of the Falklands, so her military intelligence staff miscalculated the ability of Britain's services to do so. Argentina's command structure had developed through generations of inter-service rivalry, and was dominated by the requirements of counter-insurgency campaigning. It was ill suited to the conduct of combined operations. The Falklands lay within the navy's sphere of responsibility, under the control of Admiral Juan Jose Lombardo at Puerto Belgrano on the mainland. Yet the mainland army and air force command centres were located further south at Comodoro Rivadavia, and the hapless Major General Menendez in Port Stanley was dependent on a ramshackle chain of liaison officers for communications between the services. The invasion of the Falklands had been chiefly the brainchild of the navy. But after the sinking of the *General Belgrano* its ships withdrew to their bases, and the other services became unwilling to accept direction from a service that was contributing little to the war. The reluctance of the air force to embark on hostilities was well known: 'The almost certain prospect that we would have to fight against one of the major military powers in the world ... with long experience of conflicts of various magnitudes, backed by the warlike sensibility of its ruling classes and with some of the world's most modern weapons systems was a source of constant worry to air force commanders ...' (*Aerospacio*, September 1982).

If the navy had dispersed its ships, they could have broken out by night to stage hit-and-run Exocet raids against the British. There was a certainty of losing some units to Royal Naval submarines, but the equal certainty of being able to push some through to dislocate British operations. Clearly the prospect of heavy losses deterred the Argentine admirals. The air force, to its credit, allowed no such fears to prevent it from doing its utmost. But the recriminations between the services prevented effective cooperation. The navy failed to provide the air force with the radar direction that its pilots had expected. The air force failed to profit from the technique developed by navy pilots of lobbing their bombs to provide them with enough 'air time' to fuse. The air force decision to bring returning pilots to widely dispersed bases to camouflage the scale of losses precluded effective debriefing and exchange of information about tactics.

General Menendez hesitated fatally for some days after the San Carlos landing, claiming to believe that it was merely a diversion. He could have prolonged the campaign considerably by aggressive raiding and patrolling around the British beach-head, even if he lacked confidence in his troops to mount a major counter-attack. His 5th Marine Battalion, which fought on Tumbledown, was the best unit he possessed. He might have conducted his campaign with more confidence had he been given the two battalions of mountain commandos which remained at Comodoro Rivadavia throughout the war, guarding against a possible Chilean intervention. Instead, the bulk of his forces were raw conscripts. An immense logistics effort was needed to keep them supplied, while they were of little value on the battlefield. The precarious Argentine supply system on the islands was created to meet the needs of one brigade for a month, the length of time they were briefed to remain. In the event, after heavy reinforcement, there were more than 11,000 men to be fed for three months, and the system could not cope. Menendez was also locked in constant dispute with General Joffre and General Daher in Port Stanley. The army's postwar *Calvi Report* even alleged that a mutiny was at one stage plotted, to replace Menendez with Colonel Mohamed Ali Seineldrin of the 25th Infantry Regiment.

The simple truth is that the Argentine army had no conception of how to fight a war against a major enemy. Their American training had taught them to rely too heavily on resources rather than human endeavour. An SAS officer remarked during the campaign on the problem that afflicts many Third World armies, of concentrating on acquiring expensive technology rather than applying basic training and skills. On his own travels abroad, he said, he found again and again that his hosts disbelieved all that he told them about the achievements of the SAS being based on intensive, ceaseless, meticulous training and preparation: 'They all secretly believe that there is some pill you can take if only you will tell them what it is.' The Argentinians possessed better equipment and heavier firepower than the British ashore. But their tactics, fieldcraft and motivation were lamentable. Every conversation with captured officers and the men after the war emphasised that their morale and determination never recovered from the discovery that the British proposed to fight.

If General Menendez could not have defeated the task force, he could certainly have caused it very serious difficulties, even with the human material at his disposal. But his refusal to do more than hold fixed positions condemned him to inevitable defeat. There was a ritualistic quality about the battle for the mountains around Port Stanley. Its outcome was inevitable, yet Menendez clearly believed that honour, *machismo*, demanded that he should fight a battle before surrendering. It is remarkable that he failed to make more than token use of his Pucara ground-attack aircraft, which the British greatly feared. It may be a tribute to the much-abused British Blowpipe missile that this was the one form of air threat against which it proved effective early in the campaign, and the Argentinians never made significant use of their Pucara after the landing on Mount Kent.

The government in Buenos Aires appears to have maintained its sense of fantasy about the military situation until the bitter end. When Menendez told General Galtieri on 14 June that a showdown in Port Stanley could mean 'a total massacre', Galtieri ordered him, 'Look, General, grab all the forces you have left and counter-attack.' Menendez's decision to ignore Buenos Aires and surrender was the most sensible, courageous and determined step he took throughout the war. Within a month, he and all his senior commanders together with Costa Mendes and all the members of the junta had resigned or been stripped of office. Argentina once more returned to chaos and uncertainty.

The Whitehall War

The Falklands dispute should never have led to hostilities. That it did so was the result of a series of miscalculations by both sides: by the British, that Argentina would not resort to force to assert its claim to the islands; by the Argentinians, that Britain would not go to war to regain them. Argentina had harboured a grievance for a century and a half. In 1964, she took it to the United Nations, which promptly referred the issue back to the two parties on terms which evaded the central issue of self-determination. British and Argentine negotiators then began seventeen years of discussions with the ostensible purpose of achieving partial acceptance of the Argentine claim. No one believed it could be in the interests of the Falklanders to remain in a state of perpetual antagonism with their adjacent mainland. Their islands were not Taiwan or even Gibraltar.

The policy that Lord Chalfont, Ted Rowlands, Nicholas Ridley and Richard Luce struggled in turn to implement was eventually refined to the principle of a 'leaseback'. This would acknowledge Argentine claims to sovereignty, yet protect the rights and lifestyle of the islands' people. The Argentinians never wanted to recolonise the Falklands. Britain did not want to defend sovereignty by force of arms. As Perez de Cuellar remarked after the collapse of his peace initiative in May 1982, 'It was the sort of problem which would take ten minutes to solve if both sides were willing.'

A compromise settlement was never achieved because the British Foreign Office proved far more competent at negotiating with another government than with its own. Successive cabinets regarded the political price of compromise as always just too high. American diplomats take it for granted that an essential function of their job is to lobby politicians, to sell policies that they consider desirable or essential to those who have the power to implement them. In Britain, the Foreign Office existed in a world of its own. Diplomats failed to mobilise any constituency of political opinion for a compromise over the Falklands. Their ministers, whose responsibility they believed this to be, were never in office for long enough or were never sufficiently interested to do the job for them. The Foreign Office rejected the overtures of William Hunter Christie of the Falkland Islands Committee, who wrote to Robin Edmonds in 1975 suggesting a collaboration between them similar to that enjoyed by the Malvinas Institute with the Argentine foreign ministry. Yet this tiny group proved capable of mobilising formidable backbench pressure and ultimately wrecking what the Foreign Office was trying to achieve.

It is not enough to say that politicians should have given diplomacy a clear lead. The foreign service regards itself as the custodian of continuity in policy, and that custodianship involves a measure of responsibility for generating political support. Considering the lack of this support, it is astonishing that a succession of Foreign Office officials – David Scott, Michael Hadow, Robin Edmonds, Hugh Carless, Anthony Williams, John Ure – managed to sustain the momentum of negotiation at all. On three occasions, in 1968, 1977 and 1981, British governments could have suspended talks on the grounds that the principle of self-determination represented an impossible obstacle to progress. Yet the Foreign Office's legitimate concern to protect British interests in Latin America spurred them to keep the negotiating process in being. The flaw was that a political strategy was never evolved to complement the diplomatic one. Diplomacy without politics is ultimately impotent.

By 1981, decisions made outside Foreign Office control had dramatically reduced the credibility of Britain's interest in the Falklands; the shelving of the Shackleton Report, the withdrawal of *Endurance*, the granting of second-class British citizenship to the Falklanders. British diplomats failed to perceive the impact of these measures on Buenos Aires and on the shifting sands of Argentine politics. From June 1981 until the eve of the invasion of the islands,

the Foreign Office and the Joint Intelligence Committee in the
Cabinet Office allowed themselves to be deceived by their belief
that, if Argentina were to act, she would do so only after three
phases of 'graduated escalation'. It was this delusion which caused
them successively to neglect the possible dispatch of submarines
on 5 March; to discount evidence of increased tension and rumours
of impending invasion in Buenos Aires; to commit the crucial
provocation of sending *Endurance* from Port Stanley on 20 March;
and even to disbelieve the true intention of Anaya's fleet as it
sailed towards the Falklands. The JIC assessments passed to ministers were complacent and misleading. It is a stark reflection on
the British constitution that those responsible for these assessments should have been confirmed in office by the Falklands war,
and graced with an extraordinary sequence of exonerations by
the Franks Committee (see Appendix D) while Lord Carrington
and Richard Luce remained in the political wilderness. From the
moment the British task force sailed, the focus of British diplomacy
narrowed dramatically, while the Foreign Office found itself under
fierce attack from politicians and the media. Some diplomats
insisted that the Argentine invasion could never have been predicted or avoided, and that even out of the catastrophe a lasting
settlement could be forged. The Prime Minister herself even agreed
at one point to sovereignty negotiations. As a succession of mediators were drawn into the dispute, there were hopes in the Foreign
Office that the Falklands might be lifted from Britain's shoulders
altogether and transferred to an international administration. Yet
by the end of April, Pym, Acland and Palliser in London, together
with Parsons and Henderson in the US, faced diplomacy's ultimate
challenge: finding some means of averting a war already scheduled
to begin. In the event, the same political forces in Britain and
Buenos Aires which had prevented a diplomatic settlement for
seventeen years had now increased the stakes to such heights that
neither side could afford to withdraw. When the game had ended,
Britain's winnings were so vast that she appeared to abandon a
long-term Falklands diplomatic policy altogether. Faced with yet

another UN resolution on 4 November 1982 requesting a resumption of negotiations, Britain found ninety nations voting against her, including the United States. She had won the war, but not yet the argument. The Falklands had merely become a costly fortress.

Nations which had willingly supported Britain when she was acting as self-appointed policeman against armed aggression, now felt the point had been made and honour satisfied. The dispute could not be left to fester and Britain ought to show magnanimity in victory – at least to the point of taking up some of the negotiating ideas suggested during the conflict. It was too petty to be made a long-term issue of national pride. Sanctions duly ended. France, to Mrs Thatcher's anger, resumed the Exocet and Super Etendard contract suspended during the war and Germany completed her frigates. It appeared from the debates at the UN that Britain ironically enjoyed less sympathy for her sovereignty claim after the struggle than before it. As in so many limited wars, the cause of the dispute returned precisely to the status quo ante, wholly unresolved.

The Foreign Office, shattered by the outbreak of the South Atlantic war, was largely ignored by its government when it ended. The new Foreign Secretary, Francis Pym, had been appointed in the hope of 'clearing the air' between Downing Street and his department. Yet he found that his persistent support for a negotiated settlement set him at loggerheads with the Prime Minister. Once, she even hazarded the opinion that the Falklands war would never have happened had she possessed the same sort of 'in-house' advice on foreign affairs that she received from Professor Alan Walters on economic policy. The Foreign Office was initially appalled by the appointment of her favourite diplomat, Sir Anthony Parsons, to her private staff. A 'shadow Foreign Office' was burgeoning in Downing Street, with the prospect of the same divisions and rivalries as exist between the State Department and the White House in Washington. Was Mrs Thatcher now going to generate the sort of friction she had seen between Reagan and

Haig? (She resolved these doubts by simply replacing Mr Pym in June 1983.)

Yet the British foreign service came out of the Falklands experience with some remarkable successes to its credit. Parsons's UN Resolution 502 was a tour de force of diplomatic manoeuvring, matched by similar success at the EEC on 9 April. British diplomats could look with pride on Henderson's orchestration of American public opinion; the war cabinet's finessing of de Cuellar's peace plan in the last week before San Carlos; and the containment of any world opposition to Britain's military actions throughout the sea and land war. British public opinion was satisfied by the justice of its own cause, yet the support or even acquiescence of the rest of the world in a 'colonial' war was by no means a foregone conclusion.

The most notable casualty of the diplomatic interchanges was Britain's relationship with the United States. London did not fully comprehend Washington's inevitable divided loyalty between hemispheric and historic friendship. At the same time, Britain not unreasonably argued that it was for Washington to sort out its own mind on what was surely a moral not pragmatic issue and to act decisively thereafter. Instead, the Reagan government demonstrated a divisiveness and lack of direction which dismayed many observers, in Latin America as much as in Europe.

The Haig team criticised the Buenos Aires junta for its inability to make up its mind and deliver consistent decisions. Yet this often seemed a charge which could equally be levelled at Washington. Tom Enders failed to realise the seriousness of the issue, subordinating it, like Jeane Kirkpatrick, to the dictates of an anticommunist strategy in Latin America. Reagan's incomprehension of his problem; the ham-fisted manner in which successive peace initiatives were launched by the State Department; the confusion between 'even-handedness' and 'tilt'; the antipathy towards the UN peace effort; the fiasco of the Kirkpatrick veto; the blatant disagreements between the key figures shaping American policy;

all suggested an executive machine ill-suited to the needs of modern international relations – let alone to the possible demands of nuclear confrontation. Many American officials interviewed for this book were refreshingly frank at the shortcomings the Falklands war exposed in American foreign policy. 'We misread Britain, we misread Argentina, we were complete amateurs at the UN, we ended by pleasing no one and offending everyone,' said one US ambassador. The western alliance might reasonably enquire whether any of these lessons have now been learnt.

If the Falklands war began in part because the British civil service had failed adequately to define and fulfil its functions, the struggle gave it a new sense of purpose. The machinery established in Whitehall on 4 April emerged triumphant and without modification at the end of the war. The Prime Minister created a war cabinet that not only embraced the key departments of foreign affairs and defence, but also protected her political flanks. Whitelaw and Parkinson represented important strands in the government and party without getting in the way of the work being done. The inclusion of Sir Michael Palliser in the supporting civil service team, along with Sir Robert Armstrong, Sir Antony Acland and Robert Wade-Gery, kept the Prime Minister in touch with outside departments, as well as providing a long-term view which might otherwise have gone by the board. The war machine was small yet effective, both politically and administratively. Mrs Thatcher's constant reference to the 'Falklands Spirit' when peace returned demonstrated the well-known yearning among prime ministers for the executive as well as political simplicity of war. It seemed a far cry from the intricate network of power-broking and negotiation which is the lot of modern cabinet government.

The military hierarchy was kept equally close-knit. The chiefs of staff and the defence bureaucracy were continuously, carefully consulted. Their invitations to Chequers – roughly every other week – enabled them to share in informal debate about the conduct of the war, though most decisions were taken on a closed circuit between the cabinet, Sir Terence Lewin and Sir John Field-house. Lewin's success in gaining the Prime Minister's confidence, together with his personal friendship with Fieldhouse, were critical to the chain of command. Just as Parsons secured advancement from his Falkland success, so Lewin even found himself tipped as a possible defence secretary, an extraordinary tribute for a Chief of Defence Staff. The service chiefs also enjoyed the remarkable, almost eerie, sensation of being able to take defence decisions without concern for cost. For the first time in two decades, the British government detached itself wholly from economics. 'It made us rather light headed,' said a senior Ministry of Defence official. 'We didn't ask the Treasury for anything. We just told them.' The mounting cost of the war was simply fed into a Treasury calculator week by week.

The intelligence community received no more than a mild rap over the knuckles from the Franks Committee (see Appendix D), though Franks did conclude it was 'too passive in operation'. We have commented in the course of the narrative on the dangers of an increased reliance on electronic and signals intelligence at the expense of human analysis. One result of this, noted by most western intelligence sources, is the lower status accorded to 'humint' on the ground and a higher one to its 'assessment' at headquarters, where it is vulnerable to distortion by other views and interests. When departmental policy can exert a direct influence over the assessment of raw material passed to ministers, there is clearly a risk of what should be an open flow of information becoming blocked or misdirected. In Britain's case, the dominance of the Foreign Office over the JIC machine is a classic instance of this risk. Intelligence staff might be forgiven for not predicting Anaya's pre-emptive invasion – though it was surely a strong possibility. But they should have been at least aware of one planned for later in the year. Once the decision to forestall any British military reinforcement in the South Atlantic had been taken by the junta, probably on 26 March, the intelligence machine appears to have responded swiftly. It was always understood that, in a race, Britain could never get to the Falklands as fast as Argentina.

More worrying to some are the implications of the communications gap which occurred in the morning and afternoon of Friday, 2 April. Allegedly as a result of freak weather conditions, the British government were quite unable to communicate with their 'tripwire' force on the Falklands, from the moment the Argentine invasion began right through to the eventual surrender. It is known that after a certain point, both the radio station and the Cable and Wireless office were in enemy hands. But no alternative channel of communication existed and news of the crisis came exclusively from Buenos Aires for at least seven hours. The result was that the British cabinet was unable to confirm its key retaliatory decisions. It simply did not know what was happening and was unable to provide clear leadership. As one minister said grimly, 'We did not even know enough to be able to resign.'

This 'communications hiatus' is a central obsession of nuclear strategists. An attacking missile system only has to knock out a key point in the information circuit for ministers to have insufficient information for their response. At 2 p.m. on the afternoon of the Argentine invasion, six hours after it had been completed, the British cabinet was still treating it as hypothetical. Not until evening did they have enough information formally to approve their retaliatory measures. It was perhaps as well that these involved the laborious process of putting ships to sea. The Falklands war may seem a puny theatre in comparison with that of an inter-continental nuclear exchange. The fact is that it commenced with a prolonged paralysis of decision.

The Media War

A more hotly debated feature of Whitehall's war concerned the handling of the media. The Falklands war was the most controversially reported of Britain's conflicts since 1945. From the beginning

– because the only means of reaching the islands lay with the task force – coverage of the British side of the war was entirely at the mercy of the Ministry of Defence. Uniquely, there was no scope whatsoever for independent enterprise. The Royal Navy, which traditionally values its privacy and has little recent experience of the media, at first flatly refused to take reporters with the task force. After a heated argument between Fleet Street and the Ministry of Defence and on the Prime Minister's personal insistence, three British television reporters, two camera crews, two radio reporters, two photographers and fifteen newspaper correspondents were accredited to the task force, sailing in *Canberra*, *Hermes* and *Invincible*.

Most of the disagreements which followed between the Ministry of Defence and the media both at sea and at home were the product of the lack of a considered policy or plan for the reporting of a British war. As the First Sea Lord later admitted, 'Our learning curve was rising right through to the end.' The correspondents with the task force were accompanied by a team of civilian Ministry of Defence public relations officers whose normal functions were merely to answer telephones in their department, or to arrange visits to service establishments. They lacked knowledge either of media needs or of military affairs, and failed to gain the respect or trust of either the correspondents or, more important, of the senior officers of the task force. Their only contribution to the reporting of the war was rigorously to enforce increasingly erratic restrictions on outgoing news. These became a matter of much bitterness among the press corps on the ships when they learned that far more information was being made freely available in London by the Ministry of Defence.

The anger of the media in London stemmed initially from the plain lack of news from the task force. All background briefings were stopped with the sailing of the task force – though they were later resumed under pressure from the Downing Street press officer, Bernard Ingham, who ill concealed his contempt for the ministry's information performance. No equipment for transmitting television pictures was embarked. Editors became increasingly concerned that they were being used by the Ministry of Defence to channel misinformation – above all after Sir Frank Cooper asssured them that there would be no 'D-Day type landing' in the Falklands twenty-four hours before the amphibious assault at San Carlos. The ministry's choice of Ian Macdonald as spokesman, who in his television announcements seemed more like a maiden aunt than a government representative, added a note of eccentricity to what was otherwise merely a farrago of indecision and incompetence. The lack of television pictures was attributed to the technical impossibility of transmitting them without interfering with vital electronic equipment aboard British warships. The difficulties raised by the navy were viewed with some scepticism when it was remembered that television reporters had been able to transmit freely from the American carrier task force in the South China Sea in May 1975, following the fall of Saigon. At any rate, television pictures reached England two weeks or more after the events they described, a lag almost unprecedented in modern media history. Argentine pictures were made available freely and tended to dominate foreign newscasts throughout the war. It is impossible to avoid the conviction that, given the known difficulties of conducting a campaign in front of television cameras, the British authorities at home and afloat did not exert themselves to make a satellite link possible.

There is no doubt, also, that much more information and many more news stories could have been allowed to reach newspapers in Britain if a more intelligent and imaginative censorship policy had been followed. Once the war began, most censorship with the task force was carried out efficiently and sensibly by service officers. However, material reaching London was then subjected to recensorship by a variety of uncoordinated interests in the services and the defence bureaucracy. Much was lost that need not have been, and much was delayed for days by petty scruple. Meanwhile the intense pressure placed upon Whitehall by the media meant inevitably that some individuals in the Ministry of Defence, Westminster and Downing Street privately 'leaked' – or used the lobby correspondents to indicate – material of often critical sensitivity. The most notorious episode was the advance news of the British attack on Goose Green. The official denial of a 'leak' is, as we have shown, impossible to accept. Interdepartmental rivalry in the media war was often intense.

If Whitehall's role in the propaganda war was mishandled, that of the British media was not creditable. After so many years of peace, few reporters possessed any knowledge of military affairs. Most of those who sailed with the task force found that their ignorance increased the difficulty of gaining respect and trust from service officers. Because many editors doubted that there would be a war when the fleet sailed, most of the correspondents dispatched were ordinary newsdesk reporters rather than specialists or feature writers. Some were physically unfit for the rigours of a campaign in the South Atlantic, and could contribute little to its coverage after the landing at San Carlos. The most serious breach of relations between the correspondents and the command occurred a few days before the final British attack, when it was discovered that one reporter had telephoned another correspondent on the civilian telephone circuit, and talked freely about the details of the forthcoming attack. Although it was later learned that the line had been cut well short of Port Stanley, Brigadier Thompson was sufficiently dismayed by the possibility of the conversation having been monitored by the enemy to consider changing his plans. Thereafter, all correspondents were forbidden to attend brigade or unit orders groups, and faith in the trustworthiness of the journalists was never recovered.

At home, very early in the war, the British press proved itself incapable of self-censorship. There was constant speculation about future British intentions, guided by battalions of retired admirals and generals. Any scrap of interesting information, such as the failure of Argentine bombs to explode, was published without thought for the operational risks. Newspapers announced that SAS and SBS patrols had landed on the Falklands often on the basis of the most unreliable American 'sources'. They discussed possible

dates for the launching of the British offensive, evidently taking
the view that the preservation of security was solely the problem
of the Ministry of Defence. The reason – though not the excuse –
for this was indeed the plethora of print censorship. Some tabloid
newspapers, notably the *Sun*, sought to work their readers into a
fever of mindless belligerence in the weeks after the task force
sailed. This performance reached its lowest level with the newspaper's 'Sponsor a Sidewinder' feature and competitions for abu-
sive jokes about Argentinians. The British press at large found it
difficult to set aside the normal rules of peacetime competitive
journalism in response to the demands of war. There seems a
strong case in any future British conflict for the wider use of 'D'
Notices prohibiting newspapers from reporting or speculating
about some sensitive areas.

This step could only be justified, however, if there was a far
more intelligent and enlighted public relations policy within the
Ministry of Defence. It should not be unrealistic to hope that
higher-calibre civilian public relations officers might be employed
at the ministry. One sensible course must be to make more use of
serving officers to handle the media in time of war. By far the best
public relations officers of the war were those appointed by individual units on the battlefield. It was extraordinary that the importance of news management was not recognised long before the San
Carlos landing, and a senior officer – of at least the rank of colonel
– sent south to handle it. The ministry appear to have acknowledged this in evidence after the war to the Commons defence
select committee. Whether Whitehall yet recognises the crucial
role that propaganda and well-managed publicity can play,
especially in limited conflicts, remains to be seen.

The Politicians' War

Just as war galvanises the executive branch of government, so it
tends to enervate the legislative. During the Falklands conflict even
the full cabinet found itself stranded in a no-man's-land between

the two. The cabinet was informed every Tuesday of the progress of the task force, but kept ignorant of any information which 'if leaked would cost lives'. Special sessions were only summoned to Downing Street when the war cabinet felt need of support: on 2 April, before the task force sailed; on 5 May to approve the Peruvian concessions; and on 18 May to receive the full chiefs of staff's presentation three days before the San Carlos landing. But full cabinet heard nothing of the differing views expressed in war cabinet (except on the grapevine), and therefore could not seriously challenge its collective decisions. The war cabinet was probably more constrained by opinion on the Tory backbenches than by other members of the government.

Parliament meanwhile found itself a frustrated bystander. For so many years, members of the House of Commons had spurned Foreign Office advice and policy, and done nothing to educate themselves about the Falklands issue before rushing to judgement on junior ministers. Even those who supported diplomatic compromise in office opposed it to score easy points in opposition. The mindless harrowing of Nicholas Ridley by such MPs as Peter Shore and Sir Bernard Braine on the floor of the House in December 1980 was a major contribution to the failure of diplomacy. The Commons' questioning of Richard Luce on 30 March 1982 undoubtedly encouraged Buenos Aires to hasten its invasion. The notorious Saturday debate on 3 April provoked a display of hysteria worthy of Galtieri's army council. The antagonistic structure of Britain's Parliament precluded the sort of informed concern that was essential to achieve a diplomatic settlement to the Falklands dispute. Once the task force had sailed, MPs lapsed into either belligerent enthusiasm for victory or outright opposition to force. Neither was particularly suitable in assisting a delicate escalation of pressure on Argentina to achieve a settlement which might stop short of war. It was noticeable that the war cabinet more often betrayed signs of stress – as in the week before Goose Green and after Fitzroy – when the Commons was in session and baying for action than when it was in recess.

The government bore some responsibility for this shortcoming. Neither the House of Commons nor any of its committees was kept abreast of official thinking as a Washington congressional committee would have been. Indeed, it was said that American politicians were being told more by the British Foreign Office and their own defence briefings than MPs were learning at the dispatch box from ministers. The only government step towards informing MPs was the Prime Minister's offer of confidential briefings for opposition party leaders. This was rejected by Michael Foot as too damaging to his freedom of action, and accepted only by David Steel and David Owen. As a result, the debates in the House of Commons during the negotiating phase revealed how ill-informed MPs were being left. It was the same vicious circle of secrecy breeding political inertia which had played a major part in the genesis of the conflict. More people could have been told more about the South Atlantic war without compromising military or diplomatic security in any way.

Finally, there remains the Prime Minister. The figure of Margaret Thatcher towers over the Falklands drama from its inception to the euphoria of the final triumph. Her personality matched its often eccentric sense of proportion. Her single-mindedness, her belief in the futility of negotiation, even her arch phraseology at moments of crisis, all seemed to armour her against any suspicion that this might be a dangerous, even absurd, adventure. 'Defeat – I do not recognise the meaning of the word!' and 'Rejoice, just rejoice!' passed into the Falklands lexicon. In a world which was accustomed to brand war as an ugly obscenity, the Prime Minister was determined that the Falklands conflict should be seen as a noble and principled crusade. Her longing undoubtedly matched the mood of the nation and captivated those working round her. Each of the participants interviewed for this book made similar remarks: 'It was Mrs Thatcher's war. She held us to it. She never seemed to flinch from her conviction about its course. She took the risks on her shoulders and she won. She emerged as a remarkable war leader.'

Nations are fortunate to have such leaders in time of conflict, but there are also advantages in leaders who avoid conflict in the first place. Some of Mrs Thatcher's critics point out that it was her Whitehall and her cabinet which deluded the Argentinians into believing that they could invade British territory with impunity. Others argue that, after the invasion, the dispatch of the task force was a costly and disproportionate overreaction to a situation in which neither Britain's borders nor her economic interests were at stake. A task force might have been necessary to save the Tories at the next general election, or at least to save Thatcher's administration from immediate collapse. But that should not be the reason for war.

Mrs Thatcher cannot escape her share of responsibility for the original debacle. She was unsympathetic to Ridley's final attempt to settle the Falklands issue by diplomatic compromise. She did not understand what he wanted to achieve, or what he feared. At the same time, she never considered reinforcing the Falklands' defences even in the light of Ridley's failure and Carrington's warnings. She was over-conscious of the threat from her right wing if she compromised diplomatically, yet reluctant to accept the economic price of military preparedness. Her inexperience in defence and foreign affairs was exacerbated by her lack of personal rapport with Lord Carrington and John Nott. Downing Street was clearly more vulnerable to external crisis than it should have been.

Even the most experienced Prime Minister is at the mercy of her briefings. In the first months of 1982, the JIC told Mrs Thatcher little to suggest an imminent crisis in the South Atlantic. When she was alerted by the South Georgia incident, she swiftly dispatched *Endurance*, though she seems to have been unsure what to do with it next. She sent submarines when she was warned of the serious threat the weekend before the invasion. Yet it was only on Thursday, 1 April, taking strength from Sir Henry Leach, that she began to feel her way towards a dramatic, definitive response to the Argentine threat.

Mrs Thatcher's failure to send an ultimatum to Argentina is

one of the mysteries of the pre-invasion week and is known still to exercise a number of those present at Thatcher's various crisis meetings. The usual reason given is that the sending of the task force was seen as part of a diplomatic exercise, not a military one. It is also said that, even if Britain had told Buenos Aires in the most unmistakable terms that massive retaliation would follow any invasion, it would not have been believed. Yet that is hindsight. There is force in the argument of a senior Argentine official: 'We simply never dreamed for one minute you would send a task force. Had we known then what we know now, the sceptics would have had powerful evidence to counter Anaya's proposal for invasion.' The sense of two nations drifting almost unintentionally to war that first week of the crisis is a vivid one, and makes the conflict all the more tragic. In an age of 'total communication', the lack of clear advance signals between Britain and Argentina is astonishing and a poor comment on both governments.

Once Mrs Thatcher had become convinced that a task force was feasible, she was utterly tenacious. Almost alone among her colleagues, she maintained from the earliest days that only a task force, rather than diplomacy, could achieve the cabinet's declared aim of total removal of the invader from the islands and the restoration of British administration. She wavered only once and briefly in her commitment to this aim – during cabinet debate on the Peruvian initiative (see pages 210–11). Otherwise, her certainty of Argentine intransigence, fully justified in the event, reflected a remarkable ability to think herself into the junta's mind. Haig repeatedly commented to his staff on the uncanny similarity between the two protagonists' intransigence. Mrs Thatcher sensed Galtieri's precarious political position, judging that he could no more withdraw his troops and survive than she could withhold sending the task force.

Mrs Thatcher's judgement of her own position is debatable. Had she treated the loss of the Falklands as a tragic fait accompli, accepted the resignation of her Foreign Office team and mobilised whatever international support she could to secure better terms for the islanders, she would certainly have endured painful and traumatic moments in Parliament. However, supported by military advice available to her that a task force would be a most risky undertaking, she would certainly have found majority support in Parliament. Her own backbenchers would have been disgruntled and furious, but they would scarcely have evicted her in favour of a 'task force faction' – which Labour would surely have opposed. And for the Tories to have risked a general election on the issue would have been suicidal. Even had Mrs Thatcher felt personally obliged to resign, as Whitelaw suggested she would, this would not have brought down the Tory government.

Yet costly and destructive wars are not justified by party considerations. On 2 April, any responsible government had to ask itself three questions: Was the dispatch of a task force militarily sound? Was it essential to honour Britain's obligation to the Falkland Islanders? And was it politically desirable to set an example against aggression, to restore the self-respect of the British people and to maintain the credibility of their defences?

On the first question, John Nott's initial hesitancy and that of some service chiefs was soundly based. It is hard to escape the conclusion that Sir Henry Leach's enthusiasm for sending the navy to the South Atlantic was, albeit subconsciously, fortified by his enthusiasm to show what his service could still do. Mrs Thatcher sent the task force with full awareness that she was taking a gamble, but without knowledge of the true odds against success. The decision was further complicated by the fact that, on 2 April, the finer points of strategic balance did not seem to matter. She herself may have believed from the beginning that Britain would have to fight. But most of her colleagues, whose support she needed to dispatch the fleet, believed that nothing worse than a naval demonstration in the South Atlantic was at stake. Had the gamble failed, or even had it succeeded through no effort on Mrs Thatcher's part, the task force could have been branded a reckless use of Britain's armed forces. Since it did succeed, and did so in large measure through her qualities of leadership, she is entitled to the credit for luck and judgement. It is doubtful if any other British Prime Minister since Eden, with the possible exception of James Callaghan, would have sent the amphibious task force and supported it right through to victory. The soundness of the operation must in this case be assessed by its success.

As to the obligations to the Falklanders, they must be the judge of whether they feel the debt of honour to them has been met. They might reasonably claim the British government's duty was to deter the Argentinians from invading in the first place rather than turn their homes into battlefields. A war on the islands was virtually certain to destroy the fragile lifestyle they were hoping to preserve, and indeed it has done so.

Self-determination cannot be considered an absolute concept. Were wider issues not involved it would have been patently disproportionate to send 1,000 men to their deaths simply to enable 1,800 British citizens (and half-citizens) to keep the government of their choice. It was inevitable that what was won back by force would have to be retained by force, and for a sufficiently long time to render inconceivable any hope that the islands might be restored to their previous isolated state. On this subject, all that can be said is that if the islanders now want to be left alone, they should settle as soon as possible for the solution available to them in 1981, of 'leaseback'. It is still the only solution which might ensure their security from risk of further attack without a massive and dominating British military presence. But it will only be achievable through a positive act of will on the islanders' part.

It is the answer to the third question which will dictate Mrs Thatcher's claim to the respect of history. Arguments for war based on the principle of 'setting the world an example' are always dangerous. They can be used to justify quite disproportionate responses, as occurred in South-east Asia in the 1960s and 1970s. They tend to be selective: why for instance did Britain not use force in 1965 to uphold the concept of majority self-determination in Rhodesia? And there is the risk, as an American official remarked during the Falklands war, that 'Far from proving that

aggression does not pay, Britain has only proved that resisting it
can be ridiculously expensive.'

Future historians of this war cannot let the matter rest there.
Their task will be not simply to assess the actual consequence of
the operation, but the hypothetical consequence of it not having
been fought. What would have been the impact on both strong
and weak nations if Argentina had been left in victorious possession of territory seized by force in the course of UN negotiations? Mrs Thatcher and her war cabinet cannot be accused of
seeking war eagerly, or of cynicism in the pursuit of peace, though
certainly some ministers thought a peaceful settlement more
feasible than others. The compromises offered in good faith
under the terms of the Peruvian and UN plans were substantive
retreats from the British government's initial promises to Parliament. They would have granted Argentina considerable reward for
her aggression and incidentally caused a major political crisis in
Britain. They were justified in the cause of averting war. These
concessions were plainly rejected by Argentina. Those who argue
that such conflicts should be made the testbed of a new international order must face the fact that the Argentine invasion was
a breach of that order and there was not the slightest chance of
any UN or other force acting as policeman in Britain's place. It was
a case of action by Britain or a victory for armed aggression over
peaceful negotiation. It was an argument which the large majority
of world states were ready to acknowledge throughout the conflict.
It requires a strange ethic to maintain that the world is a less safe
place now the crisis is over.

The case is more than that. The fact that a conclusion to any
political or military event may be inexact and unquantifiable must
not be allowed to rule it out of account. Had Britain left the
Falklanders to their fate on 2 April, the British people's respect for
themselves and their confidence in their political and military
leadership would have experienced a severe blow. True, colonial
wars can have dangerous side effects on the nations which fight
them. A people can turn to jingoism as they watch a distant game,

played on their behalf by professionals safely out of reach of homes and loved ones. Yet the popular media's image of the Falklands war should not become the actual one. On 14 June, Britons did not fill Trafalgar Square with the hysterical chants of victory. In many ways their response was more dignified and less strident than that of their leaders, as it was when the task force sailed. This was a war which the British people should not have had to fight. Yet after so many years of what seemed like national failure and decline, they were confronted with a disaster which they still had the strength to rectify. They were reassured by the way the services performed. They were pleased that a job which had to be done was done so well. They felt justified in a renewed national pride and self-confidence.

Appendix A: Chronology of Military and Political Events

2 April	Argentine invasion of Falklands	British cabinet approves sending of task force to South Atlantic
3 April		UN passes Resolution 502 demanding Argentine withdrawal
5 April	Carrier group sails from Portsmouth	
7 April		Reagan approves Haig peace mission
8 April		Haig team arrives in London
9 April	3 Commando Brigade sails aboard *Canberra*	EEC approves economic sanctions against Argentina
10 April		Haig arrives in Buenos Aires
12 April	Maritime exclusion zone comes into operation round Falklands Submarine *Spartan* on station off Port Stanley	Haig returns to London
14 April	Argentine fleet leaves Puerto Belgrano	Haig returns to Washington to brief Reagan
15 April	British destroyer group takes up holding position in mid-Atlantic	Haig back in Buenos Aires

17 April	Admiral Fieldhouse chairs conference at Ascension with Admiral Woodward and 3 Brigade	Haig presents junta with 5-point plan Service councils debate terms
18 April	Argentine carrier returns to port with engine trouble	
19 April		Argentine response to Haig passed to London
21 April	South Georgia operation begins	
22 April		Pym to Washington with UK response to Haig
24 April	Woodward's task group rendezvous with mid-Atlantic destroyers	
25 April	South Georgia recaptured	
26 April	'Defence area' declared round fleet	
27 April	Chiefs of staff present Operation Sutton to war cabinet	Haig's 'final package' sent to London
29 April	Task force arrives at exclusion zone Vulcan arrives at Ascension	
30 April	Total exclusion zone comes into force General Moore flies to Ascension for conference with Brigadier Thompson	Reagan declares US support for Britain, promises 'matériel' aid
1 May	Initial SAS and SBS landings on the Falklands First Vulcan raid on Port Stanley, Sea Harrier raids and naval bombardment	Pym returns to Washington as 'ally'
2 May	*General Belgrano* sunk on orders of war cabinet	Pym returns to Washington as 'ally'

3 May	Argentine patrol boats attacked	Galtieri rejects Peruvian plan, citing *Belgrano*
4 May	*Sheffield* sunk. First Sea Harrier shot down	
5 May		Emergency meeting of full cabinet approves acceptance of Peruvian plan
6 May	Two Harriers crash in fog	Junta rejects Peruvian plan for second time
7 May	Total exclusion zone extended to 12 miles off Argentine coast	De Cuellar discusses 'ideas' in New York with British and Argentine delegations
8 May	War cabinet dispatches landing force south from Ascension	
9 May	Trawler *Narwhal* attacked Final plans drawn up for San Carlos landing site	
11 May		Walters sent by Haig to Buenos Aires
12 May	QE2 leaves Southampton with 5 Brigade aboard	Junta concedes 'sovereignty not a precondition' to de Cuellar
14 May	SAS attack on Pebble Island	Parsons and Henderson summoned back to London for consultation
16 May		Chequers war cabinet draws up final British proposals for de Cuellar Parsons returns to New York
18 May	San Carlos landing plan goes to full cabinet Landing force rendezvous with Woodward's task group	

19 May	War cabinet gives Woodward go-ahead for landing	
20 May		Thatcher tells Commons of collapse of peace process. White paper published
21 May	San Carlos landing begins *Ardent* sunk. 16 Argentine aircraft lost	Open debate commences at UN Security Council
23 May	7 Argentine aircraft lost	
24 May	*Antelope* sunk	
25 May	*Coventry* and *Atlantic Conveyor* sunk	
26 May		War cabinet questions lack of movement out of bridgehead. UN Resolution 505 bids de Cuellar to seek settlement
27 May	3 Para and 45 Commando set out for Teal Inlet SAS land in strength on Mount Kent 2 Para set out for Goose Green	
28 May	Battle of Goose Green 5 Brigade trans-ships from *QE2* at South Georgia	
30 May	General Moore arrives at San Carlos	
31 May	42 Commando land on Mount Kent	
1 June	5 Brigade begins disembarkation at San Carlos	War cabinet debate Foreign Office–Washington peace proposals Further Shackleton Report ordered

2 June	2 Para leapfrog to Bluff Cove	Argentine military envoys arrive at UN: 'ready to surrender to UN'
3 June		Versailles summit opens Reagan's 5-point plan given to Britain
4 June		Britain vetoes ceasefire resolution in Security Council US vetoes then tries to change mind
5 June	Scots Guards embark for Fitzroy	
6 June	Scots Guards land at Fitzroy, Welsh Guards embark for same	
8 June	Disaster at Fitzroy. *Galahad* and *Tristram* bombed: 51 die Moore finalises battle plan for Stanley	War cabinet asked not to reveal Fitzroy casualties
11 June	Battle of Port Stanley begins Mount Longdon, Harriet, Two Sisters	
12 June	5 Brigade moves into position	Thatcher and Nott go to Northwood
13 June	Battle for Tumbledown and Wireless Ridge	
14 June	Argentine surrender at Port Stanley	

Appendix B:

The Falkland Islands Task Force

Senior Commanders

Chief of the Defence Staff Admiral of the Fleet
Sir Terence Lewin, GCB, MVO, DSC

First Sea Lord Admiral Sir Henry Leach, GCB, ADC

Commander-in-Chief Fleet Admiral Sir John Fieldhouse, KCB

BRITISH NAVAL FORCES COMMITTED TO THE FALKLANDS TASK FORCE

Flag Officer, First Flotilla Rear-Admiral John Woodward

Commodore Amphibious Warfare Michael Clapp

Commodore of the Royal Fleet Auxiliary Captain S. C. Dunlop

Notes   Dates given when ships entered operational area.
The numbers for aircraft are those that were on board the aircraft carriers
at the beginning of hostilities

Abbreviations   ASW = Anti-Submarine Warfare   RFA = Royal Fleet Auxiliary
Char = Chartered   Ro-Ro = Roll-on, Roll-off
GWS = Guided Weapons System   SAM = Surface to Air Missile
Req = Requisitioned   SSM = Surface to Surface Missile

Aircraft Carriers

Hermes   25.4.82   Capt. L. E. Middleton

28,700 tons   2   Quad Seacat SAM launchers (GWS.22)
1,350 crew   12   Sea Harriers
28 knots   18   Sea King

Invincible   25.4.82   Capt. J. J. Black, MBE

19,810 tons   2   Sea Dart SAM launchers
1,000 crew   8   Sea Harriers
28 knots   5   Sea King

Destroyers and Frigates

Type 82

7,100 tons   2   Sea Dart SAM launchers
407 crew   1   Ikara ASW launcher
29 knots   1   4.5 in gun + 2 × 20 mm Cannons
                    Facility for a Wasp helicopter

Bristol   23.5.82   Capt. A. Grose

County Class

6,200 tons	4	MM.38 Exocet SAM
471 crew	2	Seaslug Mk. 2 SAM launchers
30 knots	2	Quad Seacat SAM launchers (GWS. 22)
	2	4.5 in guns
	1	Wessex HAS.3 ASW helicopter

Antrim   17.4.82   (damaged)   Capt. B. G. Young

Glamorgan   25.4.82   (damaged)   Capt. M. E. Barrow

Type 42

4,100 tons	2	Sea Dart SAM launchers
268 crew	6	Mark 32 ASW torpedo tubes
29 knots	1	4.5 in gun + 2 × 20 mm cannons
	1	Sea Lynx HAS. 2 ASW helicopter

Cardiff   23.5.82   Capt. M. G. T. Harris

Coventry   20.4.82   (sunk)   Capt. David Hart-Dyke

Exeter   19.5.82   Capt. H. M. Balfour, MVO

Glasgow   20.4.82   (damaged)   Capt. A. P. Hoddinott, OBE

Sheffield   20.4.82   (sunk)   Capt. S. Salt

Type 22

4,000 tons	12	Sea Wolf SAM launchers
223 crew	4	MM.38 Exocet SSM
30 knots	6	Mark 32 ASW torpedo tubes
	2	40mm guns
	2	Sea Lynx HAS.2 ASW helicopters

Brilliant 20.4.82 (damaged) Capt. J. F. Coward

Broadsword 25.4.82 (damaged) Capt. W. R. Canning

Type 21

3,250 tons	4	MM.38 Exocet SSM
235 crew	1	4.5 in gun + 2 × 20 mm cannons
30 knots	1	Quad Seacat SAM launcher (GWS.24)
	6	Mark 32 ASW torpedo tubes
	1	Sea Lynx HAS.2 ASW helicopter

Active 23.5.82 Cdr. P. C. B. Canter

Alacrity 25.4.82 Cdr. C. J. S.Craig

Ambuscade 18.5.82 Cdr. P. J. Mosse

Antelope 18.5.82 (sunk) Cdr. N. Tobin

Ardent 13.5.82 (sunk) Cdr. A. West

Arrow 20.4.82 (damaged) Cdr. P. J. Bootherstone

Avenger 23.5.82 (damaged) Capt. H. M. White

Leander class – Exocet Group

3,200 tons	4	MM.38 Exocet SSM
223 crew	3	Quad Seacat SAM launchers (GWS.22)
28 knots	6	Mark 32 ASW torpedo tubes
	1	40 mm gun
	1	Wasp (or Sea Lynx HAS.2) ASW helicopter

Argonaut   13.5.82   (damaged)   Capt. C. H. Layman, MVO

Penelope   23.5.82   Cdr. P. V. Rickard

Minerva   23.5.82   Cdr. S. H. G. Johnston

Leander class – Broad-beamed converted Group

2,962 tons	12	Sea Wolf SAM launchers
260 crew	4	MM.38 Exocet SSM
28 knots	6	Mark 32 ASW torpedo tubes
	1	Sea Lynx HAS.2 ASW helicopter

Andromeda   23.5.82   Capt. J. L. Weatherall

Rothesay class

2,800 tons	1	Quad Seacat SAM launcher (GWS.20)
235 crew	2	4.5 in guns
30 knots	1	Limbo depth-charge mortar
	1	Wasp ASW helicopter

Yarmouth   25.4.82   Cdr. A. Morton

Plymouth   17.4.82   (damaged)   Capt. D. Pentreath

Ice Patrol ship

3,600 tons   2 20mm cannons
                  2 Wasp ASW helicopters

Endurance   Capt. N. J. Barker

Submarines

Swiftsure class

4,500 tons   5 21 in. torpedo tubes with 25 Mark 24 Modified
97 crew   Tigerfish torpedoes
30 knots

Spartan   12.4.82   Cdr. J. B. Taylor
Splendid   19.4.82   Cdr. R. C. Lane-Nott

Churchill & Valiant class

4,900 tons   6 21 in. torpedo tubes with 32 Mark 24 Modified
103 crew   Tigerfish torpedoes
30 knots

Conqueror   16.4.82   Cdr. C. L. Wreford-Brown

Valiant   16.5.82   Cdr. T. M. Le Marchand

Courageous 30.5.82   Cdr. R. T. N. Best

Oberon & Porpoise class

2,410 tons   8 21 in torpedo tubes (6 bow, 2 aft)
69 crew   Mark 24 Modified Tigerfish torpedoes
12 knots
17 dived

Onyx   28.5.82   Lt.-Cdr. A. P. Johnson

Amphibious Warfare Vessels

Landing Platform Dock (LPD)

12,120 tons   4 Quad Seacat SAM launchers (GWS.20)
580 crew   2 40 mm guns
21 knots   4 Landing Craft Unit (LCU) (100 tons load each)
                 4 Landing Craft Vehicle & Personnel (LCVP) (5 ton load
                    each)
                    Facility for 5 Wessex or 4 Sea King helicopters
                    Accommodates 400 troops for extended period or
                    700 troops for short-time

Fearless   13.5.82   Capt. E. S. J. Larken
Intrepid   13.5.82   Capt. P. G. V. Dingemans

Landing Ship Logistic (LSL)

5,674 tons	2	40 mm guns
68 crew		Facility for helicopter operations
17 knots		Accommodates 340 troops for extended period or 534 for short-time
		(These ships are RFA-manned)

Sir Bedivere	18.5.82	Capt P. J. McCarthy
Sir Galahad	8.5.82	(sunk) Capt P. J. G.Roberts
Sir Geraint	8.5.82	Capt. D. E. Lawrence
Sir Percivale	8.5.82	Capt. A. F. Pitt
Sir Tristram	8.5.82	(damaged) Capt. G. R. Green
Sir Lancelot	8.5.82	(damaged) Capt. C. A. Purtcher-Wydenbruck

Troop Transports and Equipment Ferries of the Royal Fleet Auxiliary and ships taken up from trade

QE2	23.5.82	Req Cunard Liner Facilities for helicopter operations	67,000 tons
Canberra	13.5.82	Req P&O Liner Facilities for helicopter operations	44,807 tons
Norland	13.5.82	Req P&O Ro-Ro ferry	12,000 tons
Tor Caledonia	6.6.82	Req Whitwill Ro-Ro ferry	10,000 tons
St Edmunds	7.6.82	Req Sealink Ro-Ro ferry	9,000 tons
Nordic Ferry	25.5.82	Req Townsend Thoresen Ro-Ro ferry	6,500 tons
Baltic Ferry	25.5.82	Req Townsend Thoresen Ro-Ro ferry	6,500 tons

Elk 13.5.82	Req P&O Ro-Ro ferry 2 × 40 mm guns.	5,463 tons
Europic 13.5.82	Req Townsend Thoresen Ro-Ro ferry	4,190 tons
Atlantic Conveyor 13.5.82 (sunk)	Req Cunard Container Ship converted to aircraft ferry	14,946 tons
Atlantic Causeway 25.5.82	Req Cunard Container Ship converted to aircraft ferry	14,946 tons
Contender Bezant 7.6.82	Req Sea Containers Ltd container ship	11,000 tons

Supply Ships

Fort Austin 26.4.82	Cdre. S. C. Dunlop, MBE RFA Fleet replenishment ship. Facilities for 4 Sea King helicopters	23,600 tons 185 crew 22 knots
Fort Grange 26.5.82	Capt. D. G. M. Averill, CBE	
Resource 25.4.82	Capt. B. A. Seymour RFA Fleet replenishment ship Facilities for 4 Sea King helicopters	22,890 tons 171 crew 21 knots
Regent 8.5.82	Capt. J. Logan	
Stromness 13.5.82	Capt J. B. Dickinson RFA Stores support ship	16,792 tons
Saxonia 20.5.82	Req Cunard freighter	8,000 tons
Lycaon 21.5.82	Char China Mutual Steamship freighter	11,804 tons
Geestport 6.6.82	Char freighter	9,750 tons

Support Ships

Uganda 8.5.82	Req P&O Liner Converted into a hospital ship	16,907 tons
Hydra 14.5.82	Cdr. R. J. Campbell RFA Casualty ferry	2,744 tons
Herald 15.5.82	Cdr. R. I. C. Halliday RFA Casualty ferry	2,744 tons
Hecla 9.5.82	Capt. G. L. Hope RFA Casualty ferry	2,744 tons
British Enterprise	Req BUE North Sea oil-rig support ship (manned-submersible support)	1,600 tons
Stena Seaspread 8.5.82	Req Stena North Sea oil-rig support ship	6,061 tons
Stena Inspector	Req Stena North Sea oil-rig support ship	7,000 tons
Engadine 2.6.82	RFA Helicopter support ship	9,000 tons
Pict 18.5.82	Req United Trawlers. Minesweeper tender	1,478 tons
Cordella 18.5.82	Req J. Marr Trawler Minesweeper	1,238 tons
Farnella 18.5.82	Req J. Marr Trawler Minesweeper	1,207 tons
Junella 18.5.82	Req J. Marr trawler Minesweeper	1,615 tons
Northella 18.5.82	Req J. Marr trawler Minesweeper	1,238 tons
Salvageman 2.5.82	Req United Towing ocean tug (2,000 hp)	1,568 tons
Yorkshireman 9.5.82	Req United Towing ocean tug (9,000 hp)	689 tons
Irishman 9.5.82	Req United Towing ocean tug (9,000 hp)	689 tons

Wimpey Seahorse 2.6.82	Req Wimpey Marine ocean tug	1,599 tons
St Helena	Req United International Bank Ltd islands supply ship	3,150 tons
Iris 21.5.82	Char British Telecom cable ship	3,873 tons

Tankers

Bayleaf 9.6.S2	Capt. A. E. T. Hunter RFA tanker	40,000 tons
Scottish Eagle 10.6.82	Char King Line tanker	33,000 tons
Alvega	Char Finance for Shipping Ltd tanker	33,000 tons
Balder London	Char Lloyds of London tanker	33,000 tons
Olmeda 25.4.82	Capt. G. P. Overbury RFA tanker	36,000 tons
Olna 23.5.82	Capt. J. A. Bailey RFA tanker	36,000 tons
Tidespring 17.4.82	Capt S. Redmond RFA tanker	27,400 tons
Tidepool 13.5.82	Capt. J. McCullough RFA tanker	27,400 tons
Pearleaf 4.5.82	RFA tanker	25,790 tons
Fort Toronto 12.5.82	Char Canadian Pacific water tanker	19,982 tons
Eburna 27.5.82	Char Shell tanker	19,763 tons
G. A. Walker	Char Canadian Pacific tanker	18,744 tons
Dart 14.5.82	Char BP tanker	15,650 tons
Test 21.5.82	Char BP tanker	15,653 tons
Tay 23.4.82	Char BP tanker	15,650 tons
Trent 5.5.82	Char BP tanker	15,649 tons
Wye 25.5.82	Char BP tanker	15,649 tons
Esk 22.4.82	Char BP tanker	15,643 tons

Avon	Char BP tanker	15,640 tons
Anco Charger 15.5.82	Char P&O tanker	15,974 tons
Blue Rover 2.5.82	Capt. D. A. Reynolds	
	RFA tanker	11,522 tons

Naval Air Squadrons deployed in the South Atlantic

800, 801, 809*, 899	Sea Harriers
845, 846	Mk.iv Sea King helicopters
847*, 848*	Wessex v helicopters
820, 824, 825*	Mk.ii anti-submarine Sea Kings
826	Mk.v anti-submarine Sea Kings
737	Wessex iii helicopters
815	Lynx helicopters
829	Wasp helicopters

A total of 171 naval aircraft were deployed, most permanently based aboard ships of the Royal Navy and Royal Fleet Auxiliary, but some transported south and subsequently operated from shore bases.

---

* Squadrons specially formed for Task Force operations.

BRITISH LAND FORCES COMMITTED TO THE FALKLANDS TASK FORCE

Land force commander Major-General Jeremy Moore, Royal Marines
[arrived at San Carlos 30.5.82]

Deputy land force commander Brigadier John Waters

HQ 3 Commando Brigade
Brigadier Julian Thompson, RM

29 Commando Regiment Royal Artillery
>   Lt.-Col. Mike Holroyd-Smith
>   18 × 105 mm light guns + 148 Naval Gunfire Observation Battery

59 Independent Commando Squadron Royal Engineers
>   Major Roderick Macdonald

40 Commando RM
>   Lt.-Col. Malcolm Hunt

42 Commando RM
>   Lt.-Col. Nick Vaux

45 Commando RM
>   Lt.-Col. Andrew Whitehead

2nd Battalion Parachute Regiment plus attached units
>   Lt.-Col. Herbert Jones
>   29 Field Battery RA, Blowpipe Troop of 43 Air Defence Battery,
>   Field Troop 9 Parachute Engineer Squadron, Troop 16 Field
>   Ambulance, Detachment 81 Ordnance Company, 613 TACP

3rd Battalion Parachute Regiment plus attached units
>   Lt.-Col. Hew Pike
>   I × Section Field Ambulance, 1 × Ordnance Coy Detachment

Commando Logistics Regiment RM
       Lt.-Col. Ivar Helberg

3 Commando Brigade HQ and Signals Squadron RM
       Major Richard Dixon

3 Commando Brigade Air Squadron
       Major Peter Cameron
       11 × Gazelle, 6 × Scout helicopters

2 × Medium Reconnaissance Troops, B Squadron the Blues & Royals
       Lt. Mark Coreth
       4 × Scorpion, 4 × Scimitar Combat Tracked Reconnaissance
       Vehicles, 1 × Samson Field Recovery Tractor

T Battery 12 Air Defence Regiment
       12 × Rapier missile launchers

Air Defence Troop
       12 × Blowpipe missile launchers

1 × Raiding Squadron RM
       Capt. Chris Baxter
       17 × Rigid Raiding Craft

Mountain and Arctic Warfare Cadre, RM
       Capt. Rod Boswell

2, 3 & 6 Sections Special Boat Squadron, RM
       Major Jonathan Thomson
       20 all ranks + 11 strong command element with naval task group,
       3 × 4-man detachments and 2-man command element in
       submarine *Conqueror*, 22 all ranks in further submarine

D & G Squadrons 22nd SAS Regiment
       Lt.-Col. Michael Rose
       100 all ranks + 7-man command element in assault ships,
       remainder with naval battle group

3 × Tactical Air Control Parties

Air Maintenance Group

Rear Link Detachment 30 Signal Regiment (Satellite and High Frequency
communications)

3 × Mexefloat detachments 17 Port Regiment Royal Corps of Transport

5 × Landing Ship Logistics Detachments 17 Port Regiment

3 × Surgical Support Teams

Postal Courier Communications Unit Detachment of 1 PC Regiment 402

Detachment RAF Special Forces

Detachment 47 Air Despatch Squadron RCT

Detachment 49 EOD Squadron 33 Engineer Regiment
> 1 × two-man bomb disposal team

Y Troop Detachment (Communications)

Commando Forces Band (stretcher-bearers)

HQ 5 Infantry Brigade
Brigadier Anthony Wilson

Began landing at San Carlos, 1 June 1982

2nd Battalion Scots Guards
> Lt.-Col. Michael Scott

1st Battalion Welsh Guards
> Lt.-Col. John Rickett

1st/7th Duke of Edinburgh Own Gurkha Rifles
> Lt.-Col. David Morgan

97 Battery Royal Artillery
> 6 × 105mm light gun

HQ 4 Field Regiment RA

656 Squadron Army Air Corps
> 6 × Gazelle, 3 × Scout helicopter

10 Field Workshop REME

16 Field Ambulance

81 Ordnance Company

Forward Air Control Party
> 2 × FAC

ROYAL AIR FORCE SQUADRONS EMPLOYED IN THE SOUTH ATLANTIC

1	Harrier GR3s transported on *Atlantic Conveyor* or flown directly to the Task Group, operating from HMS *Hermes*
55, 57	Victor tankers
44, 50, 101	elements of Vulcan squadrons engaged in bomber sorties
42, 120, 201, 206	Nimrod maritime reconnaissance
24, 30, 47, 70	Hercules C-130 transport aircraft, some specially fitted with long-range tanks
10	VC10s operating Brize Norton–Ascension Island link
63	RAF Regiment equipped with Blindfire Rapier embarked with 5 Infantry Brigade
18	Chinook helicopters – 4 embarked on *Atlantic Conveyor*, of which 1 became operational; 4 embarked on *Contender Bezant*, which became operational ashore on 14 June

PRINCIPAL COMBAT AIRCRAFT ENGAGED
IN THE SOUTH ATLANTIC

Harrier GR3

Speed   maximum at low altitude, 640 knots / 1,185 kph / 736 mph

Payload   maximum external weapon load, 5,000 lb / 2,270 kg

Range   with one in-flight refuelling over 3,000 nautical miles / 5,560 km /
3,455 statute miles

Sea Harrier

Speed   maximum level speed, as GR3

Payload   maximum weapon load, 8,000 lb / 3,630 kg

Range   varies according to mission performed: high-altitude intercept
radius with 3 minutes combat and reserves for vertical landing
400 nautical miles / 750 km / 460 statute miles; strike radius,
250 nautical miles 463 km / 288 statute miles

Pucara

Speed   maximum level speed at 3,000 m or 9,845 feet altitude, 270 knots / 500 kph / 310 mph

Payload total external stores, 1,620 kg / 3,571 lb

Range   with maximum fuel at 5,000 m
or 16,400 feet altitude, 1,641 nautical
miles / 3,042 km / 1,890 statute miles

Mirage III-E

Speed   maximum level speed at sea level, 750 knots / 1,390 kph / 863 mph

Payload approx 3,000 lb

Range   combat radius, ground attack. 647 nautical miles / 1,200 km / 745 statute miles

Super Etendard

Speed   maximum level speed at low altitude, 650 knots / 1,204 kph / 748 mph

Payload maximum weapon load, internal fuel only, 4,630 lb / 2,100 kg

Range   radius of action, with AM.39 Exocet, 350 nautical miles / 650 km / 403 statute miles

Appendix C:
The Falklands Honours List

CIVIL

Life Peer

Baron

Admiral of the Fleet Sir Terence Thornton LEWIN, lately Chief of the Defence Staff

Knight

Rex Masterman HUNT, HM Civil Commissioner, Falkland Islands

Order of the Bath

CB

K J PRITCHARD, Ass Under-sec., MoD

Order of St Michael and St George

CMG

D H Anderson, FCO

Order of the British Empire

CBE

Capt D A Ellerby, Master, MV *Norland*

I McL Fairfield, Chmn and Chief Exec Chemring

Miss P M Hutchinson, HM Ambassador Montevideo

R T Jackling, Ass Sec, MoD

Capt D J Scott-Masson, Master, SS *Canberra*

Capt J P Morton, Master, MV Elk

N H Nicholls, Ass Sec, MoD

E J Risness, Dep Ch Sc Off., MoD

W B Slater, Man Dir, Cunard Steam-Ship Co

J R C Thomas, Dep Ch Sc Off., MoD.

OBE

P D Adams, Prin Sci Off., MoD

R G Algar, Sen Prin, MoD

The Rev H Bagnall, Dean of Christchurch, Falkland Is.

M J Beynon, Chief Map Res Off., MoD

Mrs A A Bleaney, Actg Sen MO, Falkland Is

Mrs M J Bourne, Sen Prin Sci Off., MoD

R Butcher, Man Dir. Wimpey Marine

D W Chalmers, Constructor (C), MoD

Capt W J C Clarke, Master, MV *Europic Ferry*

Capt A Fulton, Master, cable ship *Iris*

R O Gates, Exec Dir. Aircraft Engineering, Marshall of Cambridge (Eng) Ltd.

A J Glasgow, Pro Dir. Marconi Underwater Systems

E J Harvey, Prin Prof and Tech Off., MoD

S S Holness, Sen Prin, Department of Trade

V E Horsfield, Works Man. Woodford Aircraft Group, British Aerospace

C Hulse, FCO

Miss M M Jones, FCO

D Lewis, Prof and Tech Supt, MoD

A F G Moss, Div Man. HM Dockyard, Gibraltar

J P Raby, Proj Dir. Humber Graving Dock and Eng Co Ltd

Capt D M Rundle, Master, MV *British Wye*

Capt M J Slack, Master, MV *Wimpey Seahorse*

The Rt Rev Mgr D M Spraggon, Prefect Apost, Falkland Is.

R S Tee, Prin Prof and Tech Off. (Con), MoD

P Varnish, Prin Sci Off., MoD

R Watson, Local Dir. Qual Ass. Swan Hunter Shipbuilders Ltd

R Weatherburn, Sen Prin Sci Off., MoD

J A Weldon, Prin Prof and Tech Off., MoD.

MBE

Mrs V E Bennett, Actg Matron, Stanley Hosp. Falkland Is

Mrs J H Bolton, Cler Off., MoD

C M Boyne, Sen Sci Off., MoD

D L Breen, Radar Systems Eng Marconi Radar Systems Ltd

R A Brown, Marine Services Off. II (Eng), MoD

T J Carey, Elec Supt, Falkland Is

E D Carr, Reg Man. Southampton, Genl Coun of British Shipping

A F G Collins, Steelwork Prod Man, Vosper Ship Repairers Ltd

A J Collman, Prof and Tech Off. II, MoD

P M J Cook, Prof and Tech Off. II, MoD

F J Cooper, Passenger and Cargo Man. Asst, British Transport Docks Board

D J Cormick, Sen Field Eng, Marconi Space and Defence Systems

R A Drew, FCO

Miss P Durling, HEO, MoD

S Earnshaw, Ch Marine Supt, Thoresen Car Ferries

Miss M G Elphinstone, Volunteer MO, Falkland Is

Miss R M Elsdon, Sen Nursing Sister, SS *Canberra*

J R R Fox, Radio News Reptr, BBC

J A French, Sen Sci Off., MoD

B A Gorringe, Catering Man Grade II, Staff Restaurant, MoD

E M Goss, Manager, Goose Green Farm, Falkland Is

M J S Hatton, Prof and Tech Off. II, Dept of Trade

Miss S M Hill, Cler Asst, Dept of Trade

GWT Hodge, Prof and Tech Off. II, MoD

W Hunter, Prof and Tech Off. II, MoD

R D Lawrence, HEO, Cabinet Office

R G J Lloyd, Asst Man. Warehouse and Distrib Services, NAAFI

D McAlpin, Flt Trials Eng. Ferranti

W Robert McQueen, Sen Sci Off., Met Off.

D Monument, Maint Supt. P & O Steam Navigation Company

T R Morse, FCO

Mrs V A Mothershaw, Exec Off., MoD

Mrs D B M Murray, Sen Sci Off., MoD

Mrs P M Nutbeem, Chairwoman, 16 Field Amb, RAMC Wives' Club, Aldershot

Sqdn Ldr T J Palmer, RAF (Retd), HQUK Land Forces, MoD

Miss E Patten, Senior Welfare Off., St John and Red Cross Service Hospitals Welfare

T J Peck, Coun. Leg. Cncl, Falkland Is

D Place, Water Supervisor, Falkland Is

J T Price, Exec Off., MoD

J F Quirk, Sen Exec Off., RN Supply and Transport Service

P Robinson, Higher Sci Off., MoD

J R P Rodigan, Prof and Tech Off. II, MoD

K W Shackleton, Contract Eng., Ames Crosta Babcock Ltd

M S Shears, Prodn Man., Vosper Thorneycroft (UK) Ltd

Capt D Sims, Sen Cargo Surveyor, Hogg Robinson (GFA) Ltd

Miss A Slaymaker, Cler Off., MoD

Sqdn Ldr J M Smith, RAF (Retd), Sen Op Man., Dynamics Group, British Aerospace

R L Start, SEO, Dept of Trade

Mrs A E Thorne, Exec Off., MoD

J Turner, Sen Sci Off., Met Off.

P J Watts, Dir. Broadcasting Svce, Falkland Is

R S Whitley, Vet Off., Falkland Is.

British Empire Medal

A J Aldred, MoD

A A Dairyman, Falkland Is

G Bales, Tug *Irishman*

Mrs I Bardsley, club manageress, Portsmouth, NAAFI

R S Barrett, chief steward, Cable Ship *Iris*

D P Betts, Able Seaman, Tug *Irishman*

R S Blanchard, foreman shipwright, Vosper Ship repairers

M H Boyes, lab mech, MoD

Mrs N D Buckett, housewife, Falkland Is

T Dobyns, farmer, Falkland Is

E C Emery, Prof and Tech Off., Dept of Trade

Luis Estella, HM Dockyard, Gibraltar

J S Fairfield, lately cpl. RMS, Falkland Is

R J Ford, senior storeman, MoD

J A Goldie, stores officer, RFA Resource

L S Harris, senior elect. Falkland Is

R J Hatch, marine Serv Off. IV (deck), MoD

J Haywood, progressman Planner Tech (Shipwright), MoD

J Johnston, Snr Storekeeper, RFA *Fort Austin*

J J Jones, Prof and Tech Off., MoD

B J Joshua, Catering Mgr, Pan American Airways, USAF base, Ascension Is

S M Kang, laundry man, HMS *Brilliant*

G J Lane, Lab. Mech, MoD

A J Leonard, chief cook, SS *Atlantic Causeway*

J A Lynch, stores officer, MoD

P McEwan, RFA *Regent*

M McKay, farmer, Falkland Is

P Miller, tractor driver, Falkland Is

E G Morgan, Prof and Tech Off., MoD

A J G Nisbet, Prof and Tech Off. (III), MoD

B Oram-Jones, Prof and Tech Off., MoD

B Oram-Jones, Shipwright. MoD

Mrs H B Perry, telephone Supt, Falkland Is

P R Peterson, Mech Fitter, David Brown Gear Indust

R A Robjohn, Supt exp flight shed, Westland Helicopters

D R T Rozee, plumber, Falkland Is

E W Sampson, stores off. grade C, MoD

V Seogalutze, asst ch inspr, Bridport Gandry

D A Smerdon, Prof Tech Off., MoD

V Steen, guide, Falkland Is

L K Suen, laundryman, HMS *Antrim*

D V Threadgold, telecom tech off. grade II, MoD

Miss K L Timberlake, nursing sister, Falkland Is

R Todd, Prof and Tech Off. III, MoD

F J Tough, Prof and Tech Off. III, MoD

Mrs E Vidal, radio telephonist, Falkland Is

Miss B Vaughan Williams, nursing sister, Falkland Is

C W Wilson, foreman, repair support area, Marconi Radar Systems

C J Winder, Prof and Tech Off. III, MoD.

ROYAL NAVY

Order of the Bath

KCB

Major General John Jeremy
   MOORE, Commander Land
   Forces Falkland Islands
Rear Admiral John Forster
   WOODWARD, Commander
   British Naval Task Force

CB

Commodore M C CLAPP
Brig J H THOMPSON, RM
Rear Adml A J WHETSTONE

Distinguished Service Order

Capt M E Barrow
Capt J J Black
Capt W R Canning
Capt J F Coward
Capt P G V Dingemans
Cdr S C Dunlop, RFA
Lt-Cdr BF Dutton
Capt C H Layman
Capt E S J Larken
Capt L E Middleton
Capt D Pentreath
Capt P J G Roberts, RFA
Lt-Col N F Vaux, RM
Lt-Col A F Whitehead, RM
Cdr C L Wreford-Brown

Distinguished Service Cross (Posthumous)

Lt-Cdr G W J Batt
Capt I H North, Merchant Navy
Lt-Cdr J M Sephton
Lt-Cdr J S Woodhead

Distinguished Service Cross

Lt-Cdr A D Auld
Lt A R C Bennett
Lt-Cdr M D Booth
Cdr P J Bootherstone
Lt N A Bruen
Lt-Cdr H S Clark
Cdr C J S Craig, Fleet Ch PO (Diver)
M G Fellows
Capt G R Green, RFA
Lt R Hutchings, RM
Capt D E Lawrence, RFA
Lt-Cdr H J Lomas
Sub Lt P T Morgan
Cdr A Morton
Lt N J North
Capt A F Pitt, RFA
Lt-Cdr N W Thomas
Lt S R Thomas
Lt Cdr S C Thornewill
Cdr N J Tobin
Cdr N D Ward
Cdr A W J West

Military Cross

Capt P M Babbington RM
Maj C P Cameron RM
Lt CI Dytor RM
Lt C Fox RM
Lt D J Stewart RM

Distinguished Flying Cross (Posthumous)

Lt R J Nunn RM

Distinguished Flying Cross

Capt J P Niblett RM

Air Force Cross

Lt-Cdr D J S Squier
Lt-Cdr R J S Wykes-Sneyd

Distinguished Conduct Medal

Cpl J Burdett RM

George Medal (Posthumous)

Sec Eng Offr P A Henry RFA

George Medal

Able Sn (Radar) J E Dillon

Queen's Gallantry Medal (Posthumous)

Actg Colour Sgt B Johnston RM

Queen's Gallantry Medal

Ch Eng Offr C K A Adams, RFA
Lt J K Boughton
Marine Eng Artificer (M) 1st Class
    K Entick-napp
Third Offr A Gudgeon RFA
PO Medic Asst G A Meager
Lt P J Sheldon
Third Eng B R Williams, Merchant
    Navy

Distinguished Service Medal (Posthumous)

PO Marine Engrg Mech (M) D R
    Briggs
Act Cpl Aircrewman M D Love RM

Distinguished Service Medal

Colour Sgt M J Francis RM
Ldg Aircrewman P B Imrie
PO J S Leake
Sgt W J Leslie RM
Act PO (Sonar) (SM) G J R Libby
Ch Marine Engrg Mech (M) M D
    Townsend
CPO (Diver) G M Trotter
CPO Aircrewman M J Tupper
Ldg Seaman (Radar) J D Warren

Military Medal

Act Cpl A R Bishop RM
Sgt M Collins RM
Sgt T Collings RM
Cpl M Eccles RM

Cpl D Hunt RM
Marine G W Marshall RM
Cpl S C Newland RM
Cpl H Sid-dall RM
Cpl C N H Ward RM
Sgt J D Wassell RM

Distinguished Flying Medal

Sgt WC O'Brien RM

Mention in Dispatches (Posthumous)

Lt A Curtis
Weapon Engrg Artfer 1st Class
   A C Eggington
Sub Lt R C Emly
Sgt A P Evans, RM
Lt N Taylor
Actg Ch Weapon Engrg Mech
   M G Till
Weapon Engng Mech 2nd Class
   B J Wallis

Mention in Dispatches

Radio Op (Tactical) 1st Class R J Ash
PO Aircrewman A Ashdown
Marine R Bainbridge RM
PO Aircrewman J A Balls
Lt P J Barber
Sub Lt R J Barker
Marine N J Barnett RM
Sgt P Beevers RM
Ch Air Engrg Artfer (M) R J Bentley
A/Ldg Med Assist G Black
Lt-Cdr M S Blissett

L/Cpl F W Boorn RM
A/Ldg Marine Engrg Mech (M)
   C R Boswell
Sgt I W Brice RM
Ch O J K Brocklehurst, Merchant
   Navy
Able Seaman (Missile) N S
   Brotherton
Cpl C J G Brown RM
WO Class 2 R J Brown RM
Lt-Cdr B W Bryant
Sgt E L Buckley RM
Marine Engrg Artifer (H) 1st Class
   D A Bugden
Sgt B G Burgess RM
PO Aircrewman R Burnett
Lt-Cdr R G Burrows
Lt N A M Butler
Sgt E R Candlish RM
Lt C T G Caroe RM
Marine Engrg Mech (M) 1st Class
   L Cartwright
Lt-Cdr J S M Chandler
Marine Engrg Mech (M) 1st Class
   M L Chiplen
Lt-Cdr J N Clark
Lt C H T Clayton
Capt M A F Cole RM
Marine D S Combes, RM
Cpl G Cooke RM
Sgt R T Cooper RM
AB (Missile) A Coppell
Lt-Cdr G R A Coryton
Lt R L Crawford
Marine Engrg Mech (M) 1st Class
   C Crowley
Marine G Cuthell RM
Sgt G Dance RM

Marine L Daniels RM
Colour Sgt B Davies RM
Sgt C C De La Cour RM
Sgt B Dolivera RM
Marine S Duggan RM
Lt A J Ebbens RM
Marine Engrg Mech (M) 1st Class
    D J Edwards
PO Marine Engrg Mech (M) J R Ellis
Cdr R D Ferguson
Lt W J T Fewtrell
Sgt I D Fisk, RM
Midshipman M T Fletcher
Weapons Engrg Artfer 2nd Class
    J M C Foy
Lt-Cdr R V Frederiksen
Lt-Cdr D G Garwood
L/Cpl B Gilbert RM
Ch Marine Engrg Artfer (H)
    K W Goldie
Marine L J Goldsmith RM
Ldg Seaman (Missile) R M Gould
Sub-Lt D E Graham
CPO (Ops) (M) E Graham
CPO (Diver) B T Gunnell
Lt-Cdr A C Gwilliam
Lt F Haddow RM
Sgt D K Hadlow RM
Ldg Aircrewman J A Harper
A/Ldg Marine Engrg Mech (M)
    S W Hathaway
CO P F Hill RFA
A/Cpl G Hodkinson RM
Lt R I Horton
Lt-Cdr L S G Hulme
Sub-Lt P J Humphreys
Ldg Radio Op (Tactical)
    R J Hutcheson

AB (Missile) S Ingleby
Lt-Cdr I Inskip
Marine Engrg Artfer (H) 1st Class
    P G Jakeman
Sgt K M James, QGM RM
PO (Missile) H Jones
Ldg Seaman (Diver) P M Kearns
Lt-Cdr R S G Kent
Marine Engrg Artfer (M) 1st Class
    K S Lake
Maj P R Lamb RM
Cdr R C Lane-Nott
AB (Radar) M S Leach
Marine Engrg Artfer 2nd Class
    D J Leaning
Lt H J Ledingham
Cdr T M Le Marchand
L/Cpl C K Levett
Sgt W D P Lewis RM
Lt-Cdr J A Lister
Lt D A Lord
Lt-Cdr I B Mackay
Lt A N McHarg
Sgt M Mclntyre RM
Cpl T W McMahon RM
Lt P C Manley
CPO Airman (AH) N C Martin
Marine Engrg Mech (M) 1st Class
    T Miles
Lt J A G Miller
Lt P G Miller
Marine Engrg Artfer (M) 1st Class
    S D Mitchell
Weapon Engrg Mech 1st Class
    P R Moir
Lt A G Moll
Lt-Cdr C R W Morrell
Sgt H F Napier RM

Lt-Cdr K M Napier
Marine M A Neal RM
Capt A B Newcombe RM
Med Assist M Nicely
Marine G Nordass RM
Maj M J Norman RM
Lt-Cdr M J O'Connell
Marine D L O'Connor RM
Capt E J O'Kane RM
Lt R J Ormshaw
Lt C L Palmer
Maj D A Pennefather RM
Capt A R Pillar RM
Lt R F Playford RM
Lt C J Pollard
Marine Engrg Mech (M) 1st Class
  H B Porter
Capt N E Pounds RM
Lt A Pringle
Lt P I Rainey
PO Air Engrg Mech (M) S Rainsbury
Lt-Cdr A A Rich
Lt F W Robertson
Leading Aircrewman I Robertson
WO2 A S Robinson RM
Actg PO Marine Engrg Mech (M)
  D M K Ross
Sgt T A Sands RM
Marine C J Scrivener RM
Marine Engrg Mech (M) 1st Class
  D J Serrell
Marine Engrg Mech 1st Class
  A G Siddle
Lt R E J Sleeman
Lt D A Bereton Smith
Chief Marine Engrg Mech
  T G Smith
Ldg Seaman (Diver) C A Smithard

Marine Engrg Mech (M) 1st Class
  A Stewart
Ch Eng J M Stewart, Merchant Navy
Sgt W J Stocks RM
Sgt C R Stone RM
Marine J Stonestreet RM
Marine R S Strange RM
Marine Engrg Artfer (M) 1st Class
  S P Tarabella
PO Aircrewman C W Tattersall
Cdr J B Taylor
Cdr B G Telfer
Marine P Thomason RM
Ldg Seaman (Diver) A S Thompson
Lt C Todhunter
Fleet Ch Marine Engrg Artfer (P)
  E M Uren
Maj R C Van Der Horst RM
Marine Engrg Mech (L) 1st Class
  W G Waddington
AB (Diver) D Walton
Seaman (ops) D J Whild
Lt-Cdr R E Wilkinson
Marine P K Wilson RM
Sgt R D Wright RM
Leading Aircrewman S W Wright
Colour Sgt E Young RM
Ldg Med Assist P Youngman

Queen's Commendation for Brave Conduct

Marine P A Cruden RM
PO2 B Czarnecki, Merchant Navy
Chief Marine Engrg Mech (L)
  A F Fazackerley
Weapon Engrg Mech (R) 1st Class
  J R Jesson

PO Weapon Engrg Mech (R)
G J Lowden

Second Officer I Povey RFA

Chief Weapon Engrg Mech (R)
W Rumsey

Radio Op (Tactical) 1st Class
D F Sullivan

Marine Engrg Mech (M) 1st Class
T A Sutton

Acting Col Sgt D A Watkins RM

Order of the British Empire

GBE

Admiral Sir John David Elliott
FIELDHOUSE, Commander-
in-Chief Fleet Northwood,
Middx

KBE

Vice-Admiral David John HALLIFAX,
Chief of Staff to Commander-in-
Chief Fleet

CBE

Capt P Badcock

Capt N J Barker

Capt C P O Burne

Capt R H Fox

Capt J Garnier

Capt M H G Layard

Capt R McQueen

Capt I J R Tod

Capt J P Wrigley

OBE

Cdr T A Allen

Cdr L S J Barry

Cdr P Birch

Maj R J Bruce RM

Maj J S Chester RM

Cdr M Cudmore

Capt J V Dickinson RFA

Cdr F B Goodson

Cdr C J Esplin-Jones

Cdr L T Hickson

Surgeon Lt-Cdr (Actg Surgeon Cdr)
R T Jolly

Capt J S Kelly

Cdr D A H Kerr

Cdr M L Ladd

Capt P J McCarthy RFA

Cdr P J McGregor

Maj D J Minords RM

Cdr A W Netherclift

Cdr (A/Cpt) A J Oglesby

Capt G P Overbury RFA

Cdr G S Pearson

Capt C A Purtcher-Wydenbruck
RFA

Capt S Redmond RFA

Cdr A S Ritchie

The Rev A M Ross

Cdr R A Rowley

Cdr J T Sanders

Cdr R J Sandford

Maj J M G Sheridan RM

Cdr D W Shrubb

Maj S E Southby-Tailyour RM

Maj J J Thompson RM

Cdr C W Williams

Cdr G A C Woods

MBE

Lt S J Branch-Evans

Lt-Cdr M J D Brougham

Lt-Cdr R C Caesley

Lt R S Collins
Lt A D Dummer
Lt-Cdr C J Edwards
Fleet Ch Radio Superv D J Eggers
Lt-Cdr R Goodenough
Lt-Cdr M Goodman
Lt-Cdr R W Hamilton
Capt C F Howard RM
Lt-Cdr G M J Irvine
Lt-Cdr P J James RNR
Fleet Ch Wtr C G Lamb
Fleet CPO (Ops) (S) M J Legg
Lt-Cdr J H Loudon
Lt-Cdr H A Mayers
Lt-Cdr I S McKenzie
Lt-Cdr J M Milne
Fleet Ch Marine Engrg Artfer (H)
    P W Muller
Fleet CPO (Ops) (S) R J Nicholls
Lt D C W O'Connell
Lt-Cdr L D Poole
Lt B Purnell
Capt M J Sharland RM
Surgeon Lt-Cdr P J Shouler
Lt D F Smith
Capt D Sparks RM
Lt-Cdr J N O Williams
Lt-Cdr D J R Wilmot-Smith

British Empire Medal

PO Medical Assistant K Adams
Air Engrg Mech (R) 1st Class
    J L Bailey
Ch Air Engrg Mech (M) N R Barwick

Marine Engrg Artfer (H) 1st Class
    T J Bennetto
Ch Air Engr Artfer (R) 1st Class
    D M Childs
Master-at-Arms A F Coles
Ch Marine Engrg Mech (P) G S Cox
Ch Engrg Mech (L) W D Eaton
Air Engrg Artfer (M) 1st Class
    S J Goodall
Ch Air Engrg Artfer (M) D J Heritier
CPO (D) L B Hewitt
CPO Caterer J A Jackson
Air Engrg Artfer (H) 1st Class
    D E Jones
Air Engrg Artfer (L) 1st Class
    R A J Mason
Med Tech 1st Class S McKinlay
CPO Cook M G Mercer
Ldg Wren Stores Accountant
    J Mitton
Ch Wren Educ Assist A Monckton
Air Engrg Artfer (L) 2nd Class
    A J Smith
CPO (Ops) (M) O G Stockham
Air Engrg (L) 1st Class R J E Strong
Chief Air Engrg Mech (L) 1st Class
    T L Temple
Ldg Wren Dental Hygienist K Toms
Ch Wren Family Srves B M Travers
A/Ldg Stores Accountant G J Walsh
PO (Missile) J J T Waterfield
PO (Missile) E L Wells
Air Engreg (M) 1st Class
    D J Williams
Sgt B Winter, RM

ARMY

Victoria Cross (Posthumous)

Lt-Col Herbert JONES, 2 Battalion,
    The Parachute Regiment
Sgt Ian John MCKAY, 3 Battalion,
    The Parachute Regiment

Distinguished Service Order

Maj C N G Delves, D and D
Maj C P B Keeble, Para
Lt-Col H W R Pike, Para
Lt-Col M I E Scott, SG

Distinguished Service Cross

W02 J H Phillips, RE

Military Cross (Posthumous)

Capt G J Hamilton, Green Howards

Military Cross

Maj M H Argue, Para
Capt T W Burls, Para
Maj D A Collett, Para
Lt C S Conner, Para
Maj J H Crosland, Para
Maj C D Farrar-Hockley, Para
Maj J P Kiszeley, SG
Lt R A D Lawrence, SG
Capt W A McCracken, RA
Capt A J G Wight, WG

Distinguished Flying Cross

Capt S M Drennan, AAC
Capt J G Greenhaigh, RCT

Distinguished Conduct Medal (Posthumous)

Pte S Illingsworth, Para
Gdsmn J B C Reynolds, SG

Distinguished Conduct Medal

Cpl D Abols, Para
Staff Sgt B Faulkner, Para
Sgt J C Meredith, Para
W02 W Nicol, SG
Sgt J S Pettinger, Para

Cconspicuous Gallantry Medal (Posthumous)

Staff Sgt J Prescott, RE

Military Medal (Posthumous)

Pte R J de M Absolon, Para
L/Cpl G D Bingley, Para

Military Medal

Cpl I P Bailey, Para
L/Cpl S A Bardsley, Para
Sgt T I Barrett, Para
L/Cpl M W L Bentley, Para

Sgt D S Boultby, RCT
Cpl T Brookes, R Sigs
Cpl T J Camp, Para
Pte G S Carter, Para
Gdsmn S M Chapman, WG
Cpl J A Foran, RE
Sgt D Fuller, Para
Pte B J Grayling, Para
Cpl T W Harley, Para
Bdr E M Holt, RA
Sgt R W Jackson, SG
L/Cpl D J Loveridge, WG
Sgt J G Mather, SAS
Sgt P H R Naya, RAMC
W02 B T Neck, WG
Gdsmn A S Pengelly, SG
L/Cpl L J L Standish, Para
Sgt R H Wrega, RE

Mention in Dispatches

Sgt I Aird, Para
Pte S J Alexander, Para
Lt-Col J Anderson RAMC
Maj the Hon R N Bethel, SG
Capt A P Bourne, RA
Pte A E Brooke, Para
Dvr M Brough, RCT
Capt C C Brown, RA
Gdsmn G Brown, SG
Capt I A Bryden, SG
Maj W K Butler, R Sigs
S/Sgt W H Carpenter, SAS
L/Cpl L A Carver, Para
Lt (QGO) P Chandrakumar, 7 GR
S/Sgt T Collins RE
Pte K P Connery, Para
Chaplain D Cooper, RAChD

Lt M R Coreth, RHG/D
Pte A M Corneille, Para
Cpl I C Corrigan, REME
Lt M T Cox, Para
L/Sgt A C E Dalgleish, SG
L/Cpl N J Dance, Para
L/Sgt I Davidson, SG
Maj P E Dennison, Para
S/Sgt G K Dixon, RA
Piper S W Duffy, SG
L/Cpl K P Dunbar, Para
Gnr G Eccleston, RA
Capt M P Entwistle, RAMC
Lt-Col K R H Eve, RA
Capt P R Farrar, Para
Cpl D Ford, RE
W02 J Francis, RA
Lt D P Frankland, RCT
L/Cpl R Gillon, RE
Pte (now L/Cpl) D J Gough, Para
L/Sgt D Graham, WG
Pte D Gray, Para
Maj P H Gullan, Para
Pte (A/Cpl) J Hand, Para
L/Cpl (A/Cpl) S P Harding-Dempster,
  Para
Pte P J Harley, Para
Maj R B Hawken, RE
Lt (now Capt) R C Hendicott, RE
Cpl (A/Sgt) J Hill, Para
Lt-Col G A Holt, RA
W02 G Hough, WG
Capt (Now Maj) E H Houstoun,
  Gren Gds
L/Bdr (A/Bdr) O D Hughes, RA
Capt S J Hughes, RAMC
Cpl S D Iles, RE
Lt the Lord R A Innes-Ker, RHG/D

Bdr J R Jackson, RA
Gnr J Jones RA
L/Cpl K B Jones, RCT
Sgt R R Kalinski, Para
Capt S J Knapper, Staffords
S/Sgt (A/W02) A la Frenais, SAS
Maj B C Lamb, RA
Lt C R Livingstone, RE
Lt J G O Lowe, RCT
S/Sgt C D Lowiner, Para
L/Cpl D MacColl, SG
Maj R Macdonald, RE
Piper P A MacInnes, SG
L/Cpl J D Maher, RE
Capt R J Makeig-Jones, RA
Pte A Mansfield, Para
Maj T A Marsh, Para
Sgt P J Marshall, ACC
L/Sgt T McGuinness, SG
Capt J H McManners, RA
Lt A M Mitchell, SG
2 Lt IC Moore, Para
Pte R P G Morrell, Para
Maj P Neame, Para
Cpl T K Noble, Para
Pte E O'Rourke, Para
Lt J D Page, Para
Pte (A/Cpl) D J Pearcy, Int Corps
Cpl J F Phillips, Para
Pte (A/Sgt) B W Pitchforth, Queens
Pte A Potter, RAOC
L/Cpl B J Randall, RE
Sgt P Ratcliffe, SAS
L Cpl G Rennie, SG
W02 M D Richards, RA
L/Cpl J J Rigg, AAC
Lt Col J D A Roberts, RAMC
Maj B P S Rolfe-Smith, Para

Capt C R Romberg, RA
Lt-Col (now Col) H M Rose, Coldm
  Gds
Sgt I Roy, RE
Capt J D G Sayers, WG
W02 M J Sharp, AAC
Cpl J Sibley, Para
Maj C S Sibun, AAC
Spr (A/L Cpl) W A Skinner, RE
Maj G W Smith, RA
Capt R J Southworth, RAOC
Col H P Stretton, RHG/D
2 Lt J D Steuart, SG
Lt W J Syms, WG
Cpl (A/Sgt) R C Taylor, R Sigs
Maj A Todd, RCT
L/Cpl G Tytler, SG
Pte (A/Cpl) P A Walker, Staffords
Sgt R J Walker, AAC
2 Lt G Wallis, Para
Lt M E Waring, RA
Capt J N E Watson, RA
Lt G R Weighell, Para
Lt (now Capt) M G Williams, RA
Lt (now Capt) M S H Worsley-Tonks,
  Para.

Order of the British Empire

Col I S Baxter, late RCT
Col J D Bidmead, late RCT
Col (now Brig) D B H Colley, late
  RCT
Col B C McDermott, late RAMC

OBE

Lt-Col A E Berry, RGJ
Lt-Col IJ Hellberg, RCT

Lt-Col M J Holroyd-Smith, RA
Maj (now Lt-Col) P J Hubert, Queens
Lt-Col W S P McGregor, RAMC
Lt-Col D P de C Morgan, 7 GR
Lt-Col J F Rickett, WG
Lt-Col (QM) P J Saunders, RE
Lt-Col R. Welsh, RAMC

MBE

Maj E L Barrett, RCT
Maj C G Batty, RAMC
Maj CM Davies, RE
WOl (RSM) A J Davies, WG
Maj J A East, RAMC
WOl L Ellson, WG
Maj A R Gale, R Sigs
Maj C Griffiths, RAMC
Maj (QM) G M Groom, RCT
W02 (Act WOl) R Haig, RE
Maj L Hollingworth, RAOC
Capt T G McCabe, RAMC
WOl M J McHale, RAMC
Capt R Marshall, Int Corps
Capt (QM) N E Menzies, Para
Lt (now Capt) F J Moody, SG
W02 D Moore, RCT
WOl R G Randall, RE
Maj (OEO) J M Ridding, RAOC
Maj J R Stuart, R Sigs
Maj M G Taylor, R Sigs
W02 P M Williams, RCT

Maj T J Wilton, RA
Maj G J Yeoman, RCT
W02 R C Yeomans, R Sigs

Civilian Awards (Army Sponsored)

MBE (CIVIL)
Mr A M Cleaver, Corr PA
Mr J R R Fox, BBC Rep.

British Empire Medal

S/Sgt W F Blyth, RCT
S/Sgt E G Bradley, RE
Sgt R J Brown, RE
S/Sgt M J Dent, RE
S/Sgt J Fenwick, REME
S/Sgt R L Griffths, R Sigs
Cpl N J Hall, RE
Sgt D Harvey, RAOC
S/Sgt C L Henderson, ACC
Cpl G J Herrington, RPC
S/Sgt J D Holmes, RAOC
Cpl W II Hopkins, RAOC
Pte D J Hunt, ACC
Sgt D R Pasfield, RE
S/Sgt P Rayner, RE
S/Sgt (A/W02) M Reid, RAMC
S/Sgt C G Taylor, REME
Cpl (A/Sgt) A Worthington, RE

ROYAL AIR FORCE

Order of the Bath

CB

Air V-M G A CHESWORTH
Air V-M K W HAYR

Distinguished Service Cross

Fit Lt D H S Morgan

Distinguished Flying Cross

Wing Cdr P T Squire
Sqdn Ldr R U Langworthy
Sqdn Ldr C N McDougall
Sqdn Ldr J J Pook
Flt LtWFM Withers

Air Force Cross

Wing Cdr D Emmerson
Sqdn Ldr R Tuxford
Flt Lt H C Burgoyne
Sqdn Ldr A M Roberts

Queen's Gallantry Medal

Flt Lt A J Swan
Flt Sgt B W Jopling

Queen's Commendation for Brave Conduct

J Tech A Thorne
SAC K J Soppett-Moss

Queen's Commendation for Valuable Service in the Air

Sqdn Ldr E F Wallis
Sqdn Ldr M E Beer
Flt Lt J D Cunningham
Flt Lt J N Keable
Flt Lt M M MacLeod
Flt Lt G D Rees
Flt Lt R L Rowley
Flt Sgt S E Sloan
Wing Cdr M D Todd
Flt Lt P A Standing
Sqdn Ldr T N Allen
Sqdn Ldr A F Banfield
Sqdn Ldr G R Barrell
Sqdn Ldr J A Brown
Sqdn Ldr P Bayer

Mention in Dispatches

Sqdn Ldr J G Elliott
Sqdn Ldr R D Iveson
Flt Lt E H Ball
Flt Lt M W J Hare
Flt Lt G C Graham
Flt Lt A T Jones
Flt Lt I Mortimer
Flt Lt H Prior
Flt Lt R J Russell
Flt Lt R D Wright
FO P L Taylor
FO C Miller
Flt Sgt D W Knights
Cpl A D Tomlinson

Order of the British Empire

KBE

Air Marshal Sir John Bagot
   CURTISS

CBE

Group Capt C E Evans
Group Capt AFC Hunter
Group Capt P King
Group Capt J S B Price

OBE

Wing Cdr A J C Bagnall
Wing Cdr D L Baugh
Wing Cdr P Fry
Sqdn Ldr B S Morris
Wing Cdr J K Sim
Wing Cdr A P Slinger
Wing Cdr C J Sturt
Wing Cdr B J Weaver

MBE

Sqdn Ldr C G Jefford
Sqdn Ldr D M Niven
Sqdn Ldr J E Stokes
Flt Lt E M Clinton
Flt Lt P A Room
WO D P Barker
Sqdn Ldr W F Lloyd
Sqdn Ldr T Sitch
Flt Lt J Dungare
Flt Lt B Y Mason
A/Flt Lt A Neale
Master Air Ldmstr A D Smith
Flt Sgt J H Bell
Sgt J M Coleman
Flt Sgt K Kenny
Ch Tech T J Kinsella
Sgt P Tuxford
Ch Tech R K Vernon
Sgt J C Vickers
Cpl D J Vivian

Appendix D:
The Franks Report

The report was published on 18 January 1983. The first three chapters consisted of an analysis of the background to the Falklands conflict. The fourth comprised the report's conclusions and is printed here with some historical passages edited out. The paragraph numbers are Franks' originals.

The Government's Discharge of Their Responsibilities

260   In this Chapter we address the central issue of our terms of reference, the way in which the responsibilities of government in relation to the Falkland Islands and the Falkland Islands Dependencies were discharged in the period leading up to the invasion. We have had to consider many questions, but two are crucial. First, could the Government have foreseen the invasion on 2 April? Secondly, could the Government have prevented that invasion? We deal with the first question at the outset of the Chapter. The second question is more complex and in our view cannot be answered until we have examined how the dispute became critical and how it was handled at various stages by the present Government. We consider the answer to this question at the end of the Chapter.

Could the Invasion of 2 April Have Been Foreseen?

261   We consider first the question whether before 31 March the Government had warning of the invasion of the Falkland Islands on 2 April. We have described in detail the events of the days leading up to the invasion and all the information available at the time, including all relevant

reports from the intelligence agencies. We believe that our account demonstrates conclusively that the Government had no reason to believe before 31 March that an invasion of the Falkland Islands would take place at the beginning of April.

262   All the information, including intelligence reports, that has come to light since the invasion suggests that the decision to invade was taken by the Junta at a very late date.

263   Argentine naval forces were at sea between about 23 and 28 March, in the course of annual naval exercises, which included a joint anti-submarine exercise with Uruguay (press accounts of which the British Naval *Attaché* in Buenos Aires reported on 27 March). The Argentine news agency reported on 2 April that the fleet had sailed south from Puerto Belgrano on 28 March with a marine infantry battalion, an amphibious command section and troops embarked. The actual order to invade was probably not given until at least 31 March, and possibly as late as 1 April. Dr Costa Mendes was subsequently reported as saying that the Junta did not finally decide on the invasion until 10 p.m. (7 p.m. local time) on 1 April. It is probable that the decision to invade was taken in the light of the development of the South Georgia situation; but it seems that the violent demonstrations in Buenos Aires on the night of 30/31 March were also a factor in the Junta's decision.

264   It may be thought that, although the Government could not have had earlier warning of the invasion, they must have had fuller and more significant information of Argentine military movements. The fact is that there was no coverage of these movements and no evidence available to the Government from satellite photographs. We discuss these matters further below in the context of the arrangements made for gathering intelligence.

265   We specifically asked all those who gave evidence to us – Ministers and officials, the British Ambassador in Buenos Aires and other Embassy staff, the Governor of the Falkland Islands, Falkland Islanders and persons outside Government with special knowledge of and interest in the area – whether at any time up to the end of March they thought an invasion of the Falklands was likely at the beginning of April. They all stated categorically that they did not.

266   In the light of this evidence, we are satisfied that the Government did not have warning of the decision to invade. The evidence of the timing of the decision taken by the Junta shows that the Government not only did not, but could not, have had earlier warning. The invasion of the Falkland Islands on 2 April could not have been foreseen.

Foreign and Commonwealth Office Judgement on How the Dispute Would Develop

293   At the beginning of 1982 there was evidence from several sources that Argentina, and particularly the new government of President Galtieri, was committed to achieving success in its Malvinas policy in a much shorter timescale than most previous Argentine Governments had envisaged. There were clear indications that it attached particular significance to achieving a solution of the dispute on its terms, in which the sovereignty issue was the overriding consideration, by January 1983, the 150th anniversary of British occupation. These indications included General Galtieri's remarks in his speech in May 1981, intelligence about the attitude of different elements in the Argentine Government, the press comment at the beginning of the year and, definitively, the terms of the *bout de papier* at the end of January 1982, which called for serious negotiations with a timescale of one year, culminating in the recognition of Argentine sovereignty.

294   The Foreign and Commonwealth Office recognised clearly that the situation was moving towards confrontation, as is shown by the advice they gave their Ministers at the beginning of the year, notably in connection with the Annual Report of the Governor of the Falkland Islands. They believed, however – and their belief was supported by evidence – first, that Argentina would not move to confrontation until negotiations broke down; secondly, that there would be a progression of measures starting with the withdrawal of Argentine services to the Islands and increased diplomatic pressure, including further action at the United Nations; and thirdly – and the intelligence bore this out – that no action, let alone invasion of the Islands, would take place before the second half of the year.

Contingency Planning

295   Nevertheless, in recognition of the deteriorating situation, the Foreign and Commonwealth Office had set in hand in 1981 contingency plans to provide alternative services for the Islands, and, at its request, the Ministry of Defence prepared a paper on the military options available in response to possible aggressive action by Argentina. A paper on civil contingency planning was also prepared in September 1981 in expectation of a meeting of the Defence Committee, at which Ministerial authority might have been obtained to take the plans further. Chartering ships would have required appropriate financial provision and also Ministerial agreement to acknowledge such measures publicly, and this could have been seen as a form of pressure on the Islanders. As it turned out, the inability to give more substance to these civil plans did not matter, as Argentina did not escalate the dispute in the way expected. On the military side the absence of detailed contingency plans for responding to aggressive action by Argentina did not inhibit a very swift response once it was clear that an invasion was imminent, as can be seen from the remarkable speed with which the task force was prepared and sailed. We discuss in paragraphs 324–332 the separate question whether earlier military steps should have been taken to deter an Argentine attack.

The View in the Foreign and Commonwealth Office at the Beginning of the Year

296   We believe that the view taken by Foreign and Commonwealth Office Ministers and officials early in 1982 of how the dispute would develop was one which could reasonably be taken in the light of all circumstances at that time. In the event it proved to be a misjudgement, but not one in our view for which blame should be attached to any individual. There were, we believe, three important factors in the misjudgement: first, in underestimating the importance that Argentina attached to its timetable for resolving the dispute by the end of the year; secondly, in being unduly influenced – understandably and perhaps inevitably – by the long history of the dispute, in which Argentina had previously made threatening noises, accompanied by bellicose press comment, and indeed backed up its threats with aggressive actions, without the dispute developing into a serious confrontation; and, thirdly, in believing, on the basis of evidence, that Argentina would follow an orderly progression in escalating the dispute,

starting with economic and diplomatic measures. Sufficient allowance was not made for the possibility of Argentina's military government, subject to internal political and economic pressures, acting unpredictably if at any time they became frustrated at the course of negotiations. The July 1981 intelligence assessment had warned that in those circumstances there was a high risk that Argentina would resort to more forcible measures swiftly and without warning.

The Response to Events Following the New York Talks

297 We acknowledge the skill with which Mr Luce and Foreign and Commonwealth Office officials handled the formal talks between the Argentine and British Governments in New York on 26 and 27 February. The agenda for the talks was provided by the Argentine *bout de papier* issued on 27 January. They were held in a cordial atmosphere, and the general view of the British side was that they had gone somewhat better than they feared. A joint *communiqué* was agreed, and in the draft working paper on the negotiating commission reference to the frequency of meetings – an important element in the Argentine proposals – was avoided. At the same time, it had been clear even at the talks that the Argentine side's ability to manoeuvre was strictly limited. The Argentine Government were committed to the establishment of the commission, with negotiations being conducted at high level, at a much faster pace than in the past, and with a strict deadline of a year. They pressed strongly for a formal reply from the British Government to their proposal within a month, with a view to the first round of talks being held at the beginning of April.

298 The unilateral *communiqué* of 1 March instigated by the Junta marked an important change of attitude on the part of the Argentine Government. It in effect denounced the joint *communiqué* by making public the details of the informal working paper, and commended the proposals in the *bout de papier* for a programme of monthly meetings with the aim of achieving recognition of Argentine sovereignty within a short time; and, if those proposals were not effective, claimed the right to choose 'the procedure which best accords with (Argentine) interests'. Although Sr Ros expressed regret about the *communiqué* and accompanying press comment, and Dr Costa Mendes assured the British Ambassador in Buenos Aires that no threat was intended, it indicated a hardening attitude on the part of the

Argentine Government, and a commitment to the negotiating commission proposals and the timetable for its work.

299 The increased seriousness of the situation was recognised by Foreign and Commonwealth Office officials. They discussed it with Lord Carrington at a short meeting on 5 March, at which several diplomatic initiatives were set in hand.

300 This was also the occasion when they mentioned to him the previous Government's decision in November 1977 to deploy ships to the area covertly, though without recommending similar action at that stage. As it happens, 5 March was about the last moment at which, given that the invasion took place on 2 April, it would have been possible to sail a deterrent force to be in place in time. It would have taken nuclear-powered submarines approximately two weeks and surface ships approximately three weeks to reach the Falkland Islands. The evidence we received suggested to us that Foreign and Commonwealth Office officials did not press Ministers to consider deterrent rather than diplomatic counter-measures or prompt the Joint Intelligence Organisation urgently to update its July 1981 assessment because they believed that Argentina would not resort to military action before initiating diplomatic and economic measures.

301 Officials were also looking for an early meeting of the Defence Committee, which Lord Carrington had envisaged taking place after the February talks, and it was expected that the meeting would take place on 16 March. No paper was tabled for that meeting, however, because Lord Carrington thought it right to await the Argentine Government's reaction to the message he was proposing to send to Dr Costa Mendes.

302 We believe that Foreign and Commonwealth Office officials did not attach sufficient weight at this time to the changing Argentine attitude at and following the February talks and did not give sufficient importance to the new and threatening elements in the Argentine Government's position. We conclude that they should have drawn Ministers' attention more effectively to the changed situation.

303 We note that the Prime Minister reacted to the telegrams from the British Ambassador in Buenos Aires on 3 March reporting aggressive Argentine press comment following the New York talks, and called for

contingency plans. We regret that the Prime Minister's enquiries did not receive a prompt response. She also enquired of Mr Nott on 8 March about the timing of possible warship movements to the South Atlantic.

The Joint Intelligence Organisation

304 The reports by the intelligence agencies and the assessments made by the Joint Intelligence Committee were a key factor in the judgements made by Ministers and officials in the period leading up to the invasion, which we have reviewed above. For many years Argentina and the Falkland Islands were regarded as a priority for intelligence collection but were in a relatively low category.

Earlier Intelligence Assessments

305 From 1965 the Argentine threat to the Falkland Islands was regularly assessed by the Joint Intelligence Committee, the frequency of assessment increasing at times of heightened tension between Britain and Argentina in the dispute on sovereignty, in the light of the internal political situation in Argentina and information about Argentine intentions. The timing of assessments was often related to the rounds of formal negotiations between the British and Argentine Governments. In the period of the present Government a full assessment was prepared in November 1979.

The Assessment of July 1981

306 A further full assessment, the last before the invasion, was prepared in July 1981. This assessment was particularly important because, as was apparent from the oral evidence we received, it had considerable influence on the thinking of Ministers and officials.

Review of the 1981 Assessment

307 We were told in evidence that the Latin America Current Intelligence Group met 18 times between July 1981 and March 1982, but did not discuss the Falkland Islands on those occasions. They were, however, discussed on two occasions in that period at the weekly meetings held by the Head of the assessments staff; and on at least four separate occasions consideration was given by those concerned, who were in close touch with the Foreign

and Commonwealth Office on this matter, to the need to update the
assessment made in July 1981. These occasions were in November 1981, in
preparation for the next round of talks, which were then scheduled for the
following month; in December 1981; in January 1982, in the light of the
proposals that it was known that Argentina would put forward before
the February talks in New York; and in March 1982. On each occasion up
to March it was decided that there was no need to revise the assessment.

308   We were told that the four principal factors that the assessments
staff considered in assessing the Argentine threat were: the progress of
Argentina's dispute with Chile over the Beagle Channel; the political and
economic situation in Argentina; the state of inter-service rivalry there;
and, most importantly, Argentina's perception of the prospects of making
progress by negotiation. The information they received after July 1981 was
not thought to indicate any significant change in these factors which would
have justified a new assessment. The conclusions reached in July 1981
about Argentine intentions and the options open to them were regarded as
consistent with more recent intelligence and therefore still valid.

309   In March 1982 it was agreed that a new assessment should be
prepared, and work was started on it. It was thought, however, that it
could most usefully be presented to Ministers in the context of a more
general consideration of Falkland Islands policy, which they were expected
to discuss at a meeting of the Defence Committee on 16 March. In the
event, as we have explained, that meeting did not take place, and the new
assessment was never completed.

310   The next assessment, which we described in paragraph 230, was
made at very short notice in the morning of 31 March and was concerned
with events on South Georgia. In its conclusion it expressed the view that,
while the possibility that Argentina might choose to escalate the situation
by landing a military force on another Dependency or on the Falkland
Islands could not be ruled out, the Argentine Government did not wish to
be the first to adopt forcible measures.

The Intelligence Agencies

311   This assessment on the eve of the invasion relied chiefly on the
information available from the intelligence agencies. Throughout the
period leading up to the invasion secret intelligence was collected, in

accordance with the priority accorded to this target, on Argentina's attitude to and intentions in the dispute, in particular the views of its armed forces and Ministry of Foreign Affairs; on relevant internal factors in Argentina; and on its general military capability. In October 1981, following a general review of intelligence requirements in Central and South America and the Caribbean, the Joint Intelligence Committee notified the collecting agencies that, in view of the increasing difficulty of maintaining negotiations with Argentina over the future of the Falkland Islands, the requirement had increased for intelligence on Argentine intentions and policies on the issue. But additional resources were not allocated for this purpose. We were told in evidence that, for operational reasons which were explained to us, the deployment of additional resources would not easily have secured earlier or better intelligence of the intentions of the very small circle at the head of the Argentine Government where decisions were taken.

312   If, as we believe, the decision to invade was taken by the Junta at a very late stage, the intelligence agencies could not have been expected to provide earlier warning of the actual invasion on 2 April. It might have been possible to give some warning of the military preparations preceding the invasion, if there had been direct coverage of military movements within Argentina in addition to coverage of its general military capability. But it would have been difficult to provide comprehensive coverage of these movements in view of, among other things, Argentina's very long coastline and the distance of the southern Argentine ports from Buenos Aires. The British Defence *Attaché* in Buenos Aires told us that his section at the Embassy had neither the remit nor the capacity to obtain detailed information of this kind. By the time the diplomatic situation deteriorated at the beginning of March it would have been difficult to evaluate such information because of the absence of knowledge about the normal pattern of Argentine military activity.

313   There was no coverage of Argentine military movements within Argentina, and no advance information was therefore available by these means about the composition and assembly of the Argentine naval force that eventually invaded the Falklands. There was no intelligence from American sources or otherwise to show that the force at sea before the invasion was intended other than for normal naval exercises. No satellite photography was available on the disposition of the Argentine forces. The

British Naval *Attaché* in Buenos Aires reported the naval exercises when he became aware of them, mainly on the basis of Argentine press reports.

314 We have no reason to question the reliability of the intelligence that was regularly received from a variety of sources.

Did the Intelligence Assessment Machinery Function Effectively?

315 As to assessments, however, we were surprised that events in the first three months of 1982, in particular the Argentine *bout de papier* on 27 January, the unilateral *communiqué* on 1 March and the Prime Minister's comments on the telegram of 3 March reporting Argentine press comment, did not prompt the Joint Intelligence Organisation to assess the situation afresh. As we have explained, the assessments staff considered the need for a new assessment on several occasions in this period. Work was started on one early in March, but not completed because of the intention to link it to a meeting of the Defence Committee. It was decided not to prepare a new assessment before the beginning of March because of the view in the Joint Intelligence Organisation that the conclusions of a new assessment were unlikely to be significantly different from those of the July 1981 assessment. The assessment of 31 March 1982, although focused on the South Georgia incident, tends to support this view.

316 We do not regard the view taken by those concerned of the need for a new assessment as unreasonable in the light of the information available to them at the time. But in our consideration of the evidence we remain doubtful about two aspects of the work of the Joint Intelligence Organisation. First, we are not sure that at all important times the assessments staff were fully aware of the weight of the Argentine press campaign in 1982. As a result it seems to us that they may have attached greater significance to the secret intelligence, which at that time was reassuring about the prospects of an early move to confrontation. For instance, the intelligence referred to in paragraph 131 pointed out that the press campaign was probably designed to exert pressure on the United Kingdom in the negotiations. Our second doubt is whether the Joint Intelligence Organisation attached sufficient weight to the possible effects on Argentine thinking of the various actions of the British Government. The changes in the Argentine position were, we believe, more evident on the diplomatic front and in the associated press campaign than in the intelligence reports.

317   We do not seek to attach any blame to the individuals involved. But we believe that these factors point to the need for a clearer understanding of the relative roles of the assessments staff, the Foreign and Commonwealth Office and the Ministry of Defence, and for closer liaison between them. The aim should be to ensure that the assessments staff are able to take fully into account both relevant diplomatic and political developments and foreign press treatment of the sensitive foreign policy issues.

318   We are concerned here with defects in the Joint Intelligence machinery as we have seen it working in an area of low priority. As we have seen only the papers relevant to the subject of our review, we are not able to judge how the assessment machinery deals with areas of higher priority, but we believe that, in dealing with Argentina and the Falkland Islands it was too passive in operation to respond quickly and critically to a rapidly changing situation which demanded urgent attention.

319   We consider that the assessment machinery should be reviewed. We cannot say what the scope of such a review should be in respect of the machinery's wider preoccupations, but we think that it should look at two aspects in particular. The first, to which we have already referred, is the arrangements for bringing to the Joint Intelligence Organisation's attention information other than intelligence reports. The second is the composition of the Joint Intelligence Committee. On this, consideration should be given to the position of the chairman of the Committee: to the desirability that he or she should be full-time, with a more critical and independent role; and, in recognition of the Committee's independence in operation from the Government Departments principally constituting it, to the Chairman's being appointed by the Prime Minister and being a member of the Cabinet Office.

Impact of the South Georgia Incident

321   If the Joint Intelligence Committee machinery had operated differently, we have no reason to believe that it would have increased the intelligence available to the Government about the operations of Sr Davidoff, which led to the South Georgia incident preceding the invasion. There are still uncertainties about the full scope and character of those operations. The visits to South Georgia, by Sr Davidoff himself in December 1981 and by his party in March 1982, were both made on Argentine naval

vessels, and the Argentine Navy was no doubt aware of them. But there was no evidence at the time, and none has come to light since, suggesting that the whole operation was planned either by the Argentine Government or by the Navy as a follow-up to the occupation of Southern Thule. The intelligence available indicates that, when the incident grew more serious it was seized on to escalate the situation until the Junta finally decided to invade the Falkland Islands.

322   We recognise that the response of Ministers had to take account of conflicting pressures at home, especially from Parliament, and from Argentina. The initial reports of the incident appeared alarming – shots having been fired and the Argentine flag run up – and it was a reasonable reaction to order HMS *Endurance* to sail to South Georgia to take the men off. Thereafter the Government went to great lengths to avoid exacerbating the situation and made every effort to offer constructive ways of enabling the Argentine party to regularise its position. These were all rejected by the Argentine Government, which by then were clearly intent on raising the temperature.

323   Nevertheless we believe that, if Sr Davidoff s operations had been more closely monitored from December 1981 onwards and there had been better liaison between the Foreign and Commonwealth Office, the British Embassy in Buenos Aires and the Governor in preparation for the second visit in March 1982, Ministers would have been better able to deal with the landing on South Georgia when it occurred.

The Possibility of Earlier Deterrent Action

324   We next examine whether the Government should have taken earlier military action to deter Argentina. We have considered two possible actions that the Government might have taken: the earlier despatch of a task force on a sufficient scale to defend, or if necessary retake, the Islands; and the deployment of a much smaller force in the form of a nuclear-powered submarine, either on its own or supported by surface ships.

325   We believe that it would not have been appropriate to prepare a large task force with the capacity to retake the Falkland Islands, before there was clear evidence of an invasion. As we have explained, this was not perceived to be imminent until 31 March. Sending such a force would have been a disproportionate, and indeed, provocative, response to the events

on South Georgia, and would have been inconsistent with the attempts being made to resolve the problems there by diplomatic means.

326 A smaller force might have been deployed, either overtly as a deterrent measure or covertly as a precautionary measure, whose existence could have been declared if circumstances required. There were three occasions when such a force might reasonably have been deployed: before the New York talks at the end of February; at the beginning of March in the light of evidence of increased Argentine impatience at lack of progress in negotiations; or later in March, as events on South Georgia moved towards confrontation.

327 In this connection parallels have been drawn with the action taken by the previous Government in November 1977, when two frigates and a nuclear-powered submarine were deployed to the area. On that occasion the deployment was made covertly to buttress negotiations. The closest parallel is therefore with the talks in New York in February 1982. At that time there were signs of growing Argentine impatience, in the form of the *bout de papier* and the accompanying hostile press comment in Argentina, but in other respects the circumstances were different from those obtaining at the time of the 1977 talks. 1977 was a tense period in Anglo-Argentine relations and there was a sharper risk of Argentine military action. Ambassadors had been withdrawn at the beginning of the previous year; there had been a much more recent infringement of British sovereignty in the form of the establishment of an Argentine presence on Southern Thule; and there had been physical acts of aggression by Argentina against foreign shipping. Before the talks in 1977 the Joint Intelligence Commission assessed that, if negotiations broke down, there would be a high risk of Argentina's resorting to more forceful measures; in those circumstances action against British shipping was seen as the most serious risk.

328 It was believed that the round of talks in December 1977 could lead to a breakdown of negotiations. The circumstances leading up to the February 1982 talks were different, and we consider that they did not warrant a similar naval deployment.

329 There was a stronger case for considering action of this nature early in March 1982, in the light of evidence of increasing Argentine impatience, culminating in the threatening *communiqué* issued on 1 March by the Argentine Ministry of Foreign Affairs and the accompanying bellicose

Argentine press comment. As we explained in paragraph 148, Lord Carrington was informed of the action taken in 1977 at the end of a short meeting
on 5 March. Lord Carrington told us in oral evidence that the matter was
mentioned only briefly. He asked whether the Argentines knew about the
naval deployment, and, when told that they did not, he took the view that
this reduced its relevance to the situation he faced. Lord Carrington also
told us more generally that, although the situation had become more
difficult, he did not believe that the prospect of continuing negotiations at
that time was hopeless. In his view nothing had happened to trigger the
sending of a deterrent force. He was concerned that, if ships were sent, the
fact would have become known. This would have jeopardised the prospect
of keeping negotiations going, which was his objective. With hindsight he
wished he had sought to deploy a nuclear-powered submarine to the area
at an earlier stage, but on 5 March it did not seem to him that the situation
had changed in such a way as to justify such action.

330   We do not think this was an unreasonable view to take at the time,
but we believe that there would have been advantage in the Government's
giving wider consideration at this stage to the question whether the
potentially more threatening attitude by Argentina required some form of
deterrent action in addition to the diplomatic initiatives and the contingency planning already in hand.

331   Finally, we consider whether earlier action should have been taken
to deploy ships to the area in response to the developing crisis on South
Georgia. In Lord Carrington's judgement a deployment involving surface
ships was likely to carry too great a risk of becoming known at a time
when the Government were concerned to avoid any action that might
have appeared provocative. That could have provoked escalatory action by
Argentina against the Falkland Islands themselves, which the Government
had no means of resisting effectively. This objection would not have
applied so strongly to sailing a nuclear-powered submarine, since there
would have been more chance of keeping its deployment covert. The
decision to sail the first nuclear-powered submarine was taken early on
Monday 29 March.

332   We consider that there was a case for taking this action at the end of
the previous week in the light of the telegram of 24 March from the
Defence *Attaché* in Buenos Aires and the report of 25 March that Argentine

ships had been sailed for a possible interception of HMS *Endurance*. We would have expected a quicker reaction in the Ministry of Defence to these two reports, which were the first indications of hostile activity by the Argentine Government.

Final Warnings to Argentina

333   The British Government took several opportunities in the weeks leading up to the invasion to state publicly their commitment to the defence of the Falkland Islands and the Dependencies. In the House of Commons on 23 March Mr Luce stated that it was the 'duty of this Government and of any British Government to defend and support the Islanders to the best of their ability'.* On 25 March the British Ambassador in Buenos Aires, on instructions, warned Dr Costa Mendes that Britain was committed to the defence of its sovereignty in South Georgia as elsewhere. As soon as a threat to the Falkland Islands themselves was perceived, the Prime Minister contacted President Reagan on 31 March and asked him to make it clear to the Argentine Government that the Government could not acquiesce in action against the Falkland Islands. As the Prime Minister explained to us in evidence, without the collective advice of the Chiefs of Staff on whether an operation to retake the Islands was feasible and the approval of Cabinet, it was not possible for her to go further. In the event, when speaking personally to General Galtieri, President Reagan stated forcefully that action against the Falklands would be regarded by the British as a *casus belli*.

334   We conclude that warnings by the British Government of the consequences of invading the Falkland Islands were conveyed to the Argentine Government.

Could the Present Government Have Prevented the Invasion of 2 April 1982?

335   Finally we turn to the more complex question we posed in the opening paragraph of this Chapter. Could the present Government have prevented the invasion of 2 April 1982?

---

* (1) *Official Report*, House of Commons, 23 March 1982, Col. 799.

336   It is a question that has to be considered in the context of the period
of 17 years covered by our Report: there is no simple answer to it. We
have given a detailed factual account of the period, and we attach special
importance to our account of events immediately preceding the invasion. It is essential that our Report should be read as a whole – and to
recognise, as we do, that there were deep roots to Argentina's attitude
towards the 'Malvinas', and that the present Government had to deal
with that within the political constraints accepted by successive British
Governments.

337   As to the Argentine Government – and this is quite apart from the
influence on the Argentine Government of actions of the British Government – the Junta was confronted at the end of March 1982 with a rapidly
deteriorating economic situation and strong political pressures at a
moment when it was able to exploit to its advantage the developments in
South Georgia. We have already stated at the beginning of this Chapter
the reasons why we are convinced that the invasion on 2 April 1982 could
not have been foreseen.

338   The British Government, on the other hand, had to act within the
constraints imposed by the wishes of the Falkland Islanders, which had a
moral force of their own as well as the political support of an influential
body of Parliamentary opinion; and also by strategic and military priorities
which reflected national defence and economic policies: Britain's room for
policy manoeuvre was limited.

339   Against this background we have pointed out in this Chapter where
different decisions might have been taken, where fuller consideration of
alternative courses of action might, in our opinion, have been advantageous, and where the machinery of Government could have been better
used. But, if the British Government had acted differently in the ways
we have indicated, it is impossible to judge what the impact on the Argentine Government or the implications for the course of events might have
been. There is no reasonable basis for any suggestion – which would be
purely hypothetical – that the invasion would have been prevented if
the Government had acted in the ways indicated in our report. Taking
account of these considerations, and of all the evidence we have received,
we conclude that we would not be justified in attaching any criticism or
blame to the present Government for the Argentine Junta's decision to

commit its act of unprovoked aggression in the invasion of the Falkland Islands on 2 April 1982.

FRANKS, *Chairman*
BARBER
LEVER
PATRICK NAIRNE
MERLYN REES
WATKINSON

A. R. RAWSTHORNE, *Secretary*
P. G. MOULSON, *Assistant Secretary*   31st December, 1982

Glossary

Battalion Military formation normally some 600 strong in the British army

Blowpipe Hand-held, wire-guided ground-to-air missile designed by Short Bros.

Bofors 40mm Swedish-designed automatic anti-aircraft weapon first used in Second World War

Bren Magazine-fed light machine-gun, pre-Second World War design

Brigade Military formation of variable size, normally three battalions in the British army, although five battalions were under 3 Commando Brigade control in the Falklands

BV 202 Tracked towing vehicle and trailer built by Volvo, purchased by Royal Marines for Arctic warfare, highly effective load-carrier in the Falklands

CAP Combat air patrol – standing patrols flown over designated areas by Harrier aircraft

Chaff Radar-reflecting tinsel curtain blown into the sky by ship-mounted projectors to decoy homing missiles

Chinook Giant twin-rotor helicopter capable of carrying up to 10 tons, as much as five Sea Kings. American-built, used by both Britain and Argentina

CVRP Combat vehicle reconnaissance and patrol, i.e., Scorpion or Scimitar light tanks

Division Military formation of variable size, normally some 10,000-plus strong, composed of three brigades and supporting arms

84 The 'eighty-four' or 'Charlie G', Carl Gustav tube-launched infantry anti-tank rocket

EOD Explosives and ordnance disposal team, i.e., bomb disposal

Exocet French-built anti-ship missile used by Argentina

FOO Forward observation officer, normally a gunner directing the fire of an artillery battery by radio

Gazelle British-built reconnaissance and attack helicopter, invaluable for communications and casualty evacuation, but vulnerable through lack of armoured protection

GDP Gun direction position on a warship, normally sited above the bridge

GPMG General-purpose machine-gun – belt-fed Belgian-designed 7.62mm weapon, one or two per section carried in every British battalion

Harrier Vertical takeoff and landing strike aircraft. Sea Harrier version fitted with Blue Fox radar, RAF GR3 version designed for ground-attack role

Hercules American-built C-130 transport aircraft extensively used by both Britain and Argentina

Hexamine Portable cooker burning solid-fuel tablets carried by every British soldier

LCU Landing craft utility – large steel landing craft capable of carrying up to 100 men, of which four carried by each British assault ship

LCVP Landing craft vehicle and personnel – small landing craft of which four carried in each assault ship's davits

LSL Landing ship logistics – 5,700-ton ocean-going troop and supply ships manned by merchant navy crews, six in Royal Fleet Auxiliary

Lynx Westland armed helicopter carried aboard some British warships, probably the finest of its type in the world

Milan Wire-guided anti-tank missile, issued to British battalions'

support companies and used to great effect in the Falklands for bunker-busting

Montonero Peronist urban guerrilla group of the 1960s and 1970s

Oerlikon 20mm Swedish-designed anti-aircraft cannon, Second World War vintage, fitted to many British ships

'O' Group Orders group – gathering of officers to receive commander's directions

OP Observation post – normally a carefully camouflaged entrenched position well forward of main lines

PNG Passive night goggles – image-intensifying night vision equipment, made in several models, most American, used by both sides, but more effectively by the British

Puma Anglo-French-designed medium-lift helicopter used by the Argentinians in the Falklands

Rapier British-built ground-to-air missile mounted on quad launchers. Most of those used in the Falklands demanded visual guidance, although 5 Brigade brought with them a squadron equipped with Blindfire radar capability

RAS Replenishment at sea – by steaming alongside a supply ship or tanker with hose and cable connections, a delicate feat of seamanship in which the Royal Navy excels and of which the Soviet navy was demonstrably envious

RFA Royal Fleet Auxiliary

Sangar A stone protective wall built by troops on ground too hard to dig trenches

Scimitar Alvis-built light tank – CVRP – equipped with 30mm automatic cannon, with superb cross-country high-speed capability

Scorpion Alvis-built light tank – CVRP – equipped with 76mm gun and high-quality night-vision equipment

Scout Westland-built British army communications helicopter

Seacat Obsolescent sea-to-air medium-range missile. Range: 5,000 yards

Sea Dart Long-range, high-altitude sea-to-air missile. Range: 38 miles

Sea King Westland-built naval helicopter, capable of carrying 20 men or acting in an anti-submarine role, fitted with sonar

Seaslug Obsolescent sea-to-air medium-range missile. Range: 28 miles

Sea Wolf Short-range, low-level, sea-to-air missile

Shrike American-built air-to-ground radar-homing missile

Sidewinder AIM9L American-built heat-seeking air-to-air missile fitted to Sea Harriers, by far the most successful missile of the Falklands war

66 The 'sixty-six' – an American-built rocket (known as the LAW in the US), a throwaway short-range bunker-buster or anti-tank weapon carried over an infantryman's shoulder

SLR Self-loading rifle – standard British infantry weapon, 7.62mm semi-automatic modified from the original FN design

SSN Ship submersible nuclear – submarine

Start line The point from which troops advance to attack tactically deployed

Sterling Standard British army 9mm sub-machine-gun

STUFT Ships taken up from trade – the urgent requisitioning of civilian ships

Wasp Obsolescent British naval anti-submarine helicopter

Wessex Obsolescent British troop-carrying helicopter

Yomp Royal Marine slang originally describing cross-country ski move, then meaning any non-mechanised march

Index